FREDERICK THE GREAT

PUBLISHED ON THE FOUNDATION ESTABLISHED IN MEMORY OF

PHILIP HAMILTON MCMILLAN OF THE CLASS OF 1894 YALE COLLEGE

ALTHOUGH no one, with the possible exception of Napoleon, has been more written about than Frederick the Great, there has been, oddly enough, no single outstanding book in English that tells the story of his extraordinary life. Pierre Gaxotte, the author of this biography, is a Frenchman and historian, and so peculiarly fitted to be the biographer of a Prussian king who spoke French better than German, who was the patron of Voltaire, a lifelong admirer of French life and letters as well as the ally and enemy of the Court of Versailles.

Frederick was one of the strangest, most contradictory characters in history. Narrowly educated, disciplined and beaten in childhood, compelled to witness the execution of his closest friend, pent up in the drafty rooms of Prussian castles, forced into a military discipline that he detested, Frederick revolted against his father only to be broken and molded in the image of the soldier-king and then to appear as one of the great military commanders of history. A poet, unstable, brilliant, with a burgher's mind for details of business, he was able to face a coalition of all the great powers of Europe and to leave behind him a Prussia that was destined in its turn to dominate the Continent.

With a wealth of anecdotes, with a superb understanding of the deeper currents of history as well as of the people that guided them, Pierre Gaxotte tells the story of Frederick, the men and women around him, and the Europe of Louis XV, Catherine of Russia, and George III. It is also the story of a later Europe, that of 1870, 1914, and 1939, for without Frederick there would have been no Bismarck, or William II, or Adolf Hitler. Frederick literally made history, and his mark will be on it for a long time to come.

Frederick the Great

Frederick *the Great*

BY PIERRE GAXOTTE

TRANSLATED BY R. A. BELL

New Haven Yale University Press *1942*

TO

MADELEINE DUMÉZIL

The English version is for
J. S. B., *who came into the world at the same time.*

CONTENTS

ILLUSTRATIONS

From the *Almanac,* which adds: "During a journey the King made in July, 1779, to a colony lately founded near Neustadt to visit a variety of improvements he had ordained, he arrived among others in a village where General von Zieten was in front of the castle. Bailiff Fromm, who was on horseback beside the King's carriage, was the first to notice him & mentioned it to the King. The latter had the carriage stopped forthwith, got out of it, & displayed the greatest delight to the general, for having thus met him unexpectedly. While the King was discussing a variety of things with this general, & a certain Herr von Kleist, he noticed a big man in a white suit, & asked Bailiff Fromm who it was without anyone noticing the fact, when he had found out, & after having exchanged a few more words with Messrs. von Zieten and von Kleist, he turned suddenly upon him, & said to him, *Your servant, Mr. District Councilor!* whereupon, as the latter wished to come near him his Majesty said to him: Wait! I know you, you are District Councilor *Quast.*"

Drawn by Robert W. Galvin.

𝕱𝖗𝖊𝖉𝖊𝖗𝖎𝖈𝖐 *the Great*

I

Father and Son

I

WHILE Louis XIV was growing old amid the splendors of Versailles, Berlin was still nothing but a town of wood and brick drowsing by the dark, slow waters of the river Spree. Long before its promotion to the rank of capital city the town had been formed by the union of two small forts, originally built in the land of the Slavs by colonists, fishermen, and mariners from Brandenburg in the thirteenth century. A wall with bastions, defended by ditches, surrounded the old quarters—the arsenal, the mint, the bridges, the castle, the cathedral, four or five churches, and the brand new statue of the Great Elector. Beyond the ramparts the town thrust out its first suburbs over sandy fields, stretches of heath, and boggy meadows, where it was hard to find a solid bottom for piles. . . .

The earth seemed still to be damp from the glaciers which had once covered it. In their retreat they had left behind them mud, stones, and blocks of granite half embedded in the fertile soil. There was no margin to this gloomy waste. It had not any pronounced or notable features. Sluggish streams merged into strings of lakes which had no clear banks. The wind, which brought with it the scent of resin, showed that a forest was quite close: birches, beeches, and above all pines—pines with ruddy trunks and gloomy foliage. Even after the finest days cold mists crept along the spongy ground at dusk.

Between two arms of the Spree rose the royal castle, a huge unfinished building in a mixture of styles, vaguely Dutch on one side, and on the other severely classical. Facing the river, towers with bell turrets roofed in copper; facing the square, a fine, regular façade—two heavy wings each adorned with four colossal columns, three lines of windows above the ground floor, and a terraced roof hidden by a square balustrade. The State apartments were vast and well furnished; they had fine tapestries, long rooms leading one into the other, ceilings where the tales of heroes of old were portrayed, doors carved and gilded, and cornices overloaded with a mass of cupids, trumpeters, garlands, and crowns. Visitors were astonished at the huge amount of silverwork that was displayed. In the Hall of the Knights the torches, the brackets, the chandeliers, the tables, the seats, even the balcony, all were of solid silver. In short, considerable luxury and extravagance for a sovereign who was reigning over less than two million people and whose title dated from 1701. But it would have needed a brave man to tell him that a king's dignity depended on revenue or age of title.

Frederick I was poor and in debt, yet he used to get up early to have more time to relish the pleasure of being a king. He was stunted, deformed, with common but prepossessing features; he had a serious and benign manner and he nobly maintained the outward shows of sovereignty. He used to load himself with diamonds, eat to a fanfare of trumpets, retire to bed in a procession, and import from Paris enormous periwigs in the Spanish manner, which concealed beneath a cascade of extravagant curls the very ugly swelling he had at the base of his neck. He sported a Grand Chamberlain, a Grand Master of the Arms, some Swiss Guards, fifty cooks, and an Academy of Learning. He had lost two wives and had consoled himself by arranging gorgeous funerals for the defunct ladies; and he had taken for his third wife Sophia Dorothea of Mecklenburg, who was twenty-three years old and just a bit wrong in the head. He was a Calvinist. She adhered to the strictest form of Lutheranism: during their five years of marriage she nagged at him about Efficient Grace and Predestination. He bore with her like a Christian, for he possessed that abundance of patience which is essential to a good husband. Nevertheless for the honor of his profession he forced himself to take a mistress to imitate Louis XIV. She was the Countess of Wartenburg, wife of the Grand Chamberlain. She was included in the *Almanac:* the editors enrolled her in the high rank demanded by her occupation among the one hundred and forty-one titles which formed the hierarchy of the Court.

Two grandsons of the King had died in early infancy. A third was born on Sunday, January 24, 1712, between eleven o'clock and midday. The grandfather wanted the boy to be called

Frederick like himself, because, he wrote, "This name has always brought luck to my House." The christening took place on the thirty-first. The bells pealed for an hour together. "The child, dressed in a robe woven with silver and studded with diamonds, the train of which was carried by six countesses, was borne to the chapel of the castle, under a canopy upheld by a princess and two princes. The King was awaiting him under a baldachin, the four poles of which were held by four chamberlains, and its silken pendants by four Knights of the Black Eagle." The godfathers and godmothers who had sent representatives were the Emperor Charles VI, the Tsar Peter the Great, the States-General of Holland, the Canton of Berne and the Elector of Hanover; the Empress Dowager, the Electoress and the Electoress Dowager of Hanover, the Duchess of Brunswick and the Dowager Duchess of Mecklenburg. The guns on the ramparts boomed three times, telling the loyal people of Berlin that another Christian had been added to the royal family.

Fritz had the will to live. His grandfather was delighted, and sent the good news to all the family. "He is fat and rosy . . . a very healthy child . . . he tugs stoutly at the nipple of his nurse." He cut his teeth early and without pain. "In this can be seen a kind of predestination."

But Fate decreed that King Frederick should see no further. He died on February 27, 1713, of a disease of the lung.

His son, Frederick William, was by no means stingy about the obsequies. The dead man himself could not have done better. The preparations lasted two months. Clad in cloth of gold and ermine, the corpse lay in state for seven days on a ceremonial bed of red velvet embroidered with pearls; the crown was at its head, the scepter and sword under its hand, and its breast was crossed by the collar of the Black Eagle. The coffin was escorted to church in the presence of almost the whole army. Along the route regiments presented arms. The new King wore a long cloak of mourning and its train was carried by the Master of the Horse. The courtiers followed in heavy wigs and in rich costumes. When divine service was over Frederick William himself gave the order for firing the salute, and then in ominous silence returned home.

Truly he had given a rare proof of his filial piety by spinning out to eight weeks a ceremony which maddened him and cost him so many ducats. The very next day the liveries made their exit. Pages, gentlemen, chamberlains, bodyguards, masters of the ceremonies, Marshal of the Court, Master of the Posts, Master of the Wardrobe, heralds, and musicians all went to the devil or to the army. That left only a trumpeter, two pages, and four officers, who with a round dozen of valets, orderlies, and batmen formed the complete household of the King. He kept for himself a five-roomed suite: a Hall of Banners where the standards of the garrison were placed, an antechamber, an audience chamber which was also used as a dining room, a closet, and a bedroom and dressing room combined. The ground floor of the palace was turned into offices and housed the staffs of the ministries, while the cellar was made into the treasury: through one door and down one flight of stairs, and Frederick William could be sure that his people were at work and the money was safe. The silver plate, the medals, the rare wines, the diamonds, the extra carriages, and the animals were sold to pay the creditors: the King of Poland bought the wild beasts and the merchants of Frankfort the carriages. The Jewess Liebmann, who had taken advantage of Frederick's passion for jewels, was thrown into prison. A new regulation fixed the order of precedence. First came the military, the marshals, the lieutenant governors, the generals. . . . Last, in the sixth rank, came the ministers.

Frederick William did not dismiss the Court painters. This was because he loved being painted and gloried in portraits both of himself and of his family. But he was on his guard. Artists were rogues and loafers: each one had to contract to produce a fixed number of canvases at stated intervals. They still adorn the royal palaces of Berlin, Potsdam, Charlottenburg, Monbijou, and Wusterhausen.

Frederick William was twenty-five years old at his accession to the throne; he was a little over middle height, and inclined to be thick and sturdy; his face was red and his chin already fleshy, his mouth very small for his broad face, his lip haughty, his nose too short, but straight enough, his eyes large, protruding, round, and gray, laughing when he was in a jovial mood but of a terrifying steadiness when he wished to intimidate. As a child he had been like a cherub. In afterlife his hair remained fair and silky:

he was ashamed of it and had it cropped close. He covered his clipped pate with brown wigs tied informally and later with flat little white wigs. After giving up civilian dress he was only known to wear two costumes—green hunting kit with black facings and the uniform of his regiment, dark blue with copper buttons, scarlet lapels, chamois leather breeches and waistcoat, and white boots or gaiters. Under the affected pomp of official portraits you can feel him bubbling with impatience and anger. He grasps his commander's baton like a cudgel.

By nature he was anxious, cruel, miserly, despotic, and finicky, unable to stand delay or contradiction, inclined to rough-handle life. But life was to return his brutality a hundredfold. Though very clean in his personal habits and though changing his linen every day, in everything else he was deplorably unhygienic, eating too much and too fast, almost without chewing, and over-indulging in beer, spirits, and tobacco. Soon enough he complained that headaches drove him mad. He slept badly—a sleep troubled by nightmares which made him foam at the mouth until he went off into a stupor. By day he had fits of drowsiness and dozing and also sudden impulses at which he leaped into the saddle and galloped aimlessly for hours. Attacks of gout followed one another and grew more painful from year to year. Red and blue blotches marbled his bloated face. He went deaf. He suffered horribly. An ambassador relates that "at times the skin beneath his thighs would hang loose, like the bladder of a freshly killed pig." Every autumn during the hunting season he weighed himself night and morning in the hope that exercise and sweating had made him thinner. Yet he ended by weighing 270 pounds. In his last years, swollen with dropsy to the shape of a barrel, with legs the size of a human body, he was to measure eight feet six inches round the belly.

For money he had a low and sordid affection. "Whoever's got the cash," he used to say, "controls army and administration, and in addition gains the respect and admiration of the world." Therefore the kingdom had to be exploited so as to yield an increase every year. "To make a bit more," *"ein Plus machen,"* that summed it all up. With the bit more soldiers were equipped; if need be they were bought. And it was through soldiers that kings became "formidable."

"I would not go out of my way to get the most beautiful wife or mistress in the world, but soldiers! they are the chink in my armor, and for them I can be made to go to any lengths you like."

This terrible, ludicrous, abominable man had virtues which compel admiration: frankness, honesty, hatred of trickery and spying, fidelity to family duties—above all, love of his country and devotion to public business. To use the happy phrase of Lavisse, he thought of himself as only the head servant of an ideal, eternal being, the King of Prussia. "I am," he would say, "the Commander in Chief and the Finance Minister of the King of Prussia." All his life he worked under the eye of this master, whom he knew to be exacting and formidable. He spared neither trouble nor energy to satisfy him. Insatiable curiosity, unfailing application, incredible exertions to be everywhere at the same time, cares innumerable, plans for everything, precision, speed, perpetual alertness which let nothing escape it: he was killing himself, but everything must run smoothly and must be ordered "like a sheet of music."

The sovereign's slavery had naturally to be mirrored by the obedience of the subjects. Let them carry out orders without delay, without discussion—if need be, without comprehension. *Nicht raisonnieren!* That was the motto of the reign. "We are the Lord and King, and we do what we will." As for those who opposed him: "We will deal out exemplary punishment to them, as in Russia."

Two years after his coronation he discovered that certain Prussian officials were not carrying out his orders. At once he flew into a passion against this "pack of mongrels" who must "dance to his tune," otherwise he will have them "strung up and roasted"; he will treat them as rebels, he will act the "nabob." "I am in command of my army, and a thousand dirty quill drivers shall issue no commands. I should be a fool if I put up with that."

In 1716 the nobles were restive. "I am marching toward my goal, I am strengthening my rule, I am establishing the throne as firmly as a rock of bronze, and I leave to these fine gentry the hot air of the Diet. When a man is gaining his ends, he leaves hot air to others."

II

THE bureaucracy and the army lay in wait for the Crown Prince: his position in them was appointed from the cradle. As an inner, executive Councilor of State, as a Commissioner for War or as one of the jury of the Chamber of Domains, he was a cog in the machine and must, like the rest, play his part without flinching. Frederick William explained at length how he meant his son to be trained for his duties in the Instructions he gave to the boy's governors when Fritz was seven years old. Instructions of this type dated from the Great Elector's day. They had been used for Frederick I, and, after the influence of Leibniz had amended them somewhat, for Frederick William himself. It was the code of a gentleman, according to the meaning that word had at Versailles: good Christian, accomplished horseman, man of honor, stoical, courteous, pious without bigotry, a good judge of works of culture, with all the manners, graces, ease, and self-control which come from frequenting good company—a rare mixture of serious virtues and amiable qualities.

Frederick William improved on this training in his own way. The chapter dealing with social life was ruthlessly curtailed; it was enough that the Prince should have "seemly manners and deportment." Physical exercise was to be carefully graduated so as not to overtax the child's strength, but his instructors must remember that he was destined for a hard life and must give him a distaste for laziness, "one of the greatest of all vices." He must deny himself "operas, comedies, and other follies of the laity." He must get accustomed "to planning, thrift, and moderation."

In the same way the chapter on intellectual training was curtailed: "As for the Latin tongue, my son will not study it." Frederick William gave no reasons, but as he foresaw that he might be asked for some, he added, "I forbid anyone to mention this subject to me." History must be cut down to a detailed knowledge of European politics of the last hundred and fifty years. The Prince must see how his predecessors had acted; he should consider their behavior and distinguish the strong from the weak sides of it. He must visit the archives to get used to State papers and reports, and also to find there real history, free from moralizing and from purple passages. Without skipping a line, he must read through the *Theatrum Europæum,* a huge, unedited catalogue, where battles, treaties, and changes of rulers were set down year by year starting from 1617, with maps, plans, and references. As for Ancient History, that would only be referred to in passing.

Let us not be too quick to smile. In the days of Frederick William, which were also those of Bayle, the history of the Ancient World was not yet written. Previously legends and traditions had been quietly accepted, but at last they had been torn to shreds by a generation of skeptics. Scholars and wise men were still groping in search of a sure method, based on verifiable facts and not on words. How then could such a scrap heap of myths and errors merit any attention? Could a king of Prussia get any enlightenment from it?

Frederick must be made familiar with an elegant, terse style in both French and German. He should know how to speak in public and he must declaim before a child of good family, who would reply to him in little speeches proper to his station in life: thanks, congratulations, encouragement to soldiers before battle. . . . He must study the Rights of Nations (a great novelty, this) and the science of agriculture; he must know enough of mathematics to lay out a camp, to understand "fortifications and the other arts of war."

His tutors and governors must supervise the company he keeps. Never should they leave him to himself, not even at night. At the period of puberty they must redouble their vigilance, "otherwise they will answer for it with their heads."

Helped by the royal chaplain, they must mold the Crown Prince into a pious prince who respected the Commandments, loved virtue, and feared God. He must be brought up to have a horror of atheism, Arianism, Socinianism, and Catholicism, which "can with reason be put in the same basket," because it is "artificial and absurd." But here arose a difficulty of dogma: the Protestant Church was troubled by the disputes of the Calvinists and the Lutherans. The former thought that a part of mankind had from the Fall been destined by God for salvation, and the rest to damnation; the latter, on the other hand, believed that all could attain to Grace. The Calvinists were particularists and the Lutherans universalists, but universalists were to be found among the Calvinist flock, and Frederick William was of that number. He thought the doctrine of predestination a danger to the State because it did away with the subject's sense of responsibility. He forbade the clergy to preach it to the troops, lest they should think themselves destined for desertion and should take to flight in good earnest. Besides, he was not anxious to be damned in advance.

He desired passionately to unite the Reformed churches and obstacles angered him. "The difference between our two evangelical religions," he wrote one day to Pastor Roloff, "is really just the wrangling of the clergy. For if on the face of it there is a great difference, when the matter is inspected at close quarters it is the same faith on all points, alike for Divine Grace and for the communion; but in the pulpit one lot gives us a sourer sauce than the other. May God pardon all the clergy, for at God's throne they will have to answer for having stirred up controversy among those verminous Schoolmen, and for having thrown the work of God into confusion." Conclusion: Christ died for all men, and the Prince must believe in Universal Grace. He must be taken to churches to hear sermons, and examined on his return to see if he had remembered any parts of them.

Last comes the essential point, military education. "From childhood" Frederick must be prepared by his tutors to become an officer and a general. "They must fill my son with a real love of the soldier's trade and impress on him that nothing in the world can bestow glory on a prince as can the sword; that in it and by it he must seek for the only true glory, or else he will be a figure of shame to all the world."

When Frederick was thirteen, the King completed his first Instructions by a detailed timetable. Weekdays, up at 6 A.M. The Prince will not roll over in bed. He will rise at once, kneel down, and repeat a short prayer aloud: "O Lord God, Holy Father, I thank Thee with all my heart for the gift Thou hast made of this night, through the work of Thy grace. In the name of our Saviour, Jesus Christ, make me obedient to Thy Holy Will, that I may not commit, either this day or the next, any deed which shall take me further from Thee. Amen." This said, Frederick will put on his shoes, will wash his face and hands without soap, will dress himself, and have his hair combed but not powdered. While a servant hands him his clothes, he will drink his tea or coffee. At 6.30 his teacher and the servants will enter. Reading of the Bible. Morning Prayer. Hymn. 7–10.45, lessons. Then the Prince "swiftly," "at the double," will wash his face and hands, using soap for the hands alone. He will put on his suit, have his hair powdered, and at 11 A.M. be at the King's for the family breakfast and conversation. At 2 P.M. lessons go on again till 5; the Prince is his own master till bedtime, provided he gets some fresh air and "does nothing which may be contrary to the will of God." Having wished his father good night, washed his hands and face, said his prayers and sung a hymn, he will be in bed by 10.30. The governor who sleeps in his room will put out the lights at once. Saturday: general revision. Sunday: Frederick will get up an hour later and do no work. The morning is to be filled with religious duties—reading and comment on the Gospels, questions on the Catechism, and a service at church.

Thus, having foreseen everything, regulated everything from the way to believe in God to the way to sit at table, Frederick William was sure that all would be for the best, and that his beloved son and heir would improve "a bit more" each year and would rapidly become like himself. But Frederick William was no judge of men, for he distrusted everybody. He imagined, quite falsely, that implicit and complete obedience could be obtained by speaking loudly and by raising his stick. Most of the people he chose to carry out his program were not in the least suited to fulfill his purpose. Fundamentally they disagreed with him, and without ill will they betrayed him at every turn.

Up to the age of seven Fritz had a governess, Madame de Rocoules, who had already brought up the King. She was a Frenchwoman, an exile since the Revocation of the Edict of Nantes, a wise, discreet person, who was said to love intrigues. She had a knack for versifying, liked a spicy jest, and kept a *salon*. A beautiful portrait at the castle of Potsdam shows her in extreme old age, wrinkled, toothless, mantled in lace, with much kindness in her face and mischief in her eye. After twenty years in Prussia, she knew not a word of German, and the first kind words, perhaps the only ones Frederick ever heard, were in French. Till her death Madame de Rocoules was for him "his dear, kind Mamma."

The tutor Duhan was also a Frenchman, born at Jandun in Champagne in the year of the Revocation. His father, who had formerly been secretary to Turenne and a Councilor of State, had left France two years later and had settled in Berlin, where he became secretary to the Great Elector. Frederick William noticed Duhan at the siege of Stralsund in the very thick of the fight. He engaged him there and then, in the trenches. Yet this gentleman was above all a humanist; he was passionately fond of literature, and in his eyes nothing equaled the works of the Ancients.

The governors who took up the work when Madame de Rocoules retired were gallant soldiers: General Count Albert Conrad Finck von Finckenstein was a very honest man, universally valued for his probity and belonging to a very old family, which had settled in Prussia in the days of the Teutonic Order. He had a big head, a big nose, big features. He was a veteran in European wars and had done bits of fighting all over the place, served the Low Countries against France, and France against Spain; then he had returned to his own country and covered himself with glory at Malplaquet. In the course of his roving life he had come in contact with William of Orange, Prince Eugene, Marlborough, Luxemburg, and Louvois, and besides this he had hoped to make a large fortune at Versailles: one might almost say that Frederick's childhood was encircled by France. The junior governor, Colonel von Kalkstein, was thirty-six years old. The Jesuits under whom he had studied turned him out well informed and well mannered, but he could neither make himself loved nor influence his pupil's line of thought. Finally, above them all, confusing and thwarting everything, stood his mother, Sophia Dorothea of Hanover. Fifi, as the King called her in moments of affection, was a stout woman quite without malice, well educated, and by no means stupid; a person of taste, but conceited, pigheaded, a spendthrift, garrulous, and a plotter, a lover of secrets and smuggled letters, who thought herself exiled in Prussia since her father had become King of England. She had fourteen children of whom ten survived, but her pregnancies did not stop her from intriguing. From fear of the King she involved herself in evasions, and these led to appalling interviews, from which she would emerge humiliated, in tears but unrepentant. Frederick grew up among quarrels and recriminations, surrounded by people who trembled and people who lied.

He was quiet, taciturn, often ill, and a slow learner. Pesne painted him at three years old with his eldest sister Wilhelmina, who was six. They are both pretty children. He is wearing a lownecked dress of blue velvet braided with gold, a child's drum is fastened to his sash, and a cap with large feathers sits above his golden hair. Wilhelmina holds his hand to prevent him from beating the drum; she is dressed like a French marquise and has long curls, a rose in her hair, and flowers in the folds of her cloak with a train. Behind them a negro carries a parasol on his shoulder and a parrot on his wrist. Though Pesne has given Fritz the chain and medal of the Black Eagle, he is still a fat, lumpish baby, sleepy looking, with big eyes, and a chin more firm than his sister's. Yet if they changed costumes, it would be impossible to say which was the boy and which the girl.

Frederick William loved his son and would have liked to be loved in return "fraternally," "with confidence," as the man who wished him all the good in the world. "Threaten him with his mother," he had ordered, "never with me." However, he could not find the way to his son's heart or the way to his mind. He could not express his almost heroic idea of the Prussian monarchy—he even managed to make it seem grotesque. His rages and fits of violence degraded the very thing he wished to make great; he made even the idea of ruling seem hateful because he made all too clear the pinpricks and discomforts of it and never mentioned its justification and its nobility. The "pious lords," the "good masters," who talked to Frederick of his duties, gave him a narrow pedant's picture of the profession of king: with monotonous zeal they emphasized the toil, the slavery, and the hardships of his position, but they did not give him a feeling of his destiny or the desire to fulfill it. The words which they repeated to him endlessly—soldier, gentleman, general, father of his people—all these words reached his ears like the names of icy, threatening deities. They were the idols of a repulsive cult, the meaning of which he could not grasp. Fritz was broken in, not educated.

At the age of four he began to learn the fifty-four movements of Prussian drill. All his playthings were of military design:

lead soldiers, guns, drums, tents, flags, miniature cannon. He was made to fire a pistol to get used to the terrifying bang.

Frederick William had a regiment of giants at Potsdam on which he spent fabulous sums of money. At the age of six Frederick was to have his company too, the Crown Prince's company of cadets, 131 hand-picked young lads, who would be gradually recruited up to the strength of a battalion—gentry and sons of gentry, soldiers and sons of soldiers. "Fritz marched in the ranks at first, under the command of Instructor Rentzell, a grown lad of seventeen years. Then he took charge of it himself. He had the honor of an inspection by the Tsar Peter, and by his grandfather, the King of England, who praised him highly. In 1721, on his birthday, the King made him a present of a small arsenal, which was set up in one of the rooms of the castle at Berlin."

Fritz endured his father's tyranny, but with his sensitive, independent, melancholy nature he suffered in silence. Frederick William was overwhelmed with work, always on the run, always supervising, and he could hardly superintend his son's lessons himself. Mother and governors made up facts to please him. They described to him the son of his dreams. "Fritz," the Queen wrote to him, "says he wants to take the large cannon in the arsenal, and find Papa and help him kill the King of Sweden . . ." (July 5, 1715). "I have the cannon fired every day so that Fritz may get used to it." "I have made Fritz fire a small pistol. I hope that when you next see him you will not find him such a coward. . . ." "I saw Fritz on horseback this afternoon, a thing I had not seen for a long time" (June 10, 1718). "Fritz learns all he can of the *Theatrum Europæum*." What a fine child! When he was behindhand with his program, his teachers were ready with excuses in their weekly bulletin: "His Royal Highness learns with difficulty, as do all minds which show promise of depth and are gifted with great strength of judgment."

There is no doubt that Fritz tried, in his early childhood, to please that terrible father of his, who frightened everybody else but had fits of rough affection for his son. We have the letters he wrote him at that time. One day he gave the King news of the state of his company and thanked him for having sent along a new officer. Another time he announced that he had shot a hare. He was learning the *Theatrum Europæum* steadily without skipping a line. Wilhelmina and he "think night and day of their dear Papa," and wait for his return with impatience. Having gone to inspect his company at Köpenik, he was not satisfied with the arms drill, "but nothing could be better than their shooting." During another visit he was pleased with the maneuvers and gave a barrel of beer to his cadets for their trouble. The barrel of beer must have gone straight to the King's heart, but the whole affair was probably inspired by a tutor.

In 1720 Frederick produced a little composition in French called "A Way of Life for a Prince of Noble Birth." This pretentious title is ridiculous enough for something penned by a gentleman eight years old, but the text must have filled dear Papa with joy. "His heart must be well inclined, his religion of the Protestant type—a fear of God not after the manner of those who do so for money or for earthly things. He must love his father and mother. He must be grateful. He must love God with his whole heart, for those who love him try to please him with all their might. . . . He must thank Jesus Christ for His goodness in being crucified for us, poor sinners. He must never forsake the Protestant faith. . . . He must not love anything too much, he must be obliging and polite, and must mix with all sorts of people. To know the right thing to do and not to do it is a sin. He must act according to the Ten Commandments, not steal, not demean himself, and always think: 'All the good I do comes from God.' He must never think of evil things; all the evil which enters the mind comes from the Devil. He must remember the passage of the Bible which says, 'Be sober, be vigilant; because your adversary the devil, as a roaring lion, walketh about, seeking whom he may devour: Whom resist steadfast in the faith.' "

Kalkstein swore he had neither added nor taken away a single letter of the Prince's essay—so speaks the courtier; he had at least corrected the spelling, leaving a few mistakes for credibility, since much later on Frederick spelled in such a way that it is difficult to understand his sentences at the first reading. For the rest, the child had done nothing but repeat his lessons of religious teaching, probably word for word: he was taught to read the Bible, and was made to copy out passages until he could recite them by heart. One of these exercises is preserved in the Hohenzollern Museum.

"However," writes Lavisse, "during the daily lessons, during personal tuition by Duhan, step by step all unperceived there took place a process quite unlike the training of a little soldier and a young Christian. The Prince's education was overflowing the banks drawn for it by the King. Duhan had no deliberate intention of disobeying the instructions he had received; but in spite of himself he conserved, reduced, and augmented them. He corrected the letter by the spirit." In plain English, he double-crossed his master. The King had said, "Facts, all the facts": Duhan pruned and reorganized, replacing detail by ideas, reasoning, and general surveys. The King had said, "Plenty of memory tests": Duhan used to forget the recitations and make his pupil speak his own mind. The King had said, "No works of the Ancients": the Ancients were introduced with *Telemachus*.[1]

Frederick William had no objection, for he had read this book in his childhood. But *Telemachus* took Frederick many miles from the Spree, into a world of sunshine, where there were neither gravel pits, nor giant recruits, nor cadet companies. He followed the hero across the wine-dark sea; in his company he gazed at Calypso in her grotto of rocks, carpeted with young vines, which was kept deliciously cool by the breezes. He listened to the springs which ran with a soft murmur amid fields sown with amaranth. He fled pursued by Venus, who rent the clouds in her chariot of roses drawn by a pair of doves. He drank of the wine of the nymphs, which is more sweet than nectar, from golden cups crowned with flowers. Mentor softly told him that virtue was gentle, and down in the Kingdom of the Dead he learned that conquerors, heroes, and warriors have no right to the highest places in the Elysian Fields, for these are reserved for peaceful, benevolent princes who wander, freed from earthly woes, about the scented groves, shining with rays of soft light which surround them like a garment.

"Idomeneus," Mentor told him, "is wise and enlightened, but he is too occupied with details, and does not sufficiently consider his affairs as a whole to form any real policy. The function of a king who is above other men does not consist in doing every-

1. Fénelon, Archbishop of Cambrai, wrote *Les Aventures de Télémaque* to form part of the education of Louis XIV's grandson, the Duc de Bourgogne. It was published in 1699.

thing himself; to hope to succeed in such a task is the wildest of vanities. . . . The best and most perfect government consists in controlling those who govern."

"Happy," cried the captive Telemachus, "happy are those who reject violent pleasures, and can be content with the joys of an innocent life. . . . Happy are those whose pleasure it is to cultivate the mind. . . . Happy are those who love reading, and are not deprived of books as I am."

And Telemachus would console himself by playing the flute. There was heavenly harmony in his voice. He sang of the beauties which nature has lavished on the countryside, and to hear him shepherds forgot their huts and their flocks and stood in rapture motionless around him. It seemed as if nothing fierce remained in the waste places—everything there was gentle and gay; the sweetness of the peasants was mollifying the earth itself.

How far it was from Potsdam! How far from Prussian drill! Frederick was tired of being a little soldier; he was encouraged by his sister Wilhelmina, a very intelligent girl who talked and behaved as if twice her age, and he began to devour novels he secretly borrowed. The first was *Pierre de Provence,* a tale of the love of a noble knight for Maguelone, the lovely daughter of the King of Naples. There were abductions, tourneys, pirates, tempests, and a wedding.

"I was not allowed to read it," he himself relates, "and I used to hide it. I slept between my governor, General Finck, and my valet. When they were fast asleep I used to step over the valet's bed and go into another room where there was a lamp in the chimney corner. I used to crouch there and read. But one night the marshal's cough woke him up. He did not hear me breathing, groped for me in vain, called out. I ran in quickly. I said that I had had a call of nature. I hid my book, and I kept off it after that. 'Have a care, my Prince,' and I did take care."

Fritz spent his happiest hours far from the parade ground in the company of his mother and his sister. Both of them loved him, Wilhelmina with passionate tenderness, his mother in her own way, with restless, forceful jealousy. She helped estrange him from his father by compelling him to side with one or other of his parents. Her voluble conversation was always full of complaints; foreign envoys bear witness that as a talker she rivaled the

prophet Jeremiah. She complained of her husband's cruelty, of
the wretched life he forced her to lead, *her*, the daughter of the
King of England. She complained of the ministers who incited
him against her, and who were certainly planning to assassinate
the Crown Prince to confirm their control of policy. She knew of
all the intrigues of the Court and the town and explained them
in detail to her daughter, disclosing to her dreadful stories quite
unfit for the ears of a child.

The two children saw that their parents were at loggerheads,
and that their mother resented any unpleasant duty the King
imposed on her. When the master of the house was away, the
mistress gave a different tone to the establishment. Then in the
little castle of Monbijou, which was a gift to her from Frederick I
filled with costly curios, there was society, gambling, music, and
dancing. One day the King returned unexpectedly and blun-
dered right into the middle of the dancers; in a rage and without a word he left the company frozen by his presence. After one
of these humiliating scenes Sophia Dorothea began making plans
quite openly for occasions when the King was likely to be away,
and Fritz knew well enough that such times would mean liberty
for her and a more pleasant life for him.

Between their games the children gossiped. The little brother
was a telltale, and the sister, on her side, passed on all she had
picked up: their mother's bickerings and household gossip, both
above and below stairs. Her governess, Letti, snores like a police-
man, and men visit her room—she has nicknamed Frau von
Kamken the Fat Cow, the Queen the Great Donkey, and (so she
says) Frau von Sonsfeld is a silly creature. Grumbkow, the minister and all-powerful favorite, is a coward who feigned death in a
ditch at Malplaquet to avoid joining in the attack. The King has
stayed up all night with his generals drinking. The Queen has
been crying again this morning. An astrologer has foretold that
Frederick will become one of the greatest princes who have ever
reigned. The King has said that the loss of a woman is like the
extraction of a rotten tooth, for it hurts to have it pulled out,
but the moment afterward what a glorious relief it is to be rid
of it.

Frederick and Wilhelmina kept to themselves. They egged
each other on in their loves and hatreds. They accustomed each

other to look at the ugly sides of their home life and to despise
the people around them. They were silent and reserved at table,
and they exchanged looks of distaste and understood each other
without words. The King, who noticed this tacit disapproval, was
annoyed by it.

Things happened around the Queen and the Crown Prince
which displeased him and which were kept from him. Once he
surprised the tutor redhanded in the very act of disobedience,
teaching his son Latin. They had thought he was far away, when
he suddenly entered the schoolroom.

"What are you doing?"

"I'm declining *mensa, mensae,* Papa."

"You knave! A son of mine learn Latin! Out of my sight!"

Propelled by blows from the royal stick and by kicks from
behind, Duhan fled. The King came back and found Fritz
crouching under the table, so he pulled him out and cuffed him.

Here was a "dandy," a reserved, speechless, retiring "milksop,"
who no longer loved soldiers but was interested in romantic
rigmaroles—"the wind, the blue of the sky!"—this was no son
of his. He was maddened by the bored face and martyred expression assumed by Fritz; he contrasted him with his brother William, a fine child who looked you straight in the eyes and was
quite willing to do drill. In due course he came to think that if his
eldest son were to fail him, Prussia would fall into much better
hands.

In March, 1724, at Grumbkow's house, the King suddenly
pointed at the Prince and said: "I would like to know what goes
on in that little head of his. I know he doesn't think as I do.
Certain people give him ideas unlike mine and encourage him
to find fault with everything. They are rascals."

"Rascals," he repeated and turned to his son: "Fritz, mark
my words: always keep up a large, efficient army; you cannot
have a better friend, and without that friend you will not be able
to survive. Our neighbors would like nothing so much as to make
us come a cropper; that's their aim, I know. You will get to know
them. Believe me, you must not think about imaginary things;
fix your mind on real ones. Have money and a good army; they
ensure the glory and safety of a prince."

As he spoke he gave Fritz little pats on the cheek, which ended
by being like slaps.

Every day the King worried about the danger which threatened
his life's work. When he was dead, what would become of his
kingdom? And the army? And the Treasury? What had he done
to the Lord God to deserve such a child? Why did Fritz resist all
his efforts? Yet he loved him: he had spared neither trouble nor
money in his upbringing. But the dandy met his advice, as well
as his rages, with an obstinate look. It was obvious the good-for-
nothing was laughing up his sleeve at his father.

Frederick William was out riding alone, in his usual way,
tortured by the desire for movement and change, and brooding
upon his troubles. Fritz is lazy. He does not work. He writes
rotten German which bristles with ugly blunders. He is haughty.
He is a dreamer. He does not know how to speak to an officer.
On a horse he sits in the saddle crumpled up like a rag. He is
grubby and affected. He does not wash, but puts on lace, has his
hair curled, and likes fripperies. He's as soft as a little girl. He
wears gloves at the meet. He's a bad shot. He walks on the tips of
his toes like a fop. He wriggles in his chair. Instead of singing
hymns to the organ, he plays on the flute and spends all his spare
time at it. At table he keeps his nose in his plate and makes
idiotic faces. (Not content with the old-fashioned two-pronged
fork his father used, he once wanted to employ a silver fork with
three prongs for eating. That day Frederick William boxed his
ears, but blows were as useless as reproaches.) His grandparents in
London have asked the Queen for a portrait of Fritz: "The
Queen need only have a portrait made of a big monkey." Those
rogues the governors have caused the trouble with their indulgent
stupidity. They deserve to be thrashed or sent to the vaults of
Spandau. But what is he to do? It would be best if Fritz were
always with his father. Perhaps he can still be reformed. . . .

It is easy to imagine Frederick William's thoughts. He was
not the sort of man who kept his mouth shut: we have only to
piece together the various growling phrases which he let fall.
From now on the discord between him and his son was public,
and foreign envoys regularly informed their Courts of it. On
May 1, 1725, Frederick William made up his mind to be person-

ally responsible for Frederick. He appointed him captain at the age of thirteen in a royal regiment at Potsdam. His lessons were reduced and replaced by more complete military training. The army was to save the Crown Prince by inspiring him with respect for his uniform and with knowledge of his duties.

III

POTSDAM was Frederick William's favorite palace. He found Berlin too "ministerial"—too many councilors, too many diplomats, too many civilians. At Potsdam he was only a soldier, a colonel of the giant grenadiers. Every day he took part in parades and drill, and Fritz must come with him. When maneuvers were successful, he called the men his "dear children in blue" and listened gently to their complaints. They were his second family. Once, when ill, he made two hundred of them march past his bed to distract his mind from his suffering. He knew nearly all by name and could remember what the tallest had cost him. Indeed, for economy's sake he would have liked to produce giants cheap on his own lands. He used his authority to marry giants to giants, and when the result of the union was a child with large hands and feet he used to send with all speed for the mother and the child. But as this breeding device gave only poor results, he collected giants from abroad, from Sweden, the Ukraine, Ireland, Hungary, Wallachia, wherever he was given leave. When recruits arrived he measured them himself. One day his recruiting sergeants surprised him by producing a Norwegian eight feet eight inches tall. A lucky day! In his bedroom were hung head-and-shoulder portraits of all the captains in his regiment: this was to help him keep them in mind from the moment he sprang out of bed. In two other rooms he had hung the portraits of the colonels of his army, and under each of them the complete equipment of the regiment regularly laid out on a board. When a colonel died, his picture was taken down and placed respectfully in the Hall of the Dead, and the newly promoted officer took his place. Finally, in another gallery were lined up life-size effigies of the giant grenadiers. If gout stopped the King from going out he had himself wheeled past this huge, dumb troop. A fine life! Fritz was about to learn what it was to be a Prussian officer.

But the Prince's constitution could not endure the hardships put upon him by his father. The King so drove and harassed him that an ambassador found the child looking prematurely aged and walking with a stiff and heavy tread as though he had already been through numerous campaigns. He was a poor soldier, fell from his horse in front of the generals and wounded himself with the pommel of his sword. He was a poor Christian, and came so ill-prepared to his confirmation that the Court chaplain could only get him to scrape through the test by doubling his lessons. Each year Fritz was ill from exhaustion: in 1726 from vascular fever which left him "weak and thin as a hop pole"; in 1727 from jaundice. Family life got more and more unbearable by degrees. "A cloud of terror hangs over the house; every day the Queen weeps; the Prince's face is pitiful to behold." Everyone noticed his gloom and was secretly sorry for him. "His father," said a Saxon diplomat, "has taken him from his lessons too early. He has to follow his father everywhere, without hearing anything of public affairs. Thus if he learns anything, he does so indirectly, in disconnected scraps and without any general foundation. . . . His father thwarts his inclinations and desires. . . . He has only to know what will please his son to refuse it him." Rather was he trying to impose his own pleasures on the boy.

At nightfall he used to hold a gathering of the "evening company." People collected in the smoking room around a long wooden table. The King sat at one end on a four-legged stool which had two elbow rests but no back; his guests and cronies sat to left and right on two benches or on chairs. In front of each place stood a jug of beer, a glass, a pipe, and a basket full of coarse tobacco. Peat was burned in copper braziers. After an hour or two bread and butter, cheese, ham, and cold veal were brought in. The King used to make the salad himself. When there was a distinguished guest Hungarian wine was drunk. The company was an odd collection—some generals, some ministers, some ambassadors; old Dessau, who organized the army; the indispensable Seckendorff, who was the Emperor's officious representative; Gundling, the president of the Academy of Berlin, who used to get horribly drunk and was the clown of the gathering; sometimes one or two clergymen; when in the country a village schoolmaster, of whom Frederick William had had a high opinion ever since his pupils had refused to shout at the end of lessons at the royal command, "Our teacher is an ass."

The King smoked and drank continuously. Sometimes he had a gazette or a report read to him. He harped on his memories of Malplaquet, spoke of his ambitions, drank the healths of sovereigns who had pleased him during the day, and, glass in hand, criticized one or other of them ceaselessly. The conversation was haphazard—there was talk of hunting, strategy, politics, and religion, also guard-room gossip, oaths, and dirty jokes about women were to be heard. Sometimes the men danced together. There were also traditional jests, such as sawing a chair's legs in two and making a newcomer sit on it as the seat of honor or confronting him suddenly with a tame bear. A painting at Monbijou shows a meeting of the Tobacco Circle; Frederick is there on the right of his father, looking small and awkward. These affairs were like awful spells of forced labor for him, and he cut a wretched figure at them. The King treated him as a milksop and twitted him with not having manly tastes.

Every year in May Frederick William used to review the garrison of Berlin, doing one regiment a day. After the drilling the King inspected the men one by one. "My son, are you getting your fair share of everything?" he asked each in turn. The last day came the general inspection, when Frederick had to be on horseback at 2 A.M., and the parade did not finish till nightfall. After that the King used to leave for the provinces. In 1725 Frederick went with him to Magdeburg; in 1726 to Prussia and Westphalia. They traveled fast, so as to see everything. No escort, except on the Polish border. Five or six well-harnessed post chaises, but no window curtains whatever the weather. The idea was to catch the colonels, judges, tax collectors, and farmers of royal lands off their guard. The King examined accounts, visited the countinghouses, and asked questions by the hundred. When he was dissatisfied, his rage was appalling and his terrible cane came down on cringing backs. Once he had a deceitful councilor hanged before his eyes and forced his colleagues to come and see him slung from the gibbet. He also had moments of jollity, for he loved good fare, especially when others paid the bill. He invited himself en route to this or that man's house and gorged himself full. Like all good Germans, he preferred pork and goose however they were cooked, but he also liked truffles in oil and he could easily eat eight dozen oysters. Whenever he came upon a good dish, such as tripe with cabbage, he used to go down to the kitchen to ask for the recipe, and at the same time he got to know the prices of the ingredients.

Although Fritz—always the fop—had a leaning toward dainty dishes, he was not a bad trencherman and began to show interest in wines. But at Magdeburg and Stassfurt, so as to shine beside his father, he refused the ducats which the town council offered him as a gift of welcome and ordered them to be given to the poor. He refused ducats! At Magdeburg the King forced him to get them back, but he had the impudence to declare that he would keep them till his accession and then return them to the wretched taxridden inhabitants. In Westphalia he dined with the King at General von der Mosel's. They were to go hunting after the meal, but the old general, who had drunk a bit too much in honor of his guests, could not get into his saddle. The Prince had played him the dirty trick of shortening his stirrups. He watched the scene this caused with much amusement. Now the King liked playing practical jokes well enough but only on professors, and Fritz ought to have respected a military man.

From incidents of this sort it can be seen that the character of Fritz hardened in proportion as the King tried to break it. He learned to control himself better under restraint, he hid his humiliation, he lied, he kept back his tears but he did not bend. "Firm in his decisions to the point of being opinionated"— thus a perspicacious diplomat described him. He despised his father for not being able to dominate him. Sometimes he set out to madden him by playing the innocent. One day Wilhelmina and he burst out laughing in the middle of a sermon, and then they evaded the anathemas of the Church by putting on a contrite expression. Above all, for his moments of freedom he organized a second life of which we know little—but it presupposes accomplices and many secret absences. At the age of fifteen he had already a debt of 7,000 thalers with a Berlin banker —about $10,000 in the money of today.[2] It is difficult to believe

2. These modern equivalents are notoriously inaccurate. The Germans reckoned by crowns, or thalers, or reichsthalers, which have been called rixdollars; thalers minted in Prussia were worth from three to four French livres, and from

that all this enormous sum was used to buy music paper or to pay transcribers of music. It is true that he owned a hidden library in the town, which was near the palace in a private house belonging to Councilor von Peyne; it contained exactly 3,775 volumes in 1730, and the catalogue fills eleven large pages in Bratuscheck's work on the education of Frederick. The great French and English periodicals, an English encyclopædia, dictionaries and grammars in French, English, Italian, and Spanish, a French rhyming dictionary, anas, manuals of poetry, style, and conversation, French translations of the great writers of Greece and Rome, a number of biographies, memoirs, and tales of travel almost all in French, a short history of Brandenburg in French, atlases, all the great French writers since Rabelais, all of Voltaire that had so far been published, works on mathematics and physical and natural sciences published in Paris and in Holland, books on the Fine Arts and music, books on political theory— Machiavelli, Thomas More, Bodin, the Abbé de Saint-Pierre— treatises on moral philosophy, the works of Descartes, Bayle, and Locke. The Prince wrote out the catalogue of his first library with his own hand, but it is obvious that he alone could not have planned a collection embracing almost all the knowledge of the human race. Duhan had chosen for him and had brought the books together. Frederick must have read haphazard, piecemeal, like a pilferer who tastes forbidden fruit.

The money he borrowed so mysteriously was also spent on finery. He had court suits made and used to wear them on the sly, after he had cast off his uniform, which he called "his shroud." One evening the King surprised him in a brocade dressing gown: he tore it off him and threw it in the fire. Perhaps he bought himself jewelry, snuffboxes, and rings, for which he had a passion at one time. Perhaps he bought the silence of his servants. . . .

After the Prince's confirmation in 1727, the King, knowing a little and suspecting much more, dismissed Duhan and put in his place Major Senning, a famous disabled soldier, who had charge of the Prince's military training. In addition a few months later he gave Fritz four new companions, who were also to be

60 to 75 cents in English money of the time. The florin or gulden was worth from two to three livres, and from 40 to 60 cents.

his overseers. He told them that his son was at a dangerous age and liable to every evil impulse, that they must keep an eye on his conduct, and that on their heads would fall the responsibility "for the least excess or irregularity from which they had failed to dissuade the Prince" or of which they had not warned him, the King.

Frederick William said all this in front of the Prince; a more humiliating procedure cannot be imagined. But the King knew very little of his son, and Frederick possessed in the highest degree that natural knack of the weak, which is to make use of their weakness to gain pity and love. About a dozen of his letters of 1727 and 1728 have been printed; they were to one of the four, Lieutenant Frederick Louis Felix von Borcke, younger son of the president of the Chamber of Domains of Minden. The overseer had been captivated; he had become the chosen crony, the dearest companion, from whom the Prince demanded the pleasure of a passionate friendship—a friendship such as sometimes exists at an age when love has not yet taken shape in a man's heart. One day the King praised Borcke; Fritz at once sent him the news: "It has pleased me more than I can say because of the love I feel for you." When Borcke was ill, he got anxious: "Every time I think of you, and I often do, I cannot stop myself from falling into a fit of melancholy, from which only you can save me. . . . Do not die, for death is the one thing in the world which I fear most for my friends and least for myself." When Borcke got better, he thanked him for it as for a gift: "You alone could inspire me with such joy, and no one else but I alone can feel it." He excused himself almost humbly for worrying him: "I am afraid of boring you with my importunate friendship which can give pleasure to no one but myself. . . . Finally, my tiresome tenderness shows itself, and lays bare to your eyes these feelings of a heart which is full of you, and which cannot be quieted except by the knowledge that you are fully aware of the tender affection with which it adores you."

Fritz had soon the chance to make use of this charm of his under circumstances calculated to enrage his father. At the beginning of 1728 the King was getting ready to set out for Dresden, where he was expected on a visit. He kept up cordial relations with Augustus II the Strong, Elector of Saxony and King of Poland. Augustus II was a veritable colossus of a man and when in the smoking room never missed one round of drinks. Between them they even founded a club, the Anti-Temperance Club, and exchanged huge tankards as tokens of esteem, which it was a point of honor to empty at a draught. They also did business together. Augustus II had bought his father's collection of antiques off Frederick William, and gossip says he paid for them with two regiments of dragoons. But Dresden was the most brilliant, sumptuous, dissolute Court in Germany, and therefore the King had decided not to take Fritz, and Fritz was deeply disappointed. To console him, Wilhelmina intrigued so skillfully with Suhm, the Saxon envoy at Berlin, that King Augustus was won over by his maneuvers and asked for the Crown Prince himself; Frederick William had to give way to his host's entreaties and call Fritz to his side. So that his son should make a good impression, he ordered him a suit laced with gold and had a new livery made for his attendants.

There they were, both of them, amid a round of fetes, ballets, and masked balls, in an elegant and cultured society, surrounded by witty, easygoing women, dancing, dining, talking, listening to comedy and opera. . . . Fritz accepted all invitations. He had discovered the life of his dreams. He was at ease in this grandeur and magnificence; he was treated respectfully, as befits a prince. Puffed up by the arrogant idea he had of his own worth, which no snubs had shaken, he laid himself out to captivate all who came near him. He played the flute in public, in an orchestra of professionals. He was applauded. He knew how to please and how to charm. He sent his sister intoxicating accounts of "the great world," which he signed "Frederick Filosopher." Frederick William, on his side, was put in a good temper by the wine of Hungary, and took some trouble to be pleasant. But among other misfortunes he split his ballroom trousers. As he had brought only one pair, he had to send a courier to Berlin for some more. He saw that his son was more popular than he, and as it filled him with angry jealousy, he humiliated him in revenge.

Still he had not seen everything. Augustus the Strong kept a kind of harem of the finest women of his country. When he died it was reckoned that he had had three hundred and fifty children by his mistresses. He would willingly have lent some of these ladies to his guest. One night, Wilhelmina tells us, he took Frederick William into a richly furnished room. Suddenly a tapestry was drawn aside, and his eyes beheld a novel sight indeed. "It was a girl in Eve's costume casually lying on a day bed. She was a more lovely creature than the paintings of Venus or the Graces; she caught the eye with a body of ivory, whiter than snow and with a better figure than that of the Venus de Medici at Florence. The resting place of this treasure was decorated with so many wax tapers that their light was dazzling, and the goddess' beauty gained a new brilliance from them. The authors of this masque had no doubt that the King's heart would be moved by this display; but it was quite otherwise with him." Frederick William was a faithful rather than a tender husband. No sooner had he set eyes on the beauty than he made a scandalized retreat and roughly pushed Fritz, whom he saw behind him, out of the room. But Venus had not aroused the same horror in Fritz, and Wilhelmina affirms that he won the favors of the dazzling Formera from King Augustus. "She was his first mistress," she adds.

What must we think of this? Court gossip is always unreliable. Wilhelmina herself was too much of a scandalmonger for her word alone to be believed. On the other hand, Fritz was quite capable of telling her of imaginary escapades from pure braggadocio, to pose as a fashionable young man. This side of a man's life is always very private, but it is highly probable that Frederick awoke late to the pleasures of love and was never much interested in them.

Back in Berlin he fell ill of a sort of slow fever which took away his appetite and made him grow visibly thinner. (It was said later that this illness was badly treated and made him impotent for the rest of his days, but we can by no means accept this statement for lack of real proof.) "Caused by despair at the prospect of no more debauchery," wrote Wilhelmina without a qualm; the beginning of tuberculosis, said the doctors, who were probably right; but also despair, boredom, and weariness with life— these attacked him when he was under the old rod once again. The King thought his life was in danger, which distressed him. "When children are well," he wrote to the Prince of Anhalt-Dessau, "we do not know how much we love them." "My eldest son is ill of consumption. You can imagine how it grieves me. I am going to wait till Monday: if things do not improve, I will have a consultation of all the doctors, for none of them can say what is wrong. He gets as thin as a shadow, and yet he does not cough." Frederick William listened patiently to the Queen's reproaches; he even regretted his past severity and tried to make up for it with caresses.

However, in these days of reconciliation he alone was sincere. Abetted by the doctor, who belonged to "the right side," Fritz exaggerated his illness to get some rest, and Sophia Dorothea for the chance of a good nag at her husband. When the King of Poland came to Berlin to repay the visit of the year before, Frederick at first made a point of not appearing at meals. Vanity, not fatigue, was the reason, for he did not wish to yield precedence to an electoral prince. He came to the fetes and illuminations. It is also said that he used to meet a Polish countess secretly, who dressed in men's clothes and had favors for him. This is the epilogue of the tale of Dresden, and is no more likely than the rest.

When the illuminations had burned themselves out, the King left on a tour of inspection without taking Fritz, who was still thin and pallid. There was an orgy of music behind the back of the disagreeable tyrant. Augustus II had lent the Queen his chamber orchestra. Every day there was a concert at Monbijou, and Frederick and Wilhelmina played duets together; Wilhelmina lovingly called her lute "Principe," and Frederick his flute "Principessa."

In autumn the King returned, and as was the custom each year they had to follow him to Wusterhausen for the hunting. Wilhelmina has described with "fierce distaste" the residence which Frederick William liked so much: "This enchanted castle, this so-called palace . . . which only consisted of one main block, the beauty of which was heightened by an old tower, which contained a spiral staircase of wood. The main block was surrounded by a terrace, round which a ditch had been dug, and the black stagnant water in it was like the river Styx and spread an awful, suffocating smell. Three bridges, one at each façade of the house, communicated with the courtyard, the garden, and a windmill opposite. The two sides of this courtyard were two wings where the gentlemen of the King's suite were lodged. It was bounded by a palisade, at the entrance of which were chained two white and two black eagles, and two bears to act as guards—very wicked beasts, it must be remarked in passing, who attacked everybody. In the middle of this courtyard stood a well, which had very cleverly been made into a fountain for the use of the kitchen. This magnificent group was girt around with steps and outside with an iron trellis, and this was the agreeable spot where the King chose to smoke of an evening."

The castle still exists. When the bell turret, the steep roofs, the high gables, and the ivy-clad walls come into sight among the trees its appearance is not unpleasant. It is the home of a country squire built upon an old castle. The walls of the ground floor are thick enough to stand a siege. The tower divides the frontage into two unequal parts, three windows to the right, one or two to the left. The rooms are divided in the same way, on either side of a large corridor which begins behind the staircase. The whole ground floor is vaulted. The King slept in a very narrow corner room which still possesses in the thickness of the wall the deep sink in which he used to wash. The Queen had an enormous room, but like the others it was merely whitewashed, with a very rough floor and with wooden chairs, for not a single upholstered seat was to be found in the house. On the first floor were the smoking room, a little playroom, and six or seven rooms where children, ladies in waiting, governesses, and officers were jumbled together.

The ornaments have been replaced, but must have been made up as they are today of antlers, wild boar heads, weapons of the chase, boar spears, hunting equipment, and copper lamp brackets. In the gray days of September and October the little deepset windows let in only a weak, gloomy daylight; night fell early and the evenings were cold. As there were only three hearths to heat the whole place, Fritz often lay between damp sheets at night. The main torture of that house was living one on top of the other in a perpetual state of being spied upon. When there was a large party they ate outside in a marquee, with their feet in water if it had rained. The food was bad because no one ever knew when the King would get back and because he insisted on sitting down to table twenty minutes after his arrival. The Queen grumbled and scowled while waiting long hours for him;

she played quadrille with three ladies, and her daughters were kept in with her, "not daring to breathe the fresh air, nor go into the garden, because she forbade it."

Frederick William used to hunt the bear and wild ox in Prussia and Pomerania, and deer, wild boar, pheasant, heron, hare, and partridge at Wusterhausen. He showed a real passion for this sport, firing up to 600 shots a day, and remaining twelve hours at a time in the open. His books record the fact that from 1717 till 1738 he shot 1,455 pheasants, 1,145 hares, and 25,066 partridges at Wusterhausen. But the greatest sport was hunting the stag, at least three times a week. The King and his guests were driven to the meet sitting back to back on the benches of a long cart, or rather on a beam on wheels, without rails or roof. The pack, however, was a large one and carefully chosen; the grooms looked well in their uniforms, and at the death the chief huntsman presented the King with the foot of the beast on a silver tray. The stag was brought back in a cart adorned with branches, and after a steward had cut off the steaks for the Court, the animal was eaten by the pack in front of the palace and in the presence of the ladies. Frederick William wanted everything to be done royally, for in this matter alone he loved extravagance and etiquette: his correspondence with the Prince of Anhalt-Dessau is full of hunting talk and of discussion about the proper usages —it is almost like reading a book by Jacques de Fouilloux.

Fritz loathed this life. He used to give the hunt the slip, and sit under a tree playing the flute like Telemachus, out of defiance. In the evening at dinner he never opened his mouth. "My dear Borcke," he wrote to his friend, "we have here the silliest collection of people—a motley, ill-assorted crowd, for neither the tempers, the ages, nor the tastes of those who compose it harmonize. . . . There is plenty more I could tell you, but I got up at five o'clock this morning, and now it is midnight. . . . I am so sick of all I see that I would like to wipe it from my memory, as though it had never been. Nevertheless, one thing I can tell you is that in the smoking room my amusement consists of cracking nuts, an amusement fully worthy of our present abode."

Two clergymen who spent several days at Wusterhausen in 1727, young Francke and his brother-in-law Freylinghausen,

have each written a journal which lets us get a glimpse of the
private life of the King. They were with him especially at meals,
which lasted two hours. Prince William said grace and Frederick
carved the meat. Their father kept his caresses for William.
Once he took his hand, and raised a big knife as if he wished to
cut off his fingers. "The Prince went pale, but at once cried out
confidently, 'Oh, Papa, you love me too much to do that,' and his
father embraced him." One Sunday he asked him point-blank,
"William, what do you remember of Mr. Freylinghausen's sermon?" The little fellow replied quite unabashed, "And you,
Papa?" Whereupon the King began to laugh heartily, and everyone else joined in.

Frederick William had been ill and he took advantage of the
visit of two theologians to harry them with questions about
Heaven, the prophets, permitted pleasures, the conditions of
salvation, the dangers of play acting, the division of the Protestant
churches and Christian resignation, and also about the expenses
of the orphanage at Halle, of which they were in charge.

"Yes," he said to Francke, "it is very difficult to get to Heaven."

"That which is impossible to men is possible to God," replied
Francke.

"Yes, I know my wickedness as well as anyone else does," the
King went on. "I am a wicked man, and if one day I am good, I
am bad again the next. I know it well, but I cannot do otherwise."

He also remarked before a crowded table, "It may be that I
shall live some time longer and that I shall make perfect my religion (so help me God), or else it will become worse. But if I do
become worse, I will consider all priests who perceive it and fail
to inform me as unmitigated scoundrels."

At that he got up and distributed pious works to the Queen's
ladies. In the middle of one of these edifying conversations,
Gundling arrived drunk. He made some surprising gestures,
rose from the table, fell among the pages, got up, bellowed, and
stumbled out again.

The two learned men asked for an interview with the Crown
Prince, whom Freylinghausen had had to question publicly on
the Scriptures by royal command. Frederick replied to one that
he was engaged for the whole day and to the other he spoke eight

ungracious words on the fifth day. Before leaving Wusterhausen the wretched man learned that the Prince referred to him as a Pharisee, and that he and his sister had made fun of him because of his belief in ghosts.

The rages of Frederick William became daily more terrible. Frederick complained of them in almost every letter to Borcke. The King is still in a bad temper, the King scolds everybody, the King is fearfully put out, "There are cursed scenes here every day, I am so tired of them that I would rather beg my bread than live on the footing on which I do." He no longer even hoped for a reconciliation, but only for "a lull in the storm of abuse."

He made an attempt to obtain this truce in the middle of September. He did not dare to speak to the King but wrote to him instead. He began by excusing himself for not coming to see his dear Papa, because he fears he will get a worse welcome than usual. It is by letter that he begs his dear Papa to be more gracious toward him. He assures him that after having searched his conscience at great length he finds no cause for self-reproach; but if, unknowingly and unwittingly, he has done anything to offend his dear Papa, he humbly asks his pardon, and he hopes that his dear Papa will put aside the cruel hatred of which his son is made conscious by his whole behavior. He, Frederick, cannot get used to the idea that, after having always thought he had a kindly father, he must henceforth believe the very opposite. Thus he is full of confidence and hope that his dear Papa will consider all this, and will become gracious to him once more. In any case, he assures him that he will voluntarily commit no fault, and that, even in disgrace, he is with the most humble and faithful respect his dear Papa's most humble and faithful son and servant.

This servile, sugary letter full of "dear Papas" and cumbersome circumlocutions still further irritated the King, and his reply was a scornful note written in the third person: "He who does not love his father is self-willed and wicked. Love of a father means doing his will, not only when he is present but even when he is out of sight. Secondly, he knows very well that I cannot stand an effeminate boy, who has no manly tastes, who is shamefaced, who cannot ride a horse or shoot, and who crowns all by not washing himself; who curls his hair like a madman and does not have it cut. And I have reproached him a thousand times for all this but to no purpose. Moreover, he is proud and vain. Apart from a very few, he speaks to no one. He is not popular. He is not affable. He grimaces like a madman and only does my will when constrained and forced to it. He does nothing from filial love; his only pleasure is to follow his own inclinations; he is good for nothing. That is my answer."

No, Fritz was not the pliable creature, the yielding paste which the brutish obstinacy of Frederick William desired him to be. But every atom of despotism, violence, and even madness in the father's character was aroused by the idea that this sickly body housed a rebel soul, that for years this skinny dandy, this little woman, this flute player had never ceased to combat his orders and scorn his rages, that he, the King, had found beneath his hand, among his own flesh and blood, the only living thing which dared defy him. On such occasions he was no longer master of himself. He would thrash his son, from jealousy, from hatred, from rage at feeling himself despised, to make the boy feel humiliated also and to rejoice at his shame.

Six weeks passed, weeks of terror. Then Frederick made what Lavisse calls a heroic bid. It was at the Feast of St. Hubert, at dinnertime. He was seated opposite his father beside the Saxon minister, Suhm, who recorded the incident. He began to drink heavily, contrary to his usual habits. "I shall surely be ill tomorrow," he said to Suhm. Soon the wine went to his head, and he complained to his neighbor of his life of slavery. He talked so loud that he could be heard on the other side of the table, and the Queen anxiously made signs to Suhm to calm him. But Frederick proceeded with his mournful confidences and frequently interrupted his tale to point at the King and say, "Nevertheless, I love him."

"What does he say?" asked the King.

Suhm replied that the Prince was drunk and not responsible for his words.

"Bah!" answered the King. "He's shamming. But what does he say?"

"The Prince says that, though the King makes him drink too much, he loves him a great deal."

"He's shamming," repeated the King.

The Queen, obviously in agony, got up, and all showed signs

of following her. At a gesture from the King the men sat down again. Suhm offered to lead out the Prince, who could no longer stand up, but Fritz swore he would not leave without having kissed his father's hand. The King, who was enjoying this farce, gave him his hand with a laugh. Frederick seized the other and covered both of them with kisses and then he drew his father to him; all the company burst into applause and shouted, "Long live the Crown Prince." Then Fritz reeled around the table and flung himself at the feet of the King, hugged his knees, and repeated with endless protestations that he loved him with all his heart, that he had been slandered, that people wanted to make them quarrel, but that he would love him and serve him passionately all his life.

"Good, good," said the King. "Only let him be a good boy."

That evening in the smoking room Frederick William was extremely gay.

The change did not last long because his father was persuaded that Fritz had been acting a comic part, which is possible and even probable. Yet historically it matters little: drunken vows could not change the harsh decrees of Fate.

The Deserter

I

IN the drama which follows allowance must be made for political factors: they played a great, almost a decisive part, for if such factors did not begin the misunderstanding between father and son, they were responsible for aggravating it and pushing it to its final stages.

The matter went back a long way. The Queen, Sophia Dorothea, was the daughter of George I, King of England. The families of Hanover-England and Brandenburg-Prussia had a mutual promise of long standing to "cement their close relationship with further marriages." It had been agreed that Wilhelmina should marry her first cousin, the Duke of Gloucester, son of the Prince of Wales and grandson of George I, and that Frederick should marry the duke's sister, the Princess Amelia. "The two mothers discussed these plans in their correspondence; even the children exchanged letters and little presents."

That her daughter would reign in London was an article of faith to Sophia Dorothea. It used to console her wounded pride. She told herself that she would one day be the mother of a king of Prussia and of a queen of England, that she would be honored by two kingdoms and that she would cut a fine figure in the world. But this double marriage was not a mere family affair; it was an affair of state which was going to link Prussia to the maritime powers for a considerable time—that is to say, it would make her join one of the two systems which divided Europe between them; it would place her on the side of France and England against the Emperor and Spain. Diplomatic bargaining soon took a hand in the negotiations: the royal family of Prussia became a field of battle for the leagues and counterleagues of contending chancelleries.

Besides, the King's very character was of such a type as to

complicate the intrigues still further, making them oscillate by leaps and bounds from one extreme to the other without system or plan. Frederick William had the greatest respect for the wealth of the United Kingdom but he had little enough for the House of Hanover; he had known it poor and needy in spite of its proverbial arrogance, and it had been hoisted onto the British throne by the merest chance, by a distant family connection, because Parliament had put aside the real heir, James Stuart, on the charge that he was a Papist.

Things became far worse when George I died, for Frederick William had played with George II in the days when he was only a German princeling—he had even licked him. He could not bear seeing his old playfellow beating the big drum now, so he nicknamed him the Comedian, the Coxcomb, the Red Cabbage, and when he was angry everything connected with his brother-in-law became "English riffraff." Besides, by any reckoning, what would he gain through this union? The reversion of Jülich and Berg which he coveted? Holland would never want such a well-armed neighbor at her gates, and France was not anxious to run the risk of installing the Prussians at Düsseldorf. The Red Cabbage was himself too ambitious to play a big part in Germany to work wholeheartedly for the aggrandizement of a rival elector. In the other camp the Empire was blessed of God, and the Emperor was formidable; without any doubt, anxiety for his own dominions, which had to descend to his daughter, would force him to be more accommodating than that Englishman. What was he to do? From which side would he get the more?

Lavisse has summed it up extremely well: Frederick William did not wish to act alone and disliked all possible associates. He dreaded isolation but he had no sooner entered a coalition than he would try to get out of it. He mocked at the Great Powers, whom he called quadrillers. Yet he would have been very glad to join in a dance with them, had he not feared he would be treated as an inferior. Most of all he was afraid of not being paid on the nail in "good spadefuls of earth" and "a good piece of well-populated land." No territory, no Prussians! this was one of his mottoes. When he found his plans were discovered, he used to be furious, he would withdraw, return, falter, and recover himself. Then he was the laughingstock of Europe. People mocked at his grenadiers who were so clean that he would never send them into battle for fear of their getting dirty. They mocked at his finances which were so orderly that he did not dare to set a regiment on the march for fear of upsetting the account books. They mocked at his hectoring ways and his endless tergiversations. Peter the Great said of him, "He likes fishing but will not wet his feet," and an English minister remarked, "The King of Prussia is only a wolf in his own sheepfold."

After Prussia had joined the Hanoverian Alliance in 1725, the marriage plans grew more specific. Frederick William moved from Herrenhausen, where he had met his father-in-law, and left the Queen there to arrange the date of the betrothals. King George pleaded the necessity of consulting his Parliament and evaded the issue. As Frederick William pretended not to understand the reasons for this delay, he was told from London that "a romance must not be begun from the tail end," and that matters of State must be decided before thinking of the trousseau. But at this point the King in a fit of nervous remorse had been unfaithful to the League of Hanover, and had already signed a neutrality pact with Russia and a secret agreement with the Emperor.

This *volte-face* was the work of General Count von Seckendorff, whom the Emperor Charles VI and Prince Eugene had been clever enough to send to Berlin. Frederick William had a great liking for him: he had been acquainted with him in the past, in the Low Countries during the war against France. Seckendorff had the build and manners of a good farmer, and he was intelligent, wily, an indefatigable talker, a good soldier, and a firm Protestant. He was always in the smoking room, drinking and smoking without crying off, and he could cap the King's remarks on any subject, quote the Scriptures at Francke, and boast of the superior qualities of the detachable bayonet with the veteran Dessau, the "graybeard." He studied his Frederick William, and in a few months, by overlooking his rages, encouraging his manias, and humoring his prejudices, he acquired a knack of leading him without his noticing it.

Furthermore, at the Prussian Court everyone was for sale.

Seckendorff discovered the prices paid by France and proceeded to outbid them. He made certain of the help of the principal minister, Grumbkow, who was master of the particulars of the Department for War. "Monsieur de Grumbkow," Wilhelmina wrote, "is a very civil man whose conversation is smooth and witty. His mind is cultured, supple, and insinuating, and his talent for pitiless satire—that fashionable accomplishment of our times—makes him universally popular. He knows how to combine serious and amusing talk. This fine exterior hides a crafty, calculating, treacherous heart. His life is most dissolute; the whole of his character is just a mass of vice." "He is stuffed with malice, spite, cowardice, falsehood, and impertinence," a Saxon envoy said of him. Truth to tell, Grumbkow was well versed in business of every sort. He was the godson of the Great Elector and the son of a minister; a general at thirty-one and a minister himself at thirty-five; he was well informed, affable, worldly wise, and an uncommonly hard worker. But he was one of the most dishonest, crafty men to be found in any cabinet in Europe. Frederick I, on his deathbed, had called him a great rogue. "Change your nature," he said to him, "or else you will never get to the home of the blessed, where I am going." Grumbkow had not changed his nature. For cash he delivered to Seckendorff the secrets of the royal household and even its diplomatic correspondence. He would advise him of the right moment to make certain moves; he used to prime him in the art of bringing up matters before Jupiter (i.e., the King) "in a way that he will find tasty" and also in a way that would spike the guns of Olympia (i.e., the Queen). Seckendorff saw to everything: he even bought Gundling, who could say things of importance when in his cups, and Eversmann, the lodgekeeper at the castle, a good spy to whom Frederick William liked to tell his worries.

The strangest thing of all was that the King was more or less aware of the treacheries which surrounded him but was not shocked by them. He often wrote across a ministerial report, "You are too fond of *louis d'or*," or, "You are too fond of guineas," but he did not dismiss the minister. He was convinced that no one would ever succeed in affecting his decisions and it amused him to see foreign powers giving his councilors an income: their generosity allowed him to reduce salaries and brought money into the kingdom.

At heart he was passionately eager for his daughter's marriage, but he thought he was acting very shrewdly by not being the first to speak of it and by feigning indifference. "The lady is worthy of the gentleman," he used to say, and "I do not wish to commit myself for a few apples and pears." When the news from London was good he advanced his pretensions. The young lady was to have no dowry, at the most "a few jewels, some crockery, and some silver." If the Prince of Wales could not make up his mind, there would be many other suitors. After all, he did not care whether Wilhelmina was a queen or not: the House of Brandenburg was sufficiently illustrious to do without a further royal title.

When reports were bad, when his tricks did not come off, how he raged! The English riffraff wanted to embroil him with the Emperor, to "dishonor" him, to "confound him from top to bottom." But he would not let himself be treated as a pawn and he worked off his temper on his family—on the Queen, to whom he would not speak for a fortnight because she did not know how to make her children appreciated; on his daughter, who was a whore and a harlot, whom no honest man would ever want to take for his wife; on his son, whose fault it was that he had been shamefully bamboozled by the Red Cabbage.

It was in fact on his son's account that the negotiations did hang fire. George II insisted that the weddings of Frederick and of Wilhelmina should take place at the same time. He was afraid that when Frederick William had provided for his own daughter, he would not want to have *his* as a daughter-in-law. This was not bad reasoning, for the King of Prussia was not anxious to welcome a princess who was a great lady brought up amid luxury and likely to bring expensive habits to Berlin. And then he thought Fritz too young and was afraid this emancipation would give the boy pleasure.

"I don't in the least want," said he to the Queen one day, "I don't want a daughter-in-law who gives herself airs, and will fill my Court with intrigues as you do. Your son is only a sniveler, and rather than marry him off I'll give him the strap. He has a horror of me but I can bring him to heel" (this was his usual phrase). "Devil take me, if he does not change for the better, I'll treat him in a way he don't expect."

During 1729 negotiations hung fire, with the Queen running to her brother and her husband by turns as a suppliant, with George II standing firm on the principle of the double alliance, and with Frederick William demanding an engagement for Wilhelmina alone, while Grumbkow and Seckendorff kept throwing oil on the fire.

"If you and your English family were at your last gasp," the King shouted at his wife, "I would not even lend you my doctor."

But when Wilhelmina was quite worn out and seemed ready to take another fiancé from her father's hands, then it was her mother's turn to abuse her: "I would rather throttle you with my own hands." It was also Fritz's turn to encourage her to resist: "It is better to put up with anything than to fall into the hands of our enemies; England is our only support, and if your marriage with the Prince of Wales is broken off we shall all be destroyed together." Domestic scenes became so frequent and so painful that the governors, Finckenstein and Kalkstein, could stand the sight of them no longer and asked leave to resign. The King attached two new officers to his son's person, Colonel von Rochow because of his staid character, and Lieutenant von Keyserlingk because he was brisk and a good horseman.

Frederick William loved to mess about with pen and paper, so he gave Rochow a new set of Instructions, wherein he repeated that the Prince was a weed who liked the activities and pleasures of an idler. The colonel is to explain to him "that all effeminate and lascivious activities are highly unbecoming in a man; they are fit for fops and dandies, but a dandy is a doll, a villain, the type who needs a box on the ears." He is also to teach him to sit a horse, to look people in the eyes, to walk without mincing, and to speak and laugh without making faces. He is to prevent him from wearing a nightcap, fill him with the spirit of sincerity and candor, and make him question everybody, great and small, "for it is the way to discover everything and to become sharp-witted."

Once again Frederick William dwelt upon his disappointments as a thwarted educationalist—futile recriminations, for at seventeen Fritz was forever immune from those influences he had not freely chosen to follow. The very nature of the conflict had altered: for the last two years the Crown Prince, urged on by his mother and his sister, had been up to the neck in diplomatic intrigue. As heir to the throne, he made himself the tool of the Anglo-French camp against the Austrians.

Certainly Wilhelmina and he had every right to defend themselves against the Court of Vienna; they had every right to despise and hate Seckendorff and Grumbkow. However, since the matter was a political one, they were on dangerous ground, where they had to take care not to encroach upon the rights of the King's Majesty and thus slip into treason. Unfortunately, their mother was not the sort of woman to preserve moderation, for when her vanity urged her on this stout party lost all restraint and was irresistibly drawn toward perilous attempts.

From the first she established herself on an intimate footing with the English and French envoys, Du Bourguay and De Rottenbourg: she was always consulting them, she showed them the letters she sent to England, she asked them for couriers to evade police censorship. As she paid spies to hang around the King, she sent in their reports to the envoys, and in return they told her what they had learned from Knyphausen, the minister in the pay of France.

She encouraged Frederick to ask Rottenbourg about the best way to become popular, and Rottenbourg advised him to be as affable as his father was severe. Frederick was spurred on to tell the Frenchman of conversations in the smoking room, of the maneuvers of the Imperialists, of all he could learn of his father's schemes. He loaded Rottenbourg with attentions, assured him of his sincere friendship, took his hand in public, and frequently begged him "to persevere in the good cause." After having recalled the Prince to more prudent and discreet behavior a number of times, Rottenbourg yielded to his insistence and finally wrote to Versailles: "The King is universally hated by men of every status in the kingdom. To weaken the father it would be necessary to form a party around the Crown Prince and gather round him a number of officers. . . . I believe this plan would succeed." *A party.* For what purpose? The Queen had got used to the idea that Frederick William would not live much longer; the King himself in moments of depression spoke of abdicating and retiring forever to Wusterhausen with a pension of 10,000 thalers. But, since there was no need of a party to ensure that the crown should revert in due course to the legitimate heir, what then?

There were plots against the King. Once forty of the giant grenadiers had been exasperated by ill-treatment and had considered setting fire to Potsdam and burning him alive in it. At army maneuvers he sometimes heard the whistle of bullets without knowing from which musket they came. Did the mother and the son themselves think of some palace revolution? Did they think of certifying him insane and shutting him up? When Frederick was closeted with the ambassadors there may have been strange, criminal innuendoes—Rottenbourg did not even dare put them into writing. However, there is not the slightest indication that things went any further than words. It is true that Frederick had for his father an overwhelming hatred and wished for his death. For instance, while Frederick William was traveling in Saxony the house where he was staying caught fire: "The conflagration was so sudden and so fierce that they had all the trouble in the world saving that prince." Fritz, who was staying at Count Flemming's, was awakened so that he could go to the King's side: "Why should I?" he asked. "I can't put out the fire," and he went to sleep again. Also in a letter to Borcke he described in a singularly detached manner an accident which nearly killed his father—it was on the way back from hunting: "One of the horses which was in front of the cariole shied and pushed the cariole so near the ditch" that it only needed to go an inch farther "to drown the King and all the luggage." Yet in spite of his hatred and his precocious dissimulation Frederick was too frivolous and inexperienced to make a good conspirator. His mother was even more inexpert; impulsive, credulous, now peevish and now arrogant, swift to anger and swift to give offense, her pride rebuffed those who were most attached to her, while her habits of misplaced confidence dashed the hopes of her fellow conspirators. Her chambermaid and favorite, Frau Ramen, with whom every night she would share "her most secret thoughts," was in the pay of Seckendorff, and also spied on the King's account. As for Frederick and Wilhelmina, they rigged out their enemies

with nicknames borrowed from Scarron's *Roman Comique:*
Grumbkow was "Rancour," Seckendorff "Rapine," and the
King "Scarecrow." There was much that was bookish and infantile in all this. If Fritz plotted at all, it was a plot of useless
correspondence and of conferences which led nowhere.

He wrote far too much. A frontier incident had occurred between Prussia and Hanover: Prussian recruiting sergeants had
carried off some Hanoverian peasants by force, and the English
Court had arrested some Prussian soldiers and kept them as
hostages, though their passports were quite in order. Frederick
William was touchy on this score. He mobilized 44,000 men, and
it seemed that war was imminent. This was the moment Frederick chose to send "very secret pledges of his friendship for the
King of England and the Prince of Wales, saying that he is convinced that his feelings will always be truly understood, in spite
of the present alarms." A fine display of personal diplomacy!
Elsewhere he boasted of having reconciled the arrangements of
his father and of his uncle: England wants the double marriage,
Prussia the single match; let England be content for the moment
with Wilhelmina's marriage, in exchange for which he gives his
word of honor, confirmed in writing, never to marry anyone
except the Princess Amelia.

Frederick William did not know all this in detail, but with
the help of Grumbkow and Reichenbach, his envoy in London
who was also a pensioner of Austria, he knew enough of it to
keep him on the boil. Wilhelmina's memoirs tell of scenes that
were terrible—or ridiculous. One day she and her brother were
in the Queen's bedroom, where the King had forbidden them
to set foot. The carelessness of the people on guard allowed Frederick William to come near to surprising them. There was no
other way out of the room, so Fritz hid in the cupboard of the
commode, and Wilhelmina went flat on her belly under the bed.
The King, who had been hunting, sat down in an arm chair
and dozed off. Frederick was suffocated in his nook, and Wilhelmina from time to time poked out her head to breathe. This
torture lasted two hours, until the King left.

At table one of his daughters complained of not having enough
to eat, and he flew into a rage but vented all his anger on the
two eldest children: he threw a plate at the head of Fritz, who

dodged it, and another at Wilhelmina's, which she also avoided. A storm of insults followed these preliminary attacks, and then he started to sermonize with his eyes on the Prince. "You ought to curse your mother," he told him, "for it is she who is the cause of your being badly brought up. I had a teacher who was an honest man: I always remember a story he told me in my young days. At Carthage there was a man who had been condemned to death for several crimes he had committed. He asked to be allowed to speak to his mother while he was being led to execution. She was fetched, and he came close to her as though he wanted to whisper to her and bit a piece out of her ear. 'I treat you thus,' he said to his mother, 'to make you an example to all parents who do not take the trouble to bring up their children in the practice of virtue.' Apply the story to yourselves."

As no one answered he started railing at his son again, until he was in such a state he could speak no more. At last the company rose. Frederick William, who was seated in a wheel chair because of his gout, dealt a great blow at Wilhelmina with his crutch as he passed by, "which," said she, "I was lucky to avoid, for otherwise I would have been stunned." He continued to chase her for some time in his vehicle, but the people who were pulling it along took care to let her get away.

Wilhelmina declares in her memoirs that before serving her and Frederick the King used to spit on their plates, and that he forced both of them to eat and drink things which disagreed with them, "which sometimes made them bring up all they had eaten before his very eyes." This is hardly credible, but on the other hand worse details are to be found in ambassadors' reports. For a long time the King had been in the habit of beating Frederick, but these blows seemed more humiliating as the boy grew older. One day—it was in December, 1729—as the Prince entered his room he beat him with his stick, seized him by the throat, threw him on the ground, and forced him to kiss his feet and beg his pardon. This horrid scene was repeated. The King displayed his son's humiliation; he flouted him in public and threatened him with unheard-of punishments, "You know," he would add, "that I keep my word."

In this inferno the Queen and Wilhelmina, who had so often feigned sickness, nearly died in good earnest—the Queen of a difficult pregnancy and Wilhelmina of smallpox, which the King treated by making her drink extremely strong Rhenish wine. As for Fritz, he found some consolation in devoted friendship with a page named Keith, whom he loved passionately and to whom he gave his entire confidence. Wilhelmina reproached her brother for allowing such familiarities to Keith, but he always excused himself by saying that the boy was his intelligence officer, that he had to humor him, and that he was spared much suffering through the news he provided.

II

In the month of March, 1730, the dispute over recruiting was swiftly settled by arbitration, and at the request of Sophia Dorothea the Court of St. James's announced the dispatch of an ambassador extraordinary, Sir Charles Hotham. It always flattered Frederick William to have attention shown to him, and Sir Charles was an eminent man of very old family and, as a final piece of good fortune, colonel in the Grenadier Guards of His Britannic Majesty. Frederick William promptly changed sides and moods simultaneously. He invited the English envoy, Du Bourguay, to the smoking room, drank the health of King George and forgot to drink the Emperor's, and made ponderous fun of the indigence of that wretched creature, Charles VI, whom he called Charles the Guttersnipe. The object of Hotham's mission was to fix up both marriages. As a last resort he had been authorized to put off that of the Princess Amelia, provided that the engagement was publicly announced and confirmed by treaty. In the course of the negotiations he was permitted as a maximum to guarantee to Amelia a dowry of £100,000 sterling and the government of Hanover until Frederick ascended the throne of Prussia. On the other hand, Frederick William had his plan, which was the same as ever and consisted of fixing up Wilhelmina at top speed without committing himself to anything for Frederick.

Hence arose a remarkably comic scene. Charles Hotham arrived on April 2, and on the fourth he was invited to dine at Charlottenburg. As the conversation revolved around the recent marriage of the Princess Frederica to the Margrave of Ansbach,

the King began to shout, "Girls must be married off! A health
to Wilhelmina and the Prince of Wales!" Then all the company
rose with cheers and repeated this in chorus, Grumbkow with
the rest but green with terror. That was Hotham's first surprise.

Frederick William was drinking heavily and told him that
Wilhelmina was ugly and pock marked but that this slight dis-
figurement did not prevent her from being honest, that she
would be faithful, that she would content her husband, and
that damn it all if he had taken her three years sooner she would
have been in better condition. In the end he seized his neighbor and started dancing.

Sir Charles was astounded and withdrew all the more anxious
from having overheard a scrap of conversation between Grumbkow and the King. "Are you to be congratulated?" Grumbkow
had said.

"Yes."

"Twice over?" Grumbkow had then asked in a low voice.

"No," had been the reply.

Next day at a conference the Englishman tried to put things
straight. Frederick William did not seem unsympathetic, and
Hotham had a feeling that he had made difficulties so as to extract
from London some titbit in return for Frederick's hand. "If they
want the double match and want to detach me from the Emperor, let them make a proposal for Jülich and Berg." And
again, "I loathe my son and my son loathes me. It would be all
to the good for us to keep apart. They can nominate him Regent
[*Stadthalter*] of Hanover with his Princess." Now King George
was the most conciliatory of men: he even suggested taking Wilhelmina without a dowry. Without a dowry! Frederick William
had no more reasons for hanging back, yet he still beat about
the bush. He could come to no decision in his irresolute mind,
he was a prey to anxiety and held council after council. The
ministers weighed and weighed again the pros and cons, especially the cons, for the Imperialists had picked up heart again
and played their trump cards. Seckendorff staged a grand pathetic scene. Schooled by Grumbkow, Reichenbach sent from
London news well calculated to anger and upset the King—he
assured him that the English were sure they could lead him by
the nose, once they had removed his most faithful servants from

him; Amelia was an intriguer who wanted to lay down the law in Berlin; King George only agreed to everything because he hoped to get it all back again; moreover, his seat on the throne was not a very firm one, the Hanoverian dynasty was unpopular, a Stuart restoration was not an impossibility. . . . Finally Reichenbach revealed a dangerous point—the promise made by Frederick to marry none but the Princess Amelia.

That was enough to upset everything. Frederick was anxiously following the debate wherein his destiny and liberty were at stake, and he guessed the mishap had occurred when he saw a triumphant smile on Seckendorff's face once again. On two occasions he wrote to Hotham imploring him to consent immediately to the marriage of the Prince of Wales alone. "As for mine," he added, "the only real reason the King has for not putting his hand to it is that he wants to keep me under his heel, and bait me for the rest of his life whenever he is in the mood for it." He expected "terrible things" to befall him, but he would remain faithful to his word.

The negotiations finally broke down at Mühlberg in Saxony, where the Prussian Court had moved to join in the festivities arranged by the King of Poland. Reviews, maneuvers, drinking bouts, parades followed each other in fine confusion. There was a feast of thirty thousand covers for the army. The Kings rode on horseback between the tables, and the sweet turned out to be a cake which had used up six hundred eggs, three tons of milk, and a ton of butter. When the Kings drank each other's healths sixty pieces of artillery were fired. Betweenwhiles Hotham and Frederick William exchanged reminiscences, but the King of Prussia was pigheaded and there was no longer any hope of a settlement. Faithful to his habit of revenging himself on his family, he humbled his son with much publicity. One day he thrashed him black and blue in public, threw him on the ground, dragged him by the hair, and took him on parade in soiled clothes. "If I had been treated like that by my father," he shouted, "I'd have killed myself; but to you it's all the same, you stand for anything"—terrifying words which encourage the thought that Frederick William wished to drive his son to suicide, or at least to push him to some desperate act which would be his undoing.

Sir Charles had nothing more to do in Berlin. The new minister, Guy Dickens, had arrived and it was up to him to continue the talks. All the same, to wind up his mission Hotham decided to strike a decisive blow. The English postal authorities had intercepted several letters from Grumbkow to Reichenbach, and Guy Dickens had just brought one along with him. It provided decisive evidence: it proved that Frederick William had been fooled by the two rogues and showed how it had been done. Charles Hotham and Guy Dickens were received on July 10 at midday. After the presentation of the new minister they talked of indifferent matters. The King was in a good temper and Hotham, returning to serious topics, reminded him of the suspicions of which he had already made mention. He concluded by saying that, as General Grumbkow had always denied them, "The King my master has ordered me to place this autograph letter of the general's in Your Majesty's hands." He held out the letter; the King took it and glanced at it, recognized Grumbkow's writing, and red with anger threw it on the ground, crying, "Sirs, I have had enough of this damned business." Then he rushed out, slamming the door behind him.

Such manners were current in Prussia, but they were out of place in dealing with an English gentleman. Hotham had acted in the name and by the orders of the King his master, and the affront was thus addressed to George II; it was therefore impossible for the ambassador to remain a moment longer. But Frederick William was repentant: "It's my spleen," he said; "when I am in a bad temper I must give vent to it." He could not understand Hotham's touchiness. What a fuss about a crumpled letter! If indeed it had been a letter from the King of England—but a letter from that scoundrel Grumbkow! Twice he sent a minister, Borcke, to present his excuses to Hotham and to ask him to dinner: both times the reply was the same—Hotham could not reappear at Court. He left on the morning of July 12.

From that moment Fritz decided upon flight.

III

FOR the last two years at least he had been thinking of getting out of Prussia, both to escape ill-treatment and to breathe a different air. Perhaps it was his father himself who had put the idea into his head by saying good-humoredly one day that "he would like to be Fritz's governor and take him through foreign lands." In the summer of 1729 there was a rumor current that the King was going to send the Crown Prince to finish his education in Italy, France, or England. Moreover, rivalry between father and son was almost a rule in the Hohenzollern family, and separation had always seemed the most discreet method of appeasing dissension. The Great Elector had spent four whole years in Holland and had only come back under compulsion and with obvious distaste. His son, the future Frederick I, had withdrawn into Hanover with his young wife, and Frederick William himself had been lucky enough to visit the Low Countries in the company of the Prince of Orange. However, he did not want to be separated from his own son: first, because he was afraid he would not return, and secondly, because he got too much satisfaction out of tormenting him.

The first definite plans of escape began in November or December, 1729. Frederick confided them to Keith, the page whom Wilhelmina detested, but the conspiracy got no further than the ordering of two trunks and a carriage through the agency of Lieutenant von Spaen. Soon afterward Keith was sent to garrison duty at Cleve with the Mosel regiment and Fritz was left alone. Not for long, however, for chance soon gave him a new bosom friend. One evening when he and his mother were going by water to Potsdam, he had heard through the darkness the notes of a flute. He had quietly gone up to the musician and spoken to him. It had turned out to be Lieutenant Hans Hermann von Katte, a twenty-five-year-old officer; he was the son of a general, the grandson of a marshal, and a servant of the Hohenzollerns by tradition, and he seemed born to be the companion of the Heir Apparent. Fritz had some scruples about him at first but they broke down after Keith had left, and he adopted him as a friend.

Katte was not handsome: very swarthy, pock marked, with heavy eyebrows and a look which struck Wilhelmina as baneful. But he had much to commend him: he was a great reader, witty, elegant, well mannered, and a facile, brilliant conversationalist; he played the flute and the harpsichord; he could draw and paint.

He wrote French fluently, loved liberty, talked and laughed at everything without restraint, and surrounded his friend with an anxious, uncritical tenderness. In just the same way a few of the younger officers were fanatically attached to the Prince; Spaen once said that he felt such love for him that he endured real anguish when separated from him, and Katte added that his misfortunes so affected him that he could refuse him nothing.

On May 31, 1730, while traveling in Saxony, Fritz revealed his intentions to Katte, who at first was frightened by them. At the camp at Mühlberg he returned twice to the subject. There was no time to lose; he wanted to leave at once and take advantage of the confusion. One day he asked Count Hoym, the Saxon minister, to get him some post horses for two officers who wanted to travel incognito to Leipzig. Hoym easily guessed who the officers were and refused the horses. Katte himself had begged him to make difficulties, but to soothe the Prince's impatience he bought him various maps. On June 16 the English envoy, Guy Dickens, had a long secret meeting in a tent with Fritz and left the camp bearing a secret message from him—the Prince explained to his uncle that he could no longer bear the wretched way in which he was treated. The Prussian Court was soon to go to Ansbach to see the Margrave Charles William, who had married the King's second daughter, and then on to Stuttgart and Cleve; he would escape en route and get to Strassburg. He would remain six weeks or two months in France and from there he would travel to London. He expressed the hope that England would take measures to prevent any harm befalling his sister and to assure him of a good welcome in France.

Katte was told everything by the Prince and offered to come with him, if need be to follow him from post to post disguised as a postilion until the right moment—a wildly imprudent idea. But Frederick was so inconsistent in his decisions that twelve days later during a hunt he begged Augustus II to ask the King on his behalf to let him travel.

The reply from London reached Berlin on July 9; at 10 P.M. Frederick had an interview with Guy Dickens at one of the gates of the castle, while Katte kept watch. In a note drawn up in official language King George gave his nephew the strongest assurances of his sympathy but advised him to attempt nothing

for the moment. Particularly he begged him to consider the
political repercussions of his flight and the international consequences which would not fail to ensue. Fritz did not grasp the
importance of this objection, but on the other hand, as George
II offered to pay his debts, he boldly declared them to be 15,000
thalers—double their real size. During the night of the fourteenth to fifteenth he had a last interview with Katte in the
park at Potsdam. Hidden in the bushes they talked for two hours
tenderly, feverishly. Fritz had just been beaten again and henceforth he feared for his life. He asked his friend for help, and
Katte tried once more to restrain him but could not and so he
swore not to forsake him. However, as he was not taking part in
the progress to Ansbach, he had to get leave from his colonel. If
he got it, he hoped to join Fritz at Wesel, not at Stuttgart, and
they would both make for Holland instead of going by Strassburg. They even agreed to correspond under cover of a cousin
of Katte's, the Rittmeister von Katte, who was on a recruiting
round in Franconia. Then they parted company. It was past
midnight; Katte returned to Berlin on horseback. Next day he
received a note from his friend fixing their meeting place and
listing some odds and ends he wanted to have with him in his
exile. They had already sold the diamonds from Fritz's decorations to raise money, and Katte had borrowed from his friends.
Their funds came to nearly 3,000 thalers.

The wretched boys were surrounded by spies and their secret
was not their own. Rumors of the flight were hawked from embassy to embassy. The sympathetic Rochow awaited a false move
by the Prince and kept careful watch. One night, after a scene
with the King, he had seen him return completely beside himself and he had begged him in a friendly way never to undertake
anything in the grip of anger, for fear of having to repent of it
sooner or later. Frederick William had only resigned himself to
taking his son with him to keep a closer watch on him after
considerable hesitation. Such was his mistrust that he gave orders
that Colonel von Rochow, General von Buddenbrock, and Colonel von Waldow should travel in the same carriage and never
lose sight of the Prince.

At dawn on the fifteenth the expedition set out. The King
kissed his wife affectionately before leaving and expressed his

regret for having foolishly offended Hotham. "You are beginning to talk a little more reasonably," replied the Queen, "but the minute you see so much as a spire in Monsieur de Seckendorff's country where you are going first, you will change your tune, and when your travels are over you will return to plague your family and your wife too and to make us suffer as usual."

"No, no, I promise you," replied the King. "I love you much too much, my dear wife. Give me a kiss."

In spite of a terrific storm which had destroyed the roads they reached Meuselwitz on the first evening. On the eighteenth the King went on his way accompanied by Seckendorff. He was at his son-in-law's on the twentieth and he stayed there a week. Fritz was worried by the lack of news from Katte and had already questioned the Rittmeister in vain, when at last he gave him a letter from his cousin: leave was unobtainable and Katte could not come. Fritz burned the letter at once and answered within a quarter of an hour by the same messenger that Katte should keep calm until the arrival of new orders. But the Prince wanted at all costs to be certain of having an accomplice and he asked the Rittmeister point-blank to come with him. When he tried to treat this as a joke, Frederick gave him many details of the route, even urged him to look for horses, and handed him a letter of credit to cash immediately at Nürnberg; then the good man took cover behind his oath as an officer, entreated the Prince to think things over, and withdrew much disturbed (July 23). Without divulging anything definite, he advised Rochow, "as a good friend," not to lose sight of his "exalted subordinate," and he added that moreover in this matter he committed himself to the grace of God to escape all misfortune.

To whom could the Prince appeal? Among the King's pages was a younger brother of Keith's, who was as dull as the elder one was bright. When they halted Frederick called him and spoke to him privately.

"Are horses to be found everywhere?"

"In certain places," replied Keith, "some are left, in others none."

"Do you always have to remain beside the King's coach? Can you be half an hour ahead or half an hour behind?"

"I have to stay by the carriage, for when the King gets down he asks for all who are attached to the carriage."

"Order some horses for me."

"Where does Your Highness wish to go?"

"Where do you think I am going?"

"I don't know."

"If I once get away I shall never return."

Frederick thought it was arranged and wrote on the twenty-ninth to Katte telling him to go to The Hague, where he would be hiding himself under the name of the Count of Alberville. He sent him, to inform the public, a sort of manifesto to justify his conduct and on the same day he ordered Keith, his friend at Wesel, to desert from his regiment and go to Holland with all speed.

On July 31 the caravan reached Augsburg: it goes without saying that the fields of battle where Marlborough and Prince Eugene had won renown were visited. Then they proceeded toward Württemberg. The ducal Court awaited them at Ludwigsburg. Frederick, who treated desertion like a visit to a ball, used the delay to have a scarlet cloak made for him. He was able to get in touch with young Keith once again: perhaps he spoke to him, or perhaps he slipped him a note. At Heilbronn the carriages left the valley of the Neckar and headed for the Rhine. Fritz had decided to fly on the following day, August 5, at half-past two in the morning. Keith knew of this and was to obtain horses at the stage.

Frederick thought this would be Sinsheim, but the King suddenly decided to stop two leagues short of that and sleep at Steinsfurt. As usual the retinue dispersed and spent the night in barns. "We are not much farther from Mannheim," said the King; "if we leave here at five o'clock we shall have plenty of time to get there."

At about quarter-past two Fritz got up, took his money, put on his scarlet cloak, and went out quietly, expecting to find Keith and the horses. However, Keith was late. For half an hour he waited for him by the door. His valet, Gummersbach, had heard him get up and had asked him where he was going so early. "To the King," Fritz had answered. Gummersbach had thought that answer was odd. He sent a messenger to wake Colonel Rochow, who had gone to bed fully dressed and came at once. He found the Prince standing beside his carriage as though waiting for the company to set out. They exchanged "Good mornings," and Fritz, seeing that the game was up, went back into the barn. Rochow and Gummersbach stood on guard by the door. At that moment Keith arrived.

"Good morning," said Rochow. "What horses are these?"

"They are for the pages," replied Keith.

"Go to the devil with your horses!"

Day began to break. Seckendorff, Buddenbrock, and Waldow arrived in due course. The noise made the Prince come out.

"How does Your Excellency like the costume of His Highness?" Rochow asked the Austrian.

In despair the Prince took off his cloak and, so as to bear out his statement to Gummersbach, he did in fact go in to his father, who told him to set out ahead as his coach was a very heavy one. Fritz went and drank his tea, hid himself, delayed as long as he could, and reached Mannheim two hours after the King. But he had been able to meet Keith and once again ordered him to bring the horses in the small hours.

Keith was too frightened to repeat the performance. On Sunday, August 6, he flung himself at the King's feet as he was leaving church and confessed to him his all-too-weighty secret. As he had to go to dinner at once the King restrained himself. On the way he noticed Rochow in an antechamber and drew him into a window recess. "Fritz has tried to desert," he told him hurriedly. "I am amazed that I haven't been told. You, Rochow, you will bear the blame on your head, your neck, and your throat if you do not hand him to me at Wesel, alive or dead. Now I have no time to say more, and as I may not be able to get a chance to speak with Buddenbrock and Waldow alone you will tell 'em this in my name and inform 'em that they're held to be responsible." Rochow answered briefly, "He cannot escape us; he would not have escaped. I had taken my precautions. The Prince's valet is reliable: he and the footmen can be trusted."

Henceforward Fritz was closely guarded, but the journey continued as though nothing was up. Darmstadt, Frankfort, Mainz, Bonn, Cologne—for six mortal days the Court dawdled from the lands of one princeling to those of the next. Nursing stormy thoughts in his great bubbling brain, the King would not modify the prearranged program of visits for fear of offending his hosts; he made an effort to go against his whole nature, but it stifled him. At Mannheim on August 6, when he saw the governor and officers of Landau come from France to pay homage to him, he imagined they were waiting on the Prince to help him in his flight, and that evening he could not resist flinging this remark at his son: "I'm surprised to see you here. I thought you'd be in Paris by now." Frederick, who did not yet know of his betrayal but was beginning to get anxious, replied boldly, "In Paris? I would be there, if I'd wanted to go," and he slipped a final note to Keith: "Things are taking a turn for the worse. Arrange for our departure." On the eighth the procession arrived at Frankfort, the town where emperors were elected. The King left his carriage at seven in the morning. He ordered that Frederick be conducted on board the boat which was to take them to Wesel. For his part he went to the Town Hall, the *Römer,* where he accepted the compliments of the citizens and had them show him the Golden Bull. He too went on board at nine o'clock.

On the tenth they were at Bonn, where the Archbishop Elector of Cologne awaited his powerful neighbor. The Heir Apparent could not miss the reception. As they started Frederick William in a loud voice ordered Rochow and the officers not to leave the Prince for a second and to deliver him alive or dead. Fritz heard everything but did not so much as blink, yet his anxiety increased as he felt himself more strictly guarded. Guessing that Seckendorff already knew the truth, he drew him aside and played a part for his benefit. He confided in him as to a generous adversary and to a man of honor. He blended truth with falsehood and told him that he had wished to escape but that he had been held back by the thought of his mother and his sister; that he did not fear for his life but that he was tortured by the danger to Katte and to his friends. "If the King is willing to promise me that he will pardon them, I will make a clean breast of everything. If not, they can cut off my head, but I will betray no one." He ended up by begging Seckendorff to help him out of "this labyrinth" and by assuring him of his eternal gratitude: the Austrian murmured a few vague words of sympathy in reply.

On the eleventh the King learned of the flight of Keith, and a preliminary inquiry revealed that Fritz had received a letter from Berlin when at Ansbach. Frederick William no longer mastered his impatience and he had Fritz sent on ahead to Wesel. At midnight he himself arrived in Prussian territory and at half-past eight he called the Prince to the castle.

He adjured him before God on his sense of duty and his conscience to tell the whole truth and to confess all the circumstances of his proposed desertion. Then came the formidable question—"Why?"

Frederick replied, "Why? Because every day you become more hostile toward me, because you keep on giving me tangible proofs of your hatred. The very idea of flight was put into my head by the state of despair to which you had reduced me."

Frederick William felt himself on the edge of madness. He thought his son wanted to have him assassinated and bit by bit he extracted from him the preliminary details—the purchase of the carriage by Spaen, the sale of the decorations, the rendezvous given to Katte, the orders given to young Keith, the purchase of the scarlet cloak. . . . At the end Frederick was shut up in a room guarded all night by armed sentinels.

On the morrow there was a second cross-examination by Colonel von Derschau on lines laid down by the King. At what moment had Katte learned of the plan of escape? Had there been a third party? How much had the Prince got from the sale of the diamonds? How much money had he? What had happened to that money? To whom had he given it? To the question "whether anyone had recommended Katte to him" Fritz replied that he had chosen him of his own accord because he considered him one of the "devil-may-care" type of people and just the man to take a big risk. In the first of these examinations he showed the very qualities he displayed up to the end of the inquiry—he was dry, cunning, always in control of his nerves, insolent whenever possible, without a single sign of remorse. On August nineteenth he wrote to his father, "My dear Papa, I once more take the liberty of writing to my dear Papa to ask him in all obedience to free me from arrest, assuring him that all I have said or have had told to my dear Papa is true. As for the suspicions against me, time will show that they are without foundation, and I affirm I never had the evil intentions imputed to me. I beseech my dear Papa for mercy and I remain, while there is breath in my body, with the most respectful humility, his very devoted son." Frederick William was wrestling with dark thoughts and his sole reply was to hand him over to Buddenbrock on the same day with orders to take him to the fortress of Cüstrin, where two rooms opening into each other, well guarded and with "good doors," were being made ready.

Of course Buddenbrock was provided with detailed instructions under fourteen headings. Frederick, who was henceforth referred to as the King's son or the suspect—the "Prisoner"—will travel in a carriage with Buddenbrock, Waldow, and Rochow. This will be followed closely by a second chaise, in which a major and three captains will sit. They must carry good pistols and swords. The carriages will leave very early, secretly, with food and wine for the whole journey. They will avoid the territories of Hesse and Hanover where the Prince might find accomplices. As far as Halle, where they will first meet a Prussian garrison, they will drive day and night, all of them eating, drinking, and sleeping on the seats of the coaches. "During the journey General Buddenbrock will take all precautions humanly possible to prevent the prisoner from escaping. He will not allow him to leave the carriage to enter a house. All natural functions will be performed in open country, where the landscape is open for miles around and there are no hedges or bushes." Buddenbrock must take the Prince to Cüstrin "alive or dead." If the carriages are attacked en route by overwhelming numbers, he will see to it that only a corpse is captured.

The King left a little later but took a week to reach Berlin: this delay was a proof of his worry and uncertainty.

IV

In her usual way Sophia Dorothea had taken advantage of the King's absence and had given herself some pleasant days at Monbijou. There were dinners, balls, and concerts. Katte played the flute and Wilhelmina accompanied him on the harpsichord. He was calm and gay, confident that Frederick would not try to escape without him and without the money. On August 15 he asked for leave to spend a day in the country. He was arrested the next morning between six and seven. Two letters from the King arrived on the same day: one for the Queen, which has been lost, and the other for the Grand Mistress of the Robes: "My dear Madame de Kamken," he wrote, "it is my unfortunate misfortune that my son has tried to desert with a page called Keith. I have had him arrested. I have written to my wife. I trust you to see that she does not fall ill, though she may grieve for a day or two. I am your devoted friend, etc."

The Queen and Wilhelmina spent some dreadful days waiting for the master's return. They trembled for Frederick but also for themselves. In the midst of their agitation they yet had the presence of mind to destroy certain compromising papers. Their meeting was such as might have been expected. "We all hurried to kiss his hand," Wilhelmina relates, "but he had no sooner set eyes on me than rage and fury seized upon his heart. He became black in the face, his eyes sparkled with anger, and he foamed at the mouth. 'You damned bitch,' said he to me, 'do you dare appear before me? Go and keep company with your rogue of a brother.' While uttering these words, he snatched hold of me by one hand and gave me several blows on the face with his fist; one of these struck my forehead so violently that I fell backward. . . . The King then lost control of himself and would have redoubled his blows and trodden me underfoot. The Queen, my brothers and sisters, and the rest of the company prevented him. They stood all round me. . . . It is impossible to describe the melancholy position we were in. The Queen was giving shrill cries, wringing her hands, and running distractedly about the room. The features of the King were so disfigured with rage that he was fearful to behold. My brothers and sisters, the youngest of whom was only four years old, were at his knees, trying to soften him with their tears. Madame de Sonsfeld held up my head, all bruised and swollen from the blows I had endured. Can a more moving scene be imagined?"

Frederick William had Katte brought to the castle immediately. He had not thought to catch him. Having lost Keith, who had luckily fled to England, he directed all his rage against him. But for Grumbkow he would have put him and Frederick to the torture to make them confess imaginary crimes. To every question Katte replied with complete frankness. He even wrote with his own hand a long confession relating all that had happened since the occurrences in Saxony, and he was content to plead in his defense that on all occasions he had done his utmost to restrain the Prince and that, besides, he had felt quite confident that Frederick would return as he himself had kept control of the money. They never had the least design either against the State or against the King; their aim had merely been to save Fritz from his anger. At the last examination, on September 20, to the question "Does he agree that, if he had been able, he would have escaped?" he answered, "If the Prince had left, I would have followed him, but I was always sure that he would not go."

Fritz was in prison in solitary confinement, without pen or ink, with only a Bible and a book of Psalms for company. Every morning the door of his room opened at eight o'clock and two officers came in to make sure that everything was in order. In their presence a soldier brought the Prince water for his toilet, a basin, and something to eat. The orderly removed the slops and yesterday's dishes. All this had to take no more than a few minutes. The officers withdrew, locked the door, shot the bolts, and did not return until midday, when the orderly placed lunch on the table and removed the breakfast dishes. The King had forbidden knives and forks, so the meat was cut up beforehand and Fritz ate with a spoon. The same program was carried out for supper at six o'clock. "Thus," Frederick William had specified, "the door will be opened three times a day, and each time it will not remain open for more than four minutes, and each time two captains will be present at the opening and the closing of it. As far as sentries are concerned, you will post as many as are needed, for in this matter you are responsible. The two captains who attend to the opening and closing of the doors risk the deepest disgrace should they speak to the prisoner. If he asks them anything— what is happening here or there, what is the news of the world —they must make no reply, and this is my strict command and they must obey it and answer for it with their heads."

Fritz still did not fear for his life but he was mortally anxious for Katte and for his friends. He remained in bed nearly all day, trying to drop off to sleep and even lacking the spirit to put on his clothes. The solitude and the silence horrified him. He tried to speak to his jailers; so as to see new faces and hear a human voice, he asked to be allowed to make disclosures, even to go to communion, which was forbidden him in terms which contained a hidden menace: "It is not yet the time for that; the court-martial must be concluded first; after that the time will come."

The King had nominated a committee of investigation, which was composed of Grumbkow, another general, a colonel, and the commissioners Mylius and Gerbett. The committee saw to the arrest of Lieutenant von Spaen, who had bought the carriage at Leipzig, and of Lieutenant von Ingersleben, who had held Katte's horse on the night of the talk in the garden at Potsdam. It questioned the four prisoners, Katte's servants, Rochow, the Ritt-meister von Katte, and the valet Gummersbach. The King himself dictated an account of what he had seen and heard during the journey to help the investigators. They reconstructed the whole story without much trouble and only Frederick's accounts remained in rather a muddled state.

The main examination took place on September 16. Frederick was asked 185 questions, which the King had either composed himself or revised carefully.

"Who is the prisoner's father?"

"Who is his lord?"

"Who is his military chief?"

"Does he recollect that, during his childhood, His Majesty the King, as father and sovereign, gave him all his affection?"

The questionnaire followed the sequence of events closely, but was composed in such a way as to remind the Prince over and over again that he himself was responsible for his unhappy child-hood, because he had willfully rejected the help, friendship, and advice of his father.

In the course of it the King cast himself as playing the part of a generous person: "Did he not say one day that he would pay his son's debts with pleasure, for he did not lack money, provided Frederick behaved differently and with honest intentions?"

The answer was "Yes," which straightway led to this other re-proach, a surprising example of vainglorious meanness: "Did not the son, by begging foreign powers for money, give them reason to think that his father had none?"

Sometimes Frederick was silent; more often he replied with a simple "Yes," as though in approval of a tale he was being told. He only expanded a little to plead his youth as an extenuating circumstance. To question 178, "Has he anything to add in his defense?" he replied that he had nothing more to say and that he admitted he was guilty. Then came seven questions which were so unprecedented in law that the chief commissioner, Mylius, only consented to ask them at the written order of the King.

"179. What does he deserve and what punishment does he expect?"

"I submit myself to the mercy and the will of the King."

"180. What does a man who soils his honor and plots a desertion deserve?"

"I do not consider that I have been lacking in honor!"

"181. Were there not enough good examples before his eyes in his regiment?"

"Yes."

"182. Does he still deserve to spend his days with men of honor?"

"I regret what I have done, but I have never looked at things in that light."

"183. Does he deserve to be King?"

"I cannot be my own judge."

"184. Does he wish to be given his life, yes or no?"

"I submit myself to the mercy of the King and to his will."

"185. As he has by a breach of honor made himself incapable of succeeding to the throne, does he wish, to save his life, to abjure and renounce his succession in such a way that the renunciation will be confirmed by the whole Roman Empire?"

"I am not so devoted to life as that, but His Majesty the King will not treat me with such severity."

At that moment Frederick must have been at the end of his tether. However, when he heard the final questions he saw that his father had counted upon this deep lassitude of his to extract from him a renunciation of his rights. His replies are extraordinary for their dignity, moderation, and precision. He was disturbed nevertheless by the threat to his life and had the following declaration added to the protocol: "He admitted that in everything, in every way, and on all points he was in the wrong; that what gave him the greatest sorrow was the vexation of His

Majesty; that he begged His Majesty to believe that his intentions had never been of a criminal nature; that he had never sought to harm His Majesty the King in any way; that he submitted himself in all things to the will and mercy of the King; that His Majesty could deal with him as he thought fit, and that he asked pardon of him."

When the protocol was given to Frederick William he tore out the page containing the request for mercy. Throughout the month of September he turned over frightful schemes in his mind. After an evening in the smoking room the Dutch minister wrote that he would not have believed it possible for a man to conceive "such abominable and impious designs." "If the King of Prussia continues in this state of mind," he added, "we shall see the bloodiest scenes that have occurred since the beginning of the world." The inquiry had disclosed a little love affair of Frederick's with Dorothea Elisabeth Ritter, the daughter of a rector at Potsdam. He had caught sight of her one evening as he was lounging about the streets with Lieutenant Ingersleben. He had spoken to her on the doorstep and had visited her home several times when her parents were out. They had played music together. He had given her a flowered dressing gown, a pale blue house frock of Tours silk, two bracelets, and a few yards of ribbon. As soon as he learned this story the King sent a surgeon and a midwife to Elisabeth Ritter, who found her to be innocent. All the same he signed this savage order: "His Majesty orders Klinte, councilor of the court, to have the daughter of the teacher who is here under arrest whipped tomorrow. . . . She will be whipped first before the Town Hall, then before her father's house, then in all corners of the town." After which she was sent to do hard labor at the prison at Spandau "forever." She was sixteen and a half years old.

With childish fury Frederick William attacked everything which concerned his son. An examination of Katte had revealed the library arranged by Duhan. The books were seized, put in barrels, and sent to Hamburg to be sold there. The King sent for the librarian, questioned him personally for an hour and a half, and ended up by asking him how much he was paid. "Twenty heller a week," replied the wretched man (six cents in the currency of today). "That's certainly not too much," cried the King with momentary satisfaction. The librarian was exiled to Memel and Duhan along with him. At the same time Frederick's servants were dismissed, his horses sold, and the regiment of which he was colonel given to his brother William: the succession might almost have been said to be open.

Frederick William certainly thought of putting his son to death. During those dreams of his which were full of ghosts he saw and saw again the corpses of the Tsarevitch Alexis and the Infante Don Carlos, but he shrank in horror from the crime. Already, in the name of the Protestant religion, the Low Countries, Sweden, and England had written letters interceding on behalf of the Prince. The Elector of Saxony, King of Poland, had also written. The Emperor was getting ready to speak as supreme head of the German peoples. Further requests for mercy came from St. Petersburg. Then he considered at greater length forfeiture of the succession. But in fact, if Fritz was ready to renounce his rights to the crown, his renunciation would not be sincere; at his father's death he would hasten to reclaim his rights and the kingdom would be rent by civil war. And then Frederick William was not only King of Prussia, he was also Elector of Brandenburg and a member of the Holy Roman Empire. Frederick's abdication would only be valid after confirmation by the Diet. There was a procedure to follow, a long scandalous business, which would expose to the eyes of the princes the hidden motives of the drama, the brutalities, the scenes, and the betrayals. Frederick William foresaw that it would be he and not his son who would be in the dock.

As the inquiry proceeded he came to understand how exaggerated his first suspicions had been. The commissioners discovered neither plans for assassination, nor military plots, nor foreign encouragement. In vain did Frederick William get angry with the "good-for-nothing," the "guttersnipe," the "rogue" who defended himself with such impudence, in vain did he repeat that his son was his "redoubtable rival"; the case was turning into such a family feud that he thought of circulating a manifesto to the sovereigns to substantiate the grounds of his complaints. On September 11 he wrote to the Prince of Anhalt, "As for the inquiry, it goes ahead. Katte's is finished with. As for Frederick's, the scoundrel has to be questioned again at Cüstrin before it can be discussed. All the same it is certain that England knew every-thing and advised against desertion. That scoundrel wrote to the King of England and complained that I treated him badly. . . . The King advised him not to desert. . . . God save honest folk from having unnatural children. It is a great blow to me. Never-theless, I have a clear conscience before God and mankind. Warnings, punishments, kindness, mercy: nothing had any effect on him. I have more than a hundred witnesses and my only consolation is that you, my dear fellow, are one of them. . . ." A desire for self-justification lurks in these last sentences and it showed itself still more strongly in the recommendations to Mylius. The magistrate must bring out in high relief the fact that "His Majesty has not done what he has done without good reason. Otherwise for every six who support the King there will be half a dozen who will support the Prince." People must not believe "that the King denied his son bread and that the Prince has been forced by necessity to act as he did, whereas the King had his reasons for putting under the Prince's control no more than his actual needs required." He almost put himself into the position of the defendant; he gives us the feeling that he no longer knew what he wanted.

However, this "witch trial" had to come to an end. From the beginning the King had described his son's action as desertion, therefore it was on the charge of desertion and of complicity therewith that he decided, on September 21, to send Colonel Frederick and his four accomplices before a court-martial, that is to say the Lieutenants von Keith (absent), von Katte, von Spaen, and von Ingersleben. The court was composed of three major generals, three colonels, three lieutenant colonels, three majors, and three captains; Lieutenant General von Schulenburg was to preside and it was to be in session at Köpenik from October 25 on. Each group of officers had one vote and the chairman one vote, which would be a casting vote if there was an equal division.

On the twenty-fifth and the twenty-sixth the court took the oath and heard the evidence from the inquiry read. On the twenty-seventh the judges separated for deliberation, each rank on its own. In the matter of Keith they were unanimous; Keith had shamefully deserted the colors, he should be summoned by a roll of drums, and if he did not reply his sword should be

broken and his effigy hung on a gallows. In the matter of Ingersleben the captains, the majors, and the generals accepted the
charge of his having run errands disagreeable to His Majesty to
the daughter of the teacher of Potsdam. The lieutenant colonels
and the colonels remarked that the lieutenant had Katte brought
to Potsdam on the Prince's orders, but knew nothing of his plans.
Proposed punishment—two to six months' imprisonment. In
the matter of Spaen the court was unanimous over the purchase
of the carriage at Leipzig. The captains, the majors, and the
lieutenant colonels added that during the journey to Ansbach
Spaen had read a letter written by the Prince to Katte, that he
was thus aware of the preparations for flight, and that he had
failed in his duty by not denouncing them. Proposed punishment
—to be cashiered and two to six years' imprisonment.

In the matter of Katte the most detailed and precise decision
was that of the majors. They set forth and enumerated his crimes
under eleven heads: preparations for desertion (the word turns
up again here), interviews with the ministers of foreign powers,
secret correspondence. In the ninth section they blamed Katte
for pleading in his own defense that the King had treated the
Prince badly, for it was not fitting that Katte, as officer and subject, should intervene in the very least "between father and son,
between his King and the successor of his King." Katte deserved
death. The colonels and the lieutenant colonels also voted for
the death penalty. Nevertheless, mindful of the fact that the
accused had not carried out his wicked plan, that however much
the enterprise had been considered, it had had no results, that the
accused had clearly repented from his heart, and that if he was
beheaded the Crown Prince would never find peace of mind
again in this life, they besought the King to remit the penalty.
The captains and the generals recorded that Katte had frequently
tried to hold back the Prince and that in Saxony he had even succeeded in preventing his escape. They therefore decided on life
imprisonment.

In the matter of Frederick captains, majors, lieutenant
colonels, colonels, and generals agreed that he had been badly
counseled and that he had had evil intentions. But they tacitly
refused to distinguish between Frederick as colonel and Frederick as Crown Prince, between the guilty officer and the son mis-

used by his father. They let it be understood that their loyalty was directed not only to the reigning sovereign, in virtue of his title, but to all his family. They stated that they, as vassals and subjects, could not pronounce judgment on the son and family of their King. They handed back the Prince to the exalted and paternal mercy of His Majesty.

There remained the casting vote of the chairman, who held Katte's life in his hands. He supported those who decreed the death penalty for Keith, lack of jurisdiction over the Prince, six months' imprisonment for Ingersleben exclusive of time already served, and cashiering for Spaen followed by three years' imprisonment. As for Katte, he stated that although the lieutenant had promised to help Frederick, he had fixed neither a place nor a time for it, and that the intention and the act must always be distinguished. As a result he could not bring himself to vote for the death penalty and he fixed upon imprisonment for life. When the King heard the judgment he wrote to Schulenburg a note three words of which are barely legible: *"Votum Regiis (sic).* They must do justice and not whitewash the whole affair, and as Katte [really took action] the court-martial must meet again and judge in a different sense."

Seckendorff tells us that a few days later in his presence at table he accused the judges of "base intentions." "I thought I had chosen men of honor who would not forget their duty, who would not worship the rising sun, and would only rely upon their consciences and the honor of their King."

First cause of anger: the King relied on the judges to help him out of a dilemma, but they had evaded this by refusing to take on their own shoulders the father's responsibility. In the second place, while admitting that Frederick had wanted to flee abroad, they had continued to give him the title of Prince and Highness and had used words to describe his crime which belittled it— "departure," "escapade," "truancy." They had insinuated that at the back of all this was a lot of thoughtlessness and a lot of youthful folly. "They would have liked to gloss over the plan of the Prince and his toadies as a childish game which did not deserve such a punishment."

The members of the court-martial met once again on October 31, but refused unanimously to contradict themselves. They had

Frederick William

not the power to go back on what they had voted to the best of their knowledge and conscience and in accordance with their solemn oath. Next day the King in his turn gave judgment. He declared himself satisfied with the verdicts on Keith, Spaen, and Ingersleben and he even ordered the immediate release of the last of these. "With regard to Lieutenant Katte, his crime and the sentence passed on him by the court-martial, it is true that His Majesty the King is not in the habit of stiffening the awards of courts-martial; more frequently he reduces them when this is possible. But this Katte is not only an officer under my command in the army, he is on the force of the Guards. And if in the whole army all my officers ought to be faithful and devoted to me the strongest reasons bind in this way the officers of regiments such as this, which are privileged to be immediately attendant upon the most exalted person of His Majesty the King and his Royal House. . . . As then this Katte connived at desertion with the rising sun and has intrigued with ministers and envoys of foreign powers . . . His Majesty the King does not understand what vicious train of argument has prevented the court-martial from condemning him to death. This means that His Majesty will no longer be able to trust any officer or servant who is held by oath and duty, for in this world things which have happened once can happen again, and those who are going to do the same thing, taking as a precedent the case of Katte, who will have emerged from the affair so easily and well, will think the same will happen to them. His Majesty the King, who also went to school in his youth, learned there the Latin motto: *Fiat justitia et pereat mundus.* He therefore wills, in the name of the right, that this Katte, although he has deserved according to the laws to be tortured with red-hot pincers and hanged for committing the crime of *lèse-majesté,* yet out of consideration for his family be removed from this life to death by the sword. The court-martial, when announcing the verdict to Katte, will tell him that this gives pain to His Majesty the King but that it is better that he should die and that justice should not perish from the earth."

There is in this letter a homely grandeur which is not counterfeit. Frederick William visualized his life as a very hard and busy one, he had thought of Prussia and of the future, but had he analyzed his underlying motives? Had he admitted to himself that he wanted Katte to die because the supreme penalty would justify his own conduct? A pardon would have been an admission that he had not a clear conscience. He had spoken of the "rising sun" because he had seen himself lying in the grave and had imagined Fritz, newly crowned, hurrying to open the gates of his friend's prison, flinging his arms around him, and bringing him to his side at Berlin.

The days which followed were days of terror. On November 2 Katte was brought before the court-martial to hear his sentence read.

"I put myself," said he, "into the hands of Providence and of the King. I have committed no fault and if I die it is for a good cause."

However, he tried to save his neck. Already his father, Lieutenant General Katte, had made an attempt on September 5 and had asked for mercy for him, but he had only drawn this answer from the King: "Your son is a scoundrel and so is mine. What can we fathers do about it?" Katte besought his grandfather, the old Marshal of Alvensleben, to transmit to His Majesty a petition which glows with passion for life: "The error of my youth, my weakness, my thoughtlessness, my spirit which purposed no evil, my heart full of love and pity, the vain delusion of my youth which concealed no evil schemes ask in all humility for mercy, forgiveness, compassion, pity, clemency." To this despairing cry the marshal added "the tears and prayers of a very old man." He had dedicated his life to his country, and his son's after him. Both of them had offered their blood in the service of His Majesty the King. In all submission and confidence he flung himself at the feet of his master: "Your Majesty will not wish to bring down my gray hairs with such sorrow to the grave." The King replied that he was not in a position to grant a pardon, that in sparing the condemned man torture and hanging he had shown all the mercy possible, that an example was necessary, and that, moreover, he forbade anyone to speak further to him on the matter. At the same time he ordered his ambassador in London to make a strong declaration to the Court that even if there were a hundred thousand Kattes they would be beheaded all together. "As long as God shall give me life, I shall maintain myself as despotic lord [als Herr despotique], even if I still need to cut off the thousand noblest heads in the land, for the English must learn that I will never endure a coregent in my territory."

On November 3 Frederick William informed General von Lepel that Katte was to be transferred to Cüstrin for his execution. This was to take place on the sixth. "At seven in the morning you will parade one hundred and fifty men of the garrison who will form the ring under the windows of the Crown Prince. If there is not sufficient room there, you will choose another spot which will also be well within sight of the Prince." When the circle had been formed, Katte accompanied by a pastor would be brought out under escort of thirty military police. He would be read the sentence of death and after a prayer "the headsman will chop off his head." The body, guarded by sentinels, would remain exposed on the spot until two o'clock in the afternoon. Finally, he would be put in a coffin and carried silently to his grave.

Cüstrin was two and a half days' journey from Berlin. On the third Major Schack presented himself in Katte's room. "By His Majesty's order," he told him, "I have to be present at your execution. Twice I have tried to refuse, but I have to obey. God knows what it is costing me. May heaven change the King's heart and grant that at the last moment I may have the joy of telling you of your reprieve."

"You are too kind," replied Katte. "I am content with my lot. I die for a master whom I love and I have the consolation of giving him by my death the greatest proof of my devotion."

That evening, at the stage, he asked to be allowed to write to his father, but he was so disturbed that he could not find words for a beginning. At last, after pacing up and down for a long time, he wrote: "Tears well into my eyes when I think, dear father, that this letter is going to cause you the greatest pain the heart of a father can feel." He recalled all the trouble that his father had taken over him, in the hope that his son's success in the world would be the consolation of his old age. "How I believed in my happiness, in my good fortune! How full I was of certainty of my own greatness! Vain hope! How empty are the thoughts of men! How all things crumble in a single day! How sadly does the scene of my life come to an end! How far I am from my dreams! I must follow not the road of honor and glory but that of shame and of an ignominious death. Yet, O Lord, Thy ways are unpredictable and Thy purposes are inscrutable. The ways of God are not the ways of men and the ways of men are not those of God." He gave himself up to the will of God, apart from whom nothing happens on this earth. "The more bitter and hard is the manner of my death, the more sweet and comfortable is the hope and certainty of eternal salvation. . . . Be comforted, dear father. God has given you other sons to whom He will perhaps grant more happiness on this earth and who will give you, my father, the joy you have expected in vain from me. . . . I thank you with filial respect for the faithful, paternal love you have shown me from my childhood until this day. May God, the Omnipotent, return a hundredfold to you this love you have given me. . . ." He added a few words to his father's second wife, whom he had loved as if she had been his real mother, and to his brothers and sisters, to whom he excused himself for not laying bare his whole heart: "I am at the gates of death. I must think of entering there with my soul purified and sanctified. I have no time to lose." That day and the next he enjoyed calm sleep. On the journey he conversed with the pastor, Müller, and vindicated himself against the charge of having denied the existence of God, excepting as a sally so as to shine in company. His piety became exalted and he convinced himself that he was going to his execution joyfully.

They sighted Cüstrin on the fifth at midday. Almost at once he learned that the execution was fixed for the following day. "All the better," said he. "The quicker it is, the more pleased I shall be." Pious conversation with Pastor Müller and the almoner of the garrison began again. In the evening a meal was brought in; Münchow, the president of the Chamber of Domains, had sent some Hungarian wine. Then came Schack and some other officers who prayed with the condemned man. On the same evening he wrote a note to the Prince, of which we know the gist from the pastor's account of it. He begged Frederick to submit to the will of God and of the King. Schack could not sleep himself and remained with Katte until three in the morning. Together they said one more prayer, asking God for the courage to die bravely. Katte was pale. He felt his flesh and blood revolt against death. He fell asleep at last, but at five o'clock he awoke to the sound of the sentinels being aroused. At the same moment Colonel von Reichmann entered Frederick's room.

V

THE Prince had had no news for some days and was sleeping peacefully. His prison life had been much ameliorated. With the compliance of the guards President Münchow had obtained knives, forks, and candles for him. In spite of the paternal prohibition he also had books, pencils, and paper, and his ordinary fare was augmented with cold meats, fruits, and sweetmeats brought him by Münchow's son. He was able to communicate with the outside world and had started to say impertinent things again. The day he was told that his daily expenses were about to be reduced by the King to eight groschen, he replied, "Starvation for starvation, I prefer Cüstrin to Potsdam."

Naturally he was compelled to take great care. Several times he advised Wilhelmina to use invisible ink: "Are there no lemons left in Berlin?" But he also talked of sending his portrait. He was confident as to the outcome of his adventures and expected at the most to be degraded in rank and forced to spend some months in solitude at a habitable prison. In the course of the examination he had felt that Grumbkow was not pushing things to their utmost limit, but that he had won the game and wished on the contrary to arrange a reconciliation. Perhaps they had a confidential interview, but at all events they understood one another. In September Frederick wrote again to his sister: "All the literature has been received, answered, and burned. One answers it and hopes that others will do the same. I live, am in good health, and amuse myself as best I can." Then, after many endearments: " 'Rancour' (Grumbkow) shows signs of breaking with me. If this is so, my stock is falling. If you hear anything about it, I beg you to see that it leaks through these walls and reaches me." A few weeks later he no longer admitted the worst: "I have drunk your health most heartily. Let me know, I pray you, on what footing you are. If you can, hint to the Queen that she should humor Grumbkow, for he has the power to arrange everything and he is behaving very handsomely toward me. Let the Queen confide in him! I do not know at all what my fate is to be, but I would rather rot at Cüstrin than be on the footing I was before. I have just learned with regret that a father is the worst possible person to have as an enemy. . . . I live here in a state of complete uncertainty, except for your affection of which I am utterly sure. . . . Love me always and be sure that neither arrest nor liberty, nor principality, nor thrones, nor death, nor life will make me abandon the feelings of respect and affection which I always have and will always preserve."

Finally, a few days before the court-martial he sent his sister an affected letter, in which he did not hide his hopes of easy treatment: "My dearest sister, they are going to make an excommunicant of me after the court-martial which is being held at the moment; for one has to do very little to pass a heresiarch, one has only to refuse complete conformity to the master's sentiments. You can therefore imagine easily enough the charming way they will dress me up as one. As for me, I am not in the least put out by the anathemas which will be launched against me, as long as I know that my darling sister declares them to be utterly false. What a pleasure it is for me that neither bolts nor bars can prevent me from showing you my perfect friendship! Yes, my dear sister, there are still honest folk to be found in this almost wholly corrupt century, who lend me the means necessary to declare myself your most obedient servant. Yes, my dear sister, provided that I know you are happy, prison will become for me an abode of felicity and contentment. *Chi ha tempo ha vita;* let us console ourselves with that. I could wish with all my heart to have no need of an intermediary to speak to you and that we should see again those happy days when your Principe and my Principessa shall kiss one another. Or, to speak more clearly, when I shall have the pleasure of conversing with you myself and of assuring you that nothing in the world can diminish my affection for you. Adieu. The Prisoner." How far he was from reality!

When he learned in two sentences that Katte was imprisoned a few feet away from him and would die before his eyes, he gave a terrible cry: "Lord Jesus, rather than that take my life!" For two hours he moaned and wept. He ran about his cell, wrung his hands, and begged forgiveness of the friend who did not hear him. Let the King disinherit him, kill him, let him rot in prison, but Katte must be saved! His friend must live!

At seven o'clock the troops were in position and the gate of the citadel was opened. Two officers conducted Frederick to the window. Katte, who had taken the communion with fervor, walked freely between two praying priests. He was very calm and behaved completely naturally, carrying his hat under his arm. As he skirted the building to reach the place of execution, on the platform which overlooked the river Oder, he raised his head and in the gloomy twilight strained his eyes to find the Prince's cell. When Fritz saw him, he shouted to him in French, "My dear Katte, I ask you a thousand pardons. In the name of God, pardon, pardon!" And he blew him a kiss.

Katte saluted and replied as loudly, "No need for pardon, my Prince. I die for you with a thousand pleasures." But the spectators were so upset that they reported the remark in two or three different ways: "My lord, you have nothing to ask of me," or again, "Not at all, my lord."

Katte listened to the sentence of death without emotion. He said good-by to the officers and to all those who had come with him. He gave his wig to Schack's orderly, put a white cap on his head, took off his coat, opened wide his shirt at the neck, and knelt on the heap of sand which had been prepared. "Lord Jesus . . ." he began, but he broke off to prevent the headsman from bandaging his eyes. "Lord Jesus . . ." The head was severed at the first blow.

At the window Fritz fell unconscious into the arms of his warders.

The Years of Apprenticeship

I

WHEN Frederick came to himself he sat down near the window with strained features in a state of exhaustion, unable to take his eyes off the black cloak which covered his friend's body. He refused to accept the least nourishment and remained sunk in his grief until the evening. He saw the corpse being removed and he begged the governor to have the bloodstained sand taken away also.

Pastor Müller had gone up to his room immediately after the execution, but seeing him "so weak and horrified" he left him. He returned at nightfall and again at seven o'clock. The King had wanted this mood of despair and to produce it he had stage managed the drama down to the smallest detail, just as a scene is arranged in the theater. He had envisaged the priest "entering the cell before the headsman had finished wiping his sword" and he had imagined Frederick staggering, frozen with fear and horror. "My son has been sacrificed," wrote Katte's father in a heartrending letter. Yes, Katte had been sacrificed to break the Prince's pride and to humble his spirit to the ground.

Müller himself had received detailed instructions: "I do not know you, but I have heard much good of you, that you are a pious, honest minister and servant of God's word. As you are going to Cüstrin to witness Lieutenant Katte's execution, I command you to go up to the Prince's room, immediately after the execution, to reason with him. . . . Let him search his own conscience; let him ask God's pardon with all his heart for the grievous sin he has committed and for having led astray his fellow men, one of whom has had to pay for it with life and limb. If you find the Prince is cast down, you must get him to fall on his knees with you and also with the officers who are with him, to ask for God's grace with melting hearts. But you must act with tact and circumspection, for his is a head full of trickery and you will take good care that all comes from true penitence and a contrite heart. . . . As indeed I hope that the present situation and the execution, which will be fresh in his mind, will have touched and softened his heart, I make it a matter for your conscience" to test his repentance and confirm it. "If you cannot get into his confidence, you will go out and you will write to me, and if I go to Berlin you will come and speak to me. But if you find a contrite heart, you must write to me about it and stay there."

The pastor stayed. On his first two visits he had found Frederick sobbing, talking continuously of his friend and accusing himself of having killed him. Müller gave him Katte's will and he had a new bout of weeping when he read it. All night his mind wandered. The pastor, an officer, and a valet took it in turn to sit by him. In the morning he said, "The King imagines he has taken Katte from me, but I have him always before my eyes." Nevertheless he sent for a doctor and as though to come to terms with life once again, he asked him for some powders he was in the habit of taking.

In the life of the human spirit there are some contortions that are so subterranean and so inconsistent that it is hard to express what is happening beneath the surface by the use of words, which confuse the issue. While Fritz gave himself up to deep confusion within, while his thoughts seemed to have become formless and flaccid, his whole being cried for oblivion and for escape with all the impetuosity of his eighteen years. For twice twelve hours he had groaned in a fearful wilderness, full of revulsions, of questions without answers, of exhausting nightmares, of imaginary exaltations, and of humiliating relapses. With smarting eyelids he rose from sleep as from the grave, sensible of his own courage, proud at not being as other men, determined to win through by abandoning himself to the eddies of chance so as to attain one day to mastery and to his true nature. But from his dungeon what could he do to soften the King and bring him to be merciful?

Frederick William had treated his son's negotiations with England as an attempt at personal politics and even as a sort of revolt: "It needed," writes a recent biographer of Frederick, Gerhard Ritter, "the King's heavy fist to crush that network of intrigues, to safeguard the sovereignty of the Crown from the factions of the Court, to save the too-youthful heir from manifest high treason. Viewed from this angle, the terrible storm of his anger appears almost as a studied revelation of statecraft." Nevertheless —and on this point another recent biographer, Arnold Berney, is in the right—Frederick had not realized the political significance of his attempt. He had been maddened by maltreatment and had wanted to shelter from the storm; he had thought that the English marriage envisaged by his mother would give him at one and the same time money, amusements, and liberty. He always spoke of his intended escape as of a piece of devilment, a youthful escapade, an impulsive gesture. He was never willing to look upon it as a serious act of rebellion and he never paid more than lip service to the idea of repenting of it.

If he also made friendships and found sympathy among the army and among the nobility, it was not in the least as a result of a conspiracy but because under an absolute monarchy all malcontents and dreamers naturally place their hopes on the heir apparent. Thence arises a kind of hidden, inherent opposition which is the inevitable consequence of each generation succeeding the last. But a factor which an ancient monarchy like France could meet without embarrassment endangered the very existence of Prussia, which was a new, half-finished country composed of scattered fragments joined under one crown as a result of various marriages and by the chance of various deaths—a state without frontiers, without geographical unity, without traditions, without common memories, inhabited by subjects who called the people in the next province foreigners and owed a common allegiance to one thing alone, the person and power of the sovereign. The intrigues of the Queen and of Frederick, though impotent and obscure, subverted Prussia because they subverted the principle of discipline on which precisely the whole of Prussia relied.

It was the deep conviction of Frederick William that even the Crown Prince had no right to have a personality at variance with the nature of the kingdom. By desiring to satisfy his personal wishes, by making claim to spiritual delights and disinterested culture, he had revolted against the needs of the Prussian State; for neither literature, nor art, nor music, nor luxury, nor elegance, nor mental pleasures, nor refinement of manners went to make up the essential features and the *fact* of Prussia. Everything he gave himself was therefore stolen from the State; all the trouble he took to develop himself was a blow to the preservation and development of Prussia.

For some years Frederick William had watched a King of Prussia who would not be a Prussian growing up beside him, and he was all the more irritated because he had known in his own youth all that he had refused his son and had scornfully rejected it at his accession. He had been familiar with a brilliant, sumptuous Court, French in taste, manners, and speech. He had seen his mother presiding over a crowd of intellectuals, writers, musicians, and artists. He had heard her talk of Bayle and Fénelon, philosophize with Leibniz and tire him out with her "Wherefores?" But he had also plumbed the misery which was hidden beneath this brilliant exterior: the debts, the financial chaos, the ruin of agriculture, the poverty of the countryside—this was in his opinion the price of the festivities and the witticisms. Therefore Prussia could only accept a sovereign in her own image, rough like herself, a soldier like herself, a peasant, worn, pious, loving hard facts, believing in force and despising all else. When on November 7, 1730, the Crown Prince called for his doctor, the near future was already decided. What Frederick William expected of Katte's execution was that Fritz would be washed by the blood of the victim and would become a Prussian of his father's type. What Fritz had discovered from his testing was that to save his life and keep the crown he must thenceforth don his father's tastes and wear them everywhere like a garment.

II

IN the opinion of the King the first task was to bring Frederick back to the true religion, for, with his usual inconsequent methods, to instruct his son in his own belief of mankind's freedom of choice he had chosen a pastor who did not believe in it, and Frederick had remained faithful to the doctrine of predestination as a convenient theory for explaining the order of things. When he saw Müller return he was indeed far from thinking that the pastor was going to tackle him on Divine Foreknowledge, Grace, and Destiny. Though understanding little of it all he bent his mind to the theological argument, but every time Müller spoke of God's grace, he replied with the King's grace. In the end he was unable to restrain himself and risked the remark, "Must I not conclude from your visit that you wish to prepare me also for death?" Müller protested: there was no question of that! He was only concerned with teaching the Prince his error and bringing him to repent of it. Frederick understood: they wanted to make him say that his flight had not been destined from all eternity in the Divine Will and that he was wholly to blame. Was that all? He was ready to give up predestination, but he was skillful enough not to surrender too soon. He argued in such a way as to foster belief in his sincerity, but in the end he admitted he was beaten: "Then destiny does not exist and I alone am the cause of Katte's death and my own misfortune."

The same evening the pastor sent the King the good tidings—Fritz was a heretic no longer. Next day he settled in the castle in a room so situated that Fritz had only to tap on the wall to summon him. He stated in his reports that he had not been able to discover the slightest trace of duplicity in the prisoner's heart but only sincere repentance. He begged his master "to dart forth a glance of his royal mercy soon" for fear of the Prince falling into a dangerous mental state "as a result of persistent and increasing melancholy."

The reply came on November 9: "You have assured me on your conscience and before God that the Prince has been converted to God at Cüstrin, that times innumerable he begs the pardon of the King, his lord and father, for all he has done, and that he has suffered deeply for not having submitted eagerly to his father's will. If then you find the Prince willing to promise this firmly before God, if it is true that his heart suffers for his sins, if it is his real intention to improve himself in the way I have just described, you can give him to understand in my name that in truth I cannot pardon him completely, but nevertheless with a mercy he does not deserve I will relax his arrest and I will once more give him attendants to supervise his conduct. All the town shall be his prison. He will not be able to go out of it. I will give him work from morning till night in the Chamber of War, of Domains, and of Government. He will work at matters of revenue, receive the accounts, read the laws, and take notes on them. But before this happens, I will have him take an oath to act in all obedience according to my will and in all things to do as pertains to and befits a faithful servant, subject, and son. But if he kicks and rears again, he will lose his right to succeed to the throne and to the Electorate, and even, in certain circumstances, his life. . . ."

The oath must be taken by Frederick in a loud, clear voice without mental reservations or any sort of pretense. Let him think it over, for the matter was a serious one. Frederick William concluded, "May God the most high give His blessing! And as often by marvelous guidance, miraculous paths, and bitter steps He leads men into the Kingdom of Heaven, may He take back to His communion this thoughtless son! May He bow down his impious head! May He soften and change him! May He snatch him from the clutches of the Devil! May the Omnipotent Lord and Father so will it, by the grace of our Lord Jesus Christ and by His suffering and death. Amen."

As soon as he got this letter Müller went to see the Prince, who did not expect any news and greeted him with a speech on the merits of our Saviour Jesus Christ. The parson let him have his say and then in the King's name read him the pardon and the sermon which came with it. "Is it possible?" cried Frederick through his tears. However, as too prompt an acceptance would not have inspired confidence, he replied that an oath had to be considered, that he took his seriously, that he wished to commit himself deeply and therefore begged the King to let him know the wording of it in advance so that he might absorb it and conscientiously prepare himself to observe it strictly.

The idea of leaving Frederick at Cüstrin had been inspired by Grumbkow and Seckendorff, who had maneuvered since his arrest to save "the renegade colonel" and to win the gratitude of "the rising sun." The marriages were broken off, the English party was crushed, Knyphausen in disgrace and succeeded by Podewils, Grumbkow's son-in-law—their victory was complete. Yet the King might die suddenly and by gaining the friendship of his heir they enhanced their credit and strengthened their policy. Moreover, the course they envisaged was the only sensible one. Frederick could not be brought back to Berlin without stirring up fresh trouble. Since the father and son did not agree, a

separation was indicated and the education of the son far from
his father's side. At the request of Frederick William, Seckendorff arranged every detail of his son's release in writing. He
even tried to have himself sent to Cüstrin with the commissioners
appointed to hear the oath, but Frederick William did not
want it to look as if a foreigner was intervening as arbiter in such
an important matter and he chose Grumbkow with five other
generals and a councilor. They arrived on November 17. On
the afternoon of the eighteenth Grumbkow had a long interview with Fritz. What did they say to each other? We know
nothing about it, but despite the difference of their ages, they
were men who only needed a nod or a wink to understand each
other. As a token of peace and of alliance Frederick with tears
in his eyes made a gift of Katte's will to Grumbkow—a highly
dramatic way of getting rid of a souvenir which he was perhaps
beginning to find a bit of an encumbrance.

On the next day, a Sunday, Frederick took the oath "strictly
to obey the King's orders, to do in all things that which pertains
to and befits a faithful servant, subject, and son." The general
and governor then returned him his sword, but without the
scabbard of an officer, for he was no longer a member of the
army. Guards had not to turn out for him and present arms, nor
had soldiers to salute him. Frederick was very sensitive to this
humiliation and begged the King to restore him to his status as
a soldier. The reply addressed to the Crown Prince of Prussia
said that a deserter had forfeited the right to wear the uniform.
"Besides it is not necessary for all men to have the same trade;
one has to work to become a soldier; another concentrates on
learning and other such things." Then followed, as the Prussian
historian Koser puts it, some truly regal words: the Prince must
now "learn, by putting his hand to business, that no state can
exist without economy and without a good organization. Unquestionably the good of the country requires that the sovereign
himself should be informed of everything, that he should be a
thrifty husbandman: otherwise the country is at the mercy of
favorites and of First Ministers who draw a profit for themselves and throw everything into confusion. . . ."

Frederick William also wrote to his friend the Prince of Anhalt: "I could not write to you sooner, my dear fellow, for I

have had to settle this wretched Cüstrin affair. I am placing Wolden and two gentlemen at his side. He has to spend all the day at the Chamber of War and Domains, where he will be told about everything. If he does not wish to learn of his own accord, things will be repeated to him so often that he will have to remember them. If he turns out a gentleman, and I have the strongest doubts of it, it will be a good thing for him. If there is a war, he will have to leap out of the trenches with the first sergeants of the grenadiers to make reconnaissance and to dig saps and galleries. If he does it with a good grace and if he perseveres, his pardon will be complete."

On Monday, November 20, 1730, Frederick, Crown Prince of Prussia, took his place in the Chamber of Domains in the lowest rank, right at the bottom of the table, with orders not to sign documents on the same line as the councilors.

III

THE Chamber of War and Domains (*Kriegs- und Domainen-Kammer*) had been set up seven years before by Frederick William to put some order and unity into the provincial administration, which was up till then terribly complicated and divided among rival bodies that fought over the revenues. Before the Chamber of Domains, then, day by day came fiscal and economic matters—farm rents, rates and taxes, excise duties, manufactures, rivers and forests, tolls, mills, breweries, markets, inland customs —everything which contributed to the financial power of the State, the prerequisite of military strength. Frederick went to the Chamber morning and evening; he listened to discussions, copied letters, classified reports, learned how to draw up a lease and how taxes were raised.

Up till then he had lived without a guide or ruling principles in an inward solitude that was almost complete, arrogantly sure that he was destined for a glorious life but not yet showing any particular aptitude either for politics or for letters. The most remarkable thing about him was that strength of character, that pigheaded drive for personal freedom which he had wasted most miserably in petty secrecies and intrigues, with the sole object of getting for himself the lazy pleasures of a bored and futile boy.

Katte's execution made a man of him. He forced back the desire for revenge right to the bottom of his heart, while awaiting the hour when he would rule. Already he knew how to lie: henceforth he was to learn how to be at one and the same time someone else and himself; he was to discover how to pretend without giving himself away; and to do so continuously with silence and with smiles, though as far from submission as from the loquacious little deceptions of his past life.

Another transformation was taking place in his mind. At the same time that he left his wounded adolescence behind he discovered the existence of the Prussian monarchy and his own place in the monarchy. Certainly there was no grandeur, no plan, no breadth of vision accompanying this initiation, which evolved haphazard from the jobs of every day, from practical acquaintance with the routine work of land administration. But on the ground level the Prussian monarchy was more imposing than at Potsdam. Up at the top there were deceptions, slogans, and cabals. In the humble county town of the Neumark there was silent work, orderly and productive, a tenacious struggle to people desert wastes, to overcome nature, to make the land yield the "bit more" on which year by year the might of the Hohenzollerns was built.

After prison the first month of work seemed enchanting to Frederick. "His Royal Highness is as merry as a cricket," wrote an eyewitness. But Frederick could not give himself by halves; without his being well aware of it his intellect carried him on to master details and then to relate them to general principles, to view things from outside in their logical interconnections and in their unity. This was exactly what the King did not want. The Prince was not at Cüstrin to meditate but to learn how difficult it was for a peasant to earn a thaler. He was forbidden to have any books other than the Bible, the Psalms, and Arndt's book, *Of True Christianity:* no works on jurisprudence or administration, no history, no novels, no poetry, no ancient authors. "Books don't teach anything. What is needed is experience." He forbade the making of theories, forbade the making of plans, forbade talk of politics, forbade the bringing of oysters from Hamburg, forbade argument, forbade dancing, forbade the holding of general ideas, forbade the purchase of summer clothes, forbade the hear-

ing of music, forbade lights after nine o'clock at night, forbade
suppers in the town, forbade invitation of guests. The Prince was
condemned to the company of his mentor marshal of the palace,
Von Wolden, and to that of two young nobles attached to the
Chamber, Von Natzmer and Von Rohwedell. Conversation with
these "three gentlemen" was to center on the constitution of the
country, its manufactures, its police, its farms, accountancy, and
the Word of God. If Frederick ventured to speak of war, peace,
or other subjects reserved for His Majesty the King, the gentlemen were to silence him.

In fact Frederick did touch on forbidden matters, especially
with Natzmer, but the gain from it was meager enough, for in
spite of much brilliance and imagination his companion had not
much to teach him. Their conversation only served to flatter
Fritz's vanity when he gave himself the pleasure of discoursing
for an evening as heir apparent. Of much more assistance was
Münchow, the head of the Chamber, and better still was the
director, Hille. In a letter Frederick drew a flattering portrait
of him; he praised his subtle intelligence, his clear, well-reasoned
ideas, his special aptitude for commerce, his sober life, his austere
morals, his "beautiful" culture, and his talent for writing "prettily" in French and German. All the same he blamed him for
not being regular at Holy Communion and for being satirical
and fond of applause. A little jealousy peeps through these last
words. As a matter of fact if Hille guessed at Frederick's temperament and if he felt he would do great things, he was astounded
at his ignorance: "The Prince," he wrote, "knows the *Poetics* of
Aristotle and has it at his fingers' ends, but he does not know
whether his ancestors won Magdeburg at cards, or how else they
got hold of it." The director had the gusto to give some sharp
lessons to his exalted subordinate, but also, without overriding
his instructions, he began to explain to him the part his House
had to play in Germany.

One day at the end of an explanation he roughed out for him
the commercial history of Brandenburg. He told him how the
discovery of the Cape route to India had shifted the flow of trade,
how the Mediterranean had lost its controlling position, how the
merchandise of the East was thenceforth brought into Germany
through the Baltic and how Frankfort-on-the-Oder, which used

to get it from Venice via Augsburg, had ceased to be a center for it. But the conquest of Swedish Pomerania had given Frankfort its prosperity back again. Unfortunately the upper reaches of the river Oder flowed through Silesia and were under Austrian control. Frederick William lowered the customs duties on this frontier out of respect for the Emperor and allowed Austrian merchants to compete with his own subjects. "There is no hope of good trade for Brandenburg," Hille concluded, "until the Silesians are ousted from their present trade. How will this be done? We will leave it to higher and wiser heads than ours." The teaching at Cüstrin applied in this way might have transformed Frederick, but Hille did not often venture outside the permitted limits. Frederick William called him to order from afar. As he had forwarded the King a report his pupil had drawn up about the recovery of the linen industry, he drew on his own head furious reproaches: "Do you think I am going to believe that the Prince is the author of a scheme of this sort? I know very well what connection he has with it, and furthermore it does not please me in the least to see him start by making schemes. I have told you that you must teach him hard facts. I do not want to hear any talk of things that are up in the air. Anyone can make wind without a teacher."

Frederick was held down some hours every day to jobs which he despised, was idle the rest of the time and condemned to yawn away his youth among people frozen by restraint, so he was soon bored to death. They were four in a small townsman's house, they had no talk left in them, and meals were spent in trying to find some subject of conversation or in watching each other eat in silence. When the Chamber was closed they went to look at the Oder flowing past and returned by the same streets to find the same stolid, sleepy faces in the same positions. Before going to bed Frederick went over the household accounts and counted the ha'pence with the cook. The days dragged by in the same gray light, without color, slow and dreary enough in all conscience. "We—the rest of the monastery—" wrote Wolden, "shall all break up if this sort of life continues."

The grand marshal was obliged to send frequent reports to the King. At first he had tried to be truthful: among other details he had been imprudent enough to write that Frederick still believed in predestination—and in fact, since Frederick was to be tormented all his life by the problem of human liberty, for him a belief in predestination was merely a belief in his star. The King, however, flew into a rage. What? "The scoundrel will not throw his false predestination overboard. If he wants to go to Hell, let him go there! I have nothing on my conscience!" Nevertheless it is the duty of the three gentlemen to convince him of his error and to comment on the Scriptures to him. "You will come to know this saint better and better. You will see that there is no good in him, though his tongue is a good one. Oh, there is nothing to be said against his tongue!"

How had the rogue been seduced into heresy? By reading? "Books have neither legs nor wings. Someone has brought them to him. Who? Who?" The Prince is reported to be ill. A fine state of affairs! "He is predestined: everything will be all right. If there was any good in him he would die, but there is no danger of his death. The wicked flourish like the green bay tree." Frederick hastily changed faiths a second time and Wolden, not knowing in whom to confide, submitted "the whole bag of tricks" to the care of Grumbkow, who assured him of a peaceful winter. The prisoners had only one idea, "to get out of the galleys," but the King met all the pretexts for travel with refusals: "If I had done as he has done, I would be ashamed till my dying day and I would never let anyone see me." Then all at once in the summer of 1731 he announced he would appear on August 15: "From the moment I have looked him straight in the face I shall know if he has improved or no."

Frederick William arrived on the appointed day accompanied by Grumbkow and Derschau. Followed by a great crowd of people he went to the government house, where he had his son and the three gentlemen brought to him. Frederick flung himself at the feet of the King, who bade him rise and with a very serious expression harangued him thus: "You can yourself remember what has happened, the scandalous way you have behaved and the impious plans which you have made. As I have kept you near me since your childhood and have been able to get to know you well, I have tried everything in the world, both kindness and harshness, to make a gentleman of you. As I already suspected your wicked schemes at the camp in Saxony, I treated you as roughly and harshly as possible in the hope that you would think things over and adopt a different sort of behavior, confess your faults to me, and beg my pardon. But all has been in vain and you have become more and more obstinate. When a young man behaves foolishly—courts ladies, runs after girls, breaks windows, and is generally unruly—these faults of youth can be forgiven: but to commit deliberately such an act of cowardice, to do such impious things with premeditation—that is unpardonable. . . . You have thought that by persistent obstinacy you could get your own way. But see here, my fine fellow, even if you were sixty, seventy years old you would have no right to give me orders. I have till now held my own against all the world and I shall know how to bring you to heel."

Changing his tone, he reproached him for having run up debts and let himself be robbed by usurers. Then: "You have not had confidence in me—I who do everything to make our House great and to increase the army and the finances; I who work for you; for all this will be yours if you prove yourself worthy of it." And why had he spurned his father's love? At those words Frederick fell on his knees in tears.

"Come now, it was to England that you wished to go?"

"Yes."

"Good! Listen to the consequences. Your mother would have got into the most terrible trouble, for I would have suspected her of being in the plot. Your sister I would have put for the rest of her life in some place where she would never have seen either the light of day or of the moon. I would have invaded Hanover with my army and reduced the country to ashes, even at the price of my life, my country, and my people. . . . Today I would like to put you into civil and military posts, but after such behavior how dare I present you to my officers and servants? You have only one way of reinstating yourself; it is to try to atone for your fault at the price of your blood."

Fritz knelt down again. "Did you seduce Katte, or did Katte seduce you?"

"I seduced him."

"At last! It is a pleasure to hear you speak the truth for once."

Does Fritz enjoy being at Cüstrin? Does Wusterhausen still seem to him as horrible as ever? Does he still call his old uniform a shroud? Ah, he likes neither his father's manners nor his friends! Does he want to play at being a fop, make epigrams, and wear French wigs? Much good may it do him, but no one in either Prussia or Berlin takes any more interest in him. No one even knows if he is alive or dead. Does he still believe in predestination? No? That's good, but let him beware of the ungodly, let him beseech God to deliver him from evil thoughts, and Jesus Christ who wishes all men to be saved will answer his prayer. He concluded, "I forgive all the past in the hope of better behavior." Whereupon Frederick knelt down and kissed his father's feet.

They went into another room. It was Frederick William's birthday, but Fritz did not dare to congratulate him on it. The King left after a few minutes' conversation. Fritz once more kissed his feet before the assembled crowd. The King raised him, pressed him in his arms, and told him that thenceforth he would trust in his sincerity and would watch over him as he had in the past. Then the carriage drove off.

"I never believed until this moment," said the Prince to Hille, "that my father had the slightest feeling of love for me. At this moment I am convinced that he has. . . ."

IV

A few days later Frederick William made tangible the effect of his pardon by lightening the exile's program. Henceforth he went only three mornings a week to the Chamber and he sat right at the top beside the chairman. He was allowed to go out of the town, on condition he warned the governor and only visited the royal lands on the list provided. These outings took him up to the frontiers of Poland and Saxony. Somebody from the Chamber was to go with him to explain everything to him— manuring, byres, brewing, seeds, crops. Wolden was to urge the Prince to question people and to discover things for himself, and thoroughly too. Secular books, music, gambling, and dancing were forbidden. Frederick was not allowed to speak to anyone privately and the three gentlemen were to work in relays so as never to leave him alone by day or night. On the other hand he could dine in town twice a week and have two male guests at every meal, but never a woman. Wolden was to arrange occasional shoots and water picnics for him. Morning and evening the monastery was to thank God, pray, sing psalms, and read the Bible with devotion.

For the second time Frederick had asked his father to let him reënter the army, not from a wish to flatter, said he, but from the bottom of his heart: "Do whatever in the world you like with me, I shall be pleased with everything, I shall be overjoyed, if only I can be a soldier." This wish was a real one. After living for himself the tedious, stunted, idle existence of a townsman of Cüstrin, Fritz felt that despite their machinelike monotony the toils and labors of an officer were still brightened by a reflection of glory, stamped with conscious self-denial, with a continual, impassive expectation of death, which made the slavery more admirable. However, the request was premature. The Prince was not cut out for the difficult job of accomplishing his own rehabilitation without a guide. He had to turn once more to the only man in a position to help him, Grumbkow. He hated him; and in his letters to Wilhelmina he spoke of him as a madman, as one possessed, and accused him of the blackest designs. But he had need of him. From the dry greeting "Sir" Grumbkow soon became "My dear friend," "My dear general," "My dearest general and friend," and in fact it was he who gave the best advice, or at least the most useful, in the form of a veritable textbook drawn up in gritty French (August 26).

"As I hope and wish ardently to see His Royal Highness soon entirely restored to the good graces and confidence of the King his father, I have considered that I could not better employ my leisure in the country than by laying down in writing that which I think is most able to cement this happy union and confidence, having acquired by some little experience . . . an exact appreciation of the character of a court where the ground is slippery and treacherous as may be. Knowing as I do the pious sentiments of the Crown Prince I need not reconsider our duty to the Supreme Being and to religion, as it is the fountainhead of all happiness in life and our inner tranquillity depends upon it. With regard to the behavior which the Crown Prince should display toward the King, I believe that the more consistent, respectful, and natural it is the more pleasing it will be to the King." The Prince must possess a calm face and a bearing confident and without embarrassment. He is to call his father "Your Majesty" and to answer his questions with precision and without contradiction.

With the King he must avoid "all spirit of mockery and all bantering phrases . . . but on the other hand he must give up all austere, reserved, or gloomy looks, of which the King has so often complained. It is possible to be cheerful without jeering, and a laughing countenance, when it is in season, pleases the King greatly. As for affairs, whether political, military, or domestic, he must not concern himself with them in any way, neither directly nor indirectly, nor display the least curiosity. . . . If the Crown Prince is speaking to someone and the King arrives unexpectedly, he must not as heretofore break off his conversation, but he must always be ready to reply when the King inquires, *'Was sagt er?'* Moreover, in everything the Crown Prince may do in the King's presence he must always pretend to take pleasure in it, even when it gives him none."

There was supposed to be equality between all the servants of the crown. "However, as the century is a very military one, I consider the Crown Prince would do well to appear to take more pleasure in the company of generals and officers than in that of others; a gracious little glance and a pleasant smile will compensate for this advancement of soldiers above civilians." Good sense demands that the Prince should have or should make a pretense of having a little more consideration for those whom the King honors. "As for those who have the misfortune to displease the King, without refining upon their misfortune, I consider it should be possible to avoid them and not show too much compassion toward them." The only relations the Prince will have with ministers of foreign powers will be those of politeness, and he will be content with the company of staid, experienced people of mature years. He will show to his brothers a tender, natural affection.

"With regard to Her Majesty the Queen, I consider that the tenderness and profound respect which the Crown Prince naturally feels for this worthy princess need not be laid down here in the form of a rule. As, however, all things must be done with much circumspection, it is unnecessary to advise that no preference should be shown in that quarter as against the King, and

past experience must have taught His Royal Highness that the
suspicions which have been built on this preference have produced many inconveniences for the illustrious mother and the
well-beloved son. Whatever tenderness, confidence, and friendship the incomparable Princess Royal has a right to claim, which
are her due in a thousand distinctive ways, I consider nevertheless that in the beginning it will be necessary to fix certain limits
to them. . . . Furthermore the Crown Prince is gifted with such
a mind and such discernment that he will easily supplement all
that may be lacking in this document. . . . For the rest, I place
my hope in none but God. *In te, Domine, speravi, non confundar
in aeternum.*"

Fritz had in fact enough spirit to relish in all its parts this
textbook for the perfect courtier. Its main lines were judicious,
and he conformed to it with complete docility. His request to
be readmitted to the army had drawn upon him a new avalanche
of reproaches: "You have had a company of cadets which was a
good, fine, reliable company, but you showed not the least interest in it. This is why I think that if I made a soldier of you once
more, it would not please you at heart. But what is the use? If
I set out to flatter your affections, if I had an expert flute player
brought from Paris, with a dozen or so instruments and books
of music, an entire troop of actors, and a full orchestra, if I called
only for Frenchmen and Frenchwomen, two dozen dancing masters, and a dozen fops, and if I had a great theater built for you,
it would please you more than a company of grenadiers, for in
your eyes grenadiers are so much scum, but a fop, a Froggie, an
epigram, a tinkle of music, a mangy actor—that's noble, that's
royal, that's worthy of a prince!" Frederick did not insist: before being a soldier he had to be an administrator. From that time
onward the King received from him only letters to suit his taste:
here is an account of what was to be read in them from week to
week.

Frederick visited the domain of Wollup which once brought
in only 1,600 thalers and now brought in 2,000. However, it is
still possible to introduce a lot of improvements; the most obvious one would be to drain and clean up the marshes, which bring
in no profit and would make good land for wheat. The King's
reeve has built a new barn and has replaced his livestock that are

to be leased out. The land at Carzig is far from being so fertile; there is a lot of sand and in some places lime. At the place called the "Brand" there was a forest fire; if the trees are allowed to grow again it will yield no revenue for twenty-five or thirty years. The reeve's idea is to start a tenant farm—certainly the best solution. At Quartschen the sheepfold and the brewery make a good show. At Golzow the land is good; at Lebus exceptionally fine, but little was distinguishable as it had rained heavily. The buildings looked old and dilapidated. The Prince had entertained Major Roeder, who was taking a wonderfully fine fellow to join his most gracious father's regiment. He could not look at him without feeling a pang of jealousy.

The plan, estimate, and contract for the new tenant farm at Carzig are ready. Rye, wheat, and fodder will be harvested there, and all this will bring in 10 per cent. At Himmelstadt the buildings are falling into ruins; the brewery is so dilapidated that people dare not go into it any longer for fear of the roof falling on their heads. Quite near is a derelict church: it could be made into a brewery at very little expense. The cowsheds are equally tumble down and what is more they are built three hundred yards from the homestead. It is too far, for the reeve cannot keep an eye on them as he would like to. As the cowsheds must be rebuilt anyway advantage should be taken of this to bring them nearer. Frederick has been amazed to see that sowing has not taken place: this is because of the spring frosts. He has shot a stag of eight points and seen a whole herd of roe deer on the plain. At Marienwald the new lease will bring in a "bit more"—640-odd thalers, and if a useless wood is cleared the most gracious father will get another "bit more," 200 thalers. Frederick has established an error in the survey of land and has had the operation done again. He has noticed that the peasants do one feudal service daily with one horse, which is ruinous for them. Would it not be better if they did their service only three times a week but with two horses? Everyone would gain by it: the peasants would be quite free one day in two, and the reeve of the domain did not need their help every day and preferred two-horse service. The reeve wishes to buy forty oxen; he is right as he has enough pasture to support them. At Marienwald the two glassworks ought to bring in more, and the most gracious father can hope for a "bit more," for 857 thalers, 21 groschen, and 3 pfennigs. In the boar park at Neumuhle Frederick has killed eight boars with tusks, two females, and several young hogs. At Tornow the glass-works give a "bit more," 204 thalers, 10 groschen. There is a property for sale. The domain hopes to get it for 6,000 thalers; 10,000 is being asked for it—which is too much.

Throughout, these terse reports were interlarded with com-pliments, flattery, protestations of respect, gratitude, love, and most humble submission. Certainly the rebel son had persisted too long in evil ways, but he persevered in the path of righteous-ness with even greater zeal: "I depend on you alone and desire no other happiness, no other honors than those I receive of you." A pig had been killed at Wollup. As soon as he heard of it Fred-erick sent for a fine fat roast, and as he knew his father liked that joint, he had taken the liberty of sending it to him. For himself, he had given up champagne (this was not true) and the pleasures of a fop (this was not true either). He liked beer and went to marionette shows. But the King would do him a great favor if he would send him the new infantry regulations. *As the century is a very military one . . .*" Grumbkow had said.

Frederick William was not taken in by this zeal. He believed all he wanted to. When his son sent him a very detailed plan on the trade with Silesia he knew very well that he had been helped. But at last Frederick was working. In one way or another he learned things and remembered them. He used to love money for the fun of spending it: he was now acquiring a taste for making it. And then Frederick William longed with all his heart for the reformation of his son, so he scolded but relented. Was Frederick careful of his household economy? Was the cook a good one? Was he economical? Didn't he waste butter? At the beginning Frederick checked each bill, but as he could not do his own marketing he was robbed of small sums through false prices and short measure. Then he paid so much per meal or per head. But this, in the King's opinion, was not much better. He also sent his son menus, a plan, a budget, on which to regulate his expenditure.

After the proposal relating to feudal services Frederick Wil-liam was delighted, *sehr content.* "If you thought that out quite on your own you are already well up in rural economy. It is a useful notion that the forced labor should be arranged as you have suggested, and I give it my complete approval." He also approved of the rebuilding of Himmelstadt and allotted to it a credit of 3,592 thalers. He promised presents: first a horse, *a really good horse,* then three, a carriage, an equipage, and a silver dinner service. "I am having knives, forks, spoons, and plates added and also candlesticks, so arranged that everything can fit in a case and be carried by a donkey." He even added, "If you need anything, write to me."

Thus life became extremely bearable for the exiles at Cüstrin. A few days after his father's visit Frederick had dined out for the first time, at Tamsel, near the town, at Colonel de Wreech's house. The place was very charming—a Dutch landscape of water and sky. The castle had a fine appearance, with its paneling, its high windows, and its dadoed staircase. The colonel's wife was especially charming, much younger than her husband, with wit, a dazzling complexion, gaiety, and a slight tendency to flirt. Her twenty-three years and Frederick's eighteen quickly found a great deal in common. After a few days he had leave to call her "my cousin" and send her verses in French. Ernest Lavisse has treated this affair very prettily. The colonel's wife replied in kind to the first poetic declaration, but with a sting in the tail.

> And all my household join in this reply. . . .

All the household meant the colonel himself, and there is nothing to prove that Madame de Wreech had anything to hide from her middle-aged husband; she enjoyed the banter, that was all. Frederick's graces were still those of a schoolboy. "Madam, the trespassers who ravage this land have always had enough respect for you to spare your flowerbeds. An innumerable number of intruders far more ugly and dangerous than those I have mentioned above are about to descend on you, madam. . . . They are called poetical feet; they have either heavy or light bodies, and a certain cadence is essential to them and gives them life. . . ." And the ode begins. Nothing worse could be imagined.

> In off'ring these lines, Ma'am, may I be permitted
> To share with you a fact that is certainly true?

That I have been quite heartsick since first I saw you.
You are for that feeling an object well fitted.

Still Fritz respected the cousin and felt some tenderness for her. He admired her. He spent some pleasant days with her and owed her some gentle memories—the only ones he was to have of a woman in all his life.

From living in the open air and riding about the country every day he became transformed in his physique. When he had come to Cüstrin he was a mere adolescent, slender, pale, and melancholy, with narrow shoulders and the look of a hunted doe. He now had a fuller, healthier face, broader shoulders, and a confident manner of behavior and speech. He boasted of being a poet, a musician, a moralist, and a natural philosopher, but Hille who saw his daily life wrote to Grumbkow, "He will not be content with turning out rhymes as soon as he can do other things." Schulenburg went to visit him, followed him to a hunt, and remarked that he received his guests like a King. "It is obvious that he understands who he is."

Yet in many other ways he was still a child. One day Hille asked him how he would order his life if he had control of it. "I can assure you," he answered, "but don't say anything about it, that the dearest of my pleasures is reading. I love music, but I love dancing even more. I hate hunting but love to ride a horse. If I was in control of my life I would do all those things as I felt inclined; but I would spend a great part of my time on public business." He would do himself well and give concerts and little suppers. For dress he would always wear uniform but with very sumptuous greatcoats. Politically he had stuck at the *Telemachus* period. He would try to have good ministers and would let them act without descending to details himself, "For that I would rely on you others." The program was very vague. He had indulged in further reflection upon the geographical needs of the Prussian State. To judge from a letter to Natzmer (February, 1731), he fully understood that the lands under his control lay scattered from the Rhine to the Vistula and could be attacked from all sides. On the other hand this dispersal allowed him to have designs upon and spread his rule in every possible

direction, without his victorious mind being held back by any
natural obstacles. To join together the scattered fragments, he
drew up, or rather dreamed of, a plan of endless acquisition. But
he fulminated in a vacuum, as though other states did not exist.
He ignored their forces; he was not capable of estimating their
powers of resistance. Still less did he think of playing off one
against another.

V

FRITZ had resumed his correspondence with Wilhelmina, the
carissima sorella, who gave him accounts of gloomy happenings,
for while he dallied with Madame de Wreech and visited cowsheds, scores of scenes exactly like those already described were
taking place in Berlin. The Queen talked again of the English
marriage and persisted in her hopes. The King was furious and
wished to end the matter; Wilhelmina was worn out and resigned herself to accepting the Heir Apparent of Bayreuth, of the
Franconian branch of the Hohenzollerns, a fine figure of a man,
amicable, well mannered, and good looking. But no sooner had
the engagement been announced than the King regretted that
he had not found a more moneyed son-in-law, and it was upon
the unhappy fiancé that he vented his bad temper, while the
Queen revenged herself on him by snubbing him in a thousand
and one different ways.

The nuptials were fixed for November 20, 1731. On the night
before the Queen took her daughter aside: "Promise me," she
said, "to have no familiarity with the Prince and to live with
him as a sister with her brother, for this will be the only way
of dissolving your marriage, which will be null and void if it is
not consummated." She continued, of course, to hope for a courier from England, but Wilhelmina was too weary to struggle
any more. She asked for her brother to be sent for, as the King
had promised her his pardon.

From afar Frederick had been pained by the mediocrity of the
man who was to join his family. But he knew how useless it was
to resist and his letters were very reticent. He advised Wilhelmina to follow the dictates of her heart. He regretted that she
was not going to fill the place in Europe for which her fine qual-

ities fitted her, but if the Heir Apparent was as handsome as she said he was, they might perhaps live more happily in Bayreuth than under the eye of a haughty and pretentious Parliament.

The festivities lasted several days, but Frederick only had leave to come to Berlin for the third day. He arrived unexpectedly during a ball, without anyone having been told of his journey. He was in civilian dress and clad like a provincial official who had strayed into the world of fashion. Wilhelmina did not see him come in. She loved dancing and was throwing her whole heart into it. Seven hundred couples paced and turned behind her as though no such person as a Crown Prince had ever existed. Grumbkow interrupted her in the middle of a minuet. "Good gracious, madam," said he, "you must have been stung by a tarantula, or so it seems—don't you see these strangers who have just arrived?" She stopped short and saw a young man in gray whom she did not recognize. "Go and embrace the Crown Prince," said Grumbkow, "he is before you." She did not move and had to be led toward this strange young man. She found her brother "immensely fattened; his neck seemed far shorter, his face was also much changed and no longer so handsome as it used to be." She embraced him, lavished a thousand caresses on him, chattering inconsequentially, laughing and crying as if she was out of her mind. Frederick was embarrassed and replied without warmth (". . . *it will be necessary to fix certain limits,*" Grumbkow had written). He spoke little, looked everybody up and down critically, and was polite to some people in a pretty cold manner. The next day he had a longer and more intimate meeting with his sister. They told each other their misfortunes and exchanged condolences. Finally he greeted his brother-in-law and retired. The moment he was back at Cüstrin the correspondence between Wilhelmina and himself took on the same extravagant tones as of old: "I was not able to give you such tokens of my affection on that occasion as I could have wished, as I had to show extreme discretion before the King. . . . Now, if I have the satisfaction of seeing you once more, you will find I am a brother who dares display to you his tender affection unrestrainedly and you will then see if I am not ever the same. . . ." "Never did any brother in the world love with such tenderness a sister so charming as mine." "Think of a brother who only lives for you." "Adieu, dear incomparable brother." "My heart is quite full of you." "I love you more than life itself." "I think of nothing but you." "I prefer the happiness of being loved by you to empires and crowns, and after I have returned to dust, I ask for no other epitaph to be engraved on my tomb but *'My sister loved me."*

At Berlin Frederick had had the best of reasons for being nervous on his own account. In fact, Seckendorff was back at work. To have broken off the marriage with England was an initial success for him and for Prince Eugene. Now the break had to be made quite irreparable by uniting Frederick to some docile princess chosen from one of the vassal states of Austria. Prince Eugene already had his eye on Elisabeth of Brunswick-Bevern, the Empress' niece. By the end of April the King had been well primed and sent word to his son by Wolden that he must be ready to marry at the word of command: "I will leave him the choice between two or three persons." Wolden had replied that the Prince took the affair with complete resignation to Providence and with a blind obedience to His Majesty's orders. In the middle of June Grumbkow brought the list. There were only three names in it—Saxe-Gotha, Eisenach, Bevern. Frederick would have preferred the Princess of Eisenach, who had at least the reputation of being a beauty, but his hand was forced and he agreed to the Princess of Bevern if the King wished it and provided that she was neither repulsive nor an idiot. However, to all who came near him he emphasized the horror he felt for the match. Old Schulenburg was shocked by it.

"If the King is irrevocably determined on my marriage," he told him, "I shall obey: after that I shall leave my wife in the lurch and live just as I please."

Schulenburg protested in the name of God and of common decency. "But," answered the Prince, "I shall allow my wife the same liberty as myself."

Then he found fault with the rank of his bride-to-be. She was one of a minor family. He would rather have an archduchess with lands or else the Grand Duchess Anna Ivanovna with two or three million rubles. But above all, he wrote to Grumbkow, "As long as I am left a bachelor, I will thank God that I am one, and if I marry I shall certainly make a very bad husband, for I feel neither constant enough nor enough attached to the fair sex . . . the very thought of my wife is a thing so disagreeable to me that I cannot think it without a feeling of distaste."

During his stay at Court Frederick had made great advances in his father's estimation. Frederick William had allowed him to be present at a parade, and the public rushed to see and cheer him. Three days later, following a petition from the generals presented by the Prince of Anhalt, the King readmitted him to the army and promised him a regiment. However, the regiment and the engagement went together: Frederick felt a sudden love for the farms and the glassworks of Cüstrin. In the hope of remaining in his retreat he spoke of starting "some economic measure which absolutely demanded his presence." He complained of his health, of his stomach which was in a disturbed state, of his head which ached. But these excuses were puerile and the King started grumbling again. In January, 1732, Wolden received a very ill-tempered letter from him, full of veiled threats. Fritz, who was working at a concerto for flute and hautboy, became alarmed once more and begged Grumbkow to support his falling credit. Then came presents of silver plate, promises of help in setting up house, assurances of friendship. These tokens of grace alarmed him even more than threats, for they were a sign that a climax was approaching. All the same he made a final bid for freedom: "In regard to the business of the Princess of Bevern, her repudiation can be counted upon, if I am forced to take her, as soon as I am in control. . . . No one will be able to blame my behavior, for I have been forced to a course of action for which I have no inclination." But he felt he was beaten.

On February 4 he was waked at midnight by an express messenger who brought a letter from the King. At such an hour it was obvious it must treat of important news.

My dear son Fritz,
I am very pleased that you can now get on without medicine. You must beware of the cold for some days yet, for everybody here, myself included, is suffering terribly from rheumatism. So take care of yourself. You know, my dear son, that when my children are obedient I love them dearly. Thus when you were in Berlin I forgave you from the bottom of my heart, and although I have not seen you since then, I have thought of nothing but your well-being and of setting you up

both in the army and with a nice suitable girl, and of marrying you off while I am still alive to see to it. You may be sure that I have had dozens of the princesses round here scrutinized, as far as was possible, with reference to their behavior and education. The eldest Princess of Bevern has proved to be well brought up, modest and sensible as a woman should be. You must write at once and tell me what you feel about it. I have bought Katsch's house to give to the field marshal governor; I shall have the governor's house rebuilt and furnished and will give you enough money to keep house on your own. I will give you a regiment in the army in April. The Princess is not outstanding for good or bad looks. You are not to discuss this with anyone, but you are to write to your Mamma of what I have said to you and when you have a son I will allow you to travel. The marriage will not take place before next winter. In the interval I will find occasion to heap every honor upon you and I will thus be able to get to know you. She is a God-fearing creature, and that is the vital point. She will be *bearable* both for you and for her people-in-law. May God give this match His blessing! May He bless you and your successors! May He keep you faithful to the Christian faith! Always keep God before your eyes and put no trust in those damnable particularist notions and be obedient and faithful, then all will go well with you both in this world and for all eternity. And may he who desires this with all his heart say Amen. Your father, faithful unto death,

FR. WILHELM.

P.S. If the Duke of Lorraine comes I will send for you. I think your fiancée will come here. Farewell. God be with you.

As he read this letter, so oddly put together to wheedle and convince him by turns, Frederick came to see that everything had already been made public, and it would be madness to try to swim against the current. He therefore replied "in all submission" to his father that he "would not fail to obey his orders." But as the ceremony was put off till the winter he had seven or eight months in which to think it over and curse his luck. At first he was seized by a spasm of letter writing. Pages and pages were written against marriage and against pious women. The Princess of Brunswick was delicately named the Sex, the Corpus Delicti, the Merchandise, or even the Abominable Object of My Desires. "I have always wanted to gain distinction by the sword and to obtain pardon from the King by no other means but by that alone, but at the moment it seems that I shall owe it to my ——. I pity this wretched girl, for she will be one of the most unhappy princesses in the world. . . ." "If I could be married by proxy and the proxy could remain as husband, how happy I would be!" "I would rather be a cuckold than have a monster who would madden me with her stupidities and whom I would be ashamed of in public. . . . I would much prefer the biggest tart in Berlin to a religious enthusiast with half a dozen bigots at her heels."

A fortnight later the Bevern family arrived at Court. The moment the King saw the Princess he was "smitten" by her and wrote to his son to cry up the young woman and to pledge his word that she would please him. Frederick replied that he was delighted, but that in any case he submitted to his father's will. The King was so pleased with this obedience that he read the note to Grumbkow. "Well, Sire," said he, "what do you think of this dutiful son? What more could you wish?"

"It is the happiest day of my life," replied the King with tears in his eyes and he drew the Duke of Bevern into the next room that he might the more conveniently embrace him.

However, two days later Grumbkow received a letter in quite different ink from Cüstrin. "I will never take her. . . . Whatever happens I have no cause for self-reproach; I have put up with enough for a fault which has been exaggerated and I do not wish to bind myself to prolong my troubles into the future. In the last resort a pistol shot can free me from my troubles and from my life. I believe that God in His goodness would not damn me for that; He would have pity on me and would grant me salvation in exchange for a life of misery. Such are the lengths to which despair will drive a young fellow whose blood is not so cold as a septuagenarian's."

This brought Grumbkow down to earth with a bump, and, sensing the danger of the double game he was playing, he replied on the same day. "Upon waking I received this fine letter from Your Highness, which appals me. How is it that, while Your Royal Highness is in full agreement with the King, he speaks like a desperate man and desires me to poke my nose into matters which might cost me my head? No, my lord, my shirt is nearer to me than my jacket, and since you wish to play at Don Carlos, I do not wish to play the Count de Grammont. . . . I am not obliged to ruin myself and my humble family for love of Your Royal Highness, who is not my master and whom I see hastening to his ruin. . . . I realize that after all I have written here I shall lose the good graces of Your Highness, but I am quite prepared for that. You will allow me to withdraw completely from your affairs." It is possible that Frederick had tried to do his old opponent a bad turn, but the two plotters had gone too far together to separate now and soon they began to exchange compliments once more and bottles of wine.

Francis of Lorraine had arrived at Berlin on February 23. Frederick was sent for on the twenty-sixth and on that occasion made the acquaintance of his fiancée and her parents. The Duke of Bevern seemed to him a fine man, the Duchess "a fat cats'-meat seller," and the daughter an animal quite without charm. He described her in two letters to his sister as neither beautiful nor ugly, fair, with a fresh complexion, a pleasing neck, deepset eyes, an ugly mouth, a silly laugh which showed blackened teeth, ill dressed, ill mannered, not daring to raise her eyes, with a waddle like a duck's—her belly stuck out in front—embarrassed in conversation, and almost always silent. "It is easy to predict that this will be a very bad partnership." Princess Elisabeth was better than this portrait of her. She had eyes of periwinkle blue, ash-blonde hair, a dainty mouth, and a childish charm which was ready to blossom forth. However, she had been strictly brought up by severe parents who frightened her. When she felt at ease she talked with wit and gaiety. Alas, she met with nothing but hatred at the Prussian Court! One day the Queen told Wilhelmina at table before the servants, "Your brother is in despair at having to marry her and he is quite right too. She is really a fool: she answers every remark with Yes or No accompanied by a silly laugh which makes me feel sick."

At this Princess Charlotte, who was sixteen and had an angel's face and the eyes of a cherub, capped her remark with, "Oh, Your Majesty, you don't know all her attractions yet! I was at her toilet one morning. I thought I'd be suffocated there. She stinks like carrion. I think she must have at least ten or a dozen fistulas, for it was not a natural smell. I also noticed that she is deformed. The body of her dress is padded on one side, and one of her hips is higher than the other."

It is easy to see that the poor girl must have been intimidated by such a flood of spite.

The engagement was announced on March 10, 1732. The

Prince received the usual congratulations, then he turned his back on Elisabeth and talked to various people without looking at her. On April 4 he left for Nauen to take command of his regiment.

VI

FIFTEEN months passed before the marriage was celebrated. Prince Eugene and Seckendorff decided things had been badly managed, that they had been in too much of a hurry, and that the business might still fall through at the last minute because the ground had not been properly prepared for it. The Princess had to be molded, instructed, and taught the manners of the fashionable world, the King had to be kept favorable, the Prince had to be calmed down and freed from all temptations toward impulsive action. For what profit would the Emperor reap from the match if the future Queen was condemned never to have any influence on her husband?

From his garrison post Fritz continued to sulk and threaten. The King complained that he did not write often enough to his Dulcinea: it was because he lacked subject matter and did not know what to use to fill up the pages. "They want to make me fall in love at the whip's end, but unfortunately I have not the instincts of a donkey and I fear they will not succeed. . . . I am the ruler in my house and my wife gives no orders there. . . . I think a man who allows women to rule him is the world's biggest simpleton and unworthy of the honorable name of man." However, for fear of this distaste being maliciously misinterpreted, he added a libertine's declaration, "I love the sex but I love them with a very flighty love, I only ask them for enjoyment and afterward I despise them. Thus you may judge if I am composed of the stuff of which good husbands are made."

This was by no means reassuring. Seckendorff, to whom Prince Eugene had entrusted further moneys to crown the enterprise, thought of giving Frederick himself a pension. It was an elegant manner of influencing him in favor of His Majesty the Emperor. In the end, indeed, thanks to their cordial relations, the officious ambassador trusted in his own skill to right the evil notions that factious people had put into the Prince's head. But great precautions were needed, for his whole household, valets, lackeys, and cook's boys spied on the King's account. "As it is feared," wrote Seckendorff to Frederick, "that during the stay at Cüstrin it would have been impossible not to run up some debts, it will be absolutely vital to pay them without its coming to the ears of the King. . . . But as it will cause surprise if the debts are paid all at once, it will be more prudent to pay off a part each month," while giving out to his closest friends that he was economizing on his allowance. Frederick was delighted with the arrangement. As he received the money through Grumbkow's valet who usually brought him books, he spoke with enthusiasm of this new work which he was always wanting to reread. "The book which you have been good enough to send me is charming, and I am sending you a sealed copy of the song for which you ask." The song was in fact the receipt. Seckendorff used much tact to veil his generosity; Frederick had no fear of words and replied crudely that he was "bone dry." However, at the same time he assured the ambassador that he would make a habit of showing on all occasions "the devotion and deep reverence" he felt for the person of the Emperor.

He begged for himself, his friends, his sister. The King had released the daughter of the teacher of Potsdam from Spandau, but Duhan was still pining away at Memel: Seckendorff stepped in, got a pardon after a struggle, and added some money to it. Poor Wilhelmina was in penury. Her father-in-law had given her a bad reception, bad quarters, and bad treatment. After giving birth to a girl she returned to Berlin "to console herself at Papa's trough." In vain did Frederick read her a lesson: she should display modest domestic virtues, she should play the good housewife, and above all else she should bring the child to soften the King's heart! The Margravine followed this program, but Frederick William kept his purse strings tied up. To heighten the disgrace he had taken a dislike to the poor husband and he publicly called him a fool, a donkey, and a ninny. Frederick begged, "These two unhappy people trail about the country without hearth or home. . . . I cannot conceive how it is possible to refuse help to poor unfortunates who are innocent of their own plight. . . ." Seckendorff understood. He would do anything in the world to assist the worthy Princess Royal, but in exchange for the imperial guineas Wilhelmina must praise the virtues of the

Princess of Bevern and devote herself to engendering a good understanding between the bride and bridegroom-to-be, in such a way as to strengthen the friendship and perfect understanding which united the Houses of Austria and Brandenburg.

In the summer Frederick settled at Ruppin where the second battalion of his regiment was stationed, fifteen leagues to the northwest of Berlin in a country of sand and water, of languid rivers, bitter winds, peat bogs, dunes, and woods. The little town was silent, with no other sound than that of rain falling on the roofs and the tramp of soldiers marching down the street; a town of boredom, of retreat, but also for Fritz a town of freedom, of work, of meditation, and of dreams. He had recovered his sword and his uniform. "Here," he said, "I feel that I am more honored than anywhere else," and he liked to be honored.

In his letters he made fun of his new military duties. "I come from drill, I drill, I will drill—that is all the news I can give you." On the parade ground he did not mock. He fulfilled the duties of his command with eagerness. Without admitting to it he loved to find himself in the midst of these tall fellows, primitive and healthy as they were, who were to be the tools of his deep and complex ambitions. He liked to see their big, tight-laced bodies stiffen beneath his gaze. He loved the regiment with its abundant vigor, its discipline, its huge animal strength, its simple, sober fatalism. He was the will of those docile bodies. His head was full of unwritten verses as he breathed with delight the strong, acrid scent of leather belts and close-packed humanity. Then he used to return home, wrap himself in a pelisse, and play on his flute or read a book. "Here we are in deep peace and I could wish never to be in all my life more happy, or less so. . . . Excess of splendor is a burden and infinitely tiring; poverty grinds down too low a sort of nobleness which normally forms the basis of our characters. . . . I seldom budge from here, I amuse myself with the dead, and my tacit conversation with them is more useful to me than any I can have with the living." He also scrawled over a lot of paper but had taste enough to throw his poems into the fire—which he called offering to Vulcan the works of Apollo. He was late on the parade ground, as sometimes he worked all night and then only got up at nine or ten o'clock. When the Hamburg post brought oysters from England

and fat capons he used to invite some officers to dinner, three or
four only, for his finances did not allow him to regale a larger
party with such expensive delicacies. From time to time a boating trip, a card party, a modest display of fireworks in the garden, which was in front of the town; in winter a sledge race over
the ice. On Twelfth Night Frederick drew the bean cake, and
ran a raffle and two balls, one in fancy dress where he appeared
as Scaramouch, the other a masked fancy dress ball where he
was dressed as a woman and "even as a widow."

By every courier Frederick cross-questioned his correspondents
on the King's moods. When he learned from Grumbkow what
was said in the smoking room and at Court, he hurried to send
detailed justifications of his conduct to the King: he was not an
atheist; he had not left his garrison secretly; he had not been the
lover of Madame de Wreech; he did not despise his fiancée; he
had not seen Natzmer since the King had sent him away; he had
not played a joke on the pastor at Nauen; he had not indulged
in impious talk; he had not read Spinoza; he had never thought
of encroaching on the authority of His Majesty; might he die on
the spot if he had formed any plan for the future himself; he
only desired one thing—not to come back to the thorns and
thickets of Berlin and to live incognito in his beloved garrison
town. But although he had organized the kidnaping of a giant
shepherd from the territory of Mecklenburg, he was never very
sure of the future. One day the King sent him a military tutor,
Colonel von Bredow, whose official duty it was to watch over the
behavior of the household and to keep the young officers respectful. He was in reality a spy. On other occasions there arrived
from Potsdam questionnaires, financial commissions, and even
the order to draw up alone and quite unaided a general account
of the state of the domains in the bailiwick of Ruppin, with in-
junctions to make a "bit more" on the farming. This was a four
months' job, which the master had been spiteful enough to make
even more arduous by removing the old inventories from the
archives. By great good luck kind old Grumbkow helped in the
labor and, thanks to the minister, the Prince extricated himself
fairly well from the confusion. "Between you and me and the
door post," he wrote to him, "fiscalities will never be my *forte;* I
know as much about them as I need to know, but as for fixing

prices and taxes oneself I give that up completely. It is enough to investigate the subject, to guide its general trends, and to make sure trade is not forgotten."

That autumn Seckendorff went to visit Frederick to test his feelings. He found him calm and taciturn. To all insinuations on politics he replied only with vague phrases or with silence. Not a word of the money advanced, not a word of his Dulcinea; much politeness, but nothing definite. Seckendorff returned in a quandary, but the point was that Frederick had given in, fought no more, and merely made tasteless jokes about his fiancée: "My Princess has sent me a porcelain tobacco jar which I found broken in its case. I do not know if this was to emphasize the fragility of her virginity, of her virtue, or of the whole of the mortal frame."

However, this episode was to be fertile of unforeseen repercussions. At the end of 1731 the Emperor had drawn nearer the maritime powers. As Prince Eugene felt sure of Frederick William's perpetual complaisance, he thought of a new scheme which consisted of upsetting the marriages between Prussia and Brunswick to harmonize them with the new Austrian alliances. As Wilhelmina was settled, her sister Charlotte, intended for the Prince of Bevern, would espouse the Prince of Wales, and the Prince of Bevern would get Princess Anne of England in exchange. If need be, Charlotte would keep Bevern, Frederick could take his former choice, Amelia, and the unhappy Elisabeth, left on her own, could be found another husband. A vaudeville intrigue, one would have said. When Grumbkow was told by Seckendorff he raised a great outcry. How could they play with such fantastic schemes? After all that had happened, after the King had sworn not to mingle his blood with that of England! He was not as stupid or as pliable as Vienna seemed to imagine. "He will see soon enough what you're up to, and that it all amounts to nothing more than strengthening the friendship between the Emperor and England and helping the House of Bevern. . . . All that I can promise is that if the King speaks to me of it I will be neither for nor against it—but as for mixing myself up in this—may God preserve me from that!" The offer of a property worth 40,000 crowns did not shake his decision.

Grumbkow was right: the King took it all the more hardly as

he was displeased by the Emperor's behavior at an interview they had had in Bohemia (June, 1732). He had arrived at the castle of Kladrup full of superstitious reverence for His Imperial Majesty, for the exalted head of the German peoples. He had been welcomed with an affability which at first delighted him, but then he perceived that the talk was all about trifles and that the attentions paid to him were intended to make him forget hard facts. He returned disenchanted and anxious. In vain did Seckendorff bring the matter up as a jest, letting it be understood that the marriage of Princess Charlotte might bring profit to Prussia; the King flew into a mad rage and then relapsed into despair. He retired to Potsdam and talked of nothing but death, and everybody expected Grumbkow and Seckendorff to be driven from the Court. Several times the Margravine told her brother they were in complete disgrace. After some scenes in the smoking room, however, the King's rage finally subsided and he resolved to comply with the Duke of Bevern's request that the ceremony should take place on June 12, 1733, at the young lady's home at Salzdahlen in Hanover. Frederick watched without pleasure the approach of what he called the most trying event of his whole life, but he had decided to play his part in all obedience: "I will act the comedy [in such a way] that it will be quite complete."

On the very day before it Seckendorff made one last attempt. The King of Poland was dead and Austria needed England's help to prevent the French candidate, Stanislas, from being elected; in the last resort Amelia must become Queen of Prussia. Frederick William, who happened to be in bed, listened patiently to Seckendorff. "If I did not know you personally," he told him, "if I was not sure that you are an honest man, I'd think I was dreaming. If you had spoken in this way three months ago, I cannot say what I might not have done from affection for His Imperial Majesty, though it is against both his and my interests for my eldest son to marry an English princess. But to do it now! I am here with the Queen. All Europe knows that the marriage takes place tomorrow. Can't you see that this is another instance of English cunning, designed to brand me in the eyes of the world as a man without honor, a man who breaks his word?"

Seckendorff replied that it was true that the preparations for the ceremony were public, but that none of them need be changed, and instead of Frederick his sister Charlotte could be married to the Prince of Bevern. As for the marriage of Frederick and Amelia it could be celebrated later on and elsewhere. All this impudence was drowned in a flood of words, compliments, and declarations of friendship. Frederick William kept his head and let the other's involved expressions run on until they dried up; in reply he stated that he wished to get on good terms again with England, that he had other sons and daughters, that numerous marriage connections were possible, but that he would not go back upon his word once given. When letters were brought for his signature, he let the anger he had repressed break out: he accused his wife and son of being in the plot, but Fritz had a good defense and his father soon withdrew the charge. The day passed quietly enough, and in the evening there was a pastoral masque at Court; the Crown Prince played the part of a lovesick peasant, and Apollo came down and gave him the prize. Next day, June 12, the marriage was celebrated.

The Republic of Rheinsberg

I

ON June 27, 1733, the Crown Prince and his Princess made their state entry in Berlin. At the Köpenik gate they inspected four cavalry regiments, eleven infantry regiments, and the corps of Hussars. After that the procession of sixty six-horse carriages entered the town. A few weeks later Frederick returned to Ruppin alone.

On the ancient ramparts he was having a shady park constructed, with stone satyrs bearing flower baskets, with great trees, a grotto, and a little temple decorated with paintings where he gave dinner parties on fine days. However, the two houses which had served his needs in the town were too mean to hold the Princess and her ladies. Besides the King did not want his son to have a long break in his military apprenticeship, and Frederick himself longed to recapture the studious solitude of his beloved garrison town. He lived at ease there, far away from Jupiter, far from the Court, far from spying eyes, and also from now on far from Elisabeth. "To attain happy forgetfulness," he wrote, "the regiment is the best place of all."

He had read Voltaire's *Charles XII,* which Grumbkow had lent him a few months after its publication, and he reread it frequently. Voltaire had treated his main character as a tragic prince under stage lighting, but, as it happened, nothing was more fitted to enflame Frederick's mind and to fill him with the desire for dangerous exploits and epic deeds which stick in men's memories. From living side by side with his hero he felt more than ever the insignificance of his present pursuits. Then he dreamed of war: "War," he wrote on one of these occasions, "chastens lechery and pomp; it teaches sobriety and fasting; it uproots all that is effeminate," and he sighed, "A calling such as that of war deserves more than the diligence of old age."

However, there was no lack of occasions for dispute in Europe. Almost every year the Duchies of Jülich and Berg were discussed, and the King of Prussia had rights over them which he mentioned on every possible occasion. These duchies were all that remained of a great German principality which had vanished little by little from history for lack of heirs, after having dominated for more than a century all the Rhineland on both sides of the river from Aachen to the Ruhr and from Cologne to the Low Countries. Its first crisis came with the Thirty Years' War when the two principal heirs, Brandenburg and the Palatinate, had divided the inheritance; Brandenburg took the northern territories, the Mark and Ravensberg; the Palatinate took the southern lands, Berg and Jülich. But in spite of having married three times the present Elector, Charles Philip III, had no male heirs, and Frederick William was waiting for him to die so as to collect the last bit of the heritage.

In 1732 Charles Philip fell ill, and immediately those at Ruppin received orders to stand by. Frederick heard the news with extraordinary delight. He watched the regiment in a hullabaloo and the town turned upside down: "Everybody runs about like mad; the soldiers take leave of their hosts, the officers of their mistresses, the victualers of their families." As for himself he carried out "with all possible exactitude" the instructions he had received. He had the tents pitched and saw to every detail of preparation. He was at last going to "see the King's fine army in action" and be initiated into the profession of arms "in the shelter of its victorious might." His fancy had already carried him to the plains of Westphalia and had shown him the new subjects prostrate before the feet of their new master at the gates of the captured city.

The Elector did not die; the tents were folded up, and the officers went back to their mistresses. But Europe in those days was never long at rest, and failing the succession of Berg there was that of Poland. In the autumn of 1733 the French crossed the Rhine and took Kehl to create a diversion in favor of Stanislas Leczinski, the elected king, against whom Russia, Saxony, and Austria had formed a coalition. Kehl was an imperial town: in its usual dilatory way the Empire took up arms, and the King of Prussia set about providing Charles VI with the 10,000 men he had promised him. Frederick fully expected to be one of them. "I intend to make war," he wrote to his sister, "and show these French gentlemen that there are some young gamblers in the depths of Germany with enough bravado to place themselves before all their armies without a tremor." This was trying to rush things, for the soldiers used to be dispersed during the winter. Frederick had to spend all the rainy season at Ruppin in his mouse hole swearing at the Court of Vienna and the inertia of its generals. He had sent for the famous singer and composer Graun; he worked under his tuition and composed solos for the flute. In November he received a visit from the King, who was in a gracious mood and made him a present of some property worth 7,000 crowns. At last on July 1, 1734, after having spent the night dancing at the Queen's at Monbijou, he set out along with General von Schulenburg, General von Kleist, and Colonel von Bredow, who bore an Instruction in due and correct form wherein the King had once again transcribed in minute detail the habitual confusion of his ideas.

Frederick is to behave in a way proper to a prince of the ancient blood of Brandenburg and to a brave and honest soldier. He is to fear God and keep the Lord Jesus in his heart, without Whose help man is but a sounding brass and a tinkling cymbal. He is to learn all that concerns the army, not only the main things but also the details—for example, how the musketeers' shoes are made and how they last on the march. He is to educate himself from small to great things, right up to *dispositiones generalissimi*. He is to observe, inspect, question, ask the reasons for everything and reason concerning these reasons. In an army all sorts of people are to be found, princes' sons, young counts and other scions of such families; the greater part are worth little and he is to be polite to these gentlemen but to do no more than wish them good morning. He is to seek on the contrary the company and conversation of tried men, old generals, especially of the Commander in Chief, Prince Eugene, whom he is always to follow during reconnaissance or shortly before a battle.

He will be encamped with the Prussian force. General von Röder, who is in command of the King's 10,000 men, will keep him informed and will send on all orders to him. The Prince is to live from preference with the Prussian officers; they will teach

him subordination—the principal virtue of military life. Down
to the very subalterns he must know them all by sight and by
name. On days of battle he is to remain beside Prince Eugene
until the middle of the engagement but he is to finish the day in
the Prussian ranks. He is never to take off his uniform; he is not
to put up with any word against God or the Scriptures. He is to
abstain from women, wine, and play. If by some misfortune he
should fall into sin Schulenburg and Kleist are to inform the
King by express courier. If the officers of the two armies fight
each other with pistols His Majesty the King desires that His
Serenity the Crown Prince shall not take part, nor fire to no purpose. Of course Frederick is to be economical. When he is invited out to dinner he is to take his officers along with him so
that the fire in his kitchen need not be lit. The number of dishes
on ordinary days is fixed, but if he invites generals to dine he is
to be allowed two extra courses and as many as six for Prince
Eugene. A roast is to be enough in the evening. The cost of sus-
tenance is not to exceed 4,400 thalers for the whole campaign.

This mighty surplus of good advice set Frederick's teeth on
edge, but he had saved some money, and the joy of departure
swallowed up all minor matters. On July 7 he appeared before
Eugene at the camp at Wiesenthal near Philippsburg, which the
French were besieging while the Imperialists tried to raise the
siege. His greeting was very complimentary—"I have come to
see how a hero gains laurels." But the grizzled Eugene gained no
laurels that year. He let the French take Philippsburg without
a fight and Frederick did not get much out of his expedition.
Fatigues, memories of bad roads, a few drinking bouts, numerous
carriages upset and broken, a few marching songs picked up on
the road, a sight of dilatory Austrian methods, some useless
marches, some indecisive skirmishes—this was what he called in
his notes the usual confusion. The King himself arrived a week
after his son. Because of the circumstances he set out to be ten
times more unbearable than he usually was. "We have here an
amateur who plays on an instrument which maddens the whole
camp," the Prince wrote to his sister. "For pity's sake add your
prayers to ours so that we may soon be freed of him. If he stays
here much longer I will beg you to build a little house and prepare a room in it for me, for I will come in the train of many

others who like me are beginning to lose their reason." Luckily Frederick William was not well and left at the beginning of August. "Our fat guzzler is leaving in a week," Frederick sent word to Wilhelmina. Truly he was not stifled by respect.

Nevertheless the Prince got great delight from seeing warfare that did not come out of books. He tried himself under fire and acquitted himself well, neither disturbed nor excited but naturally calm and gay. Some Austrian officers praised his steadiness in the presence of danger. By always asking questions he had learned to observe, to comprehend in a glance the fine points of a maneuver or a position. He would even have liked to spend some time with the French as a friendly observer. "I can assure you," he said later to their ambassador, La Chetardie, "that though my body happens to be among the Imperialists my heart will always be on your side and full of good wishes for you." But he was dissuaded from his Utopian plan. He got his own back by watching the weaknesses of the Austrians at close quarters.

At each reconnaissance he crammed his notebooks with sketches and regularly sent his father extremely precise reports. Prince Eugene disappointed him. He could see that old age had made him timid, that his operations lacked breadth, and that he had let slip his chance of attacking the enemy.

At the end of September the army began to disperse to take up its winter quarters, and Frederick got ready to return to Berlin. The King was seriously ill. He had worn himself out in camp by trying to live a soldier's life and on the return journey his sufferings became worse. In mid-September he was given up for lost. He was in constant pain, he complained he felt stifled and that his sides ached and he ate next to nothing. So as to enjoy the smell of tobacco he made his generals smoke all around him. At times he was suffocated and his face went black. The windows were opened wide, and his attendants pushed him to the casement while he gasped "Air! Air!" His body was swollen to above the navel and when it was shifted a sound of water could be heard. Periods of quiet were rare. The moment he felt better he squabbled with the doctors and threatened to send them to prison if they did not cure him by a fixed date. He fulminated against his son and then spoke tenderly of him, calling him Fritzchen. At times he would announce that his death was near, make himself sweat before the fire, and suddenly order the negro who waited on him, "Pray hard! I will not die."

From the moment his mother informed him of the serious nature of the complaint, Frederick had abandoned himself to fate with a highly edifying resignation. He told everyone of his submission to the Blessed Lord, who governs everything in this world without a Christian being able to rebel against his decrees. "The news we have of the King," he wrote to his sister from Heidelberg, "is very bad; he is in a wretched way and is not expected to live long. Well, I have decided to keep cheerful whatever happens; for after all I am quite sure that while he lives I will have little enough pleasure. . . . Your feeling of tenderness for him arises from your long absence from him; but if you were to see him again, I believe you would surely let him rest in peace without worrying about him." And a few days later, "The King is nearing his end; he will scarcely survive the end of the year. . . . We must prepare ourselves for it, my dearest sister, and although in a way it wrings my heartstrings, to counter this I am very glad to find that I shall *then* be in a position to help you. . . ."

The Prince arrived at Potsdam on the afternoon of the twelfth. He found the King in a pitiful state: his arms and face were fearfully thin, his complexion was like wax, patches on his face were blue, his breath was short, his belly swollen and hanging, his legs huge and full of pus. Frederick William welcomed him so tenderly that he burst into tears. "I am only forty-six years old," said the King, "I have all I could wish on earth, and the Good Lord has made a happy ruler of me. Here I am in the world's cruellest agony, but I intend to bear everything with patience. My Saviour suffered much more for me and for my sins. I have deserved the punishment of God. His will be done! May it be to me according to His Holy Will. I will always praise and bless His name, for after this trial He has sent me I am sure that the hour of my death will be happy and that He will give me the ineffable felicity which no death can destroy."

Every day the King called his son to him. He was very frank with him and told him political secrets. He cursed his wretched ministry which had given him such bad advice. He complained of the Emperor, who had treated him, an old friend like him, just like dirt, and he ran through the advantages he could have got out of an alliance with France. He advised Fritz to exile one man and to hang another. Sometimes old grudges came to the surface: "If you don't deal with things properly and everything is topsy-turvy I shall mock at you in my grave." Frederick attended assiduously to the invalid and did his best to comfort him. Twice a week five members of the Central Office came to instruct him in governmental affairs and his father let him sign documents of lesser importance himself.

The Prince was drawing up plans now night and day. The ambassadors crowded round him, and he confided to his friend Alexander von Wartensleben that he had already decided in detail all he would do the moment the King was dead—what place he would go to first; how he would receive homage; whether he would be crowned; how he would wear mourning; how he would treat ministers and envoys of foreign powers; whether he would keep on his father's favorites; whether he would dine alone on state occasions; whether he would keep the regiment of giants; whether he would keep up the levies in foreign lands; where he would set up the Queen and what pension she would receive; what new regulations he would ordain for the army and for the administration. "Yes, my dear little Count, I shall have a lot of work one day, but I hope to get through it and there is pleasure enough in being sole King of Prussia." He was so sure the kingdom was his that he ordered Grumbkow to hold up all current diplomatic negotiations.

However, the King did not die. While Wilhelmina was already thinking of setting out to be present at his last hour he sent Frederick on a tour of inspection to Ruppin. On his return the Prince found him recovering, breathing more freely, and catching up his stick to beat those servants who came within reach of his arm chair. Water trickled from his legs and feet through cracks, but the doctors could not believe it was a lasting improvement. "He will not last after January 1," Frederick repeated to himself and for weeks kept sending his sister a diary of the illness, a journal of Court life, and a newsletter of his own feelings. Turn over the pages of their correspondence and the drama lives again. Just at first the recovery was not kept up: the King suffered from a sharp fever; he had a tumor in the left calf which would take a day or two to drain. The doctors waited for it to burst before coming to a decision—if the pus was of a certain color the King would die during the week, if not he might live another month; at all events he would never leave his bed again. Then follow medical and psychological symbols mixed with words of forced pity. The Queen was charming and quite resigned. Water had collected in the right arm. The King was in a filthy temper. The end would come quickly for gangrene was inevitable. It was painful to see his father suffer. An incision had been made in the left leg, but so far nothing but a little blood and water had flowed from it. The belly was swollen; the fever did not leave him; he might drag on till the end of the year. As the doctors had not given up all hope Frederick's enemies were raising their heads again; if the fatal event did not take place terrible vengeance might be expected. "The King's recovery will be my undoing." The Princess Sophia had been married to the Margrave of Schwedt; owing to present circumstances the ceremony had been a quiet one. The best and most intelligent doctors considered the King was done for; those who spoke of recovery had certainly been ordered to do so by the ministers. The King was better, but it must be the final rallying. No, it was a change of complaint, for he had been dropsical and he was becoming consumptive. A pernicious fever was consuming him; his digestive organs no longer functioned; his liver was rotting; he could not possibly recover.

On her side Wilhelmina consulted the doctors in Bayreuth. They quoted several cases of people who had been worse than the King and had dragged on a long time. But those people were careful of themselves as the King never was. She also had her hopes. The old Margrave was ill but of an illness which never forsook its victims. There was a conjunction of fates as between brother and sister: they had passed through the same trials and would receive the crown on the same day. If the King seemed to be improving it was only so that he might die suddenly of a relapse, when the Margrave was at his last gasp: "A little patience, my dear brother, and my prophecy will be fulfilled." And Frederick replied politely, "I am charmed at the constancy with which death pursues the old Margrave. . . . I hope to hear the happy tidings of his surrender." After a good fight the Margrave died in May, 1735, and Frederick assured his sister "of his very lively satisfaction"; but though the final limit had been reached and passed, the King himself lived on. Frederick was tossed like a shuttle between Potsdam and Ruppin (where he had just acquired a chamber orchestra) and was surprised one day to see his father on his feet once again and much reduced in size. "Talking of the King," he wrote to his sister on January 10, "I must inform you of a most amazing thing; he is recovering completely, he is beginning to walk about and he is in better health than I am. I have dined with him and I can assure you he eats and drinks enough for four. In a week he will go to Berlin and it is certain that in a fortnight he will be on horseback. It is as extraordinary a miracle as ever occurred. . . . God must have had some very good reasons for giving him his life." A few days later Frederick wrote again, "Our miracle is on the high road to recovery here," and when Wilhelmina in the summer spoke of a sympathetic relapse, he added, "The King's illness is just a politic one; he is very well the moment he feels inclined and he gets worse when he finds it convenient. I was taken in at first, but now I see through the mystery. You can be sure, my dear sister, that thanks to God he has the constitution of a Turk, and he will survive far into the future if only he wants to do so."

Fritz fell from the heights. As a good son he had to show his delight and give thanks to God. But he had shown himself to be impatient, feverish, and eager to grasp at the crown. He was no longer of any account, just an importunate heir deceived by fate. He had talked too much and written too much; once again he had behaved like a youngster and had made no real use of his reading, reflection, experience, and retirement. Perhaps with his useless papers before him he wept from rage and shame. After having thought he was lord of all, he found himself once more faltering and lost without even the strength to hope, for the King might reign for another quarter of a century. "My God," he wrote on the subject of mourning garments to his sister, "I am charmed by the Duke of Brunswick's conduct; he has had the good manners to die like a man of honor to please his son. I consider that he has not misused worldly grandeur." Frederick William took pride in his strength; he seemed, now he was restored to life, to wish to revenge himself on his son for having been feeble and timorous. He set about making him feel his slavery all the more.

Besides in his confusion Frederick would have liked to flee the Court. He asked leave to return to the army of the Rhine; the King refused permission because he disliked the idea of tying himself down to helping Austria for another year, but also because he wished to keep the Crown Prince under his thumb. Without the help of this diversion Frederick had to seek within himself the courage to endure and to wait.

The crisis of 1734 left as big a mark on his life as did the death of Katte. In the opinion of the historian G. B. Volz it made even more, for though he reacted against the gloomy sights of Cüstrin with all the easy forgetfulness of youth, the illness and recovery of the King had made a lasting change in his thoughts and studies. A new tone of bitterness and gravity appeared in his letters. "Disgusted as I am with every facet of the world I throw myself into reflections which compel me to see more and more that there is no stable and permanent happiness to be found here below . . . the more one knows of the world the more one dislikes it, finding in it more sorrow and misfortune than instances of joy and happiness." Back at Ruppin he had not given up his usual amusements. "To calm body and soul" he read and wrote "like a galley slave." He had music enough "for four" and he boasted of having "got on far enough in composition to write a symphony." But he often said that he was more or less certain to die before the King did and that he must seek in his mind and conscience for the delight and repose which the chances of life had denied him. What he read in the galleys was the work of philosophers, of moralists, of all those who interested themselves in the mysteries of mankind and of the universe.

The King, however, could not leave the Prince to his meditations. At the beginning of September he suggested a pleasure trip, or rather his idea of one, instead of going on a campaign. "I want to ask you if you would like to make a pleasure trip in Prussia for five or six weeks to master the finances and get the feel of that district, to see what is still lacking and why things are not yet prospering down there. It may be useful to you to take a good look at what is happening down there both in the town and country and in the administration, since you will have to rule this land one day and you will not find it satisfactory to have to trust the specious reports of people who are most of them inter-

ested parties. I have suffered all too much from this, and although
this district is one of my finest ones I must confess, all the same,
that it is still in a wicked and shameful state of disorder. If therefore you would like to go down there, I will give you a complete
set of instructions, in which you will see what parts it is best to
observe with attention, how I have arranged the administration,
and what still remains to be done. You will have authority to gain
exact information of all the operations of the Chamber of War
and Domains and wherever else you find it necessary. You will
at the same time see if all the regiments which are in Prussia are
in the order I wish them to be in and you will be able to put right
all that is not in order. I await your opinion on this matter."
Frederick replied that he knew he was born for obedience and
he submitted with a good heart to his father's will, but he wrote
to his sister, "He wants to send me on a trip to Prussia; it is a little
more civilized than Siberia but not much so."

Prussia lay outside Germany proper, outside the Empire, right
in Slav country surrounded by Polish territory. It was here only
that Frederick William was a King. At Berlin he was the Elector
of Brandenburg, elsewhere Prince, Count, Duke, or Margrave.
The royal title only applied in this far-off province, where lay
Königsberg, the town where the kings were crowned. The country had remained almost uncultivated and had been terribly
devastated during the Thirty Years' War. On his early visits
Frederick William had seen nothing but deserted villages, ruined
houses, wasted fields, wretched natives, and packs of wolves. To
fill up the desert places, the sight of which worried him, he organized a real colonizing movement, to assist which he poured
out money, work, his genius for practical details, and his great
gifts as a recruiter of men. One year he had a windfall of fifteen
thousand Protestants from Salzburg, who had been expelled by
their bishop, and he thanked God for it. But it was his own work
there which had been heroic; he had pursued it ceaselessly, in
spite of mortifications, accidents, and ever-recurring difficulties.
By showing his son this province which he loved as the work of
his own hand and for which he had labored so hard, he wished
perhaps to compel his admiration. Nevertheless he wrote of it
as poor and wretched, as though he was modestly trying to hide
his own merit. Had Fritz understood that there was something

worthy of respect in this good workman's modesty? At all events he did what he had to do admirably well.

Naturally he made fun of himself and of his mission. In a letter to Grumbkow he compared himself to a ghost clad in the purple, which was promenaded round the country to proclaim that the overlord was alive and would come to chastise or pardon, but he followed the King's instructions point by point. He inspected the regiments, watched them maneuver, examined the men and the horses. He visited the domain lands and the villages, tasted the bread, compared the rents and the state of cultivation. He had reports given him and made notes on them like those of his father. On the way there and the way back he crossed Polish Prussia, which seemed to him like a desert. He saw Poles who were "terrifyingly filthy and slovenly"; near Königsberg he encountered the train of the refugee King Stanislas, and took the chance of dining two or three times with the wandering sovereign, who impressed him as being a great man—as much a king in adversity as he would have been on the most glorious of thrones. Frederick William was delighted: "It is particularly pleasing for me to see you going into the details of things in this way and forcing yourself to get to the root of everything: indeed that is the main thing." However, the eye of the son was sterner than the eye of the father. From Königsberg Frederick sent in so harsh a report that he was nervous about it. "As far as my journey is concerned," he wrote to Grumbkow, "I will tell you shortly that I have just been all over Prussia; I have seen its good points and also, on the other hand, its naked poverty. If the King does not decide to open the granaries toward the new year you can count on it that half the people there will die of hunger, for the harvests of the last few years have been very bad. In my earlier letters to the King I have only given a superficial account, but after completing the journey and going all round I have written him my feelings on the matter quite frankly and as I would speak them before God. I am put in charge of a commission, I am asked to examine things and make a report on them: very well! Would I not be betraying the King, the country, my conscience, and my honor if I did not pour out my whole heart and describe things as they appeared to me?" The King sent orders in accordance with his son's proposals. He was indeed so far from being annoyed with him that he hurried on with the domestic establishment he had begun in October, 1733, on which he had already spent more than 100,000 thalers.

II

ABOUT a dozen miles to the north of Ruppin lay the domain of Rheinsberg. It could be reached through woods and fields by a quiet road, the only traffic of which consisted of carts loaded with logs, faggots, or peat. The town was very small and almost entirely inhabited by French Huguenots. After having been burned down it had been rebuilt in the style of a civic center, and the houses seemed crushed by the majestic, empty streets. The park and the castle were set slightly apart at one end of a huge square planted with lime trees. An iron gate had to be opened, a bridge crossed, and a courtyard traversed to reach the edge of a lake—the Grinericksee—and to discover the land where Frederick spent his happiest days: an immense watery waste, gray and green, lightly touched with mist; with soft sand which sank beneath the feet, tall grasses yellow and sharp as swords, silver birches, beeches, green and black pines which endured the squalls of autumn stoically, pools stretching on forever and ever, joined by tiny channels choked with water herbs; a land of dunes, of grassy islets, of forests, of rivers, and of stagnating waters, made up at once of purity and putrefaction, which the autumn drenched in fogs and showers as if the water of the earth were rejoining the waters of the heavens. Winters were windy, icy, hostile. After a short spring, all astir with eager life, the hot months swam with milky brightness, with transparent moistness, and at close of day, when the rim of the horizon was like burnished copper, the waters purpled and the tree tops were tinged with glowing reflections.

There was an old seigniorial manor there which the King allowed Frederick to transform as he liked. His architect, George Wenceslaus von Knobelsdorff, pulled it nearly all down, adapted the remainder, and built a small symmetrical castle of elegant proportions in the French style. Knobelsdorff was thirteen years older than the Prince. He had served as a captain in the Prussian Army, had been a painter, and had made a wide study of ancient architecture as well as of that of Versailles. In 1736 Frederick

sent him to Italy to complete his education: he returned more of
a classicist than ever. He liked simple lines, regular façades, and
well-balanced masses. Rheinsberg consisted of three sections
joined at right angles round a square courtyard. The fourth side
facing the lake was closed by a double colonnade which supported
a terrace giving on to the first floor. A dozen steps led down to
the landing stage. On each side of the colonnade the two wings
were finished off with a pair of towers each surmounted by a
balustrade and overtopping the main edifice by a few feet. The
frontages were very simple: facing the town an attic and a cornice
bearing four statues of gods and over the main door this inscription, *Frederico tranquillitatem colenti;* facing the bridge
were wooden statues carrying lanterns; elsewhere rounded pediments above the windows, window ledges of wrought iron with
lyres worked into the design, some balconies, and some vases
completed the ornamentation of the building.

A great hall in white and gold took up the whole of the first
floor of the right wing; the remainder was arranged in small
apartments for private life—seven rooms for the Prince and five
for the Princess. While going over the plans of his house Frederick had remembered Dresden and had dreamed of Versailles,
of Versailles the marvelous, of which he had seen so many pictures and heard so many enthusiastic descriptions. Into the sandy
Mark he wished to transport a corner of France, a bit of the Trianon with its festive decorations, its painted ceilings, its marbles,
its stone figures, its airy gods and goddesses, its rings of fat genii.
The walls of his room were hung with green silk, spun with yellow and white parrots. He slept on a canopied bed between
Corinthian columns and right above his library, in the old tower
of the left. Minerva amid fluttering cupids held an open book
on the pages of which were written only two names—Horace and
Voltaire. Above the doors and windows were wood carvings of
books, terrestrial hemispheres, compasses, lyres, and T squares.
The Princess' room was in blue satin and silver; in the other
rooms the curtains, arm chairs and sofas were in linen gray,
celadon blue, violet, rose, and crimson with lashings of braid and
silver picture frames.

The work went on for years. When Frederick set up house
there in the summer of 1736 with Elisabeth and her attendants

nothing was yet finished. The great music room was never completed. The gardens were only begun in 1737 and it was not till November, 1739, that Frederick could write to his sister, "The furnishing is complete; there are two rooms full of pictures; the others have pier glasses with gilt or silver-gilt paneling. Most of my pictures are by Watteau or Lancret, both painters of the Brabant school." These *genre* pictures, to the number of twenty-two, are to be found in the inventory, after the portraits and flower pieces under the heading of "Dutch Pictures," without any details as to subject matter. Most likely they were those picnics, lessons in love, and serenades in a park which are to be found to-day at Potsdam and Berlin. Thanks to them the walls seemed to be adorned with a dream of springtime and youth.

In truth, the Watteaus were the treasure of Rheinsberg. Remove them and it was obvious enough that this was not the Trianon. For lack of money Knobelsdorff economized on materials. In 1739 the plaster in the kitchen cracked and had to be repaired, and rotten beams had to be replaced. The walls were finished in stucco, that marble of indigent princes, and the parquet was of deal like the floors of a real old tavern. The interior decoration had an unfinished, countrified look, was lacking in taste and overemphasized. It had a savor of ostentation and economy combined. Pesne, who was a good portrait painter, had been put out by this work that was new to him, and his brother-in-law Dubuisson had been no more happy about it than he. Painters and sculptors had overdone allegories which told a story —Apollo appearing in his chariot; Aurora parting the clouds; Fame announcing the future; the rising Sun chasing away the demons of Darkness—on the walls and on the balustrades all Olympus was calling for the death of the King. Yet the gods who are immortal should have been able to express their wishes rather more discreetly.

The inhabitants of Rheinsberg were numerous. First Princess Elisabeth, more beautiful, transformed, always good humored, always rapt in admiration of her Prince, who had had her painted in her riding habit; Madame de Katsch, the Grand Mistress of the Robes (sixty years old, dignified, stately, with a habit of making deep curtsies when the proprieties were in danger); the two Maids of Honor, Mademoiselle de Schack, who was not beautiful but who had a pretty foot, and Mademoiselle de Walmoden who was a blonde and was called Iris; lastly the almoner Augustin Deschamps, the son of a French refugee, a great reader, a logician, an educated and a clever man.

At the Prince's side were three people who were usually to be found near him—the honest old dotard Von Wolden, grand marshal at Rheinsberg as he had been at Cüstrin, the unpleasant Von Bredow, nicknamed the "Journalist" or the "Argus," and old Senning, the invalid with a wooden leg. But as well as the companions given him by his father Frederick had real friends of his own: the sapient, downright Knobelsdorff, a typical German who, however, never swore by anywhere but Greece; the Parisian Antoine Pesne, almost a sexagenarian, with a bevy of daughters, brothers-in-law, and sisters-in-law, all of them painters; the two brothers Graun, tenors, composers, violinists, professors of harmony, and masters of the chapel; Benda the First Violin, Quantz the flautist; Major Stille, placid, cultured, and devout, a musician who knew many languages; Baron de la Motte-Fouqué, a Protestant son of French refugees, born at The Hague and since then page to old Dessau, that sage and learned officer; the youngest Chasot, Isaac Francis Edmund de Chasot, nineteen or twenty years old, a Norman transplanted into Burgundy—Frederick had known him on the Rhine, as he had known Fouqué, but Fouqué had served on the Prussian side and Chasot on the French. He had had to flee the country after fighting a duel. Frederick had heard of his escapade and had invited him to pay them a visit, then came across him again in Mecklenburg and kept him at his side. He had a turned-up nose and knowing eyes; he played the flute, copied Frederick's manuscripts, and was always laughing.

A higher place in his master's affections was given to Charles Etienne Jordan, the son of a French refugee, born in Berlin in 1700, sometime student at Geneva and Lausanne, and a pastor at twenty-five. When he was introduced to Frederick and made a citizen of Rheinsberg he had just been on a tour through France, Germany, England, and Holland, without a glance at the countryside but without missing the smallest collection of curios. Once he got to Strassburg he had been delighted to see his fatherland once more. At Paris the religious ecstatics had shocked him and he found the bright young things used too much rouge, but he admired everything else—finding the city noisy and lively, the people kindly, obliging, and honest with strangers, the saleswomen polite and helpful, and the actors the best in the world. In the little book in which he wrote down his impressions he showed amazement at such elegant women, such rich libraries, such witty, courteous, and learned writers as Monsieur de Fontenelle, the Abbé de Saint-Pierre, the Abbé Dubois, Monsieur Rollin, Father Montfaucon who knew so much Greek, and also Monsieur de Voltaire, "a thin young man, who seems to be suffering from consumption and to be burned up with a blind enthusiasm." Jordan was small, well built, dark skinned, with large eyebrows and very dark hair. He was, depending on the day, the kind, the benign, the pacific, the theological, the impeccable, the most learned, the most profound Jordan, the man to whom Frederick wrote thus: Friend Jordan, *Doctissime doctor, Dive Jordane,* repeating to him that he placed himself "in the shadow of his knowledge, like the timid turtledove which hides itself in the hollow of an oak tree." In short, the man he needed to act as a dictionary to his insatiable curiosity.

Lastly Keyserlingk, the vortiginous, enigmatic Baron Dietrich von Keyserlingk. His correspondence has been lost; a pity, for he was the most beloved of them all. Before the attempt at flight he had been attached to the Prince's person, but he had returned to his regiment after the fiasco. Frederick would have liked to have him by him at Ruppin, but the King had forbidden it. He finally allowed him to be called to Rheinsberg, where his arrival was hailed "like the rising of the sun when it dispels the gloom of a winter night." He had been born in 1698 in Courland. The man belonged to a different race, with almost yellow skin, a flat nose, small eyes, a broad face, and a short body. He had studied at Königsberg University for five years and had left behind him a prodigious reputation for scholarship, as he had argued his theses in German, French, Latin, and Greek. He had spent two years in Paris; he drank a lot, dressed like a comic-opera shepherd, and could never keep still. When Bielfeld, who has left us some spicy gossip about the whole circle, saw him for the first time he was returning from a hunt with a great deal of chatter. "I was quite surprised," continues the narrator, "to find him in a dressing gown, his gun slung over his shoulder. He addressed me in a very free and easy manner, and his first words were designed to convince me that I had long had the honor of being a close friend of his. He took me by the arm and carried me off to his room. While he was dressing he recited bits of the *Henriade*, passages of German poetry, talked horses and hunting at me, cut one or two capers and a few steps of a rigadoon, and discussed politics, mathematics, painting, architecture, and military science." It was like that all day. Keyserlingk adored his Prince, told everybody about him, and wanted them all to love him. Frederick had nicknamed him Caesarion and called him his "best friend, his all."

The republic also had visitors: the respectable Madame von Kannenburg; Baron von Morrien, the Queen's grand marshal, a pleasant, jovial ass; his young wife, the charming and lively Dorothea von Marwitz, nicknamed "Madame Whirlwind"; the exquisite Louise von Brandt, the "Beauty," for whom Frederick had tender feelings, and who had, without seeming to be aware of it, the worst reputation of any at the Court; her sister, who told fortunes with cards and who was called the "Wicked Fairy"; her husband, who organized the theatricals, the Danish envoy, Praetorius, and the French minister, La Chetardie, the "Divine Marquis" whose conversation Frederick enjoyed—"It's a sweetmeat for us."

The "monastery" wrote a mass of letters. Frederick himself had four or five regular correspondents and was always trying to increase their number. Major, later Colonel de Camas, one of a family of French refugees, was a very cultured man, a good geometer, and not a bit of a courtier. Frederick opened his heart to him in his letters. Suhm, the minister of Saxony at Berlin, had done his best to help the Prince at the time of his misfortunes. Tender, melancholy, and delicate, he was the father confessor of the Prince's dreams, the "dear Phoenix," the "dear Translucent." When he was appointed to the embassy at St. Petersburg Frederick wrote to him, "That barbarous Court needs men who know how to drink heavily and—vigorously. I do not suppose you observe these characteristics in yourself. Your delicate body is the guardian of a fine, witty, and unfettered spirit. . . . My dear Translucent, do not commit a murder on your own person. Of what use will your immortal soul be to me after your death? The precious remains of the body which is so beloved will be of no service to me." Manteuffel was a Prussian who had been in the service of Saxony and had then retired to Berlin after a long career in politics, there to preside over a society of Alethophiles devoted to the search for truth. He was a fine philosopher, a good writer, widely known in society, very erudite, and a little inclined to play the spy. He pretended to be modest and called himself "Quinze Vingts"—the name of the hospital founded by St. Louis for the blind. For a whole season Frederick argued with him for and against Christian morality just for the fun of it.

The Rheinsberg colony was entirely French. No other language but French was spoken and Frederick ardently wished to install some famous writer at his side who would bring the air of Paris with him. Through La Chétardie he sounded Gresset, promising him 500 crowns a year, board and lodging, traveling expenses, and the reversion of a Catholic bishopric in Prussia when once "he should be in a position to control everything." Gresset was dazzled and was getting ready to start when the King was warned of his coming by a newsletter he read in the smoking room. The trip had to be put off, and Gresset, who knew of Frederick William's brutality, ended by breaking his contract.

Frederick did not live at Rheinsberg all the year round. He used to go to Berlin for the grand reviews; he would be there again in November or December for the Court festivities; in summer he almost always went with the King on a tour of inspection; finally at Easter he used to go to Potsdam to discharge his religious duties with the rest of the family. This ceremony struck him as being particularly ludicrous. "I don't know what they have done," he wrote, "but they tell me they want to repent on Sunday. I am such a good boy that I consent to it all, although I do not feel particularly contrite." The King of Prussia occupied his attention far more than did the King of Heaven. At the back of his mind he was never quite at ease. In vain did he extol in prose and verse the delights of solitude and the tranquillity of the countryside, for he was always turning his eyes toward Berlin and worrying about his father's moods. "I must never expect to be able to live in peace with a father who is so easily put out . . . " he wrote again to Camas in January, 1739, "I must look upon him as my most cruel enemy, who spies on me continually in search of the moment when he can give me a stab in the back. I must never relax my vigilance; the least false step, the least imprudence, a trifle, a mere nothing enlarged and exaggerated would be enough to damn me." But while the King disparaged him relentlessly in public, the Prince knew how to control himself and preserve on all occasions a stoical calm. He seemed to understand nothing, listened to the most bitter sarcasms, the most offensive allusions without shifting an eyelid, and after the worst insults he would begin a conversation from which it seemed as though he could not possibly have heard them.

For his defense he had also other weapons: his talents as a colonel, the excellence of his regiment, and the height of his recruits. "I have received orders to go to Berlin on Thursday: my regiment is furnished with arguments six foot high which is a blessing, for if anyone is saved by strict observance of the law, we shall be; if anyone pays court to the King with perfect drill, we will do so; if by the intercession of giants anyone can make their fortune at Berlin, I can rely on mine." (Letter to Camas, December, 1739.) To flatter his father's mania he combed all Europe. The Margrave, Suhm, Seckendorff, every one of his friends had to contribute. With their help he collected a prodigious mass of phenomena in uniform, a real menagerie—not only Germans, but also Lorrainers, Poles, Lithuanians, Tartars, Courlanders, Bosnians, and a well-made young Turk twenty years old. Once one of his correspondents discovered a Dutchman six feet nine inches high, whom "by the force of attraction of 6,000 crowns" he caused to gravitate toward Ruppin, where he shone with as much brilliance "as a comet with a tail."

Twenty or twenty-four people at table, an orchestra, numerous servants, building projects, and recruits at 6,000 crowns a time—all this cost a great deal. In spite of Frederick William's increasing his son's revenues by giving him on one occasion the domain of Zernikov, and on another the stud farms of East Prussia, which brought in 12,000 thalers, Frederick was still short of money all the time. Suhm, who negotiated his loans, would receive pathetic appeals: "My creditors harry me on all sides. Be good enough to pull me out of this mess, or else I shall be in a very bad way." The principal lender of money was the favorite

of the Tsarina Anna Ivanovna, a groom called Biren, whom she
had made Duke of Courland. But Biren himself was deep in debt,
and the two friends were forced to have recourse to some rather
shady schemes. For instance Frederick tried to get his father to
buy a bailiwick which belonged to Biren who would have let it
go for 130,000 crowns, 30,000 of which would have been transferred secretly to Frederick, who in his turn had promised Suhm
a commission of 3,000 crowns. The deal fell through because
Frederick William wanted to have the right to recruit in Russia
thrown in as well, and the Empress refused it him.

When Frederick could write in cipher or by secret methods
the gloves were off. When he had to be prudent he resorted to
the conventional vocabulary which he had had to use with Seckendorff. That *History of Prince Eugene* reappeared to indicate
money, and ten or twelve people were always fighting to possess
it with such voracity that it disappeared the moment it was received, and the library at Rheinsberg never so much as set eyes
on it. When Biren was the subject of discussion there was talk
of furs, pelisses, and marten skins. One day the *Memoirs of the
Academy* in three volumes arrived bound in the English manner; "I have found the reading of it very instructive," Frederick
wrote in reply, "and the truths which it contains of great practical value." It was, in fact, 3,000 crowns. The Prince also knew
how to wrap up in mythological endearments the forced loans
of money which he squeezed out of Suhm: "Dear Phoenix of this
epoch, make the sacred days of Orestes and Pylades live again,
the days of the good Pirithöus, of gentle Nisus, and of wise
Achates. Let men see in our times the happy results of recipro-
cated friendship!" But he also used a more realistic language:
"The King is very ill. Let that be used as an argument and let
me be advanced a good sum of money by next summer, for certainly if they want to oblige me they had best make haste."

The King came only twice to Rheinsberg; once when Frederick had just moved in, to see the house, and on one other
occasion. His time was spent in fishing, hunting, smoking, pigeon
shooting, boating trips, and banquets. There was some heavy
drinking and the King went off fairly well pleased.

Duty's the yoke which teaches me
How I ought to entertain

Him whom I honor three times three
As father, lord, and sovereign.

The Crown Princess and her ladies arrived in August, 1736. Frederick greeted them with delight: "Now that the sex has come here the place seems to take on a new brilliance from them; the conversation is more lively and our pleasure is more radiant." And Manteuffel added approvingly, "It is certain that a little of the fair sex looks extremely well in the country." All the world's chancelleries were interested in Frederick's marital relations and the King himself never stopped inciting him to procreation, *animirt zum Kindermachen*. To arouse his eagerness he even promised to allow him to travel abroad the moment he had an heir, and he had a magnificent bed made for him. In vain did Frederick declare in verse:

And in the night to Venus we our tributes pay,

for gossip went on whispering that the Princess and he were living like brother and sister. Nevertheless the spies appointed by the Courts to discover the privacies of the bedchamber said the very opposite with energy and precision. Frederick himself boasted of the charms of Elisabeth to his friends: "She has," said he, "a beautiful body and————————————————"
It is impossible to finish the sentence. But he admitted that he did not carry out his duty passionately. Manteuffel gave him a little lecture on this delicate subject.

"There is one thing to which Your Royal Highness ought to give more attention, and that is to having children. Your position would thus become more favorable and you would spare yourself many rebuffs in the future. . . . Passion is not always necessary: how many children come into the world whose fathers and mothers do not love one another!" (At that moment Frederick was still living at Ruppin while his wife stayed in Berlin.) "Your Highness comes here with one courier and leaves with the next. But Your Highness ought to take the time that is necessary and act like a peasant who sleeps whole nights with his wife."

"When I am in Berlin," replied the Prince, "I am always restless and anxious, because I meet with reproaches and unfriendly glances. At Rheinsberg I will be calm . . . and I promise you I will then consider what you have said to me."

When the move was completed Manteuffel returned to the attack: "I am convinced that Your Royal Highness knows how to carry this off excellently. . . . Nothing would advance the present interests of Your Royal Highness better than to have an heir of your own. The opinions of all your good servants are in agreement on this point. Perhaps the tranquil comfort in which Your Royal Highness will be able to work at this at Rheinsberg will have a greater effect than all those hasty, fleeting visits that you were wont to pay at Berlin. . . ."

On September 23 Frederick wrote in triumph, "I have the same destiny as the stags which are at the moment in rut; in nine months from now that which you wish may occur." And Manteuffel replied, "God grant that after nine months the country air may do its work!" Grumbkow also echoed this: "One must try to do one's duty wherever one is. . . . God grant that after nine months the country air may do its work." The country air did not do its work, and Frederick undoubtedly got tired of assisting it.

III

In spite of everything he was happy: less tense in mind, less troubled at heart. Among the twenty ways of spelling Rheinsberg a professor of Rostock kept to the form Remusberg, to which he had given the etymology *Remi mons*—the mountain of Remus. Therefore history was at fault: Romulus had not killed his brother and Remus had escaped from death and had taken refuge on the island in the Grinericksee, where a tomb was still to be seen. Rheinsberg therefore became Remusberg and Frederick was directly connected with the she-wolf which had nursed the twins. What an omen! The Princess was also happy. In a letter to her mother she gave a charming description of their monastic life: "Those who seek for art, true and clear philosophy, and wit should come here: they will find everything in a state of perfection, as our master is in control of it all. I have never seen anyone work as hard as he does: from six in the morning until one o'clock he works at reading, philosophy, and all the other noble studies. Dinner lasts from half-past one until three o'clock. After that we drink coffee till four and then he gets down to work again until seven in the evening. Next music begins and lasts till nine o'clock. Then he writes, comes to play cards, and we generally sup at half-past ten or eleven. . . . I can truthfully say that he is the greatest prince of our time." He was learned; he had so much wit that it was impossible to have more; he was just, charitable, generous, temperate. In short "he is the Phoenix and I am very proud to be the wife of so great a prince who has so many good qualities. To know him is to love him. . . ."

As a matter of fact life was not always so well ordered or so sober. One year Frederick had eight hundred bottles of champagne, a hundred of Volnay, and a hundred of Pommard sent for in a single order. Sometimes there was drunkenness and the crockery got broken. The valets had to be called in to direct the tottering steps of the topers to their rooms. Once Bielfeld when turning in for the night fell downstairs and almost broke his neck, but he got off with a mere fortnight in bed. There were also balls, masquerades, and parties which were called "flitter-mouse parties." They gave rise to such scandalous accounts being sent in by the Saxon envoy that the Dresden archivist has shrunk from publishing them. To make amends Frederick founded an order of chivalry for his friends, the Order of Bayard, the members of which wrote letters to each other in medieval French with comic solemnity. Sometimes they went in a band to some castle. The Prince tried to escape from importunate people, but he could not avoid keeping up neighborly relations with the Prince of Mirow, brother of the reigning Duke of Mecklenburg-Strelitz. Mirow lived in a dilapidated old manor house adorned with a ruined tower. He had no money, but he knew in detail the relationships of all the families in Germany. He would have been glad to invite himself to Rheinsberg frequently, for there he was certain of being able to drink his fill. Frederick got rid of him by taking him out hunting in the rain one day when he was wearing his best suit.

Tragedies were acted too, tragedies by both Racine and Voltaire. Frederick took the title part in *Mithridate* and that of Philoctetes in Voltaire's *Œdipe*. But the republic took the greatest pleasure of all in conversation—conversation of the French type, to which each gave of his best: Jordan his erudition, Keyserlingk his fire, Chasot his gift of comic repartee, Senning his experience of mankind. Frederick drew from each of them all he could in the way of wisdom, wit, and gaiety.

He would have liked to employ one of the best writers in France as his teacher. From time to time he sent admiring letters to Fontenelle and Rollin, but the patriarch and the historian merely replied by thanking him in tones so respectful as to discourage his insistence. Besides, he was really drawn to the most illustrious and the most turbulent of them all—Voltaire. He wrote his first letter to him on August 8, 1736. It had caused him a lot of trouble, but Jordan had corrected it and touched it up.

It began like this, "Sir, although I have not the satisfaction of being personally acquainted with you, you are none the less known to me by reason of your works. They are gems of wit (if I may so express myself) and productions wrought with such taste, delicacy, and art that their beauties seem to be new each time they are perused afresh. I believe that I have discerned in them the character of their ingenious author, who is an honor to our age and to the human race." Then follow some pages of flattery laid on with a pretty heavy hand: "Without lavishing upon you incense unworthy of your acceptance I can tell you that I find innumerable beauties in your works. Your *Henriade* delights me. . . . *César* shows us lofty characters; the sentiments contained in it are all noble and magnificent. . . . Corneille, the great Corneille, he who drew to himself the admiration of all his century, if he were to come to life again in our time, he would see with astonishment and perhaps with envy that the Tragic Muse lavishes with profusion upon you the favors which she was chary of bestowing upon him. . . . I would think myself richer in the possession of your works than I would be by possessing all the transitory and contemptible gifts of Fortune, which are gained and lost by the same turn of chance. . . . Your poems have qualities which render them deserving and worthy of the attention and study of men of virtue. They constitute a course in morality where thought and action may be studied. . . ." There was no glory but the glory of Voltaire and noble birth was nothing but a delusive bubble. Frederick therefore hoped that the admired Voltaire would not refuse to exchange letters with him, "which could not but be profitable to any thinking being," and he concluded, "I am, with all the esteem and consideration due to those who take the torch of Truth as their guide, dedicating their work to the benefit of the public, sir, your very devoted friend."

Voltaire was delighted. He was forty-two years old. He lived at Cirey with Madame du Châtelet. He had written *Zaïre, Œdipe,* the *Henriade, Charles XII,* the *Temple du goût,* the *Mondain,* and the *Lettres philosophiques.* He had fervent admirers and a good number of enemies. He had been imprisoned in the Bastille and his *Lettres philosophiques* had been burned by the common hangman. His fortune was large and his fame established. A prince sought his friendship in very humble terms. He was vain and liked a fuss; he hurled himself headlong into the adventure: "Sire, a man would have to be quite without feeling not to be infinitely moved by the letter with which Your Royal Highness has deigned to honor me. My pride has been only too deeply flattered by it; but the love of the human race which is always present in my heart and, I make bold to say, forms my character, gave me a pleasure that is a thousand times purer, when I saw that there was in this world of ours a prince who thought like a man, a philosopher prince who will make men happy. . . ." At the same time through his usual correspondents, Thieriot and Berger, Voltaire hastened to spread news of Frederick's letter around Paris, while the Prince on his side allowed it to be rumored everywhere that he was on friendly terms with the most celebrated writer of the day. Thus each drew some profit from the opening gambit.

Never was such a quantity of sweet nothings exchanged in prose and verse. For Voltaire Frederick was Marcus Aurelius, Titus, Antoninus, Caesar, Julian, Alcibiades, the Solomon of the North, a sublime spirit, a lovable being, a heroic and tender soul. He thought like Trajan and he wrote like Pliny. Heaven had placed him on earth to trample superstition under foot, to overthrow fanaticism, to restore virtue, and to teach kings a lesson.

> The laurels of Apollo drooped throughout the land,
> The fine arts hung their heads, the virtues all declined;
> Fraud, with deceitful eyes, and Plutus, old and blind,
> Controlled the thunderbolts beneath each monarch's hand.
> Then did indignant Nature raise her voice on high:

D'Alembert

Voltaire

"It is my will to see a just and happy reign—
To Vergil's talent add Augustus' majesty—
A hero shall appear and both shall live again,
All monarchs to instruct, the world to beautify."
She ceased; and from the sky the Virtues dropped like dew,
Olympus came in haste, the North was tempest torn,
Olive and laurel flowered, the myrtle bloomed anew,
          And Frederick was born.

With what delight must Frederick have breathed this incense and received the flatteries which were decked out with such ingenuity! What a revenge! What balm on old wounds! He was ill-treated at Berlin, spied upon at Ruppin, subject to a thousand indignities, compelled to swallow disappointments and rebuffs in silence, but now at last he knew the royal pride of being praised by the greatest poet of the century, a man whose writings conferred fame and whose slightest movement raised a stir at Rome, Paris, and Versailles. "The most sterile subject becomes fecund in your hands. You speak of me and I no longer recognize myself; all that you touch is changed to gold. . . ."

Of thy immortal lines one foot, one hemistich,
Where thou dost place my name like a saint in his niche,
Makes me participate in the immortal fame
Which has been merited alone by Voltaire's name.

Remusberg awaited the letters from Cirey with all the impatience of a lover. On days when the post was due all the servants went out to look for the package. "Soon I myself am seized with impatience, I run to the window. . . . If I hear a noise in the antechamber I am soon there. Well, what is it? Let them give me the letters—no news? My imagination is well ahead of the courier. . . . At last here are my letters coming; it's for me to break the seals; I look for your writing; and when I see it then my very haste hinders my breaking of the seal; I read, but so fast that I am obliged to read it through as many as three times before my mind is calm enough to allow me to understand what I have read, and it sometimes happens that I do not succeed in this until the following day." In reply he too was by no means niggardly of compliments. His pen transformed Voltaire by turns into Cicero, Demosthenes, Socrates, Plato, Vergil, Aristotle,

Anacreon, Thucydides, Terence, Quintilian, Sallust, and sometimes into Apollo and Jupiter. Neither Corneille nor Racine
could hold a candle to him. He outtopped them by a hundred
cubits. His epistles were woven by the hands of the Graces.
"Your letters exhale only honesty and virtue." "The better I
get to know you, the more I find that you are a unique person.
Your talent is enough to make you esteemed, to make you envied,
and to draw upon you the admiration of all. As for me, I need
titles, arms, and revenues. . . . Ah, my dear friend, you have
every reason to be satisfied with your lot. I am horribly fatigued
of knowing you only with the eye of faith. I would like those of
the flesh to have their turn also. If you are ever abducted, only
believe that I am the man who is playing the part of Paris. . . .
I am getting a more favorable idea of the perfection of men by
thinking of you. . . . It needs a God or some divine being to
assemble in one and the same person all the perfections which
you possess."

While Voltaire declared himself the subject of *Divus Frederi-
cus,* because in his sentimental geography "the marquisate of
Cirey was an ancient dependency of Brandenburg," Frederick
proclaimed himself the disciple of Voltaire: "Be my vigorous
critic, just as you are already my example. . . . I clearly see that
I will never have a preceptor other than Monsieur de Voltaire."

There was in all this much grandiloquence, much coquetry,
and much affectation, but also, as Emile Henriot has pointed
out, the elements of a real friendship. At the outset the two men
admired each other with equal enthusiasm, and they admired
each other sincerely and for very legitimate reasons. Frederick
admired Voltaire with all the ardor of a young man who attains
to intimacy with a writer close enough to him in age but already
crowned with a European reputation, skilled at giving dazzling
expression to ideas which appealed to him in such a way that
he made them his own while thinking he had invented them
himself. For his part Voltaire admired Frederick with all the
grateful fervor which a man of letters can feel for a prince who
is going to apply his ideas to the world of actual facts, and by
his zeal, his successes, and his exceptional destiny will prove
them to be excellent.

Besides this both had a selfish interest in the friendship. The poet was delighted to have a disciple who was some day to be called upon to reign, and he reckoned upon using him as a shield. Besides, by trumpeting about the friendship of the Crown Prince he gave himself the bitter satisfaction of taking revenge on his own fatherland. That is why his letters were sometimes rather fawning. He was only too happy to disparage France in comparison with Prussia and to throw mud at Louis XIV so as to magnify by contrast Frederick the scholar. He insisted on this so loudly that the pupil subjected his teacher to the minor humiliation of recalling him to common decency: "Louis XIV was a prince who was great in an infinity of manners; a solecism, an error of orthography could not in any way tarnish the brilliance of a reputation established by so many actions which have immortalized him. . . ."

Frederick, on his side, expected even more of Voltaire. "We princes," he wrote to him quite frankly, "have all of us calculating minds and we never make an acquaintance without having at the same time some particular aim in view which will be of direct profit to us." He was consumed by an appetite for books and he had gained a perfect understanding of the use the great can make of literary men as distributors of fame. Had not Louis XIV established his own by protecting those from whom he expected immortality? "Who would know that Alexander the Great had once lived, if Quintus Curtius Rufus and other famous historians had not taken the trouble to pass on to us the story of his life?" Voltaire, whom the King of France was not wise enough to keep by him, was therefore to be Frederick's herald. He would dispose people's minds in his favor. So as to be sure of keeping him the Crown Prince took care to incite him against his fellow countrymen: "What, is this same Voltaire, to whom our hands are raising statues and altars, neglected in his own country and living like a hermit in the depths of Champagne? It is a paradox, an enigma. . . ." And when a lampoon against Voltaire appeared he roused up sleeping rancors with an expert touch: "Your nation is most ungrateful and frivolous to allow some scandalmonger—some unknown hand—to dare attempt to sully your laurels." Or else, "I am furious with your nation and with those who are at the head of it, because they do absolutely nothing to suppress the cruel attacks of those who envy you.

France herself is dishonored by dishonoring you and she shows her cowardice by suffering this to go unpunished. . . ."

Frederick had a new edition of the *Henriade* printed in silver lettering adorned by a preface of his own composition. He trembled for the health of his illustrious friend; he begged him not to go in for chemical experiments; he assembled doctors to decide on his complaints; he overwhelmed him with gifts that were usually of no value but which were pretexts for effusions— a walking stick with a knob carved to represent the head of Socrates, a ring, some boxes, some pens, a writing desk, a small barrel of Tokay, and finally, after having arranged to be much solicited for it, his portrait by Knobelsdorff. In July, 1737, there arrived at Cirey as bearer of the precious likeness the irrepressible Keyserlingk, who was welcomed like an angel sent of God. The display of fireworks in his honor made the Crown Prince's name flash out in letters of fire with the motto, "To the Hope of the Human Race." Keyserlingk returned bearing the Golden Fleece, that is to say, Voltaire's unpublished works—the early chapters of the *Siècle de Louis XIV*, the *Philosophie de Newton*, and some poems. But it had needed all the tact possessed by the Marquise du Châtelet to save *La Pucelle* from the clutches of the messenger. On another occasion Frederick set Suhm to work to collect some memoirs for the production of a revised edition of *Charles XII*, and when it appeared he received one after the other, out of gratitude, the first editions of *Mérope, Mahomet,* and *La Dévote.*

Through Voltaire Frederick had come to understand the political importance of writers. By becoming philosophers they ceased to be artists pure and simple so as to exercise a growing influence on public opinion, on the State, and on society. "Authors," he wrote, "are in a certain sense public figures; their writings are spread throughout the world and, being known to the whole universe, reveal to their readers the ideas with which they are stamped. You publish your sentiments: their beauty, their charm of diction, and their eloquence—in a word all that the flame of thought and the power of style can produce as finished work— strike your readers; they are touched by this and soon by your generous impulse a whole world inhales your love of the human race. You make good citizens, faithful friends, and subjects who abhor rebellion and are zealous for the public good. How much we owe to you!" (Letter to Voltaire, November 4, 1736.) Thus between Frederick and philosophy was established a sort of alliance of two ambitions. To the future King of Prussia the philosophers brought the support of their writings. They orchestrated his renown, prepared for his reign, and built up his prestige. In return they could count on him to set up their government and help them against the Church. The pact was confirmed on August 14, 1738, at Brunswick by the acceptance of Frederick as a Freemason.

After Keyserlingk's visit Voltaire, who had been completely enlightened as to the Prince's philosophical evolution, wrote to Remusberg: "You cannot imagine, Sire, what a consolation it is for Madame du Châtelet and for myself to see how much your virtue abhors superstition. If the majority of kings have encouraged fanaticism in their states, it is because they were ignorant men and because they did not know that priests were their greatest enemies. . . . I am sure that the only course for a sovereign to pursue is to smother all the seeds of religious fury and ecclesiastical discord in his own realm. . . . Under a pious king all men are hypocrites; a king who is straightforward will produce men like himself." Joined by the same hatred, uplifted by the same passion, soldiers in the same cause, the Frenchman and the Prussian jeered together at the Jesuits, the priestly rabble, the old Jewish prophets whose infantile musings have shaken the world. As Voltaire appeared to think that Protestant ministers were worth more than Catholic ones, Frederick protested. They were all the same! Liberty was condemned at Rome but it was also reviled at Geneva. No doubt the princes of the North owed a great debt to Luther and Calvin, who had liberated them from the priestly yoke and had considerably increased their incomes by the secularization of Church property, but the Reformed Religion possessed, as the Roman faith did, its bigots, its hypocrites, its humbugs, its opinionated fanatics, who were all the more harmful because "their stupid ignorance forbade them the use of reason." And he pronounced a solemn malediction: "May the monks, cloistered in darkness, bury in their filthy baseness their miserable way of thinking; may our descendants be forever ignorant of the puerilities and stupidities of the faith, cult, and ceremonies of priests and monks!" What a recruit! Voltaire could not stop himself from communicating his joy to all his friends: "He is a philosopher prince; he is a human being. . . . He despises the throne and its pleasures; he loves knowledge and virtue alone! . . ."

But while Frederick unsealed letters in which Voltaire compared him to Trajan he also received others from Grumbkow which compared him to Arminius. With the same pen with which he jingled out

> "The throne is for me but an image illusory,
> But a cheating phantom of frivolous glory"

he also wrote to his most gracious King and father, "Everything is more or less in order in the regiment, except that a plot has been discovered at Nauen. The ringleader belonged to Major Quadt's company. . . . As soon as the second battalion is back here, I will have a court-martial held, and as the rogue's case is a serious one I think he will be condemned to death. This example will not be without its uses, and I hope that in future it will serve to restrain other traitors."

In spite of the candid Voltaire Frederick was preparing himself to be something other than the secular arm of the sect of the Encyclopedists.

V

The Triumph of Will Power

I

FREDERICK was a man of letters and a Frenchman. All his life he was tormented by an itch for writing; all his life he overcame his nervousness by versifying. He was ambitious to bestow upon posterity some great poetical work in the style of Voltaire, a tragedy like *Œdipe* or an epic poem like the *Henriade*. In 1738 he started a three-act play in verse, the plot of which was drawn from the *Aeneid* and was to show "the tender and constant friendship of Nisus and Euryalus"; but he did not feel sure of his powers and abandoned it for a refutation of Machiavelli. With the utmost politeness he repeated that it was impossible to imitate Voltaire without actually being Voltaire himself; he begged pardon that he, "the humble frog of the sacred vale," should dare to croak in the presence of the god. But he did not only ask for French lessons from the Apollo of Cirey, he also tried to extract from him some of the secrets of his art and a spark of his genius. It was true he had Jordan as corrector in chief at Rheinsberg:

> Jordan, my critic-secretary,
> You who pursue, with nose as wary
> As bloodhound's, those mistakes of mine,
> For pity's sake deign to refine,
> Erase, efface, correct, transcribe. . . .

However, he wanted more than a Jordan. In nearly all his letters to Voltaire he asked for criticism and advice. Voltaire would have much preferred to confine himself to compliments, for he was more interested in the Prince than in the scholar. Why not admit once and for all that Frederick's nurse had been Madame de Sévigné and his tutor Bossuet, that he spoke French excellently, and that he did their language a great honor by making use of it? But the Prince was insistent, and from time to time the master complied: "I find no mistakes of language in the 'Epistle to Pesne' and it breathes with good taste throughout. It is the painter of Reason writing to the common painter. I can assure you, Sire, that the last six lines, for example, are a masterpiece:

> Oh, be a traitor to designs of haloed saints,
> And subjects more polite portray now with thy paints;
> Sketch us the simple graces Amaryllis had,
> The forest with its nymphs, the Graces three half-clad;
> Keep always in thy mind that 'tis by love alone
> That thy art so divine saw the light and has grown.

That is how Despréaux would have written them. You will take all this for flattery. You are quite capable, Sire, of not knowing your own worth."

"The 'Epistle to Monsieur Duhan' is indeed worthy of you; it comes from a sublime spirit and a grateful heart. . . . On reading all that you have deigned to send me I perceive that there is not a single false thought in it. I find from time to time some small mistakes of language, which it is hardly possible to avoid; now, for example, how could you have guessed that 'nourricier' is a word of three syllables and not one of four? That 'aient' has one syllable and not two? The Epistle that you have deigned to address to me, Sire, is a fine justification of poetry and a great encouragement to me. . . . Should I dare to scrutinize this Epistle (and I must as I owe you the truth), I would tell you, Sire, that 'trompette' does not rhyme with 'tête,' because 'tête' has a long vowel sound and 'pette' a short one, and rhyme should please the ear and not the eye. 'Défaites' for the same reason does not rhyme with 'conquêtes'; 'quêtes' is long, 'faites' is short. If anyone saw my letters he would say, 'There is a complete pedant who goes and talks of long and short vowels to a prince full of genius.' But the Prince deigns to descend to every detail. When this Prince reviews his regiment, he examines the equipment of the individual soldier. The great man neglects nothing, he will win battles when he has a chance, he will confirm the happiness of his subjects with the same hand with which he turns eternal truth into rhymes." Could a lesson be given more gracefully?

To encourage Frederick to condense his style his teacher found a charming phrase, "this gold filigree will have greater weight and brilliance if made more compact." To teach him what a poetic image was he amused himself by transposing a phrase of simple prose into verse, and once again it was a compliment, "There is in the world a young and virtuous prince who is full of talents and loathes envy and fanaticism." Another time he rewrote one of the odes he had been sent, following the ideas closely but expressing them in different ways.

In spite of all this trouble Frederick was never satisfied. He compared himself to those folk who are dependent on charity and always ask for more. What Voltaire did not tell him he determined to discover on his own by making a careful study of the great writers. He learned Boileau and Racine by heart; when a new edition of the *Henriade* came out he compared the two texts and tried to discover the reason for each change. At last he ventured to put before his master some reflections of his own on the aptness of certain words, and the master replied that he had taken his advice in correcting the fourth and fifth acts of *Mérope*. What a triumph!

Before getting to know Voltaire Frederick wrote a cumbrous, slow, unpolished French. The refugees who surrounded him had brought with them the language of a certain date—deprived as it was of continuous impetus from daily life, this language preserved ways of speech which had fallen into disuse, and on the other hand it lacked those which had been brought in imperceptibly by common usage and were the most typical expressions of the spirit of the language. Finally by dint of preaching before mixed audiences pastors had weighed it down with Germanisms which went against its natural development and marked the sect, the conventicle. By hard work Frederick learned the French of France and the French of his own times, mobile, subtle, precise, admirably suitable for analysis and for the play of ideas. Frederick's verses were not good, it is true; some of them were even execrable. Anyhow, the thing they were most lacking in was poetry. But his prose was excellent and the moment soon came when he grasped and handled it in such a way that he could really hold his own against Voltaire. And then, in the long run, he ended by rhyming pretty well.

Great lyrical effusions were never to be in his line. He tried to be witty and was merely insipid, to be gallant and was coarse. But he also had some lucky finds, verses which stick in the memory quite apart from the rest. The didactic poem, the parody, the elegant display of rhetoric, the chaffing letter—such were the styles which suited his talents. Alas, "there is nothing that can restrain a poet in his rage!" Sometimes he was ashamed of sending so many bloated alexandrines to Cirey. "It is the invasion of the Goths!" cried he in mock dismay. Then he sighed a little sadly on rereading his verses:

> The good are those which are hard for me,
> As for the bad they cost me naught.

It is by no means immaterial that right up to his death Frederick thought in French, for to borrow one more of his phrases, language controls the play of the mind in the same way as pipes form a fountain. On the movements of the brain it imposes its own rules, its logic, construction, and vocabulary. At twenty-five Frederick hardly knew any German—a coachman's lingo. He rarely spoke it and only wrote it in letters to his father or in orders to his valet. His knowledge of ancient tongues was confined to a few quotations. It was in translation that he read Homer, Demosthenes, Plato, the great tragedians, Thucydides, Cicero, Caesar, Livy, Vergil, Horace, Tacitus, Marcus Aurelius, and also Ariosto, Tasso, Swift, and Cervantes. In his philosophy of history he went straight from Rome to Paris: "We are indebted to the French for having revived learning amongst us," he wrote to Voltaire. "After cruel wars, the establishment of Christianity and frequent barbarian invasions had given a mortal blow to the arts which had fled for safety from Greece to Italy, some centuries of ignorance rolled by until at last the torch was lit again in your land. The French have brushed aside the thorns and brambles which had completely closed to mankind the path of the glory which was to be acquired through literature." That was why other nations felt a filial gratitude toward them. As for the Germans, they had been given common sense as their heritage. They were industrious and profound: when they had a matter in hand they could weigh it up, but "their books were crushingly long-winded." And then "there is one difficulty which will always prevent us from having good books in our tongue; it is that we have not fixed the meanings of words. . . . Thus there is nothing left for our scholars to do but write in foreign languages; and as it is difficult to get a thorough grasp of them, it is much to be feared that our literature will never make great progress." One year he was fired by the philosophy of Wolff, a follower of Leibniz, but he only wanted to know this great man in French. As the translator timidly suggested that he would do better to read the work in the original because the German language was more suitable for metaphysical reasoning than the French, the Prince replied that he had had the curiosity to compare the two versions and that he could not see that the thought had lost anything in passing from the one language to the other.

Up till this time Frederick had done a lot of reading, but haphazard and for mere recreation; henceforward he wanted everything to be of use to him. The catalogue of his library, the program of his reading, and even the notes he wrote in the margin of a Montesquieu are still to be seen. In all this art war had little place. Day by day he learned the soldier's trade by active service and by visits to battlefields. As he assimilated everything this form of teaching was of use to him also, but his curiosity drew him toward philosophy, the study of men, countries, societies, governments, and laws; he instinctively sought for that which was universal and that which was great. Besides he devoted less time to collecting positive knowledge and more to forming a body of doctrine and an ideal of life for himself. He had a dislike for geometrical reasoning which was abstract and which "dried up the mind." He was a complete rebel against mathematics. When Voltaire tried to make him understand the use of infinity in an equation, he replied triumphantly that there were only two sorts of numbers, odd and even, and that infinity was neither the one nor the other and therefore did not exist. At one time, encouraged by Madame du Châtelet, he tried to master physics. He even had a laboratory set up, where he had "all the experiments of the pneumatic pump" carried out before his eyes; for several weeks he argued about the vacuum and the nature of light. Then he gave it not another thought. In obedience to Voltaire he still classed Newton as one of the geniuses who have honored our wretched species, but later he did not hesitate to call him an idle dreamer and to place Descartes much below the great thinkers Bayle and Gassendi.

His correspondence is full of pitfalls for the student. He sometimes took one side from pure virtuosity, "to see how far an argument could be pushed and on which side the most absurdities would be found." However, he was sincere with himself. When he settled down at Rheinsberg—after the paroxysm of despair which had followed the events of 1734—he had lost his Protestant faith forever. He rejected religion, despised it, and hated it. He never ran short of insults against the "priestly gang," the "theological brood." Beneath his pen the Pope became a charlatan, a rope dancer, a quack doctor, a decayed old Druid. Monks were rascals, prophets impostors, Luther and Calvin paupers, and the Bible a hotchpotch of senseless fables. Moreover, whether they were Papist or Protestant, the same spirit of domination and intolerance was to be found in all who called themselves the ambassadors of God so as to exploit the credulity of princes and nations. They taught childish absurdities, but in the name of these absurdities they had filled the world with wars and crime, persecuted reason, and perverted morals by putting up idle mummeries in the place of virtue. . . .

Nevertheless Frederick believed in a Supreme Being because the world presupposed the existence of a principle of life and action, as a clock presupposes a clockmaker. There was such obvious order in nature that it had to be admitted that some intelligence presided over this universe to keep the general arrangement of the machine in working order. But this God was impersonal, incomprehensible, a stranger to humanity. From him sprang the laws of nature and he was imperturbably present at all the revolutions they produced, for it was not in his power to alter them or suspend their effects. Yet if science unveiled to us little by little optic phenomena, the shape of the earth, and the movements of heavenly bodies, was it possible to go further and discover the very structure of things?

Wolff's *Logic* had inspired Frederick with immense confidence in the powers of the human mind. Wolff was obscure and pedestrian but he had the merit of having been expelled from the University of Halle by Frederick William and his fame was great throughout Germany. He endowed the philosophy of Leibniz with the strictness of a mathematical chain of reasoning; he wanted all the propositions of his system to be deduced the one from the other with demonstrative certainty. Frederick had great difficulty in understanding him. Helped by Suhm and Manteuffel he read and reread him, leaving nothing out, always fearing to lose the thread and to forget in the course of his reading one of the definitions to which Wolff attached primordial importance. At last he thought he had grasped his meaning and he congratulated himself on having reached a safe harbor. Without a shadow of doubt matter in the last analysis was composed of "simple beings," of atoms, of "I know not what," which had neither shape nor size and could not occupy space because if they possessed extent they were capable of being divided. These high speculations made Frederick both giddy and modest: "Such reading instructs and humbles me. I never feel smaller than after having read the proposition of the simple being." He tried to make Voltaire share his admiration, but the sage with many a compliment ended by admitting that he did not understand a word of this farrago and that he could not imagine bodies without extent. "I see myself suddenly transported into a climate the air of which I cannot breathe, on ground where I cannot place my foot, among people whose language I do not in the least understand." Frederick spoke no more of simple beings.

He had pleaded the cause of the philosopher as long as he could and with all his might, but little by little after much doubting and hesitation he had lost his fine confidence. The secrets of nature were impenetrable, man lived in darkness, his intelligence was limited, and if he received at birth an all-embracing curiosity, it was only that he might be the better able to appreciate the weakness of his understanding in later life and to suffer the more for it. Wretched men! At one time they believed themselves free and at another they imagined that a merciful God had arranged the creation so that everything should combine for their delight. What did they know of this? How could they reconcile their feeling of liberty with the foreknowledge of God, chance with His wisdom, the existence of evil with His sovereign goodness? Neither free will nor complete predetermination exonerated the Deity from participating in sin, for whether God had given us the liberty to do evil or whether He had condemned us to sin from all eternity, it came to more or less the same thing; it was only a question of a little less or a little more. But all this was so embarrassing, so rich in ambiguities, that it was better to admit our ignorance. The most ingenious systems could indeed divert us for a time, but they never contained more than confused reflections of unattainable truths. The mice which lived in a few dark holes in an immense building did not know if the building would last forever, nor who the architect was, nor why that architect had built it. They only tried to people their holes and escape the destructive animals which pursued them.

Yet even in the tiny circle of our interests and our earthly calculations, among a hundred people who believed that they thought there was hardly one who thought for himself. The others had only two or three ideas which were turned over in their brains without assuming new shapes. In vain did we repeat to ourselves that nothing happened without a cause, for more often than not destiny offered an incoherent sequence of surprises to our astonished eyes.

However, Frederick attached too much value to ideas to treat them as mere objects of speculation. He was not the man to doubt everything and behave as if he doubted nothing. When he wrote that skepticism was "frightful," "unbearable," it meant that he needed certainty to recover his happiness and his courage, but it did not take him long to get out of his difficulty. "That which is most real in us is life." Here was a starting point, and therefore a certainty. Second proposition: "If men are not made to reason on abstract matters, God has given them as much wisdom as is necessary for managing their own affairs on this earth." Finally comes the last question, of what does life consist? "The point is not that a man should trail the indolent and useless thread of his days to the age of a Methuselah, but that the more he meditates, the more he performs fine and useful actions, the more he lives." Thus the future King of Prussia emerged from a metaphysical crisis and regained a feeling for his destiny by doubling back upon his own tracks.

Prince Frederick's ethics consisted first and foremost of a respect for his calling. Thirty years later in a discussion with Maria Antonia, Electress of Saxony, a woman of whom he had a high opinion after having done her a great deal of harm, he said that destiny had placed him on a path where his own tastes would not have led him. "No one is master of his fate; we are born, we are given a part to play which often does not suit us, and it is for us to acquit ourselves of our task as best we can." In 1752 he had written to Wilhelmina, "If I could follow my inclinations, I would give myself up entirely to solitude. The misfortune is that a man finds himself entangled in a kind of slavery from which he cannot free himself. We are forced to bear the yoke which destiny sets upon us; our birth decides our estate and we must willy-nilly carry on the trade to which we are condemned." For all that, never, even in the revolts of his youth, had he considered himself as other than a king's son destined for rule. But it had needed obstinate work and tenacious persistence to acquaint him little by little with the duties of his position and to make him worthy of it. Then it was that he ceased to read as a humanist who admired and imitated and began to do so as a politician who learned and utilized. He no longer wished to know how the writers had made themselves into writers, he asked them what he was to make of himself. Day by day, one might almost say page by page, by the strength of his will alone he built up within himself another Frederick, the one who was to astonish Europe.

II

OFTEN he said, "I give thanks to the fate which placed my birth at the end of the great age of Louis XIV!"

It is hard for us to understand with what a glare of brilliance that age dazzled him. Doubtless we no longer have the temerity to call it the period of Wigs, but we say that it was a time of moderation and order, while allowing it to be understood that it was also one of constraint and formality. We say that French classical literature was a school of balance, serenity, harmony, and reason: we are ready to find in it lessons of commonplace wisdom, scholarly recipes for conventional art, enamored of symmetry and enslaved to ancient models. But the age of Louis XIV was firstly one of springtime and renewal, an outburst of youthfulness, an impetuous loosening of creative energy. Order was nothing if not a victory over the passions, an effort to harness one's instincts, a flame which was fanned and damped at one and the same time. The yardstick of the reign was not middle-class prudence—the decent behavior of quiet and respectable people—no, the scale was determined by magnificence confident of its own stability and by its unaffected use of the grand manner.

Right up till his death Frederick read and read again the works of Corneille, Bossuet, La Bruyère, Fléchier, Bourdaloue, Massillon, Molière, and especially La Fontaine, Boileau, and Racine. Once at Rheinsberg he called Boileau "the *divine* Boileau"; today the adjective seems a trifle strong to us, but to the Crown Prince, held in leash by his father's tyranny, Boileau brought hatred of the false, contempt for nonsense and bombast, a certain way of reaching for the truth and of crying it from the housetops, a violence, nay an effrontery, which upset all falsely gained reputations and made way for true greatness.

Frederick nearly always thought on paper, and he drew from his reading personal applications, causes for exaltation and rules of conduct. However, it was to the drama of Racine above all others that he owed the discovery of himself. The solemnity of its setting and the greatness of its passions and its interests made French tragedy into the drama of kings. In his old age Frederick went so far as to write that princes alone were capable of acting it properly, as they were the only people able to enter naturally into the feelings of the characters. On the other hand, Corneille's works retain some of the grandiloquence and romanticism of the Spaniards, and then Corneille illustrates magnificently a slightly high-flown morality; he makes an abundant outlay of patriotism, virtue, and courage, all excellent themes but very easy to coin and capable of being interpreted as military loyalty or civic virtue. "The heads of governments are social people and can savor an art only in its social virtues, which are necessary, but necessarily vulgar, and vulgar even in

their greatness": that was why Napoleon preferred Corneille.
But Frederick was kept on the shelf, suspect and as good as an
exile, and he did not think of educating the public: he prepared for his destiny, he sought for and created a hero. When
he looked back toward his adolescence, when he saw once more
beneath the window at Cüstrin the black sheet and the little
pile of reddened sand, he felt himself the brother of the heroes
of Racine. Like them he had been raised by his birth above
other men, freed from lesser joys and sorrows only to suffer a
fate of proportionate grandeur, to sink back under the harshest
laws of political duty and of duty to the State. In Racine politics was not dissolved in phrases and historical scenes, it was a
moral reality inseparable from the characters of the actors: it
was part of their heart and soul; it was their very life. The
great Prince was the man who looked on his duties ". . . with
eyes by reason taught, by honor filled with fire"; who knew
how to conquer his weaknesses, how to hide his sufferings; who
knew how to inspire armies and captivate the nation; who had
accustomed himself both to leadership and to self-sacrifice by
long and painful toil.

Had Frederick been initiated by his father into the daily
routine of affairs, the royal Council and correspondence, the
choice of servants and the worry of making decisions would
have monopolized the powers of his mind and he would have
been a king without thinking about it. Reduced to subordinate
work, obstinately limited to the narrow horizon of Ruppin, he
had been forced by contrast to reflect deeply on the nature of
monarchy. He had been taught that kings and subjects were
united by a continual exchange of obligations and services:
respect and obedience on the subjects' side; protection and
justice on the king's. He had also been taught that, although no
man on earth can rise against sovereigns to prevent them from
doing evil, God who had set them up had reserved to Himself
the right to punish them. On the Day of Judgment He would
ask for an account of His flock and He would destroy the evil
shepherds. When he lost all religious faith Frederick did not
call the foundations of his power in question. The French of
the seventeenth century and those of his time were too confident
of the benefits of the institution of monarchy to arouse in him

the least anxiety on that score. At the very most he substituted for the principle of the exchange of obligations the more legal notion of tacit contract, without admitting that the rights of the crown could be tied or divided because of it, as in Great Britain. It was for the prince himself to fix the limits of his power according to the demands of reason, the lessons of history, and the interests of the kingdom! Besides, Frederick was quite free to philosophize at his ease: in Prussia there were no great nobles, no clergy, no rich commoners who for centuries had fought, prayed, and suffered for the king; no Houses of Parliament, no traditions crystallized into fundamental laws. All such social forces were on a small scale, without concentration, strength, or rights. In truth Frederick could say he was going to be the first servant of his subjects, for no one would dispute his "complete freedom to do right" which he claimed for serving them.

However as freedom to do right does not exist without freedom to do wrong, the monarch had to be perfect. Frederick readily agreed that the perfect monarch was a rare find. He called him a metaphysical being. And yet for his personal use he wished none the less to make a speaking likeness of one to keep continually before his eyes as a model. To begin with, the ideal Prince saw and knew everything. "He guides the entire mass." Having studied history, which supplied him with "a picture of all the vicissitudes of fortune," he had "an accurate and precise idea of the things which happen in the world"; he was even capable of unraveling to a certain degree the mysteries of fate by his penetration and by that spirit of power and judgment which brought together all the evidence and discerned in the events of the present those which must follow them. He was firm in his plans and unshakable in his decisions. But as the Prussian monarchy was not one of those which are kept running by some sort of initial impulsion, the King was compelled to expend his own energies continually. He was too weak to control events and he had to know when to tack and give way to circumstances, "solely occupied in bringing his vessel to the desired port irrespective of the means used to get there."

At home and in their relations with foreign powers "the principal object of princes is justice." But here a difficulty presented itself and Frederick's thought became confused. Sometimes he thought, or at least he declared, that public morality was identical with private morality, that kings and commoners were amenable to the same duties, and should practice the same virtues. He had an inexhaustible supply of variations on this theme. His correspondence is full of them and he was all the more lavish with them because he felt further from power than ever before, and because he was impatient to shine but saw no other road to glory open to him but that of literature. Then would he preach that a prince should be contented with his lot, should by no means cover his neighbor's riches, and should never do to others anything he would not like to suffer at their hands. He taught that princes should be kind and mild, that conquests were criminal robbery, that between a conquering hero and a highwayman the only difference was that one was crowned with laurels and the other hanged from a gibbet. The best way kings could honor mankind was to ennoble those superior spirits who worked at perfecting knowledge and devoted themselves to the shrine of truth.

This sentimental phraseology forms the principal content of the *Anti-Machiavel,* which he began in the spring of 1739, and which was published at The Hague in September, 1740. He had put in so much of this stuff that Voltaire had to restrain him: "Zeal . . . has consumed your generous soul. . . . When Machiavelli has been abused with all justice, after that it is time to get down to your reasons for doing so." The book is a bad one. It is an edifying homily against rapacity, perfidy, arbitrary government, and unjust wars; but it is also a ponderous homily, of unbearable verbosity, containing emphatic truisms and here and there little Voltairean squibs, most of which are damp ones. The very dough of the pie was old; in France and Germany alone it had been kneaded by many hands for a century and a half—there were dozens and dozens of refutations of Machiavelli. The only novelty was to see an heir apparent undertaking this pedant's work: the novelty, but also the danger —there Voltaire made no mistake.

He devoted himself to a careful inspection of Frederick's manuscript. He not only corrected errors of language and of taste, but he eliminated as much irrelevant abuse as he dared, those too clear allusions, those rash statements which might in the future be used against their "illustrious" and "virtuous" author. For example, at the end of a short section on Cesare Borgia Frederick had wanted to add that Machiavelli "needed examples; but whence should he have taken them if not from the records of criminal courts or from the history of the Popes?" Instead of "the history of the Popes" Voltaire calmly wrote, "the history of Nero and other men of that type," which was perfectly inoffensive. Though lightened and shortened the book still remained a very feeble one, for it was nothing but one long misinterpretation throughout. The irreparable error was to have tried to write a criticism of Machiavelli on both moral and political grounds at one and the same time, or, as Charles Benoist put it, "to have brought together that which Machiavelli kept apart and thus to have been mistaken as to the nature, objects, and character of Machiavellianism."

Yet anyone might be misled by a hasty perusal of Machiavelli. The principal reason why Frederick did not understand him was that he believed the Florentine had written for the tyrants of the eighteenth century. He was angry with him for having foisted off as strength the base devices of weakness, for he compared the Italy of the Renaissance with the German Confederation. The Borgias, the D'Estes, the Montefeltros, the Sforzas were in his eyes exactly like the two hundred petty princes—"hermaphrodites between kings and commoners"— who divided between them the crumbs of the Empire. Then the pride of the future King of Prussia burst forth majestically, that pride of which the poor Margravine had so often to complain: "The majority of minor princes ruin themselves by prodigality . . . they drown themselves to uphold the honor of their name, and from vanity they take the road to misery and to the almshouse. . . . The best thing they could be advised to do would be to lessen the opinion they have of their own grandeur," the veneration in which they held their illustrious family, and the zeal they had for their heraldic insignia. Let them disband their armies and knock down their fortifications, for "war is the business of great sovereigns alone."

Here is a note of sincerity. Was it possible that Frederick did not feel the virtuous horror of conquests he paraded for the benefit of his literary friends? To tell the truth, this horror was part of the conventions and the atmosphere of Rheinsberg, as were love of the country, the delights of solitude, and disdain of earthly grandeur, as were all the pastorals, half mocking and half serious, which helped the Prince to forget his humiliation and to dull the edge of his impatience to reign.

> In summertime there meets my view,
> When I awake at dawn of day,
> Phoebus, just entered on his way,
> Painting the grapes a brighter hue. . . .

> Unhappy is the slavish clown
> Who lacks the wit to leave the town. . . .

If during these years of waiting Frederick wished to dupe anyone, first and foremost it was the Crown Prince of Prussia, first and foremost it was himself. Sometimes he was caught up in his own verbosity and succeeded in intoxicating himself with words. But he was too ambitious, too much of a realist, too hungry for action and glory to be misled for long. Did not historians agree that military glory was the only real glory? Was Montesquieu stopped by moral scruples when he admired the greatness of the Romans? In the opinion of posterity did not the will to power outweigh everything else?

Beneath the declamations of the *Anti-Machiavel* ran as a muted accompaniment another theory which was real Machiavellianism. After having upheld against this "Jesuit" of a Florentine the duty of princes to "observe religiously the faith of treaties," Frederick added, "I must remark in addition that there are certain grievous necessities which may make it impossible for a prince to avoid breaking his treaties and alliances." To absolve him it was enough that the necessity should be a really great one. And what of war? Most assuredly he had said in twenty separate passages that no greater crime existed. By what right, I ask you, could a man make "a plan to raise his power upon the misery and destruction of other men?" Nevertheless there were three sorts of legitimate warfare: defensive wars, wars of interest, and precautionary wars. The wars of interest were those which kings waged to maintain contested rights, and the battles decided the validity of their claims. Precautionary wars were offensive but they were none the less just wars, for it was better to forestall than to be forestalled. The same principle applied to foreign mercenaries: it was excellent to possess them but infamous to supply them to others. It is clear enough that to arrive at such conclusions there was no need whatever to begin with such a mighty flood of indignation.

III

ALL the same, these meditations were still so general, so theoretical that they almost seemed to be outside all time and place. However, sovereigns do not reign in a purely intellectual domain. They only govern a corner of the earth which is field, forest, vineyard, plain, or mountain, which is populated or deserted, whose inhabitants are stubborn or docile, good fighters or bad soldiers. All this Frederick William called "the real." Were Frederick's plans suited to the real?

He had studied Europe and knew some parts of it well. Over others he hesitated or was mistaken. Often his vision was limited. He was content with very superficial reasons to explain the greatness or decadence of states. Of Russia he had only an uncertain and confused idea. Maritime affairs were beyond him. He did not understand the rivalry of colonial powers. France bewitched, disturbed, and astonished him. He leveled against her the usual reproaches of inconsistency and frivolity but he feared her because of the constant success of her policy. He recognized that her population was the greatest, her government the most solid, her territory the most compact, her army the most reliable, her wealth the best grounded in the whole of Europe. In short "she united all the elements of power in the highest perfection." Also she did nothing with precipitation. She had natural frontiers on four sides, but her only limits to the east were those of her own moderation. However, she was not moderate, and it could be said that in the direction of the Rhine conquests lay open to her. On almost the same level Frederick placed fierce, greedy England, whose resources were inexhaustible, but who, from lack of troops, did not hold that rank among the powers which seemed to be her due.

Finally there was Germany, the Germanic Holy Roman Empire. Its territories stretched from Trieste to the Baltic Sea, from the headwaters of the Elbe to the frontiers of Holland. The Emperor claimed preëminence over the other sovereigns; he wore the crown of Charlemagne and he called himself the temporal head of Christendom, as the Pope was its spiritual head. The Empire, however, was indefinable. It had been called, by turns, a political monster, a dismembered mosaic, a medley, a masterpiece of patchwork, and a sprinkling of principalities, and all these comparisons were accurate. Germany was chopped up into small pieces, dismembered, disunited. In addition to some good-sized electorates it contained 2,000 territories entangled one with another, duchies, counties, republics, abbacies, bishoprics, towns, margravates, and mere lordships, among which more than 200 were sovereign states controlling all regalian privileges, including that of making alliances at will.

The Emperor lived at Vienna and was elected at Frankfort by the nine Electors: three churchmen, the Archbishops of Cologne, Trèves, and Mainz, and six laymen, the rulers of Bohemia, Brandenburg, Saxony, Bavaria, the Palatinate, and Hanover. Since 1438 the Hapsburgs had succeeded in keeping the imperial title in their family, but it was an empty title. True enough, the outline of a centralized organization survived throughout the country—a chancellery, a court of appeal, a Diet, a budget, and a territorial division into ten Circles. But under imperial justice it was difficult to obtain a sentence and more difficult still to get it enforced. The Diet was divided into three colleges—electors, princes, and towns; it reproduced all the territorial, political, and religious divisions of Germany and brought them to the boil in a closed vessel. Most circumstantial regulations protected the rights of each so well that the movement of affairs was infinitely slow. Finicky quibbles perpetuated their discussions; their resolutions were always vague or equivocal. Since the Treaty of Westphalia, France, as the protector of Germanic liberties, was represented at the sessions by a plenipotentiary whose real mission was to supervise the work of the assembly and preserve the vigor of its anarchy. Frederick called the Diet "a sort of phantom" and the delegates sent to

it by the princes "back-yard mongrels who bark at the moon."
Moreover the total official revenue of the Emperor only came
to 8,000 thalers a year—the price of a farm!

When the Diet had declared war, each of the Circles was
obliged to provide a contingent in proportion to its size. But
what was the use of this army? Many Circles contained dozens
of independent states each of which sent a handful of men. The
Circle of Swabia, for instance, included 97 sovereigns: 2 bishops, 2 prince-abbots, 14 secular princes, 23 prelates, 25 members of the Bench of Lords, and 31 towns, some important like
Augsburg and Ulm, others minute like Bopfingen, which had
1,600 inhabitants, and Buchau, which had 1,000. The army of
the Circles was nothing but a mob.

Surely, in spite of this political partition, some common patriotism existed, some moral and intellectual unity? Frederick
denied it with a sort of fury. To celebrate the liberties of the
nation each territory sported a different dialect. Interpreters
were needed to make the two ends of Germany understand each
other. It was true that progress had been made in the last
twenty-four years—manners were less rough and poverty less
widespread. "Everything has increased, inhabitants, equipages,
furniture, liveries, carriages, and the luxuries of the table." But
there was still neither taste, nor art, nor real literature. Well
then, what was left in Germany? The individual powers of the
more considerable princes. The Emperor Charles VI himself
drew his principal strength from the hereditary possessions of
his House, whether they were in the Empire like Austria, the
Tyrol, Bohemia, Moravia, and Silesia, or outside it like Hungary, Croatia, Belgium, or the Milanese. Thus he comprised in
his person two figures, the head of the Germanic body and an
ordinary ruler. It was not always easy to unravel the two of
them, and often enough the Emperor was accused of using the
Empire to establish the despotism of Austria.

This duality was not exceptional, for within the last century
three electors had acquired royal crowns outside the imperial
frontiers: the Elector of Hanover was King of England, the
Elector of Brandenburg was King of Prussia, and the Elector of
Saxony was elected King of the republic of Poland. Between
them there was no equality. Saxony was one of the richest prov-

inces of all Germany. "It owes this advantage to the richness of its soil and to the industry of its people, who make its manufactures flourish." But it was badly governed, it had few soldiers, and the Elector wasted its revenues on bribery, in the hope of making the government of Poland hereditary. Willy-nilly the Elector of Hanover would become English; however much he wished to domineer over his new subjects to the advantage of his old ones, he was forced to serve the interests of Great Britain and to adopt the mercantile policy which the nation imposed on him. As for the Elector of Brandenburg, he was a landowner. He was also the most German of the three: his kingdom of Prussia was a colony of the Teutonic knights which had been secularized.

The inheritance of the Hohenzollerns lay scattered from the Niemen to the Rhine.[1] However, the pieces were near enough together for the King to be able to go from Tilsit to Cleve without sleeping more than two or three nights outside his own territories. They were divided into three principal groups: in the east was Prussia, in the center the compact group of Brandenburg, Pomerania, Magdeburg, and Halberstadt, in the west were the small territories of Minden and Ravensberg on the river Weser, Mark on the Ruhr, and Cleve on the Rhine. But this catalogue is a considerable simplification of the whole truth. On the borders of all these possessions extended a sort of fringe of contested lands, of enclaves, doubtful sovereignties, and potential legacies. At one end of old Prussia, for example, the King held the lordship of Serrey, the dowry of a Radziwill who had married a Hohenzollern: it formed an enclave in Polish territory. The King nominated the parish priest, but the rector was elected by the synod of Vilna. A part of Pomerania, the lordship of Lauenburg, continued to be subject to Poland. The Duchy of Crossen, which was an integral part of Brandenburg, was held of Bohemia; the Duchy of Cottbus formed an enclave in Saxon territory. On the other hand the independent Duchy of Mecklenburg was actually subject to the King, who had obtained from the Emperor the right to police it and keep troops there following disturbances over the succession.

In Thuringia the feudal confusion was greater still. At Qued-

1. See the map printed upon the end papers of this volume.

linburg the King was hereditary attorney for the Protestant abbey of nuns, and a Prussian force held the town. However, the abbess had forbidden it to enter the quarter where her convent lay. In the County of Wernigerode the administration was shared out—the count had charge of Church matters and the King of the posts. He had the reversion of East Frisia—a pretext for placing a garrison there. In the interior of the Mark two counties and a borough had almost succeeded in safeguarding their independence. On the other hand the neighboring towns of Dortmund, Essen, and Werden endured the rule of Prussia, which was exercised without the least right but under the most diverse pretexts—now to protect the Calvinist minority of Dortmund against the Lutheran majority, now to appease the conflicts between the Abbess of Essen and the townsfolk. In return the Elector Palatine had the right to protect the Catholics of Cleve. The lordship of Lymers in the Low Countries, the town of Crefeld in the Archbishopric of Cologne, and Neuchâtel and Valangin in Switzerland belonged to the Hohenzollerns, who also held certain baronies in the district of the Meuse, which were fragments of the territories of Orange. In 1740 the whole represented 4,600 square miles and 2,200,-000 inhabitants.

To this geographical complexity was added complexity of a historical origin. In no place had the prince identical juridical standing. Sometimes he acted as sovereign, sometimes as vassal, sometimes as overlord, sometimes as a dignitary of the Empire or as director of the Circle of Lower Saxony. Frederick William called himself "by the Grace of God King of Prussia, Margrave of Brandenburg, Archchamberlain and Elector of the Holy Roman Empire, Sovereign Prince of Orange, Neuchâtel, and Valangin, Duke of Magdeburg, Cleve, Jülich, Berg, Stettin, Pomerania, of the Cassubes and Vandals, of Mecklenburg and of Crossen in Silesia, Burgrave of Nürnberg, Prince of Halberstadt, Minden, Kammin, of the Wends, of Schwerin, Ratzeburg, and Meuss, Count of Hohenzollern, Ruppin, the Mark, Ravensberg, Hohenstein, Tecklenburg, Lingen, Schwerin, Buhren, and Lehrdam, Marquis of the Vehre and Flessinges, Lord of Ravenstein, the lands of Rostock, Stargard, Lauenburg, Bütow, Arlay and Breda, etc., etc. . . ."

In reality, quite apart from braggadocio and titular conceits, quite apart from titles of commemoration and titles of pretension, Frederick William comprised in his person one king, one margrave, six dukes, five princes, ten counts, and as many barons if not a few more. His authority was so complex that it overflowed the political boundaries of his lands, while that of neighboring princes penetrated right into them.

Although it could be said that the prestige of the royal title had come to act as a connection of overriding importance between the various domains, the person of the lord was still the fount of all real unity. The aim of the Prussian bureaucracy was to transform this artificial and precarious unity into a substantial unity of institutions, laws, interests, and habits. In fact the work was well advanced. The old urban and provincial liberties had not survived the ruin of the oligarchic states. If the Prussian monarchy was to endure and grow it had to be a despotism, precisely because the territory it included and the subjects it comprised could in themselves provide no natural justification for its existence. Was it to be a paternal and brutal despotism in the manner of Frederick William, or the enlightened and philosophic despotism of the Crown Prince's dreams? There was not, perhaps, so much difference between the two of them after all.

The same internal logic pushed the monarchy of the Hohenzollerns toward conquest. Its frontiers were one long lawsuit— it had to win or lose, advance or retreat, extend or disintegrate. It was never satisfied and it was never secure; in any case, it never had a sense of completion. Before it became a nation Prussia was a political idea, an ambition on the march; it was the dream of a dynasty which had persevered in a single effort and which administered its territories like a home farm. That is why Frederick had to give his father credit for having established his rule "like a rock of bronze," though he criticized his foreign policy sharply. No doubt he restrained himself from fear and from respect. After the illness of 1734 he was miserable at having shown his eagerness to rule and had stopped all correspondence with Grumbkow, so that it was the minister himself who tried to reopen it again in October, 1735. However, Frederick found it hard to be frank with him. Sometimes he remained for weeks without writing; sometimes he would play the hermit and feign disgust at human vanities; sometimes he replied with eloquent truisms—but sometimes he broke out.

Since the Treaty of Berlin of December 23, 1728, Frederick William had remained faithful to the imperial alliance, but it had only brought him mortification. First, in Poland, where he feared he would see the Saxons obtain and establish a hereditary monarchy, Austria had in fact forced the election of Augustus III, son of Augustus II, against the national candidate Stanislas Leczinski who was supported by the majority of the nobility. Second, during the war in the west Frederick William had punctually provided the Emperor with his contingent against France but he had not gained in exchange the least guarantee for the succession of Jülich and Berg. He had hardly been informed of the peace, of the cession of Lorraine to France, and of the engagement of the Archduchess Maria Theresa to Duke Francis of Lorraine, who was set up with the Duchy of Tuscany. As a final blow on February 10, 1738, France, Austria, England, and the Low Countries had come together to settle the question of Berg: in the event of the death of the reigning Prince the four powers would offer their mediation to regulate the division in a friendly manner, but until a solution was found the "provisional possession" of the duchies would go to the Palatine of Sulzbach.

Frederick William had been tricked. As early as 1736 he had drawn up a memorandum under thirty headings for the benefit of himself and his ministers called the *Species Facti,* which was nothing but a long diatribe against the House of Austria, and a few days later he had pointed at Frederick and cried out in front of his generals, "There's the man who will revenge me!" None the less he was isolated and in the greatest difficulty. With a fairly clear comprehension of how matters stood he set about breaking up the coalition but as usual he acted clumsily, swinging from one side to the other by fits and starts, unable to commit himself deeply and inspiring nobody with fear, confidence, or affection.

A German prince said to young Seckendorff, who had taken his uncle's place at Berlin, "If the King of Prussia is measured by the size of his grenadiers he is the greatest man in the Em-

pire; but I am sure that if it ever came to an affair of snatch
and grab, half his soldiers would run away." Seckendorff replied, "The King knows it; besides, he will not make war."
Such was the opinion of all the world, and from that opinion
sprang a general feeling of contempt.

It was useless for Frederick to repeat that his personal reputation was safe and that he had no responsibility for the fiasco,
for it pained him none the less. "People have quite recovered
from their fear of our arms," he wrote to Grumbkow. "Their
rashness is such that they actually despise us." Prussian policy
had fallen "into lethargy." "We are in a strong position on the
military side, but our diplomacy is without vigor." The King's
reply to the four mediators contained "a conflicting mixture of
greatness and baseness," it resembled "the answer of a person
who has no wish to fight but who pretends he will." There
were, however, only two paths to take: either bend under the
shameful yoke or else reply "with a proud nobility," without
condescending to minor negotiations. He himself would not do
things by halves and he had a plan ready: to mass dragoons and
hussars at the gates of Berg so as to seize on the country as soon
as the Prince died, and concentrate the rest of the army in the
Marches so as to be ready to fall on the forces of whoever was
the first to make a show of opposing the annexation. "For if we
let slip the moment of the Elector's death, our stroke has
failed." And he added, "Would it not be possible to get over to
our side some officers of the Palatinate, who are quartered with
their regiments in the duchies, so that they could deliver the
towns to us? . . ." Assuredly that was not quite in the style of
the *Anti-Machiavel*.

Frederick also built up diplomatic combinations in his mind:
a reconciliation with Russia, a coalition with the Scandinavian
states and with Holland. But his real idea was to get an alliance
with France against the House of Austria. During the short
interregnum of 1734 he had piled entreaties upon La Chetardie, offering to play Gustavus Adolphus provided that Cardinal
Fleury would consent to be his Richelieu: "If I love anything
in the world, I love the French nation. So it only depends on
you to enable me to give free rein to my affection and tenderness; provided it is of some benefit to the country, you can lead

me as far as you like." At that moment he thought that Louis
XV would throw his whole weight against the Emperor to uphold his father-in-law Stanislas. When he saw Fleury quietly
liquidating the succession of Poland in exchange for Lorraine,
he was both disappointed and furious: disappointed at the "nice
treachery" of the Cardinal and furious at having been completely mistaken as to the essential aims of French policy.

He planned to arouse public opinion against the "quadrillers" and he wrote his first polemical propaganda pamphlet—
the "Considerations on the Present State of Political Forces in
Europe." The work was to appear in English at London anonymously and then in French as a translation. However, it is obvious that it was to be circulated in Germany, for clearly the argument had two objects: first, to alarm the maritime powers at the
insatiable ambition of France; second, to turn the German
princes against the Franco-Austrian block. It was this very
duality which constituted the weakness of the argument's presentation, for the author was catering for two different publics
at the same time, so that he was obliged to omit points which
pleased one side but might displease the other, and he gave
himself away by knowing much more about Europe than about
the Indies. Voltaire, who had a look at the work in the summer
of 1738, saw this error at the first glance. "Even if these 'Considerations' had been printed under the name of a member of
the English Parliament, I would have recognized Your Royal
Highness. . . . This work is pervaded by a style which betrays
you. I see in it such an air of a member of the Empire as is
never found in an English citizen. A man from the House of
Lords or the Commons takes less interest in German liberties."
Finally the "Considerations" were not published.

The episode was none the less one of great importance. Certainly Frederick was not the first to have written a political
pamphlet or to have got one compiled so as to influence
people's minds, but the tone of his was new, sensitive, humani-
tarian, philosophical, reminiscent of Bayle and Voltaire, with
virtuous indignation against the greedy kings who were divided
by pride and who refused Prussia the inheritance of the Palatinate. "If any power thinks that I have expressed myself too
freely, it should remember that fruit always keeps its native tang,

and that as I was born in a free country I am permitted to express myself with proud audacity and a sincerity which is ignorant of deceit. . . ." Frederick was the first among princes to realize what a power organized opinion was to be in his century, and with what weight the republic of letters was going to press down on the decisions of kings: half by taste and half by design he put this trump card in his hand and he was already thinking of playing it.

However, he thought better of it, not only because he was not master of his pen, but mostly because he was not yet entirely sure of what he aspired to be. Though his mind was vastly enriched he had not properly sorted out the treasures he had collected. His temperament, his reading, the need for activity, aspirations toward glory, moral theories, a French style, Prussian needs, a longing for power, philosophical systems: among so many elements how could harmony be set up? To complete it all trial by fire was needed—the daily responsibility of sovereign power. Some days he felt that himself. "It seems," he wrote to Grumbkow, "that Heaven has ordained that the King should make all possible preparations demanded by wisdom and prudence of those who are about to start a war. Who knows whether Providence is not reserving me to make glorious use of these preparations, by employing them to accomplish the designs for which the King's foresight has designed them?" (November 1, 1737.)

Moreover, as the friendship of the Emperor was nothing but trickery, force of circumstances brought both the father and the son over to desire an alliance with France, the only continental power capable of balancing the might of Austria. They came to it at the same time each in his own way, Frederick with the grace of a cat and his father with the graciousness of a performing bear. "The father enters into conversation with La Chetardie about cheese, the son about literature. The father takes an interest in Cardinal Fleury's digestion and sends him a bottle of old wine; the son flatters the pride of His Eminence the octogenarian" by writing him compliments from a nice young man who is intimidated by so illustrious a personage. At bottom it was the same thing, but there were also points of difference. The father was honest, he was a German, and he had scruples. No doubt he mocked at the Emperor but not at the Empire. He was incapable of calling in the French against a member of the Germanic body, still less capable of combining with them in a campaign on German soil. And then he feared the risk. Building up the strength of Prussia had cost him too much trouble for him to dare risk it on a throw of the dice. The son did not germanize, nor did he hesitate. In his eyes the Empire was nothing but a worm-eaten hovel and he was in a hurry to show himself to the world. In the "Considerations" he reproached France with having stolen Strassburg, the Thermopylae of Germany; but as an ally of the French he would have congratulated Louis XV on having held the pass for him. He said to those with whom he came in contact, "I will start with a sudden stroke at the risk of receiving one at the same time." Or else, "Prudence is very suitable for preserving possessions, but only boldness can acquire fresh ones." And again, "There will be no occasion to accuse me of sacrificing my interests to other powers. Much rather do I fear that I shall be reproached for too much tenacity and liveliness."

IV

IT was no longer possible for the father and the son to love each other: there lay between them too many horrible memories. However, the King was forced to acknowledge that Frederick performed his duties without flinching. On looking at him more closely he was even convinced that Heaven might have given him a worse successor. During a dinner party, after the grand reviews of 1739, in front of the royal family, the princes, and the generals, he congratulated Frederick on the care he had taken to improve his regiment and he told him among other flattering things, "There's a Frederick William in you." His common sense helped him to predict many things which sharp people missed. "When I die," he bellowed out jocosely one day, "everybody will cry, 'that old tormentor of mankind is gone'; but he who comes after me will send you all to the devil; that's all you will get from him." And he found this thought a very soothing one.

Nevertheless, he was no longer quite the man he had been; he had aged, and since 1734 his health had never been completely restored. When gout tortured him too much, he painted to keep his mind off the pain. He copied famous pictures which became extraordinary caricatures of humanity under his brush. He painted his grenadiers, his animals, Gundling smoking his pipe with a monkey dressed as a marquise while some hares served them with drinks. It was pointed out to him that Wolff had been unjustly exiled: he had the philosopher's works read to him, studied the laws of reasoning, marveled at them, and straightway thought of placing them at the service of the State. One evening in the smoking room he read a report from a general who was in command at Wesel and he showed that, logically, this soldier reasoned "like a clod." After which by way of a reply he advised him to learn how to construct his syllogisms correctly. When someone exclaimed before him, "It is a disgrace to the whole of Christendom for the Emperor to conclude peace with the Turks," he parried the sophism by crying, "Sir, have you learned to draw conclusions from the particular to the general, that is to say, from one to all?"

He had not become lavish, to be sure, but since the affairs of the State were in order he allowed himself some extravagances which were of a sort to heighten the prestige of the crown. He bought pictures by Dutch and Flemish masters. Especially did he buy silverware, very fine pieces which he ordered like a connoisseur and which were worthy of a royal treasury. But he no longer took much pleasure in anything. As early as January, 1738, he said he was tired of life, good for nothing, incurable, and a burden to his relatives and his servants. However, he wanted to ply his trade till the very end.

In July, 1739, he left for East Prussia with the Crown Prince —a tiring journey overburdened with inspections and reviews. They traveled by short stages, through dust and torrid heat, stopping everywhere to look at everything. On the way the King gave Frederick the stud farms of Prussia. In his letters to Jordan Frederick declared himself "dazed and stupid" and gave a dreadful description of the province. It was quite good enough to support bears! "If you were here," he said in conclusion, "I would give you the choice between the finest Lithuanian girl and the finest mare in the studs . . . for between a girl of this country and a blood mare of the stud the only difference is that which there is between one animal and another." However, to Voltaire he announced that he was traversing a country which was the *ne plus ultra* of the civilized world. "There are more than half a million inhabitants; there are more towns than there used to be, more herds than formerly, more riches and more fertility than in any other place in Germany. And all that of which I have just told you is due to the King, who not only gave the orders but presided himself at the execution of them; who conceived the plans and carried them out himself alone; who spared neither troubles nor care, nor immense treasures, nor promises, nor rewards to assure the happiness and life of a half million of thinking beings who owe to him alone their felicity and security. . . . Your humanity should spread its mantle over your Lithuanian brothers. . . ."

On his return Frederick William felt more tired than ever. One evening in the month of January while he held court in the smoking room the Crown Prince entered unexpectedly. The company with one unanimous movement stood up, but it was the rule there that no one should get up for anyone else. "Sit down, in the devil's name!" cried the King, and then he went out hurling insults at the worshipers of the rising sun. Back in his room he dismissed all the company and forbade them to appear before him; for a whole week he talked of nothing but making heads fly like carrots. He called Frederick "Sire," "Your Majesty," adding sometimes, "A little more patience, my son." However, he became worse and worse. His dropsy came back, rose little by little and stifled him. He could only stay in bed in a sitting position supported by cushions; from time to time he had himself lifted and moved on a wheel chair. In moments of calm he slept, his head resting on a bar of wood. He spent the winter in pain with slight improvements which brought back his old manias; he reckoned up the kitchen expenditure and twice reduced the number of dishes. His last outing in Berlin ended in a generous distribution of insults and blows. When he was in bed he wanted his room to be filled all the time with a hubbub of conversation, for silence woke him up. He had had a table placed across his bed and when he could not sleep he used to make boxes with great blows of his hammer, tapping so loudly that the noise could be heard in the street. The doctors did not know how to give him relief. Frederick advised calling in a well-known doctor from Halle. The King replied that Eller, his usual doctor, was quite sufficient to finish him off. "Blackguard that he is, he knows well enough that if I croak no one will demand a reckoning of the way he treated me."

He often thought of death but not as of eternal rest. When he imagined himself lying in the grave, he was never silent and tranquil at last, but sometimes laughing at the stupidities of his son, sometimes jumping with joy at the news that Fritz had humiliated Austria. All the same he was afraid of Hell.

"Would it be fair of God," he asked, "after having loved me enough to let me rule so many thousands of men in place of Him and at my own whim, to treat me one day as equal with my subjects and to judge me with the same severity?"

When the pastor replied that God was more severe on kings than on simple people, he dismissed him and had a search made in the town for a minister with whom he could chat and be understood. Finally he gave his confidence to Roloff, a fine man quite free from cant.

"My poor Roloff, I am going to die."

"Your Majesty will not die as soon as all that, but would do well to be prepared and before all else to be reconciled with his enemies."

"I have no enemies except for my brother-in-law the King of England, who has done me all the mischief in the world. But I have forgiven him and forgotten everything, and the moment I am dead the Queen shall write to him about it." Then he turned toward the Queen, "Do you hear that? You must not forget; you must write to your brother."

"But," replied Roloff, "why does not Your Majesty have the letter written to your brother-in-law at once while Your Majesty is still alive?"

"No. When I am dead the Queen shall write."

He was not the man to pay in advance, and Roloff's remark that he would not die so soon as all that had made him take thought. The next day he sent his lodge keeper Eversmann to ask the pastor for an explanation. Roloff replied that he was no doctor but that he had seen enough sick people to be sure that the King was not on the point of death, "which was very fortunate, by the way, for His Majesty was not yet certain of salvation." At that Frederick William had him brought back.

"From what I hear you are still in doubt about my salvation. What have I done that you should form this judgment on the subject?"

"I have often told Your Majesty that Christ is the foundation of our salvation on two conditions—the first is that we should believe in Him; the second, that we should order our lives on His conduct and example and that we should take on His spirit. If this change of heart does not take place in us, there is no hope of salvation! . . . Your army, your treasure, your country—you must leave all these behind, and you will have no servants on whom to give free vent to the passion of your rage. In Heaven thought and feeling must be heavenly."

Therefore on that day and the following days the King made public confession. He declared he had repented of his sins, but he left out on purpose certain acts which he did not consider as sins and he wrangled with Roloff when the pastor tried to make him remember them. At other times he despaired of ever being able to reform.

"I am like that: when I have money, I want more of it. It's an old habit and I can't resist it. I know well that if I were cured I would fall back into past errors, and that is why I pray God to take me from this world."

Frederick knew that his father was done for. From the beginning of 1740 he gave his sister to understand as much. But that year the carnival at Bayreuth was very brilliant and Wilhelmina was making her ladies act *Le Malade imaginaire*. On February 26 Frederick wrote to her, "Judging by appearances you will never see the King again. His ailments have worsened so swiftly that I doubt if he will live through the coming week. He has given you his blessing and has spoken very highly of you. At present his fever is so violent that he can hardly talk. . . . Keep calm and do not grieve too much; for things that are accomplished there is no remedy." However, the coming of the spring seemed to give the sick man strength. Frederick was careful to preserve the outward appearances of decent conduct. He was troubled, anxious, nervous—but to calm his inner agitation he versified with breathless haste. He wrote stories, the "False Prognostic," the "Miracle Which Failed," an "Ode on Flattery," an "Epistle on Fortune," another on "The Necessity of Filling the

Void in the Heart with Study," another on "Glory and Interest,"
another on "The Necessity of Cultivating the Arts." To his
friends he sent pieces of occasional verse, moral considerations,
regrets for his youth.

> Happy is he who, independent,
> Lives content and lives unseen,
> Who has preferred with good judgment
> To luxuries most opulent
> The frugal life and golden mean. . . .
> Ah, I am dragged, as I am feeling,
> On by a hand importunate,
> And I must mount on fortune's wheel in
> Accordance with compelling fate.
> Adieu, tranquillity divine,
> Adieu, ye pleasures sweet so lately,
> Adieu, wise solitude of mine,
> In years to come I shall not meet ye.

Moreover, he too had to take care of his health. He complained
of cramps of the stomach, of colics, of fits of choking, of palpita-
tions of the heart. When writing to Eller for news of the King he
also asked him for remedies and advice.

Thus the winter passed. On the first fine day Frederick William had himself transported to Potsdam. "Farewell, Berlin," said
he. "It is at Potsdam that I wish to die." But when he found his
regiment once more, when he saw around him "his dear children
in blue," he thought himself almost cured.

"Feel my body, friends, feel it. It is hard as a drum. Yet my
legs are swollen. But all that will disappear and soon you will
see me on horseback amongst you laying about me with cut and
thrust."

He embraced the officers and wanted them to go away singing,
but the following week the pains only became worse. On May
10 in a moment of calm he thought of his son: "I am no longer
anxious to live," he said, "since I leave a son who has all the
talents of a good ruler. I would not have said the same of him
five years ago, he was still too young. But, by God's grace, he has
changed and I am satisfied. He has promised me he will keep up
the army and I am certain he will keep his promise. I know he
loves the troops; he has spirit, and all will go well."

On the twenty-sixth he wrote to Fritz, calling him for the first time "my beloved son" (*mein geliebter Sohn*). "I have received your letter of the twenty-fourth instant, where I have seen your cordial compassion for my wretched condition and also your praiseworthy resolution to follow my paternal advice in everything. I am much touched by it and in fact I have not the least doubt about your promise and your feelings, supposing that God disposes of my life as it appears He will. That you should wish to come for Whitsun [June 5] pleases me greatly, and it would be a real pleasure to embrace you once more if God wills it. News of the countryside is still really bad, but as the heat of spring begins and the beasts find enough grass, I hope this will become bearable again. I am, with faithful affection, my beloved son, your very affectionate and faithful father."

The next day he summoned the chaplains of his regiment and had an interview with them interspersed with terrible pauses which frightened him. Once, after a long spell of silence, he cried, "Ah, I am a wicked man." In the night he had a fainting fit and another on the morrow. Frederick, without being summoned, rushed from Rheinsberg on May 28. On his arrival he noticed a noisy crowd near the castle—it was the King who was sitting in his wheel chair surrounded by an inquisitive crowd watching him lay the first stone of a house intended for his farrier. Fritz stopped short in amazement, but his father flung open his arms and he threw himself into them weeping. They remained some minutes without speaking: then the King told his son that he had been very severe with him at one time but that he had always loved him. They went home together and for two hours Frederick William explained the state of his affairs to his successor with perfect lucidity. He advised him to keep a careful eye on the whole of Europe and especially on George II. He recommended him to take care of his troops, only to treat with France from a strong position and not to undertake war lightly. On the next day, the twenty-ninth, he gave orders that the oak coffin with brass handles he had provided for himself should be placed by his bed, and he spoke of his end as of a peaceful sleep. His will had been drawn up seven years back, but he had the arrangements he had made for his own obsequies read over to him again.

He ordered that his body should be washed and dressed in white linen. Four hours after death the surgeons were to open it to see what had caused his death, but not one organ was to be taken out. The interment was to take place before the regiment of grenadiers, with drums draped in black and flags, fifes, and hautboys adorned with crepe. The officers were to have crepe on their hats, sleeves, sashes, and sword knots. The coffin was to be carried from the room to the hearse by eight captains, but from the church to the grave the King wished to be borne by staff officers, hoping that there would be some who would come to render him their last service. There was to be no funeral oration, but twenty-four fieldpieces would fire twelve successive rounds and the battalions would fire one after the other. He also hoped that officers from every other regiment would follow in the procession. Those who had come from far off should be served with a meal and some good wine. A fortnight later the clergy were to devote a sermon to him on the text "I have fought the good fight." When he had been buried the troops must disperse, but as they would no longer be his he merely added for his son's benefit, "A detachment of grenadiers will take the flags wherever you command them."

On May 31 at one o'clock in the morning the King summoned an almoner, then the Crown Prince, his ministers, his generals, and the captains of his regiment. He spoke to all of them, but he complained of loss of memory and of not being able to say his prayers any more. He was wheeled to the Queen's apartments and woke her with these words, "Get up, I am going to die." When the assembly was complete he ordered the horses to be led out of the stables, and from the window chose one for old Dessau and one for General Hacke. As the grooms were putting a blue saddle on a yellow horsecloth he sent Hacke to beat them with his stick. Finally he announced he was going to abdicate. Grumbkow had died a year back: his son-in-law Podewils walked off as if he was going to draw up the declaration, but meanwhile the King had a fainting fit. When he came to himself he remembered that the livery of his servants had just been renewed and he made them march past to show him their new clothes. He was heard to sigh, "Oh, vanity!" He chatted to his surgeon and with his eyes fixed on a mirror followed the approach of death attentively.

Toward three o'clock in the afternoon he murmured, "I am already dead." Then soon after, "Lord Jesus! I live in Thee, I die in Thee! Thou art my help in life and death." At a sign from Eller the Queen and the Crown Prince withdrew. They had scarcely gone out when the King died. He had lived for fifty-one years, nine months, and sixteen days.

Princess Elisabeth and almost all the Prince's friends had remained at Rheinsberg. They waited impatiently for news from Potsdam, unable to keep still the moment they saw a shadow on the horizon. The Princess alone preserved a decent mien. In the night Bielfeld was awakened by the noise of a cavalcade crossing the wooden bridge. A few minutes later Knobelsdorff entered his room: "Get up, Bielfeld, the King is no more." Bielfeld however had his doubts. "No, no," replied Knobelsdorff, "he is dead, dead as a doornail. Jordan's to see that they dissect and embalm the corpse. You may be sure that once he gets under those hands he will never return." Bielfeld got up, but as he jumped out of bed he upset a table where his purse lay. As he stooped down to collect the small change Knobelsdorff got indignant: "Collecting pennies when it is going to rain ducats on us!"

Downstairs they met the Grand Mistress of the Robes, Madame de Katsch, who was going to salute the Queen with the title of Majesty. At breakfast, which was a splendid one, the glory of the new reign was toasted and straightway they all set off helter-skelter for Berlin.

Frederick had already left it. One hour after his father's death he had given audience to old Leopold of Dessau, the organizer of the Prussian Army, adviser and inspiration of Frederick William I. Dessau threw himself at Frederick's feet and begged him with sobs to maintain him in the positions and the authority with which he had been invested under the late King.

"I will try to please you in every way I can," replied Frederick, "and I will not touch your position, nor those of your sons; but as for the authority in which you wish to be maintained, I do not understand what you mean. I have become King; my intention is to carry out the functions of kingship and be the only one who has authority."

Almost at once, to escape from hangers-on, he left for Berlin and on the following day withdrew to his grandmother's castle at Charlottenburg, leaving an icy note for his wife which concluded with these words: "You can still stay here, as your presence is still necessary, until I write to you. See few people or nobody. Tomorrow I will arrange for the ladies' mourning and I will send it to you. Good-by, I hope to have the pleasure of seeing you in good health." Elisabeth understood that their separation had begun and did no more than send the marshal of the palace to present her compliments to the new King.

Bielfeld, when summoned to Charlottenburg, took it upon himself to point the moral of these events. Frederick "with tearful eyes" greeted him thus, "You do not know how much I have lost in losing a father!" "It is true, Sire," he replied, "but I know well enough all that you have gained by gaining a kingdom. Your loss is great, but your reasons for consolation are very powerful."

Frederick gave a wan smile.

A few days later he summoned to him the Baron von Pöllnitz, who had been a gentleman-in-waiting to his grandfather and was an expert on ceremonial. "I entrust to you," he told him, "the direction of the obsequies of your former master. You will take notice that it is my intention that all shall be performed with dignity and nobility; therefore spare nothing that may be needful to give it a fitting splendor. Go to the merchants and get from them all the black cloth which will be needed for the funeral drapery. You will then send me the accounts and I will have them paid."

The baron withdrew, but as he went down the stairs Frederick opened the door to call after him, "No sharp practices! No agreements with the merchants! I warn you, I won't forgive that!"

Bielfeld had been right to collect his small change.

VI

The Call of War and Glory

I

FREDERICK was twenty-eight years old at the time of his father's death, the people loved him because they had pitied him, and everyone agreed that he was an attractive character. Two good portraits of him exist which date more or less from that period: a portrait in profile by Knobelsdorff (1737) and a head and shoulders portrait by Pesne (1739), the only one for which he actually sat. The most remarkable point about his head was the forehead, which was very high, flat, and open and exactly continued the line of his nose, the sharpness of which contrasted with his youthful cheeks and well-rounded chin. His complexion was too fresh and his face too full to afford as yet the least foreboding of the old emaciated Fritz of the future with his haughty manner and tight lips. He was a very nice, smiling, young man, a little fat, a little feminine, with quick movements and a habit of carrying his head bent over a trifle to his left. He had large eyes, prominent through shortsightedness and blue-gray in color, his looks were swift, penetrating, and witty and expressed every shade of gaiety and mischief. His face was bronzed, but his hands were very white and loaded with rings. He gesticulated a lot as he talked, and spoke without listening to what he was being told. He habitually wore a colonel's uniform, but as he was very subject to cold he used to wear two or three waistcoats under it, which thickened up his figure. On the other hand at Court fetes he looked svelte, trim, and beribboned, adorned with sashes, diamonds, and feathers. For the wedding of his brother Augustus William in 1742 he wore a costume of silver and gold which gave him "such a sumptuous air of youth and elegance" that an onlooker wrote, "I would not have been able to prevent myself from loving him had I been of the opposite sex."

The beginning of the reign was like a fairy tale. Frederick was

FRE-
LE,
ROI DE
DERIC
GRAND
PRUSSE.

intoxicated with the pleasure of being King. On Whitsunday he drove around the streets of Berlin throwing handfuls of money about. He enjoyed the grandeur and the diversity of the occupations which overwhelmed him; his joy broke forth from between the lines of his personal letters: "Good-by," he scribbled to Jordan, "I am going to write to the King of France, compose a solo, indite verses to Voltaire, change the army regulations, and do a hundred other things of the same sort." He was indefatigable, rose at dawn, worked without a single break, accepted volumes of poetry, sent off hundreds of letters, held reviews, founded a journal, chose ambassadors, created the Order of Merit, appointed a marshal, rushed from Berlin to Rheinsberg and from Potsdam to Charlottenburg, and complained that the days were twenty-four hours too short.

One after another appeared twenty edicts of a sort to make a philosopher swoon with delight: the abolition of torture, the opening of State granaries to prevent a rise in the price of bread, the suppression of Church dispensations for marriages between distant relatives, the suppression of the compulsory building which was ruining so many Berliners, prohibition of ragging in the army, mitigation of the penalties inflicted on women convicted of "having caused the fruit of their wombs to perish," institution of a Department of Commerce and Manufactures in the heart of the Central Office, permission given for countryfolk to make their own beer for home consumption, and a solemn declaration that everyone in the States of the King of Prussia was free to choose his own way to salvation. Wolff was recalled from exile and took possession of his professorial chair in triumph: the Academy was restored, and pensions and positions offered to Maupertuis, Euler, Van's Gravesande, Vaucason: the brothers Graun left for Italy to recruit an operatic company, while a company of tragic actors collected at Paris. The regiment of giants marched past for the last time at the late King's funeral and was at once reduced to a battalion.

To his distant friends Frederick sent charming notes: "My lot has changed; come, my dear friend, do not make me pine on your account," or else, "Your presence here only depends on your own wishes. I embrace you with all my heart in the hope of seeing you again before long." He summoned those who had

suffered with him, Duhan, his old tutor, and Keith, the lieutenant who had taken refuge in England while being condemned
to death by a court-martial. From London there also came one of
the last visitors to Rheinsberg, Algarotti the Venetian, author of
*Sir Isaac Newton's Philosophy Explain'd for the Use of the
Ladies.* But it was Keyserlingk who seemed the prime favorite.
At Charlottenburg on the doors of his apartment the King had
written with his own hand the friendly title he had given him—
"Caesarion." Caesarion was seen everywhere, in the castle and
the gardens, "skipping about with a little amber flageolet in his
buttonhole, singing, laughing, joking," reciting verses which
flowed in torrents from his "bubbling Hippocrene." From afar
off Voltaire was mad with joy. He had got permission to call his
prince "Your Humanity" instead of "Your Majesty" and he
sighed out:

"What! You are a king and love me as of old! . . ."

It was whispered in Paris that the philosopher was already on
the road to Berlin and would be made First Minister on his arrival. First minister of the King of Prussia? And why not? It was
time that the abbots and cardinals who had so often guided the
monarchies of France and Spain should be succeeded by these
new directors of conscience, who professed to think freely and
were to be instrumental in setting up a government of enlightenment. In the "Ode to the King of Prussia on the Occasion of His
Accession" Voltaire had slipped in a discreet hint:

My sweet hopes, I declare, must not now be denied!
You are king. Shall we see true philosophy rule
As a king by your side?

To be sure philosophy held an honored place. Before his
father was even buried Frederick had founded a Masonic lodge
at Court and he took the orator's chair himself for the reception
of his younger brother. However, Voltaire was not made First
Minister. Letters from Berlin did no more than talk in vague
terms of the possibility of a meeting in the autumn or the winter.
The diplomats, who were better psychologists than the poets,
had already seen through the intentions of the young King. "It
must be understood," a note sent to Versailles stated with pre-

cision, "that H.M. of Prussia will only make use of such head-pieces for his amusement. . . . Nature usually deducts from their judgment an equivalent of the surplus endowment they have of wit, and that is not what is needed for governing a state."

To his friends Frederick offered nothing but his friendship. Bielfeld expected some title at the very least: when the King told him that he intended him for diplomacy he dreamed of an embassy, but His Majesty added that such kinds of work called for a long apprenticeship and that he had chosen him to accompany Monsieur de Truchsess, his envoy extraordinary in Hanover, with that end in view. Jordan was a pastor and contented himself with the post of inspector of hospitals; Keyserlingk, who was an officer, with promotion in the army. Still, he would not have got it if he had not deserved it. One day, however, he hazarded some remarks about policy. "Listen, Keyserlingk," the King told him, "you are a nice lad and I like to hear you laugh and sing, but your advice is that of a madman." So Caesarion gave no more advice.

To pay its respects to the new sovereign the Chamber of Domains of the Kurmark thought it smart to ask for a supplementary credit of 195 thalers to improve the road from Rheinsberg to Ruppin, but Frederick just answered, "I know that road and the Chamber must take me for a great ass."

Indeed, in the bustle of the change to a new reign there was more ostentation than there were reforms. Queen Elisabeth was the only victim of the accession. Thenceforth she lived apart, the winters at Berlin, the summers at Schönhausen, a little castle lying to the north of the capital. However, when the King and Queen were obliged to appear together at some ceremony Frederick treated her with every possible attention, and when he himself was living at the royal palace he never failed to pay her a daily visit for decorum's sake.

Two of Frederick William's favorites were honored: Derschau received advancement and Hacke the first star of the Order of Merit. The ministers expected to be dismissed: they were all invited to retain their posts—Podewils, Thulemeier, Borcke, Boden, Cocceji. . . . They would have liked to deliberate under the presidency of His Majesty, but the King gave them to understand that he agreed with his dead father on that subject and that the old customs would be continued. So they began sending in reports and proposals in writing once more; the King replied as Frederick William had done and his orders were later brought together in the great register, where under the date of June 1, 1740, can still be read, "Here His Royal Majesty Frederick, King of Prussia, began to affix his signature." Even the style of the remarks does not change. On June 16 the councilors found that one of their proposals had evoked this reply, "When ministers argue about negotiations they are skilled persons, but when they talk of war it is like an Iroquois talking of astronomy." And two days later, "The Black Eagle is not an order for ——'s like Münchhausen."

In July Frederick set out to receive the homage of Royal Prussia. Before his departure he ordered the establishment of sixteen battalions of infantry, five squadrons of hussars, and a squadron of heavy cavalry. Along the roads his grandfather had traveled with two hundred carriages and coaches he went with three vehicles—one for himself, Algarotti, Keyserlingk, and Hacke; a second for his officers; and a third for his valet Fredersdorff and the baggage. On the way he refused all ceremonial entries, fetes, speeches, and "all useless and frivolous ceremonies." At Königsberg he had neither a coronation nor a religious ceremony, only a banquet, some reviews, and a torchlight tattoo. The kingdom had venerable privileges which went back to the days of the Teutonic Order and provided matter for endless discussions at each accession. This time everything was done in the simplest possible manner. Frederick claimed homage in his quality of lord and received it exactly as he demanded it. At Angerburg he inspected Katte's cuirassiers and formally presented the father of his unfortunate friend with the rank of marshal. Equally modest was the ceremony in the States of Brandenburg. Neither the Elector's cap nor the baton of the High Chamberlain of the Empire were brought out. Minister von Arnim addressed a short speech to the nobility and the burghers. Two spokesmen replied, an officer read the oath of fidelity, and all the company swore to it with one voice. Frederick went out onto the balcony of the castle in response to the cheers of the crowd. For half an hour, stiff and silent, lost in deep reflections, he listened to the shouts of joy.

In August he left for the Rhenish provinces, but he made a detour by Franconia and on the way greeted his two sisters at Bayreuth and at Ansbach. To Wilhelmina he gave a fan, a watch, a little bouquet of tiny brilliants, and some good advice on how to restore the finances of the Margrave. He thought for a moment of going in secret to Paris. Upon a rumor which had gone before him Voltaire hastened to have the Hôtel du Châtelet made ready: "Furnish the palace as best you can, as cheaply as you can, and as quickly as you can," he wrote, hoping to be able to entertain his Prince and show himself in his company. However, Frederick changed his mind and limited himself to the escapade of a visit to Strassburg incognito.

The expedition began with a comic incident: the King had forgotten to supply himself with a passport and he was stopped at the stage at Kehl. Fredersdorff had to draw up a safe-conduct on the spot, which Frederick sealed with the arms of Prussia. He christened himself Count Dufour and his brother Augustus William became Count Schaffgotsch. To avoid attracting attention Augustus William and Algarotti spent the night at Kehl while Frederick accompanied by Wartensleben and some servants crossed the Rhine before dark. At the sign of the Crow where they stopped, Frederick asked for sumptuous fare, for the very best they could get him, and told them to send round to the French officers' café to fetch all who were willing to sup with him. This invitation from an unknown source was so cavalier that when the innkeeper delivered it the lounging revelers greeted him with gusts of laughter. However two of them, captains in the Piedmont regiment, took the risk and accepted, no doubt with the idea of amusing themselves at their host's expense. To their great surprise they found a fine-looking young lord who spoke French without an accent, was witty and lively in his talk, and joined in with their bawdy songs. It was only at the end of the meal that Count Dufour allowed himself to utter some pleasantries on the gait of the French troops, which were taken up with great vivacity by one of the guests. However, when the quarrel threatened to become embittered, the other, who had kept his temper more successfully, concluded the interview, after having invited the foreign nobles to come to supper the following day.

In the course of the morning the two captains went and told the story of their adventure to the governor of the province. This was the Marshal de Broglie, an old soldier of some repute who had fought in Flanders and in Italy. Considering that so rich and so impertinent a foreigner must be either a prince or an adventurer, the marshal advised the young men to beware of him. However, at the same time Frederick felt that he could no longer pass unnoticed and sent his brother, Algarotti, and Wartensleben to offer the marshal his compliments, excusing himself for not being able to attend because of an indisposition which kept him indoors. Broglie invited the visitors to dinner, but as it was time for mass he offered to let them hear it in his private chapel. Wartensleben was embarrassed by his great height and did not know what to say; Prince Augustus William was very shy and remained silent; Algarotti was the only one to keep the conversation going and he was also the only one to attend the mass. Meanwhile Frederick left the inn and strolled about the town. He went up to the belfry of the cathedral and on the way out was accosted in the cathedral square by a citizen, who called him "Sire" and "Your Majesty," and begged him to release his son— the lad had been carried off by a press gang while traveling in Germany and forcibly incorporated in the regiment of giants. To keep him quiet Frederick promised him all he asked, but as he reëntered the inn he was again recognized by two deserters whom the police had put on the lookout. Shortly afterward the governor sent a man to take "the King's orders." In reply Frederick sent him word that he would come himself.

The interview passed off very badly. Frederick was getting tired of his prank and Broglie behaved both ceremoniously and importunately. Frederick left the room almost at once, scarcely bowing to the marshal's wife, who had insisted on being presented to him. He got an officer to show him the citadel and the arsenal, and then, while a fete in his honor was being prepared at the theater he got into his carriage, left a note for the marshal which bordered on rudeness, and departed with even less ceremony than he had come.

When he reached Wesel he sent Voltaire a burlesque account in which he made a little fun of himself, a lot of the governor, and even more of France and the French.

This gallant race is brusque and mad,
Proud in the best of fortune, servile under bad. . . .
Of the great Caesars' times your Louis' are but shadows,
Paris must yield to Rome in each point and in all.
No, Frenchmen are vile, you are not one of those, (*sic*)
You think, they never think at all.

Voltaire found no fault with these fine verses, for he did not realize that by putting up with them at all he gave them his approval. He was full of hopes of receiving the King at Brussels, where he had promised to come, and was waiting there himself.

My heart tells me I am near
To a happy, happy hour—
From the lips I am to hear
Of Apollo, crowned with power,
Shafts wise Roma would have scanned
With amazement heretofore.
I shall hear, shall see the man
Whom as writer I adore.

But Frederick was laid low by fever and could not stand the fatigue of the journey, so it was Voltaire who had to bestir himself. Madame du Châtelet would have liked to come with him, but Frederick discouraged her, because, or so he said, he could not bear the brilliance of their two divinities at the same time.

The interview took place on September 12 at the castle of Meuse near Cleve. In the courtyard Voltaire met with Councilor Rambonnet who was blowing on his fingers to warm them. He had dirty cuffs and a wig longer on one side than on the other; he was going at the head of twelve companies of men to summon the Bishop of Liége to permit the King his master to collect some dues, which had been contested for the last eight years, from the barony of Herstal. Voltaire zealously supported the expedition in a propaganda article which appeared in the gazettes. He found the King shivering on a pallet bed and huddled in a wretched covering which did not warm him. They supped together, talked of the immortality of the soul, of liberty, and of Plato's androgynes. After a huge expenditure of words they parted well pleased with each other. Voltaire had found Frederick full of gentleness, charm, and politeness, and Frederick was enthusiastic: "I have met this Voltaire whom I was so curious to meet, but I met him when I was in the grip of a quartan fever, and my mind was as relaxed as my body was enfeebled. With people of his sort one ought not to be ill, one ought to be very well and even in better health than usual if possible. He has the eloquence of Cicero, the gentleness of Pliny, and the wisdom of Agrippa. . . . His mind works without ceasing, every drop of ink is a flash of wit leaping from his pen. He recited to us *Mahomet I,* an excellent tragedy he has written, he made us quite beside ourselves with rapture, and I could only admire him and be silent."

Next day the little company broke up. Frederick returned to Berlin with Algarotti, Keyserlingk, and Maupertuis, who arrived from France. Knobelsdorff proceeded on his journey to Paris and Voltaire went back to Brussels and The Hague, where the *Anti-Machiavel* demanded his attention. For the *Anti-Machiavel,* polished, repolished, and prefaced, had been sold to Van Duren the publisher, who was busily printing it with an affectation of mystery calculated to give the author away and to produce a profitable exposure. In vain did Voltaire swear to Frederick that he was going to surpass the reputation and wisdom of Marcus Aurelius in one bound, for the modern Marcus Aurelius was nervous. He was asking himself whether he had not acted imprudently and he dreaded the effects of his mischievous remarks. Once already he had commanded Voltaire to do his very utmost to buy back the work, and in July he had sent off fat old Camas with a minimum list of the passages which it was indispensably necessary to cut out. Van Duren, however, refused to give up the manuscript. After much scheming and wrangling Voltaire resigned himself to the preparation of a mild expurgated edition, while he denounced the first one as a wretched forgery. Specimens of the new edition were sent off to Berlin in the middle of October. "All will admire you, even Enthusiasts," he wrote triumphantly. "My dear and venerated monarch . . . must surely please everyone." However, he also declared that the mine had exploded and that he ought "to step boldly into the breach."

The news does not seem to have worried Frederick. The letter in which he told Algarotti that he had been unmasked contained these glorious words, "I have no course open to me except bottomless depths of effrontery." Without losing a moment he in his turn repudiated both the Dutch editions. This was a very poor reward for his friend's assiduous efforts. He excused himself lightly enough: "I ask your pardon, but I could not do otherwise, for there is so much foreign matter in your edition that it is no longer my work . . . I beg of you not to advertise me too much, for it gives me no pleasure, and besides you know that when I sent you the manuscript I extracted a promise of inviolable secrecy."

Decidedly things were going badly. From his lodgings in the Prussian Embassy at The Hague Voltaire pompously headed his letters "At the Palace of the King of Prussia"—a beautiful heading when writing to Cideville, Helvetius, or Moussinot—but the palace of the King of Prussia was only a dirty old edifice left over from the Orange inheritance, where the rats outnumbered the pieces of furniture. And then the philosopher was on edge with all this waiting for an invitation which never arrived. The uncertainty of it was making him ridiculous. His rivals, Maupertuis the Pedant and Algarotti the Trifler, were already installed in the master's favor at Berlin. He knew that for years Frederick had got hold of all the attacks on Voltaire which were published in Paris. While he was Crown Prince Frederick had even had a tiff on this point with Madame du Châtelet, who reproached him because of his curiosity. What was happening in far-off Brandenburg? In a letter to Maupertuis Voltaire let his anxiety become apparent: "When we both left Cleve and you went to the right and I to the left, I felt I was at the Last Judgment where God separates the chosen from the damned. The Divine Frederick said to you 'Sit on my right hand in the Heaven of Berlin,' and to me, 'Go, thou sinner, to Holland.' Therefore I am in this phlegmatic hell far from the divine fire which inspires the Fredericks, Maupertuis, and Algarottis. In God's name of your charity send me some sparks of it to these stagnant waters where I am cooling my heels!" The invitation arrived at last and with it an ode to friendship and a thousand tender compliments. The reply was sent off at once:

> My heart, my features lean and spare
> Their trip are ready to begin;
> Already heart is at Berlin
> And never to return, I swear.

When he had had the news of his approaching departure blazoned all over Paris Voltaire at last left The Hague on November 7 in the company of that very learned man Dumolard, who was going on his recommendation to teach oriental languages in Prussia. The roads were deep in mud and slippery with snow. In Westphalia their coach broke down. While Dumolard was asking for the mail coach in Syriac and Hebrew, Voltaire bestrode a nag, and thus in velvet knee breeches, silk stockings, and pumps, perched on a stubborn beast, he crossed the forest of Teutoburg where Arminius had destroyed the legions of the Emperor Augustus seventeen hundred years before. He arrived at Berlin on the nineteenth and left at once for Rheinsberg where the King and his friends awaited him.

For a court of such recent formation Voltaire's visit was a formidable test. What bursts of sarcasm and disdain might not these rustic beauties and these provincial wits arouse in a man who had lived since the moment he left college in the very best society and had made powers tremble with his pen? Frederick had chosen Rheinsberg as a setting so as to be seen to advantage there, and he had picked the company with care. They had balls, concerts, suppers, walks, and recitations. Everyone strove to shine, and the King wrote a few days later at the very peak of delight, "Voltaire has arrived all asparkle with new charms and with a sociability he did not show at Cleve. He is in the best of tempers and makes less fuss about his ailments than usual. Nothing could be more frivolous than the way we occupy ourselves. We distill odes, we slash verses to shreds, we anatomize ideas, and yet do it all with scrupulous love for our neighbors. What else do we do? We dance till we are breathless, we eat till we are bursting, we lose our money at cards, we titillate our ears with the softest of melodies which incite us to love and bring forth further titillations. . . ."

Voltaire remained at Rheinsberg for a week. On the twenty-eighth he dined in Berlin at the Queen Mother's, and everyone hurried out to Monbijou to see the celebrity. On December 2 he pleaded that Madame du Châtelet's health was bad and started on his return journey, leaving the King a farewell note:

> Your virtues and your charms are all in vain,
> My soul is not content as yet,

No, you are only a coquette,
You conquer hearts, yet frigid you remain.

Frederick replied at once using the same rhymes:

Your godlike charms my heart would price—'tis vain;
Yet do not think I am contented yet.
You leave me, traitor, after a coquette.
But true to you shall I remain.

In spite of this delicate back scratching, which truth to tell was incongruous enough between a King of twenty-eight and a philosopher of forty-six years of age, thenceforth there was less confidence and less frankness between the two of them. Voltaire had dazzled and disillusioned at the same time. They had seen his ugliness and his grimaces, and his incessant jibes at religion, France, and Cardinal Fleury had scandalized good-natured folk. He had crossed out the King's verses recklessly and, in the old tower of Rheinsberg beneath the cupids on the ceiling, they had given an acid performance of the age-old comedy of the vain author and the tactless critic. Finally Voltaire had put in a claim for his expenses: a dreadful blunder, for he was rich enough to stand the expense of the journey himself, and it would have been more dignified on his part if he had not presented an invoice damaging to his prestige. On the other hand, in the last four years Frederick had sent him so many bad poems to patch up and had extracted from him so much profit and so many valuable lessons, that he had no excuse for not paying up and keeping his thoughts to himself. Unfortunately he was the son of Frederick William, so he paid but with loud groans: "Your miser," he wrote to Jordan, "will drink the very dregs in his insatiable desire to get rich. He will have 1,300 crowns. His passing visit of a week will cost me 550 livres per diem. It's a fine price to pay for a madman; never did a great lord's jester get such a good wage." Also in another letter to Jordan he wrote, "The poet's head is as light as the style of his works, and I flatter myself that the attractions of Berlin will be powerful enough to make him return there quite soon; all the more so since the marquise's purse is not always so well filled as mine."

Something more than the resentment of a plundered miser peeps out through these sentences. A kind of light-heartedness seems to permeate them, as though Frederick took pleasure in debasing the man whom he had feted, proclaimed as a genius, and desired as a guest because in the eyes of the world his presence was an honor and an ornament. No, the peaceful years at Rheinsberg had not cured his heart of the despair which had been instilled into it during his adolescence. He had suffered too much, had humbled himself too deeply, had seen too much of the seamy side of life to believe that men existed who were not calculating or cunning. Life was opening out before him and he was getting ready to extract every drop of its joy and glory from it, but deep within him lurked a ghastly compulsion like a painful, secret wound—he had to humiliate those who loved him.

II

THE occupation of Liége had surprised the chancelleries of Europe, for they did not expect so young a prince to make such a swift and brutal debut. The bishop was a member of the Empire as was the Elector of Brandenburg: the proper procedure was to leave the decision of the dispute in the hands of the imperial justice. However, by proclaiming that it was "a matter between one prince and another" Frederick had in fact grasped at a chance to show how little respect he felt for His Majesty of Vienna and for the constitution of the Germanic body. Besides this, at his death Frederick William had left his son a preliminary agreement with France (Treaty of The Hague, April 5, 1739), which regulated the succession of Berg. With the support of Louis XV the King of Prussia was to receive the full possession of the largest and best part of the duchy, in exchange for which he was to pay the Palatine of Sulzbach an indemnity of a million crowns and leave him Düsseldorf and the southern bailiwicks. The whole of this exchange was not to Frederick William's liking. In particular, France had made contrary arrangements with Austria two months earlier. Frederick William might well ask himself whether the latest promise annulled the earlier ones, but for him the essential thing was to set foot on the contested territories, because as he said, "Such queer things happen in this world that after twenty, thirty, or forty years Düsseldorf, Agger, and the outskirts may return to my House in the end."

Since his accession Frederick had thought of pressing home the advantages already obtained. Spain and Great Britain had been at war ever since 1739 over the question of contraband in the south seas. Although the ministers Walpole and Fleury were both of them sincerely desirous of peace, Frederick was able to guess that they would both be carried away by the course of events, that France could not remain detached from the conflict, and that by force of circumstance continental rivalries would group themselves around the Anglo-French rivalry. Thus his plan was fixed: it was promptly to maneuver between Louis XV and George II and take up an intermediate position between the two rival sides, which would make his friendship the more precious and would allow him to offer it direct to the highest bidder.

Custom demanded that the new King of Prussia should inform friendly courts of his accession by sending them ambassadors extraordinary. To George II, who was staying in Hanover, he sent a diplomat of the old school, Count Truchsess. To compliment Louis XV he chose one of his own set, Colonel de Camas, the son of a refugee. As Versailles expressed astonishment at seeing a person of so small account accredited to so great a king, Frederick replied that Camas had one arm, whereas the French envoy, the Marquis de Valori, had lost three fingers as a result of a wound: "The King of France has sent me an ambassador who has only one hand, I am paying my debt to him by sending him a man with only one arm."

As a matter of fact Truchsess was told to put it to London that Camas' appointment was the sign of a confidential mission, in the face of which England would do well to hurry if she wished to counteract it. For his part Camas was to hint at Versailles that he had been an intimate of the young King for some time past, that he had plumbed his ambitious schemes, and that the interest of France demanded that she should support them with all speed.

"You will attribute great importance to the sending of Camas to France," the instructions of Truchsess laid down; "you will say with an air of jealousy that he is one of my intimate friends, that he has my confidence and that he has not gone to France to spend his time there stringing pearls. If they wish to talk business with you, always say that you do not despair of success provided they make you a better offer than the ones the French are making me. . . . Try to get some idea of their secret intentions, talk at length about the leanings I have in their direction, make no positive propositions, make them hope for the best and fear for the worst."

"I am sending Truchsess to Hanover," said the instruction to Camas. "You will speak of him as of a man whom I respect deeply and who has my private ear, so that they will have to make better offers to me than to the late King my father to prevent me from escaping from their hands. . . . The increases which will take place in my army during your stay at Versailles will furnish you with the opportunity to speak of my way of thought as lively and impetuous; you can say that it is to be feared that these increases may start a fire which will set all Europe ablaze, that it is characteristic of young people to be adventurous, and that in this world ideas of heroism are disturbing and have disturbed the peace of an infinite number of people. You can say that I am by nature a lover of France, but that if I am to be neglected at this moment it may produce a lasting and irremediable break, but that if on the other hand I am won over I shall be in a condition to do the French monarchy a greater service than Gustavus Adolphus ever did. You will display unlimited amiability and civility to the Cardinal, you will repay honeyed words with honeyed words and bargaining with hard bargaining. . . . To the full extent of your powers arouse the envy they feel against England. . . ."

This was Machiavellianism of a very artless type, and in any case the plan was too perfect to achieve instant success. George II hated Prussia because she was the main power in northern Germany and she eclipsed his Electorate of Hanover. It would have needed much more than the threat of a Franco-Prussian alliance to make him work for the aggrandizement of the neighbor who was his rival. To all the insinuations of Truchsess the English ministers replied with vague friendly protestations, without showing the least desire to talk business. As for Fleury, he had governed France for a quarter of a century. He was too adept at tricks and stratagems to allow himself to be taken in by a novice. He was quite determined to keep the position of arbiter on the Continent, a position which all Europe acknowledged, and he did not want lightly to bind himself to strict undertakings which would cut away all hope of a lasting agreement with the Empire. To spur him on Frederick had him told that in Hanover "every effort imaginable" was being made "to attract him with brilliant promises," but all in vain, for Fleury was not to be caught like that. At the end of August the negotiations had not got one single step further forward. Camas hurried to Wesel to take the King's orders on his way, and set out again with the simple mission of "cajoling" His Eminence to extract from him, as better than nothing, a promise that France would carry out the Treaty of 1739 in good faith.

It was a check, but Frederick accepted it without the least show of ill-humor, with the serenity and composure of a true diplomat. By giving the appearance of a display of youthful spontaneity, he succeeded at one and the same time in hiding his disappointment, which was very great, and in leaving his hands quite free for the future. "The interests of France and my own interests are identical," he wrote to Fleury. "Everything seems to unite us; a little more good will on the part of the King of France would tighten these bonds forever. I am convinced that this will come about, especially since you will be unable to find an ally more firm and resolute than I am." This self-control is surprising, but truth to tell while Europe still hesitated to admit that something new had appeared at Berlin, Frederick was getting a more precise notion of the strength of Prussia every day, and he could assure himself that sooner or later his father's army would weight the scales heavily in his favor. That was why the partition of Berg held only a subordinate place among his ambitions. He had merely used it as a bait to start off negotiations, but he would gladly have put Düsseldorf and the Palatinate out of his mind in favor of another matter which he called "the great succession"; it was to be unexpectedly set in motion by the death of Emperor Charles VI on October 20, 1740.

III

THE Emperor was fifty-five years old and for several years past he had been a prey to deep melancholy, but no one expected his death to occur so swiftly. A chill caught while hunting and indigestion caused by a plate of mushrooms reduced him to such a desperate state in two days that he scarcely lived long enough to bless his daughter and to commend his soul and his dominions to God.

The news reached Rheinsberg on the twenty-sixth. Frederick was in bed with an attack of fever and his officers hesitated to disturb him. One of them, however, decided to enter his room. The King took the message from his hand, read it to the end without a word, and then sent by express for his minister, Otto von Podewils, and for Marshal von Schwerin, who were in Berlin. While awaiting them he wrote to Voltaire: "This death upsets all my peaceful notions and I believe it will be more a matter of powder and shot, soldiers and trenches than of actresses, ballets, and theaters. . . . This is the moment for a total reversal of the old political system. This is the stone seen by Nebuchadnezzar, which was cut out and rolled on the figure made of the four different metals and broke them all to pieces. . . . I am going to be cured of my fever, for I need my machine of a body and I must get all I can out of it."

The Emperor left as his heiress a princess twenty-three years of age, the Archduchess Maria Theresa, the wife of Francis of Lorraine, Grand Duke of Tuscany. The House of Austria has received much praise for having acquired its numerous territories not by force of arms but by the much more pacific method of princely alliances and marriage ties. This is an obvious exaggeration, for to keep Bohemia and Hungary the Hapsburgs had had to fight a number of wars, and little by little there had grown up among all the peoples of the middle valley of the Danube a vague consciousness of their own natural solidarity, which was imposed on them at once by geographical factors and by the constant threat of Turkish invasion. None the less nearly all the provinces united under the scepter of the family of Hapsburg were burdened with entails and devises which ran through almost every diversity and complication of that side of German jurisprudence which dealt with inheritance. Thus the opening of litigious claims was always a thing to be feared, and that was why Charles VI had tried to assure the perpetuity of his inheritance in his own lifetime at the request of the States of Croatia. In 1713, four years before the birth of Maria Theresa, he had issued the Pragmatic Sanction with all due solemnity; it proclaimed the indivisibility of the Austrian states and declared that, in default of heirs male, women were qualified to reign. He had afterward spent a large part of his reign in getting the Pragmatic Sanction accepted by all the interested parties, beginning with his relations and ending with the Great Powers. In exchange for concessions which were sometimes very heavy, Spain, Russia, Prussia, Holland, England, the Diet of the Empire, Denmark, and France had one after the other given their support. But the Emperor had been weakened by his recent defeats in Serbia and he had no further money, credit, or army left. "It is," said Frederick, "the old ghost of an idol which once had power and was mighty but which is of no account today. He used to be a strong man, but the French and the Turks have given him the pox and nowadays he is feeble."

On October 28 Frederick took counsel at Rheinsberg with Schwerin and Podewils. He explained to them his intention of taking advantage of the weakness and confusion of Austria to seize upon Silesia, a rich and populous province contiguous to Brandenburg, which would become part of the main body of the Prussian possessions once it was conquered. His troops could cross the frontier by surprise and capture the towns before Maria Theresa would even have time to collect an army. After that would come negotiations. This was the very method he had once recommended to Grumbkow for Jülich and Berg.

Schwerin and Podewils objected that it was dangerous to act in isolation and it might lead to great difficulties and great disasters. They declared it preferable to bargain with the Court of Vienna for a treaty and a subsidiary alliance to be paid, in fact, by the cession of Silesia. Maria Theresa would be threatened on all sides and would be glad to pay with a single province for military support which would preserve her states from complete destruction. If she was intractable Prussia would then join up with the Electors of Saxony and Bavaria, with Sardinia and Spain, who were going to try to establish rights anterior to the Pragmatic Sanction, probably with French assistance.

Nothing appears to have been decided on that day or on the ones that followed. Podewils and Schwerin did not succeed in convincing the King, but as there was no hurry he allowed himself time for further thought. The note he wrote to Podewils on

November 1 was drawn up in the form of a question but in terms which made the answer a foregone conclusion: "I give you a problem to solve. When a man is in a strong position, is he to take advantage of it or not? I am ready, troops and all. If I do not take advantage of it, I hold in my hands a force which I do not know how to use; if I do take advantage of it, it will be said that I have the wit to make use of the superiority which I have over my neighbors."

Three days later he was sending on some Austrian news to the minister, so he returned to the attack: "They do nothing but rejoice at Vienna, they are confident that they can preserve their hereditary estates, they already imagine the duke is emperor— vanity, folly, absurd illusion, we will make a tiny change in it all, but this little snippet of news will make you see that I was not wrong in judging that we would have been potting our own ball if we had tried to negotiate with Vienna."

Finally on the sixth Frederick heard that the Elector of Bavaria had already declared against the Pragmatic Sanction; thereupon he drew up his arguments in writing and asked Podewils to present him once again with his final "objections." Podewils merely raised a few purely formal difficulties in a mild way, and as he knew the decision was irrevocable he only claimed for himself the glory of obedience. Most delicate of all was the task of finding some legal pretext for the invasion. An old professor of Halle had of his own accord sent the King a memorandum on the rights of the House of Brandenburg relative to the Silesian duchies, but these rights had been annulled by subsequent renunciations (though they were more or less forced ones, truth to tell), and Podewils did not know how to put a good face on such feeble arguments.

"The formal claim," replied Frederick, "is a question for ministers; it is your affair and it is time you worked at it in secret, for the troops have been given their orders." So Podewils set to work, and when the declaration was ready Frederick accepted it with these words, "Bravo! That is the work of a good charlatan."

The enterprise could only succeed if the secret of it was well kept. Frederick therefore recognized Maria Theresa as Queen, ordered his Court to wear mourning, and had everything possible done to mislead the diplomats, who were getting anxious at the military preparations. The French ambassador, Valori, was kept outside the portals of Rheinsberg, and Manteuffel, who had extensive correspondence with Saxony, was politely asked to leave Berlin. The language of the Prussian envoys in the various capitals was reticent and contradictory, for it varied according to the place and the questioner. In one place it was thought that Frederick was going to take advantage of the turmoil by seizing Berg; elsewhere it was considered certain that he would stand as a candidate for the imperial crown. Some people even thought that he had come to an agreement with Maria Theresa at the expense of Saxony and Bavaria. During his visit Voltaire had been not a whit more clever or discerning. Before leaving for Rheinsberg he had offered Fleury a copy of the *Anti-Machiavel*. The Cardinal had understood the purpose of the invitation and had grasped at the chance of having his advice passed on to Frederick. "Whoever is the author of this work," he had written to the philosopher, "if he is not a prince, deserves to be one. The little I have read of it is so wise, so reasonable, and contains such admirable principles that *the man who wrote it would be worthy of controlling men, provided that he had the courage to put them into practice. If he is born a prince he has engaged himself to a very solemn contract with the public.*" Voltaire, for his part, guessed for whose use the sermon was intended. "I have obeyed," he replied, "the orders which Your Eminence never gave me. I have shown your letter to the King of Prussia." But he got no reply.

Guy Dickens, the English representative, made use of his position as family ambassador to gain access to the King and asked him point-blank if he intended to respect the Pragmatic Sanction and support the indivisibility of the Austrian estates. Frederick flushed: "I understand," he replied, "that you have no instruction at all to authorize you to ask me this question, and even if you have received any such order I have only one reply to make to you: England has no right to ask me the nature of my plans. I made no inquiries about her naval armaments, I limit myself to praying that you may not be defeated by the Spaniards."

Then, as the English agent asserted his good intentions, the King replied: "I have nothing in view but the general good. I have examined my plans with care, I have weighed the drawbacks and the advantages which might ensue for me and for the public against each other, and I have come to the conclusion that I could do nothing better than execute my schemes with vigor. . . . Austria as a power is needed for fighting against the Turks, but she should not have such strength in Germany that three electorates cannot keep her at bay. I well know that you are like France and would be glad to keep all the princes under your thumb, but I do not intend to be guided by either of you two powers, and as for you English, you are like the Athenians, who wasted their time making speeches when Philip of Macedon was ready to attack them."

In Vienna no one suspected anything. Maria Theresa was a woman of courageous and noble character and she had no doubts either of her rights or of herself, but she was very far from thinking that the first blows would come from Prussia. All the same, toward the middle of November her councilors began to be alarmed by the movements of troops and the purchases of horses which were taking place in the neighborhood of Silesia. Besides, Frederick's envoy at Vienna expressed opinions that were more and more disquieting. The House of Austria, said he, had too many enemies, she would not be able to survive unaided. She needed allies, but allies cost something and to save herself from worse evils it was as well to know when to sacrifice a gangrened limb. Maria Theresa became anxious and decided to send a new minister to Berlin, the Marquis de Botta d'Adorna, an old Italian full of experience. He did not need to be particularly observant during his journey to be convinced that Prussia was preparing for war. He arrived in a great state of emotion. An audience with the King did not reassure him. To turn the conversation toward the subject of armaments, he told Frederick that he had found the roads of Silesia broken up and cut by trenches. "I don't see that it matters," replied Frederick, "except that it makes travelers arrive a little muddy." Finally he informed the marquis that he was sending the Count von Gotter to Vienna with important proposals.

Gotter arrived at Vienna on December 17 and had an audience on the twentieth. "I bring," he said to Duke Francis, "the salvation of the House of Austria in one hand and in the other the imperial crown for Your Highness. The treasures of the King my master are at the service of the Queen. . . . In return for such offers and as a compensation for the dangers he runs thereby, he asks for the whole of Silesia but for nothing less."

The grand duke replied that the Queen had not the right to cede even the smallest piece of an inheritance which she had received only on condition she kept it indivisible. He then asked Gotter if Prussian troops had already entered Silesia. "They should be there by now," replied the envoy.

"Then go back to the King your master and tell him that as long as he leaves one man on the soil of this province we will die rather than treat with him."

At Berlin a similar scene had been enacted between Frederick and Botta. The Italian had lost patience and in the end had changed his tone completely: "Your troops look fine, Sire, but ours have smelled powder." And Frederick had replied, "If mine look fine, they are also excellent, as you are going to discover."

None the less many people considered the King's undertaking a piece of madness. The most common reactions among those around him were distrust and fear. To dispel anxiety he called together the officers of the Berlin garrison. "Sirs," he told them, "I am embarking on a war in which I have no other ally but your valor and no other resource but my own good fortune. Be mindful continually of the immortal glory which your ancestors gained for themselves on the plains of Warsaw and Fehrbellin, and never give the lie to the reputation of the soldiers of Brandenburg. Farewell! Go to keep your appointment with glory, for I will follow you without delay."

On December 14 there was a ball at the palace. Frederick was there in a domino without a mask. He chatted for a long time with the English envoy in a window recess. When it was time to break up he called for his aides-de-camp. "Tighten your girths, we are off."

The bells were ringing along his route. At Crossen a beam broke and the bell tower collapsed. Frederick reversed the omen by saying, "Thus will the mighty be brought low."

On the sixteenth at eight o'clock in the morning, with banners flying and drums beating, he pushed over the frontiers of Silesia. "I have crossed the Rubicon," he wrote to Podewils. "My troops are full of eagerness, my officers full of ambition, and my generals thirsting for glory. All goes as we wish. . . . I feel in my heart that every good fortune lies before me. . . . I will not appear in Berlin without having made myself worthy of the blood from which I spring and of the brave soldiers I have the honor to command."

VII

The Two Wars of Silesia

I

FROM his father Frederick received the prerequisites of activity and power—a full treasury, orderly finances, an industrious bureaucracy, a people used to obedience, and, above all, one of the best and largest armies in Europe.

The strength of the Prussian Army had been continually on the increase. From 45,000 men in 1713 it had been enlarged to 54,000 in 1719, to 70,000 in 1729, and to 83,000 in 1739, an enormously disproportionate figure as compared with those of France and Austria, whose populations were nearly ten times greater but produced only 160,000 and under 100,000 soldiers respectively. The Prussian Army was composed of natives and foreigners mixed in varying proportions, with a fixed minimum of one third natives. Foreigners were drawn in by the bait of a bounty on joining, and the certainty of high pay and good food: they were kept there by implacable discipline and the fear of terrible punishments. Eight hundred or a thousand recruiting sergeants scoured Europe for the King's service. The majority were unscrupulous in the means they employed; their violence was notorious; indeed one year the Dutch arrested and shot a Prussian sergeant whose excesses had made a marked man of him.

However, such proceedings were in current use at that time, and the great innovation of Frederick William's reign was that he compelled his people to submit to the principle of compulsory military service. "All subjects," said the regulation of 1733, "are born to arms and attached to the regiment of the district in which they are born." To this end the kingdom was divided into a certain number of cantons, at one canton per regiment: 5,000 muskets formed a regiment of infantry, 1,800 horse a regiment of cavalry. When a male child was born the minister who baptized him reported it to the local authority, and he was at once inscribed on the army list. At the time of his first communion he took the oath. From then on he wore a red ribbon on his collar as a distinctive emblem and he was forbidden to leave the country. From the age of eighteen till he was forty he remained at the disposal of the army. At the end of winter before the time for reviews the colonels sent officers to visit their cantons to take the men they needed. However, the recruits were only kept with their regiments for a few months of the year and returned to their villages for the rest of the time. Exemption was allowed for only sons, sons of widows, theological students, privileged settlers, master craftsmen, peasants who had large families or who cultivated isolated farms. . . . Each colonel had the right to thirty recruits yearly in times of peace and to a hundred in times of war. The regimental losses in foreigners had to be filled by recruiting foreigners. The roll of officers was formed by the local nobility. Frederick William would have liked to have reserved the higher ranks for Prussians. He did not succeed because of the lack of suitable persons among his subjects, but at least he managed to persuade each of the noble families to give one of their sons to the army. These young men were put into cadet companies between the ages of twelve and eighteen and later were drafted into their regiments. Thus it was that the aristocracy of the kingdom gradually turned into a military aristocracy; the Junkers who had once been so turbulent were transformed into officers devoted body and soul to the dynasty.

The best section was the infantry, which the Prince of Anhalt-Dessau had organized with especial care. "He built up the battalions in a new way," wrote Frederick; "he instilled them with that order, discipline, and astonishing precision which made these troops like the works of a watch, the wheels of which by artful gearing produce an exact and regular movement." The Prussian infantry surpassed others by its rapidity of fire. Each battalion was like "a walking battery."

The force which was to occupy Silesia was made up of 22,000 men, 13,000 horse, and 34 pieces of artillery. A siege train followed a little to the rear. Frederick himself was in command. When the Prince of Anhalt showed surprise at not being one of the party, the King replied that he respected his qualities as a young officer should respect the glory of an old hero who had

LEOPOLD PRINCE D'ANHALT
DESSAU

MARIE THERESE
Reine de Hongrie &c.
Née le 13 May 1717.

given many proofs of his "dexterity," but that the Silesian affair was a trifle and unworthy of a great captain's attention—a mere occupation of territory. Furthermore, he added, "I reserve this expedition for myself alone, so that the world shall not think that the King of Prussia goes to war along with his tutor." Frederick was acquainted only with the subordinate sides of the art of war, with details of service and organization. It was true that he had been under fire in 1734, studied the campaigns of Prince Eugene and of Turenne, gone on journeys to inspect the battlefields of Pomerania, and given thought to the theoretical works of Folard and Feuquières, but he had no real experience nor any well-considered opinions. Therefore he had thought it wise to take with him Marshal Kurt Christopher von Schwerin, who did not possess any of the humiliating superiority of old Dessau, having only just been granted a marshal's baton by Frederick himself. Schwerin was one of those wandering officers whom the wars of Louis XIV had thrown onto the world at the mercy of chance. He was born the son of a Swedish colonel in Pomerania and orphaned at the age of twelve; he had been brought up by his uncle who was colonel of a regiment of Mecklenburgers employed by Holland. As ensign and officer in that regiment he had served under Marlborough in the Flanders campaigns and had then been sent on a mission to Charles XII, who was a refugee in Turkey. In 1720 he had entered the Prussian Army as a general. He had been a member of the court-martial which judged Katte and had been in favor of imprisonment for life; besides this he had been a close acquaintance of Frederick's well before his accession, for the Prince loved to hear him tell his adventures.

Silesia was almost completely denuded of troops. Drawing inspiration from a plan which dated from the time of his ancestor, the Great Elector, Frederick proceeded up the river Oder, while Schwerin occupied the country with a mobile force. The King was welcomed by the Protestants, who had suffered under the bickerings of Austrian bishops. On December 22 he invested Glogau and on the thirty-first he arrived before Breslau, the capital of the province. The town was a small republic and a vassal of Austria, which could not garrison it without the consent of the burghers. General Browne, who had been given command by Maria Theresa, asked the municipality for permission to bring in a few hundred men. He had just obtained a vote in accordance with his wishes when a riot led by a Brandenburger shoemaker called Döblin compelled the elders to revoke their consent. As soon as the Prussians appeared the townsfolk brought them beer, bread, and all sorts of victuals. On January 1, 1741, Frederick occupied the suburbs and on the third, after having signed a separate treaty with the magistrates, he made his entry into the town.

In spite of snow the streets were filled with an inquisitive crowd which was held back by the town militia drawn up in line. Count Henckel von Donnersmarck, the Grand Cupbearer, led the procession. Next came the luggage and the silver on mules in blue velvet harness with cattle bells on their collars. Behind them came thirty policemen in straw-colored uniforms, then the royal carriage, with its hood down, containing only the King's state robe in blue velvet lined with ermine; finally, after an interval and announced by four equerries, came the King himself richly clad in a uniform embroidered with gold, and after him a long cavalcade of generals and pages all dressed in scarlet. He invited all the local men of note to dinner, calmed the fears of the Catholics on the subject of religious liberty, showed much respect for the archbishop and the clergy, and paid all sorts of compliments to the nobility and the leading burghers. He behaved mildly, affably, modestly, gave the Protestant ministers flattering hopes and made them preach on a text he had chosen himself: "We have neither taken other men's land, nor holden that which appertaineth to others, but the inheritance of our fathers, which our enemies had wrongfully in possession a certain time." (1 Maccabees xv. 33.) Döblin was given 2,000 gold thalers for his good services. On January 25 Frederick left Schwerin to complete the conquest of Silesia and came home. Only three places still held out, Glogau, Brieg, and Neisse.

Frederick returned to Berlin in triumph: all his plans had succeeded. However, he had reckoned that Anglo-French rivalry would assure him of the alliance of one or other of the two powers very shortly. Yet in spite of his victorious march neither of them had come to a decision, and the longer the uncertainty continued the more the prudent Podewils begged him to treat with Maria Theresa, so as to make sure of the profits of the ad-

venture as soon as possible. For some weeks Frederick was therefore compelled to play a very fine and complicated game, sometimes with the aim of concluding the affair to his advantage and
sometimes of pursuing it with increased forces. To get a quick
peace he would have been content with Lower Silesia excluding
Breslau, and he would even have indemnified the Queen by lending her two million thalers without security. But Maria Theresa
was inflexible: nothing could shake her determination, nothing
could make her bend to something she considered a piece of
cowardice and a dishonor.

At Versailles, on the other hand, Frederick found the ground
prepared for him by the clamorous endeavors of the war party.
He knew that the Cardinal detested the idea of declaring himself
against the House of Austria, because in his opinion she had
ceased to be formidable from the French point of view on the
day when a grandson of Louis XIV was enthroned at Madrid.
But he also knew that many people, urged on by Belle-Isle, accused the old minister of betraying the most sacred traditions of
the monarchy, and that they were loudly pressing him to complete the work of Richelieu by crushing the hereditary enemy
forever. Moreover, the Pragmatic Sanction only guaranteed the
succession of the Hapsburg lands to the Queen of Hungary and
did not mention the imperial crown. On this point France had
freedom of action. The anti-Austrian feeling became so strong
that it was Versailles which started scrounging round the Empire
for allies against Maria Theresa, and Frederick was thus transformed from client into patron. He was quick to exploit the advantage that France had given him and he made it plain to Valori,
the ambassador, that since his first overtures events had moved
forward and that a defensive pact would no longer meet his re-
quirements.

"What advantage would that be to me?" he asked after reading
a draft of it. "I do not see what help the King your master would
give me in the event of my being attacked by the powers which
surround me and make ready, when France is so much as mentioned, not only to go for her but also for her allies. . . . Would
the King enable the Elector of Bavaria to uphold his claims otherwise than in writing? If the Elector of Cologne and the Elector
Palatine are attacked by Hanover, would he give them a force of

30,000 men to resist her? And what diversion does the King desire
to make? Would he favor the designs of Spain [in Italy] to the
extent of sending troops there? Unless all these measures are
properly undertaken and expressly calculated, should I not seek
to turn to the other side and try to feather my own nest? Would
the King guarantee me in the possession of Lower Silesia including Breslau?"

After three or four interviews of this type Valori knew neither
what to think nor what to say. "The King of Prussia," he wrote
gloomily to a minister called Amelot, "does not reply as he ought.
. . . He opens negotiations on all sides and thinks to work mar-
vels by never bringing them to a conclusion. . . . As I speak
quite openly with you, sir, I am not afraid to tell you that levity,
presumption, and pride are the ruling traits of his character, and
you may well feel some pity for me since I have to steer through
all this."

To enforce his demands Frederick displayed a boldness which
terrified his ministers. In the last resort was he not running the
risk of being left with no allies at all? What would happen if he
was obliged to carry on the approaching campaign alone? By
dint of negotiating and protesting Maria Theresa had succeeded
in affecting English and Dutch opinion. The Catholic nobles of
Poland were disgusted to see a province of the faithful at their
very doors falling into the hands of a Protestant prince, and
powerful influences were brought to bear on the feeble Augustus
III to push him onto the side of Austria. Finally during the last
days of February a palace revolution threatened to make the
same feelings prevail in St. Petersburg. Would not the King be
taken in the rear and surrounded, without having concluded any
of the treaties over the signatures of which he had indulged in
such artificial bargaining? "Pandora's box is open," cried Podewils, "all evils are escaping from it at the same time." Frederick
did not allow the least anxiety to be apparent, but without delay
he increased the army of Silesia to 32,000 men and collected a
second body of 20,000 in the Mark under the command of the
Prince of Anhalt. On February 19 he set out for Silesia himself,
and on March 8 Glogau was taken.

This was only a prologue, and Frederick got ready for greater
events. He was calm and resolute, and his readings came back
into his mind. "There are no laurels for the idle," he wrote to

one of his ministers, "glory is given to the most industrious and
to the most fearless. . . . If I should have the misfortune to be
captured alive, I command you absolutely and you will answer
to me for it with your life, that in my absence you shall pay no
attention to my orders, that you shall act as advisers to my
brother, and that the State shall commit no unworthy action to
obtain my liberty. On the contrary, in that case I command that
it shall act more briskly than ever before. I am King only when
I am free. If I am killed I wish my body to be burned Roman
fashion and to be buried in the same way in an urn at Rheinsberg. In this event Knobelsdorff must make me a monument
like that of Horace at Tusculum."

The Prussian Army was spread out over a depth of a hundred
miles from Breslau to the headwaters of the Oder. The Austrian
Army was mobilized at last and concentrated under Neipperg
near Olmütz in Moravia. Neipperg set off in secret and entered
Silesia at its furthest end. On April 2 deserters warned Frederick
that the enemy was only sixteen miles away. The danger would
have been serious if Neipperg had marched directly against the
King so as to surprise him and beat him before he had had time
to assemble his forces. But the generals of those times were so
little eager to seek a decisive battle that they took care to avoid
all heavy risks and made the art of war consist of methodical re-
movals and of encircling movements: it was what is called the
war of posts or positions. One of the most celebrated military
writers of the century, General Lloyd, defined it in the following
terms: "The . . . most important object of any, to those who
aspire to the command of armies, is geography; not only that
which consists in a general knowledge of a country but a local
one: a man must be thoroughly acquainted with the face of the
country, and its productions. . . . The great and important
parts of war, as well in the formation, as in the execution, depend
on the knowledge of the country; and wise generals, will always
chuse to make them the foundation of their conduct, rather than
trust to the uncertain issue of battles. *If you possess these points,
you may reduce military operations to geometrical precision, and
may for ever make war without being obliged to fight.*" [1]

Neipperg's plan consisted of raising the sieges of Neisse and

---

1. From the Preface of *The History of the Late War in Germany,* by a General
Officer [H. H. E. Lloyd] (London, 1766). My italics.

Brieg by placing himself on the line of the Prussians' communications so that they would be compelled to retreat by the danger of being cut off from their supplies. For a week the two armies moved northward parallel to the Oder, Neipperg trying to get ahead of Frederick and Frederick keeping level while collecting the garrisons he had left behind him as he went along.

On April 9 Frederick could have escaped once again but for the exhaustion of his troops, who had been marching in snow and mud for eight days; this obliged him to stop for twenty-four hours and he had to resign himself to a battle. On the tenth toward midday he met with the Austrian Army in front of the village of Mollwitz: they were not expecting to fight and had not finished deploying. Even the artillery had not arrived. Neipperg had 18,000 men and Frederick 22,000, but the Austrian cavalry was greatly superior in numbers and in performance. On a sudden it was all flung upon the Prussian right, which was broken on two occasions. The second time it even succeeded in getting to the infantry, and the confusion was such that the foot soldiers of the second line began firing on those of the first and on their own horsemen, who were engaging those of the enemy. Toward four o'clock the day seemed lost. Frederick had taken the field in person and had come near to being captured. Schwerin felt that a rout was imminent and begged him to retire to a place of safety. After having sent word to Dessau to take every necessary measure to protect Brandenburg, he fled in the company of two aides-de-camp, a page, and his friend Rottenbourg. On the banks of the river Neisse he crossed the path of part of his army's baggage train; in his distress of mind he shouted to the men to save their own lives, and at once carters and camp followers scattered haphazard. At nightfall he was near Oppeln. Rottenbourg, who was a hundred yards ahead of him, dismounted, knocked at the gate, and asked the sentry to open to him. The reply was a gunshot. The Austrians were already in the town, and if the gates had not been shut Frederick would have been taken. The fugitives retraced their steps and decided to take advantage of the darkness to get to Breslau. On the way they halted exhausted at a house in Loewen and drank coffee which the page got for them. The aides-de-camp sat silent in a corner. Frederick paced up and down the room overburdened with grief at the retreat he imagined the army to be making. "My God!" he groaned, "it is too much, do not punish me too heavily."

At two in the morning a lieutenant arrived who had been sent by Schwerin in search of the fugitives. After the King's departure the marshal had re-formed the troops and forced the enemy to withdraw. The victory had been won by the Prussian infantry, whose rapid fire had broken all attacks (April 10, 1741).

At this news Frederick let fly a volley of oaths. Without a moment's delay he mounted his horse and rushed hell for leather to join the men he had abandoned at their moment of distress. In his *History of My Times* he makes no mention either of his flight or of the atrocious humiliation he underwent when he rejoined those who had conquered without his help and now looked at him in a way he must have found it hard to bear. Furthermore he judged himself with precision and severity: "My conduct was . . . culpable: I am warned of the plans of the enemy, and I take no steps to counter them; I put my troops in positions too far apart for a junction to be achieved; I allow myself to be cut off by the Duke of Holstein, and I let myself be forced to fight on a field where I have no means of retreat in case of mishap and run the risk of losing the whole of my army; on arriving near Mollwitz where the enemy was billeted, instead of marching briskly forward . . . I waste two hours forming up methodically in front of a village where no Austrian has yet appeared. If I had followed the first course all the Austrian infantry would have been captured. . . . But the only experienced officer in the army was Marshal Schwerin; the others groped along and thought all was lost if they departed an inch from tradition. What saved us, in spite of all this, was the promptitude of our decisions and the great exactitude with which the troops carried them out. Mollwitz was my school, I reflected deeply on my mistakes to my subsequent profit." (Draft of 1746.)

Frederick's genius was built up little by little through study and through an obstinate desire for improvement.

II

THE end of the campaign was not marked by any important events: after Brieg had surrendered the two armies spent the summer observing and harassing each other. Frederick took advantage of this by adding to his cavalry and hardening it in skirmishes. However, the interest of all Europe was concentrated on the conclusion of the Franco-Prussian alliance. Belle-Isle had traversed Germany to secure a coalition against Austria there and he came to Breslau in the hope of concluding the treaty. The King knew the marshal to be imperious and decided in his opinions. He arranged to entertain him with some days of banquets, reviews, and ceremonious delays but finally he had to receive him and give him his ear. Frederick was in his headquarters at Mollwitz. The snow and rain were appalling and every minute the tempest threatened to carry away the tent. Belle-Isle pressed him hard, but Frederick objected that a French alliance would saddle him with war against Saxony, Poland, Russia, and England before Louis XV could possibly send him effective help. Belle-Isle replied that the word of a King of Prussia was as good as his signature and that after so many promises he could not back out of it. Finally the alliance was concluded (June 3). The most important article laid down that within two months a French army of 40,000 men would cross the Rhine. Then from the glowing enthusiasm which seized hold of Frederick it seemed as though he had never desired anything else. "I now contend with you," he wrote to Fleury, "to be a better Frenchman than I am already."

This cordiality did not last very long. The alliance had the disturbing effect of strengthening French influence in Germany: it disquieted the Protestant princes, made the future Emperor a creature of Louis XV's, and revived the accusations of attempted domination lately leveled at Louis XIV. Frederick was alive to all this. On July 10 he again ordered Podewils to take up negotiations with Lord Hyndford (whom in a fit of Francophily he had called Lord Hind-part) and to "haggle" with him. Once his conquests were recognized he disliked the idea of bringing down the Hapsburgs to the advantage of the Bourbons and the other electors. Fleury for his part distrusted his ally: "Good faith and sincerity are not his favorite virtues," he wrote to Belle-Isle. "He is false in everything, even in his caresses. . . . All Europe detests him. . . . If he was offered some attractive bribe . . . he would have no scruples about thinking up a pretext for leaving our alliance." Indeed twelve days after the signing of it Frederick began to complain that everything was not yet under way —and he was still keeping some grievances in reserve.

None the less, the coalition ended by bestirring itself. From August 15 to 22 the French crossed the Rhine and advanced along the Danube with the Bavarian Army. On September 14 they occupied Linz, three days' march from Vienna, while Augustus III came out against Austria in return for a promise of Moravia and a narrow corridor in Bohemia—the first sections of a bridge thrown between the Duchy of Saxony and the Kingdom of Poland.

Frederick advised his allies to march resolutely on Vienna and to take it by surprise. However, the Franco-Bavarian Army was led by the Elector Charles Albert, an excellent, timorous man who did not dare to go far from his own territories. Belle-Isle claimed indeed to direct military and diplomatic operations simultaneously, but he had remained at Frankfort to arrange the imperial election and only imposed his will from afar, in the shape of a correspondence which did not always have much effect on what was occurring. Finally Belle-Isle and Charles Albert were both anxious to make use of their friendship with Frederick and with Augustus III in such a way as to lean on them and at the same time to prevent the King from giving his allies the slip. At the mercy of these contending forces the Elector wasted a week at Linz and then advanced with dispiriting sloth to Krems, fifteen leagues from the capital. He had taken 41 days to cover 125 miles. At the end of October he decided to branch off to the north to occupy Bohemia, the whole of which he wished to keep as a prize for himself.

However, the invasion had driven Maria Theresa to despair. She resigned herself to a provisional agreement on the conditions laid down by Prussia: near Neisse at the castle of Klein-Schnellendorf an armistice was secretly concluded between Frederick, Neipperg, and Lord Hyndford (October 9).

It was agreed that Neisse should capitulate after a pretense at resistance and that the Austrians should evacuate Silesia until the general peace. His Majesty the King of Prussia, said Article 5, "will take no further offensive action against Her Majesty the Queen of Hungary and Bohemia, nor against the King of England as Elector of Hanover, nor against any of the present allies of the Queen." Neipperg would be free to turn against the French; the definitive treaty would leave Prussia Lower Silesia up to the river Neisse; finally the secret was to be carefully kept and "on both sides small bodies would be active to continue the hostilities *pro forma*." Thus the intervention of France had the unforeseen consequence of freeing Austria from her main adversary and of allowing Prussia, who had begun the war, to leave it on her own and in her own time.

Frederick took a great deal of trouble to conceal his treachery. He enjoyed acting a farce, and must have got a particular pleasure out of this one, or else he would have spared himself many unnecessary lies: the way in which the siege of Neisse was conducted was enough, in fact, to enlighten the most incredulous. But he could not prevent himself from chaffing various individuals. On October 9, the very day on which the convention was signed, he wrote an affectionate letter to Belle-Isle which ended with these words: "To be arbiter among kings is reserved for Louis XV, to be the weapon of his power and wisdom is reserved for Monsieur de Belle-Isle." How he must have smiled to himself.

In reality Frederick's calculations were faulty. Just at first the French and Bavarians won one victory after another. Prague was taken on November 23 by Chevert and Maurice of Saxony; on January 24 Charles Albert was elected emperor under the title of Charles VII and crowned on February 12 at Frankfort. Frederick had to associate himself with this event by sending obsequious congratulations, but now that Maria Theresa was free of danger from Prussia she had ordered a mass levy of troops in Hungary and had aroused her subjects' patriotism. The Austrian counteroffensive began all along the Danube. Linz was recovered at the end of January, Bavaria was invaded and Munich occupied the very day Charles Albert assumed the crown of Bohemia at Prague. Frederick, who had increased his claims to keep pace with the successes of the allies, was forced to take up arms again when their defeats endangered his own acquisitions.

"An impartial observer," writes Reinhold Koser, "could not have the least doubt that the convention of Klein-Schnellendorf was not only liable to blemish the young King's reputation and policy in the eyes of his friends and enemies but also, since no necessity forced it upon him, was a hazardous action and a mistake. If the Austrians had succeeded in reaching Prague before their opponents, it is more than probable that the French, the Bavarians, and above all the Saxons would have abandoned the cause as a lost one. In that case would the convention of October 9 have acted as a guarantee for the King of Prussia? That convention of which Neipperg wrote immediately after the meeting that *it tied the Queen to nothing at all if the final treaty were not concluded before the end of December?* In short, from whatever point of view the convention is examined it always appears flimsy and hazardous. Weakly planned also were the expedients and the strokes by which the allies were to be deceived. And, all things considered, the profit from this double game was meager enough—undisturbed winter quarters and the surrender of a single fortress, which moreover would not have been able to hold out for long. Hyndford's remark, which is elsewhere inapplicable, can be applied to the armistice of Klein-Schnellendorff: he said that the king preferred an immediate gain, though infinitesimally small, to advantages of the greatest importance and weight in the future. An agreement patched up in a hurry for purely opportunist motives changed the course of history, and Austria was saved. The selfsame Frederick who had thrust that proud and ancient power to the edge of the abyss became its protector and its savior by merely staying his hand. The English, suckled as they were on the classics, recalled the lance of Achilles which wounded and cured at the same time. How many times in the years to come did Frederick implore Destiny to give him the opportunity to inflict a decisive defeat on his mortal foe? Never again was he to find a chance like that which he let slip in the autumn of 1741 by allowing Neipperg's army, the only one that Austria possessed, to retire intact without battle and without pursuit. Thenceforth his destiny was restricted."

III

WHEN he reopened hostilities in the middle of January, 1742, Frederick counted on rapidly pushing a wedge into Moravia and threatening Vienna from the northwest. However, the plan was badly carried out. In the first place Frederick had wanted to make the expedition "on the cheap," that is to say in his own words, by putting in it little of his own and much of his allies' resources. But this composite body of French, Saxons, and Prussians was unwieldy. The leaders did not agree; the Saxons were not reliable; Broglie and Augustus III restrained their subordinates from afar, while Frederick himself continued underhand negotiations with Grand Duke Francis. Zieten's hussars, however, got as far as Stockerau, a single post from Vienna. But the King had been imprudent enough to leave the strongly garrisoned fortress of Brünn uncovered behind him, and although he had "devoured" the countryside his provisioning was very uncertain. In his letters and in the *History of My Times* he laid the blame for this on Schwerin, whom he never forgave for the fiasco at Mollwitz. To conclude, he was afraid of seeing his communications cut by continuous attacks of Hungarian cavalry and guerrilla fighters, and so he doubled back into Bohemia with twelve battalions, while Prince Thierry of Anhalt, with nineteen others, was repulsed into Silesia by Charles of Lorraine, the brother of Duke Francis (April, 1742).

Frederick was cursed by the peoples he ground down and was gloomy and irritable himself. He gave vent to bitter words against the human race. "He was in a dreadful state," wrote Valori. "All his remarks were hard, his laughter forced and sardonic, his jokes full of bitterness. Everything plagued him, everything roused his suspicions." With Walpole's fall in London the war spread; war between England and Spain, war between England and France. Fighting was soon to break out everywhere simultaneously—at sea, in America, in India, in Italy, on the Danube, and on the Rhine. On that day too Frederick was likely to be threatened in his provinces of Cleve and the Mark, and perhaps also in his ancestral lands of Brandenburg. In the second place, since the war was spreading out from the frontiers of Germany to set the world ablaze, the leading position indubitably fell to France, and France would also be the only real gainer from a victory which would establish her hegemony on indestructible foundations.

Frederick was worn out by the retreat, threatened with famine, and led astray by false information, so he reflected on his own conduct and was attacked by doubts. Was not this disastrous march the result of his presumption? Why had he entered upon the Silesian adventure, if not from youthful arrogance, from his craving to be feared and admired? What had been the use of so many deaths, so much exertion, and so much expense? When he thought of missed opportunities he was filled with fits of rage against his deceitful allies, but the more he considered, the more he grew tired of the wretched confusion of his affairs and the more he was plagued by the desire to escape from it with all speed: "I am of the opinion that the good of the State demands that we make peace; therefore let us swallow some affronts and reach our goal." At one moment he thought that the English would arrange matters so as to have a free hand elsewhere. Then he convinced himself that mere negotiations would lead nowhere and that "a show of strength and some striking success" were needed. Meanwhile Dessau had brought up his first reinforcements and he would have liked to put off fighting a battle for a few weeks, as he needed the respite for the transport of food supplies and the recovery of his more sorely-tried battalions. Prince Charles of Lorraine did not give him time for this.

The battle took place on May 17 about fifty miles southeast of Prague. The Prince planned to reach the town by forcing his way between the Prussians and the French, but Frederick had drawn up his army in a semicircle in such a way as to bar the route on the marshy plains of Czaslau and Chotusitz (the battle is called after both places). At seven o'clock the Austrians attacked with their cavalry. At ten the Prussians were victorious.

Frederick did not pursue Prince Charles. Most historians agree in thinking that this inaction was voluntary and prompted by a desire to spare Maria Theresa, but the King, whose revictualing was always uncertain, had also powerful military reasons for not going far from his supplies. In any case the victory provided him with an extra trump card for profitable negotiation and he hastened to bang it down before his usual go-between, Lord Hyndford.

He had no first-class complaint to bring forward as a reason for leaving the French alliance. Faithful to his habit of thinking on paper he had drawn up with his own hand during the last days of March a table of the arguments for and against a separate peace. The first section on the two sides of the question was put in this way: "It is bad to break one's promise without a reason; up till now I have had no cause of complaint against France or my allies. One gains the reputation of being a changeable, fickle person if one does not carry out a plan one has made and if one moves from one side to the other frequently." But in his mind the interests of Prussia outweighed all else. He was forced to come to a decision when the Marshal de Broglie was badly beaten, being obliged to retreat under the walls of Prague and losing some of his baggage. On June 9, with much anxiety, he gave orders that matters should be precipitated: "It is a question of reaching a conclusion in twelve hours, if the thing's to be done at all; Silesia and Glatz a *sine qua non* and otherwise all you can extort from them." Three days later when Valori urged him to march to the relief of Prague he did not even take the trouble to try his usual subterfuges.

"My dear Marquis, I do not want to deceive the King; I am going to speak to you with complete frankness. Things are in a desperate state. . . . Your Monsieur de Broglie must bear most of the blame: no French Army now exists, you are cut off from your recruits and your supplies. . . . I do not wish to be gulled. I am working for my own peace: your affairs are in a state beyond all repair."

As Valori protested that the Prussians were in exactly the right position to relieve the marshal, he added, "Yes, by exposing myself to battle once more, and that is just what I do not want to do. I have made enough human blood flow and I hazard too much on the result of a battle to wish to expose myself once again. I would be destroyed along with you if I did not think of myself. . . . My dear Valori, I hope we shall meet again." Whereupon he turned his back on him.

The negotiations proceeded very rapidly. England desired a peace that would free Austria on the north so that she could turn her entire forces against France. Maria Theresa swallowed her scruples. The preliminaries laid down at Breslau by Podewils and Hyndford were ratified at Vienna, and Frederick began to evacuate Bohemia on June 19.

The French ambassador heard the news on his return from Prague and he did not succeed in concealing his feelings from the King, who took advantage of this to sketch a pitiless caricature of him: "No Punchinello could imitate the contortions of Valori; his eyebrows made zigzags, his mouth grew larger, he frisked up and down in the strangest way—and all this without having anything very much to say to me. His greatest anxiety turned on the part I would be playing after the peace. I completely reassured him on that question; that he could count on my arms never being turned against France, and that I would fulfill my alliance on all possible points, such as those which concerned the succession of Jülich, but that continual efforts and risks were not to be expected of me, and that just to get peace I had extricated myself from it all as best I could." He wrote still more clearly to Wilhelmina: "I saw all my allies with their arms crossed, and not being able to bear the burden of the war on my own, I have left them to clear up their own tangle as best they can."

The final treaty was signed at Berlin on July 28, 1742. Frederick was given the county of Glatz, and Upper and Lower Silesia less Troppau, Teschen, and Jaegerndorf. He undertook to protect the Catholic religion in Silesia and took on a loan of 1,700,000 crowns contracted in London on the revenues of the province. In September the Saxons also withdrew from the struggle; in December Belle-Isle and Broglie evacuated Bohemia; the day after Christmas the last of the French in Prague surrendered. At Berlin Frederick had just introduced the opera. . . . "The thing," he wrote in reference to his conquest, "is in itself befitting. . . . As for the future safety of our new possessions, I base it on a large, excellent army, a full treasury, strong fortresses, and showy alliances which at least impress the world."

IV

Mollwitz had not discouraged Frederick and Chotusitz had not given him a swelled head, but those twenty months of war had ripened him. While conquering Silesia he had continued to rhyme, build, philosophize, and write to Voltaire, but he had flung himself into "the chaos of affairs," he had played with the lives of men, endangered his own, diced with fortune, and, in an anguish of threatening uncertainty, taken decisions which involved his reputation, his honor, his dynasty, and even his State. On the evening of the battle he had followed up the retreat of the enemy by stepping over the corpses on which his glory was built. He was surprised to find he was still alive and he drank life up in deep draughts. Sometimes he did not recognize himself.

"Here is your friend, twice victor in the space of thirteen months," he wrote to Jordan. "Who would have said some years ago that your scholar of philosophy, your pupil of Cicero in rhetoric and of Bayle in reason, would play a military part in the world? Who would have said that Providence was about to choose a poet to overthrow the European system and to change the political combinations of the kings who govern it from top to bottom? . . . I wait for news of you with impatience, but write to me at length of buildings, furniture, and dancers. It recreates me and refreshes me after my occupations, which become difficult and serious in so far as they are all-important. I read what I can, and I assure you that in my tent I am as much a philosopher as Seneca, or even more so."

He felt the weight of his occupations and his duties: "The honor of making the great wheel of events turn is very heavy work. . . . I often think of Remusberg and of that voluntary application which made me familiar with the sciences and the arts; but, after all, no state of life is quite free from bitterness. I had then my little pleasures and my little disappointments; I sailed on calm water. Today I brave the open sea, one wave carries me to the skies, another lowers me to the depths, and a third makes me rise swiftly to an even greater height. Such violent movements of the soul are not what is required by a philosopher; for, whatever can be said, it is very difficult to be indifferent to varying fortunes and to banish sensibility from the human breast. Vainly does one try to appear cool in prosperity and untouched by affliction: the expressions of the face can be disguised, but the man, the inner personality, the recesses of the heart are none the less affected by it. All that I desire for myself is that success should not corrupt my humanity and those virtues I have always professed. I hope and flatter myself that my friends will find me such as I have always been. . . ."

However, those very friends could be judged in a new way,

as he had come to discover. In fact, in 1741 he had summoned Jordan and the little Court of Rheinsberg to attend him at Breslau, but philosophy did not shine at the front. Maupertuis climbed up a tree to watch the battle from afar and was captured by some Hungarian hussars, who stripped him of his clothes, his watch, and his money. As for Jordan, he was expiring with terror and did not conceal the fact. Frederick pursued him with cruel jibes, asked after his colic, asked if the doctors had found a medicine to abate it, if he sniveled a lot, if he missed his books, if he had bought himself a rapier and a white feather. The wretched fellow answered with a roundel:

> Could I but go to far Berlin!

It is his best production, for at least it is full of sincerity. Verse for verse Frederick retorted:

> What has become in these events,
> Of all your grave philosophies,
> On which you spread your eloquence,
> And of the Stoic insolence
> Which made you human life despise
> With danger not in evidence?

When the danger appeared the professors of virtue, the scholars, the Atlases of the library took to flight and were seen no more. The soldier alone, who braved death without flinching:

> By rights we should apostrophize
> As true philosopher and wise,
> The others are impostors all.

A hard saying. Frederick softened it by means of indulgence and affection but he never attempted to recant it. True enough, on his return he did not change his companions: he had too much need of their affection, their wit, their impiety, their talk, and their talent; but deep within him he kept his profound esteem for the men of character and courage whom he found at his side, self-possessed and ready to give their blood for him in moments of danger.

He was a Hohenzollern. He had set out on his adventure a

little mad, his head full of dreams, because his father had left him a powerful army and some money and because the moment seemed propitious. "My age, the fire of my passions, my desire for glory, curiosity itself, and last of all a secret instinct have dragged me from the sweet peace I was enjoying; the satisfaction of seeing my name in the gazettes and later in the annals of history ran away with me." (Letter to Jordan, March 3, 1741.) However, the practical mind, the landowning instinct, and the avarice of his House had called him back. "If a player who has won and leaves the game is considered prudent, how much more approval should be bestowed upon a warrior who is wise enough to guard himself against the fickleness of fortune after a run of triumphs and prosperity?" Wars, treaties, alliances, betrayals, all had to pay, all had to be to "the advantage of the nation" and the aggrandizement of the country. The policy of Frederick was the policy of Frederick William and of the Great Elector, it was the same game of seesaw between France and Austria, the same trial and error, the same ambitions, the same involved diplomacy. But Frederick applied to it intelligence, the bird's-eye view, freedom of action, and a bold sense of the possible which his father had never possessed. At the end of the operation he balanced his accounts. Debits: two campaigns; twenty thousand dead, wounded, and deserted; five millions of "incidental expenses." Credit: a fertile province inhabited by at least a million persons. A good piece of business.

But what gulfs yawned between dreams and actions! Those well-considered resolutions, those plans based on such excellent books were all at the mercy of a surprise, of a blow by the enemy. Yet then it was that decisions had to be made at high speed and in the dark with the help of nothing but lucid thought and self-possession. Frederick was sometimes rash, often too hasty and subject also to fits of sanguine ferocity; he was far from being master of the lawless emotions which made him fall from exaltation to despair; but he had become conscious of his inexperience, and the further he went, the more he endeavored to put all the resources of rational thought, "clear and distinct," at the service of his will to be a hero. The classical spirit of France and the Prussian traditions of colonization were brought together in his person.

V

THE most remarkable feature of Frederick's diplomacy after the peace of Breslau was his distrust of all and sundry. In fact he had no illusions as to the feelings of Maria Theresa, for he knew that she had only surrendered Silesia "with the knife at her throat," under pressure from her allies, and in the hope of recovering it in the near future. On the other hand, much as he dreaded the vengeance of France, the identity of English and Hanoverian interests also made him afraid of territorial upheavals in northern Germany to the profit of the dynasty of the Georges.

The defection of Prussia was indubitably a great success for English policy, which had been almost entirely isolated from the Continent for the last quarter of a century. During the months that followed the Carteret-Newcastle ministry also succeeded in detaching Sardinia from the side of France and was luring away the Empress Elisabeth of Russia. Frederick judged it to be wise to attach himself to this coalition but in a passive way by a simple treaty of mutual guarantee signed at Westminster on November 28, 1742. His anxiety increased when Bavaria was evacuated by the French, and the Emperor Charles VII had to flee from his territory to take refuge at Frankfort in the most wretched position imaginable, without help and almost without money. It was believed in various circles that he would be compelled to give up his crown and that Francis would be elected in his place, or at least named as his successor, with the title of King of the Romans. Finally in the spring of 1743 there assembled in Hanover an Anglo-German army, called the Pragmatic Army, which was intended to operate through the Rhineland against the French. Could the King of Prussia lend himself to the liquidation of an emperor who was "of his making"? Could he allow the House of Hapsburg to be "cock of the walk" once again in the Empire?

Prussian intimidation failed to stop the march of the Pragmatic Army, which beat Noailles at Dettingen (June 27, 1743), so Frederick tried as second best to reanimate Belle-Isle's shattered work in secret, that is to say, to unite the princes of the Germanic body against Maria Theresa. To his mind one of the best results of the last war was in fact the accession of a prince without power or prestige to the imperial throne, and the possibility of a new, feeble dynasty, which he flattered himself he would be able to keep under his control. In this way there might arise, under the military protection of Protestant Prussia and directed at the Catholic, cosmopolitan House of Austria, a new sort of German Empire virtually enfeoffed to the Hohenzollerns. However, in 1743 the plan was not capable of realization: the Bavarian Emperor was too generally considered a puppet of France to typify the liberties of Germany, and his weakness was such that he could only maintain himself with the help of Prussian arms. Now Frederick wished above all things to keep the fruits of victory without drawing his sword except as an auxiliary. On the other hand, he made the mistake of proposing at London that Charles VII should have wider territories, not in Bohemia by dismembering the Austrian heritage, but at the expense of some ecclesiastical principalities which could be secularized and some free towns which could be reduced to their municipal franchises and made part of his patrimony. A strange way of upholding the Germanic constitution! When the Emperor called on the Diet to take efficient measures to ensure his personal safety, he received only the usual temporizing and futile replies.

Frederick's fears were increased by the signature of the Austro-Sardinian alliance and by the standstill of the Anglo-Austrian offensive on the Rhine. In fact the British Government had promised Austria Lorraine and the three Bishoprics but they still had to be conquered: the further the hope of a victorious march into French territory receded, the more must Maria Theresa be tempted to turn against Silesia, where many of the inhabitants had remained faithful to her. In the autumn of 1743 Frederick had to make up his mind that he would be forced to start fighting again but he still temporized for six more months. The fortifications of the strong places of Silesia had not been completed, and he always hoped to gain the symbolic assistance of a few German princes. But as Podewils was the eternal opponent of a French alliance and only seconded him with intentional slackness, Frederick did not cease to urge him on throughout the winter. "You are the greatest milksop I know. I insist that a high tone must be adopted. . . . The tocsin must be sounded against the Queen of Hungary."

Paris sought anxiously to get at Frederick's real feelings. Voltaire offered himself once again to play the part of informer. It was agreed that he should have all his expenses paid and that as a reward he should receive, through his cousins the Marchands, a share in providing cloth for the army. Marchand and Son were associated with the philosopher and had already the contract for the supplies, but Voltaire claimed he was losing money over it and burned "to clothe the defenders of France."

To make his journey look like an exile he said he was persecuted by the Theatine monk Boyer, sometime Bishop of Mirepoix, who controlled the benefices and barred his entry to the Academy. The King treated Voltaire with charming friendliness. He loaded him with embraces and compliments, gave shows for him at the opera and the theater, took him along to Bayreuth, let him stay a fortnight with the Margravine, feted him when he returned to Berlin, but mocked pleasantly at his politics and his mission. Before leaving, Voltaire submitted him to a questionnaire, all of his replies to which were flippant.

"Your Majesty," wrote Voltaire, "will know that my lord Eatwell,[2] leading burgomaster of Amsterdam, has come to beg Monsieur de la Ville, the minister of France, to make proposals for peace."

"That Eatwell," replied Frederick, "is to all appearances the man whose job it is to fatten capons and turkeys for Their High Mightinesses."

"If Your Majesty was in a commanding position would he not snatch the scepter of Europe from the hands of the English, who beard you and who talk about you in a disgusting manner quite openly?"

"I worry myself very little indeed about what the English are saying, and all the less because I do not understand their lingo."

"Persons who have talked for only a quarter of an hour with the Duke of Aremburg, the Count of Harrach, Lord Stair, and all the supporters of Austria have heard them say that they burn to begin their campaign in Silesia."

They will be greeted there,
Hey nonny,

2. Literally "poultry yard": *bassecour* in the French.

In the manner of Nonny-no
My crony.

With Voltaire on the road home (October 12), the King turned
his mind to serious matters. On the eve of a war with his southern
neighbor the most urgent thing was to safeguard Brandenburg
and Prussia from all attacks from the north. Eleonora, Queen of
Sweden, having had no children, it was the responsibility of the
national Diet to provide against the coming vacancy of the
throne. In concert with Russia Frederick succeeded in obtaining
the majority of the votes for the Prince of Holstein-Eustin, to
whom he immediately gave the hand of his sister Ulrica, that
pretty girl to whom Voltaire had paid some slight attentions:

> Some shoots of truth will always spring
> Amid the greatest crop of lies.
> Last night in dream's absurdities
> I rose and took the rank of king,
> I loved you at that hour and dared to tell you so.
> When I awoke, the Gods did not take everything:
> I only saw my empire go.

. . . and he had kissed her portraits:

> 'Tis mighty bold to kiss, by scruples undeterred,
> Your sister's majesty displayed in modest charms;
> But not to kiss them when I see them in my arms—
>   That would be too absurd.

At St. Petersburg Frederick pulled off a matrimonial venture
of the same sort: the Grand Duke Peter of Holstein-Gottorp,
nephew and heir of the Empress, was espoused to Princess Sophia
of Anhalt-Zerbst, daughter of a Prussian field marshal and niece
of the successor to the throne of Sweden. "The young princess,"
wrote the matchmaker to the Tsarina, "unites the talents of the
mind and the virtues of the heart with all the liveliness and gaiety
of her youth." Such was the future Catherine II. Unfortunately
the League of Princes made no progress. Even if the "well-
intentioned" ones, as Frederick still called them, were ready to
sell themselves, he did not intend to purchase them with his own
money; he proposed to Louis XV that he should defray the cost
of the corruption. But as France was occupied in reviving the old

League of the Rhine on her own account and turned a deaf ear to him, he resigned himself to negotiating openly for a renewal of the alliance and dispatched a scout to Versailles. This was his friend Rottenbourg, who had served in the French Army, and by being well up in the fashionable world had married the daughter of the Marchioness of Parabère, the mistress of Philip of Orléans, at the time of the Regency. Each year Rottenbourg spent some weeks at Paris with his relations and his stay would not attract attention. However, as the improvised diplomat's only experience consisted of recruiting for the Berlin *corps de ballet*, Frederick made him rehearse his part in detail. He acted the French minister himself and enlarged on all the objections which might be raised at Versailles, including those which would be taken to his own character. He spoke of his versatility, his egoism, and the small trust that could be put in his word. Rottenbourg did not deny his master's faults but replied that in the present circumstances France could use them to her own advantage, so that Frederick cried in delight, "Only talk like that and you are sure to succeed."

Fleury had died on January 29, 1743; Amelot, the Secretary of State for Foreign Affairs, put in his resignation, and this change of personnel facilitated the agreement. It was concluded in a double way, on June 5 at Paris in the form of a Franco-Prussian alliance, and on May 22 at Frankfort in the form of a "union" between Prussia, Bavaria, France (by a separate clause), the Landgrave of Hesse, and the Elector Palatine, for the defense of the Emperor and of the liberties of Germany. The allies bound themselves to restore his hereditary possessions to Charles VII and to guarantee Silesia to Frederick. Furthermore, Bohemia was to be divided between Bavaria and Prussia with the Elbe as the frontier; for her part France was to receive a part of Belgium. Frederick reserved the right not to take the field until the end of August.

VI

WHEN he learned that the Austrians under Prince Charles had crossed the Rhine and entered Alsace he hurried on his military moves. On August 17, furnished with permits to requisition made out in the Emperor's name, he entered Saxon territory with

80,000 men, and before the ministers of the Elector King had time to collect their wits he crossed the frontier of Bohemia in three columns followed by a flotilla carrying provisions, which thrust its way through the gorges of the Elbe. On September 2 he arrived before Prague with all his men, on the tenth he opened his saps, and on the sixteenth the fortress surrendered. The next morning he bore toward the south to Tabor and Budweis as though to reach the Danube at the frontiers of Bavaria and Austria. It was a mistake, for the occupation of those wasted provinces could be of no use to him, and he left a free field for the army of Prince Charles, who withdrew from Alsace along the valley of the Main and was getting ready to reënter Bohemia in the far north by Eger and Pilsen, while Saxony, having taken up arms in due course, was cutting the Elbe route.

The land through which Frederick was advancing was mountainous, difficult, and barren. The peasants had buried their wheat and had fled to the forest with their livestock. The King marched through rain, lacked food, was cut off from his supplies of ammunition and from his reinforcements, and was harried ceaselessly by 10,000 Hungarian and Croatian hussars, who held him in so fine a net that he could no longer send out foraging parties or be reached by couriers; thus he was compelled to turn in his tracks. However, he made the new mistake of wishing both to hold Prague and to protect his communications with Breslau. He drew up his forces in a central position between them along the river Elbe. On November 19 the Austrians surprised and broke through the frail barrier of posts and patrols he had drawn up along the river bank. He retired into Silesia where he was rejoined by the garrison he had left in Prague, which had been too weak for the job and had lost its ammunition, its siege train, its cannon, its sick, and its transport. Seventeen thousand men had deserted during the retreat and the generals themselves were beginning to murmur against the King. "We have no army left," wrote Münchow, president of the Chamber of Domains of Breslau. "What we have got is nothing but a flock which holds together by force of habit and by the authority of its officers. These officers for their part are all discontented, many of them are in a desperate plight. The very least defeat or continuation of the war this season would be enough to make mutinies break out among the troops." And he added, "Our mistakes have set more than half the land against us."

Undoubtedly Frederick had counted on Prince Charles's army being kept much longer in the Palatinate. It is none the less true to say that of all his campaigns none was more badly executed, and it might have turned out even more badly but for the skill of the Prince of Dessau, who thrust back an invading force of Austrians in midwinter. However, for some weeks defeats and adversities mounted up. A loan floated in Holland was a failure, and to cover the expenses of the war Frederick seriously considered selling England the port of Emden, which he had just inherited along with East Frisia. At the end of January, 1745, Charles VII died, and his son, declining to solicit for the imperial crown, hastened to make peace with Austria. Finally France, in the face of protests, planned to push the war into the Low Countries and left only a watching force on the Rhine. Frederick insisted that a French army should march on Vienna along the Danube, but after the disaster of 1742 and the failure of Bavaria Louis XV was quite determined never to send troops a hundred and fifty leagues from his kingdom and put them once again at the mercy of a defection by Prussia; besides their advance through enemy country would be perilous in the extreme.

The King displayed the essential qualities of which he had given proof in the misfortunes of his youth, the same arrogant, feverish, and stubborn courage, which easily swelled into literary bombast: "I would far rather perish with honor than be lost to glory and repute for the whole of my life," he wrote to his first minister. "It is a point of honor with me to have contributed more than any other man to the aggrandizement of my House, I have played a distinguished part among the crowned heads of Europe: there are a number of personal vows I have taken, and I am quite determined to uphold them at the cost of my fortune and of my life. You think like a very honest man, and if I were Podewils I would have the same feelings. But I have crossed the Rubicon: either I must uphold my power, or else let everything perish and even the name of Prussian sink to oblivion along with me."

Can a more complete identity of state and sovereign be imagined? However he also said, "I work like a horse to put a favorable face upon my desperate position. The soldiery will do its duty, and there is not one of us who will not work himself to death rather than lose an inch of this country by our cowardice. Do not look only on the dark side of things. I have thrown all caution to the winds and make ready for every eventuality which may occur, and whether fortune is cruel or kind to me that will neither depress me nor puff me up with pride. . . . What use is it to me to foresee every misfortune if I do not imagine at the same time the remedy which will cure them?"

This time the measures taken by Frederick were excellently coördinated. The personal touch of a master hand can be seen for the first time. His plan was to make the enemy believe he had spread his 90,000 men in a thin cordon 125 miles long, whereas in reality he had kept more than half under his hand secretly concentrated at a central point on the line from Schweidnitz to Glatz, closely in touch with the detached bodies which showed themselves all about the place. To confirm Charles of Lorraine in his error he very openly repaired the roads to Breslau as though to provide for a retreat behind the Oder, and by means of false spies he also succeeded in sending incorrect information to the Prince which completed his deception.

On June 3 the Austrians and the Saxons, who were massed at Königgrätz, poured down through the passes of Landeshut in eight huge columns and marched out past Hohenfriedberg quite confidently toward Striegau, thinking that they had before them only the weak detachment of General von Winterfeldt. Frederick, who had more than 60,000 men hidden in the folds of the countryside, set his troops in motion at eight o'clock at night in the deepest silence. The soldiers were forbidden to smoke. On the fourth at about three in the morning the battle began with an attack on the enemy's left wing; this was composed of the Saxons, who broke up under the suddenness of the attack and cannonade and exposed the Austrian flank. These were hardly drawn up and had to retreat over ground intersected by hedges and ditches, of which they made use for a moment to hold up the enemy's advance. But as the battle gradually extended they were outflanked and in due course fled in disorder. "*Te-Deum* it suitably" was the victor's simple message to Berlin.

Frederick kept a short distance behind the enemy and entered

Bohemia at his heels. But from that moment he seemed to be paralyzed by the memory of his previous retreat and by the objurgations of his ministers, who begged him by every courier not to risk the fate of the country on a single day's battle. Thus he reverted to a war of skirmishes, without vigor or originality, always hindered by the delays and the bad routes chosen by his convoys. It was his intention to go and take up his winter quarters in Silesia after having devastated a strip of territory along the frontiers to form a kind of glacis, but the Prince of Lorraine brought 40,000 men against him and compelled him to fight another battle. As a matter of fact, the Austrians believed him to be already in retreat and therefore only prepared for a big rear-guard action. Although his forces were outnumbered two to one he took advantage of the speed and perfect drill of his soldiers to rush precipitately into the fight in front of the village of Soor, on a field which did not permit his adversary to make use of his superior numbers. Alternating attacks by the Prussian cavalry demoralized the Austrians, who were fighting with their backs to a sort of precipice and were hindered by woods and ravines so that they could find no room for deploying their forces (September 30, 1745).

That day cost the King a quarter of his effectives. Some hussars in flight also took away his treasure chest, his books, his luggage, his secretary, and his doctor. He was left nothing but the shirt he had on his back. However, he was able to camp for five days on the field of battle and to withdraw calmly after having made good the feeble and disjointed features of his previous operations by a display of appropriate action and tactical skill.

The autumn campaign was concluded without a decision. Maria Theresa's husband, Francis of Lorraine, had just been elected to succeed Charles VII against the votes of only Brandenburg and the Palatinate. The treasury of Prussia was empty; her exhausted people cried for mercy; Frederick was at the end of his resources and expedients, and had asked France for subsidies in vain; he became convinced that he had expected too much of his forces and he yielded to the entreaties of his followers. On August 26 he made peace with England in the hope that the British Government would compel the Empress to follow its example in the near future. But Maria Theresa was less resigned than ever to the loss of Silesia. Using the recaptured province of Bohemia and a friendly Saxony as a base, her generals had a plan of invading Brandenburg and taking the war to the gates of Berlin. Great was the alarm in the capital, and arrangements were already being made for moving the archives and the ministries to Cüstrin and to Magdeburg. Frederick was informed of the concentrations of the enemy and thought of a counterstroke which was a masterpiece of defensive strategy. His plan was to crush the allies in detail before they could arrange to join forces. The Prince of Anhalt-Dessau, *der alte Dessauer,* was first to fall upon the Saxons and seize Dresden, while Frederick, posted at the entrances to the mountain passes of Lusatia, would stop the Austrians on the right bank of the Elbe.

This beautifully combined operation only half succeeded through the fault of those who carried it out. First, though Charles of Lorraine was attacked at the bottom of the passes, he somehow managed to get away. Second, the movements of Frederick and the Prince of Anhalt were badly coördinated. The two men did not get on together—or rather, they hated one another. The Prince was one of the old school who maneuvered with careful circumspection and he held the King to be a whippersnapper. The King bore with the Prince from necessity but he plagued him with complaints and took no trouble to flatter the pride of an old officer loaded with experience and glory. Nevertheless on December 15 old Dessau, in spite of too prudent a march, crushed the Saxons at Kesseldorf, to the south of Dresden, almost in sight of Frederick and Charles, who had hurried up, one on the right and one on the left bank of the river: a little more speed on the Imperialists' side might have changed the fortunes of the day. On the morrow Frederick rejoined Dessau. Such was the negligence of the Saxons that they had not even thought of blowing up the bridge of Meissen, which was the only possible means of communication between the two Prussian armies. Peace, a peace of exhaustion, was at last signed at Dresden on December 26, 1745: Prussia recognized Francis' election to the imperial throne; Austria confirmed the cession of Silesia. Frederick had once again left his ally in the lurch but this time with much more reason than at Breslau and under real stress of circumstance.

The evening before the signature of the peace Frederick had

a conversation with Valori's secretary, Darget, whom he was to take into his service as a reader. Would the King spread the benefits of peace over all Europe? asked Darget. What a fine part for the hero of Germany to play!

"I agree," said Frederick, "I agree, but the part is too dangerous a one. At my last departure from Berlin, if fortune had been against me, I saw myself as a monarch without a throne and my subjects under the most cruel oppression. Here it is always 'check' to the King—you know that yourself; and lastly, I want to be quiet."

"But," replied Darget, "the Queen of Hungary will never renounce Silesia, and in time, sooner or later . . ."

"Ah, my friend," interrupted the King, "the future is beyond humanity's grasp. I have acquired, let others preserve. I will henceforth not even attack a cat except in self-defense. . . . Lastly, I want to enjoy myself. What are we, we men, to engender plans which cost so much human blood? Live and let live!" And he began to talk drama.

VIII

Sans Souci

I

AN idler leaving Potsdam by one of the quiet little streets which branched out from the Luisenplatz might have come upon a green iron gate, passed through it down an alley lined with lime trees, and reached a shady garden set about with a hedge: there a few minutes away from the castle Frederick William owned a kitchen garden, a bowling green, a summer-house, and a shooting butt. In derision he called the cabbage patch his Marly. Beyond stretched wretched meadows, fields of oats, and an oak wood overhung by a steep, naked hill. Sometimes Frederick and his friends went and lunched in the open air on top of the hillock. When the air was clear the endless ramifications of the river Havel could be seen, with its fishermen's houses and fir plantations soaked in bluish mist—one of those landscapes of water and forest which are the ornament of Brandenburg. On August 10, 1744, Frederick gave orders for the promenade to be arranged in six concave terraces planted with vines and fig trees and joined to one another down the center by flights of about twenty steps. However, it was not until January 13, 1745, that he had work begun right at the top of the "vineyard" upon a house of pleasure, a little summer palace which was to be called Sans Souci.

He had not yet found a home. Rheinsberg was too distant and too cramped. At Berlin he had already had the Opera House built, arranged some apartments in the castle to his taste, and planned a vast forum round which were to be built alongside the theater, the palace of the Academy, the Observatory, and the palace of the Queen Mother. But war had made him abandon this plan as too costly. And then the King was not happy at Berlin; it had unhappy memories for him, and he could not live there in his own way. In the period between his campaigns he settled first at Charlottenburg in his grandmother's castle, an enormous building with a dome and pediments, with two projecting wings framing a forecourt of noble aspect and two more spreading out like a fan onto the park in the manner of Versailles. However, the building of it had been held up since 1713. Knobelsdorff erected the right wing in a simple and gay French style. From camps in Silesia the King worried about the work, and as Knobelsdorff was no letterwriter he harried the mild Jordan: "Oblige that fat Knobelsdorff to send me word how Charlottenburg, my Opera House, and my gardens are doing. I am a child on this subject; these are the dolls with which I play. . . . Write to me at length on the subject of Charlottenburg and give me full descriptions." He would have liked "four pages for each pillar." Yet on his return he saw many disadvantages in Charlottenburg in spite of the charm of the site and the buildings. Its closeness to Berlin brought him, especially on Sundays, processions of inquisitive visitors and petitioners soliciting his help. It was then that he chose Potsdam as his residence—the castle in the winter and Sans Souci in the summer.

The castle of the town, the *Stadtschloss*, was an old, historic dwelling, squat and grim to behold; its general features dated from the seventeenth century and it had been very badly kept up by Frederick William: four blocks arranged at right angles around a courtyard, the fourth bulging in the center, having only one story and opening onto the old market place through a gateway and a loggia. Frederick had his father's apartments entirely demolished but he did not want to touch the arrangement of the exterior. Knobelsdorff did no more than raise the height of the wings, which were too low, and face the building with flat pilasters and half columns, which supported a cornice level with the roof and a balustrade which was itself surmounted by vases, statues, trophies, and shields bearing the arms of Prussia, Brandenburg, and Silesia. On the side facing the Parade Platz he added to the double flight of steps a balustrade, lanterns, statues, and sphinxes; finally he built the two Corinthian colonnades which connected the castle to the river Havel and to the stables.

At Sans Souci no previous buildings restrained the King's imagination. He himself drew up the plan of his house and the arrangement of his gardens. Knobelsdorff's plan provided for a

tall palace perched nearly on the edge of the sixth terrace, which
would have looked very grand seen from below. But Frederick
wanted clipped trees and flowers under his windows; he obliged
his architect to build much farther back a one-storied pavilion
rather squat in shape but pleasing to the eye, made for friendship,
and as it were flooded with sunlight. Nothing could be simpler
than the plan. In the center an antechamber and an oval dining
room roofed with a cupola in the form of an inverted bowl. On
the left, the King's apartments, a little gallery where hung the
Lancrets, the Paters, and the Watteaus, an audience chamber, a
music room, a study, a bedroom cut off by a balustrade and curtains, and finally a small circular library. On the right, five rooms
and dressing rooms "for strangers." Facing the garden a façade
ornamented with fauns and bacchants as caryatids. Facing the
road—here Knobelsdorff had his revenge—a semicircular courtyard enclosed by a double colonnade screening the domestic
offices and recalling the Trianon because of its balanced design.
At the peace of Dresden the roof was finished; in the summer of
1746 the interior decoration was begun; on May 2, 1747, the King
gave a supper there and on the nineteenth he slept there for the
first time. In the years that followed the property was enlarged.
The orangery was transformed into a banqueting hall and guest
rooms; in the park were built a picture gallery, a Chinese pavilion, a Greek temple, a terrace in rockwork, another terrace
flanked with wrangling cupids, and a grotto of shells dedicated to
Neptune. A stroller might have chanced upon a pond, fountains,
arbors of hornbeams, a tulip garden, beds of dwarf trees, a cherry
orchard, and all the heathen mythology in marble.

As though to flout the dark winters of Brandenburg Frederick
had had the roofs of Potsdam castle tinted blue and the walls
painted red, but for himself he liked white, rose, soft blue, silver,
linen gray—all luminous, soft, or faded colors. The ballroom of
Charlottenburg was green and rose with ornaments of green
marble and gilded stucco; his bedroom at Potsdam was tapestried
in blue and silver satin, that at Sans Souci in celadon green. In
both palaces the alcove was shut off by a silver balustrade on
which five cupids armed with bows kept watch. At Potsdam the
audience chamber was yellow picked out in silver, the little
dining room pale rose, the gallery green and rose, and one of the

drawing rooms pearl-colored. At Sans Souci the audience chamber was pale mauve, the music room white with scarlet hangings,
the guest rooms blue, white, and cream: these were the colors of
Rheinsberg but in sumptuous materials, in embroidered velvet,
in taffeta, in brocade, and in Tours silk.

Pesne and Dubuisson had worked on the interior decoration
and so had a Berlin sculptor called Nahl, who had been trained
in France and was succeeded in 1746 by the Hoppenhaupts,
father and son. Undoubtedly the style came from Versailles, but
the Frederican rococo had an exuberance, a fantasy, a rather wild
prodigality which distinguished it from its French models with
their more sober and restrained inspiration. Even if the excessive
use of silver for frames and furniture is deplored, the two royal
apartments gave a charming impression of refined and elaborate
luxury. In the center of a ceiling a spider had woven her golden
web; on a cornice cupid fishermen drew in their nets; palm trees
framed a mirror in which were reflected babies pursuing a hare;
on sculptured and painted panels were scattered garlands of
roses, clusters of grapes, fruits, shells, ribbons capriciously tied,
tambourines, guitars, trophies of war and of the garden, branches
of cherry, fountains, monkeys, storks, parrots—a flowery, caper-
ing, motley world, which amused the eye and held it by its amazing freshness of design.

The plans of Sans Souci which Frederick scribbled for Knobelsdorff bore many signs of being his handiwork. For the library he
wrote "As at Rheinsberg." He was thinking at that moment of
the old tower where he had spent the gentle, studious hours of
his youth. So as to preserve this memory and this appearance, the
libraries of Berlin, Potsdam, and Sans Souci were all in the form
of a small rotunda. The one at Sans Souci is in cedar wood with
fittings in gilded bronze. Bookcases alternate with mirrors, windows, and a fireplace. From his desk Frederick could see at the
very end of a walk of hornbeam the exquisite statue of a suppliant boy stretching its arms toward him, a Greek bronze which
had belonged to Fouquet and to Prince Eugene; he had bought
it in 1747 for 5,000 thalers, after having coveted it for three
years.

This library was one of the most harmonious and successful
examples of German rococo, but the most beautiful rooms—and

the best preserved—are at the castle of Potsdam: the music room with its Chinese paintings on a gold ground, and especially the great dining room decorated with ornaments in gilded bronze affixed to white panels. Around the doors, the mirrors, the panels, and the windows runs a light embroidery of metal, gracious and flexible, sown here and there with bouquets, garlands, and trophies. A chimney piece in red marble soberly framed in copper foliage, immense consoles adorned with shells and flowers, and numerous candelabra placed before mirrors complete this magnificent and delicate composition.

In 1742 Frederick bought the celebrated collection of antiques belonging to Cardinal de Polignac, which included not only statues and busts but also vases, urns, carved stones, marble tables, and some modern works, among others the bust of Cardinal Richelieu by Bernini. All these sculptures were scattered around the drawing rooms, bedrooms, and gardens. In the library of Sans Souci there was a Homer, an Apollo, a Socrates, and a Marcus Aurelius; in the little gallery were eight busts, some statues, and some bas-reliefs; on the terrace in niches of greenery was a whole set of emperors and philosophers.

And yet Sans Souci was not a country edition of the castle at Potsdam. Neither in the one nor in the other had Frederick allowed his triumphs to be illustrated. Only once at Charlottenburg did Pesne paint him as Prometheus in an allegory, but in the *Stadtschloss* he wanted the lives of his ancestors to be celebrated, especially the Great Elector. The decorations of the state rooms and of the marble hall displayed a veritable panorama of politics and war, vast heroic compositions, pictures of battles and apotheoses. Here was Prussia: on the other side of an antechamber could be found the world of the *fêtes galantes*. A fragile division perhaps? Frederick only clung all the closer to this unreal atmosphere of intricate grace—it was his dream at twenty, the imaginative retreat where he had soothed his sufferings and found the strength to overcome his feelings of distaste.

> In future years—and few are left me on the earth—
> I wish, whatever comes, to sow my path with flowers;
> Depicting all as fair to fill my life with mirth.
>   Hard-featured truth is nothing worth
>   Beside these soft deceits of ours.

He loved Watteau because Watteau opened for him the gate of faërie, and he would have been glad to create around him some of that fairyland at the very moment when presidents of Chambers and grenadiers were about to relax into their impassive sleep. "The boredom of the winter of 1743–44," says a contemporary account, "was dispelled by gatherings, balls, sledging parties, comedies, and operas. The King had a third gold table service made." And at the same time Frederick wrote to Rottenbourg, who was ambassador at Versailles, "If you come upon some Italian pomades which are well scented and perfumed powders of pleasing scent, you will do me the kindness of bringing me some of them." The fop had come into his own.

To complete the picture nothing was needed but a theatrical escapade. Frederick wished to embellish his opera with the most celebrated dancer of the day. This was an Italian girl born at Parma in 1721 called Barbera Campanini, known as La Barberina in the theater world and as Barberine to her friends. She had made her debut in Paris at the age of eighteen in Rameau's *Festivals of Hebe*. A pastel by Rosalba preserved at the Museum of Dresden shows her as she was then—fresh and roguish, with the blackest of black eyes, a complexion like a peach, and very brown hair, unpowdered and bound with roses and pearls. Her tiny mouth is breaking into an ingenuous smile which flatters and promises at one and the same time. Barberina was received with "unanimous applause." She did not possess the languid charm, the ethereal glamour which the romantics demanded of the sylphides of the white ballet, neither had she the noble and mannered poise of the great century. She was a fine creature, possessed of brilliant talent, neat and strong. She leaped to a great height and could do eight *entrechats*. The admirers of Mademoiselle Sallé said that her art smacked of fairs and barnstorming. Voltaire thought she had a man's pair of legs.

After Paris Barberina proceeded to the conquest of London. She had crowds of lovers—fifteen at a time, swore an intelligencer —and they had all more or less ruined themselves for her: her acknowledged lover, Prince Carignano; Lord Arundel, a wealthy English nobleman; the Prince de Conti, the Duke de Durfort, the Prince de Guébriant, a bishop. . . . Bielfeld, who had seen her in London, spoke of her to Keyserlingk. In September, 1743, the

Prussian minister, Chambrier, engaged her for the coming season. In the interval she left for Venice with a young Englishman, Lord Stuart-Mackenzie, who called her "my lovely, sweet baby" and was so madly in love that he talked of marrying her. In short at the appointed date, on the pretext that her salary was not yet fixed, Barberina refused to come to Berlin. Frederick treated her as his father used to treat the giants—he had her kidnaped. She crossed Germany in a carriage under guard, but the secretary who went with her had orders to keep her in a good humor by the use of graceful flattery and glowing descriptions of the beauty of Berlin and the luxury of the Court. Lord Stuart followed the prisoner from inn to inn sniveling all the way. Unfortunately, the English ambassador in Prussia, Lord Hyndford, knew the lover's uncle: that nobleman begged him to ask Frederick to send his rogue of a nephew to London. Lord Stuart was expelled by the police but went home to the island of Quakers convinced that Barberina would remain faithful to him and that outside the theater she would lead a life of austerity and continence for his sake.

On May 13, 1744, Barberina made her first appearance before the Court in the interlude of a comedy. It was a prodigious success. Frederick called her into his box, discovered she had some wit, invited her to supper, and felt a trifle amorous. At times he was a terrible impresario. When singers did not want to sing he threatened them with prison and had them brought onto the stage by soldiers. However, for Barberina he softened considerably: "Mademoiselle, I have given very precise orders to the Baron de Sweets to ensure that he will not annoy you in any way. I only ask you to have the kindness to dance when the ballets at the Opera House require it; as for comedies, unless ballets are made for them, you will have the choice of dancing or not dancing as you please. Farewell, charming Barberina, until the first supper." He paid her as much as three ministers, 5,000 and later 7,000 thalers (about $10,000 in today's currency), with five months' holiday a year and the right to go on tour abroad. All the society of Rheinsberg was to be found in her apartment in the Behrenstrasse; for four years she was queen of Berlin. Pesne painted her as a statue, surrounded by loves and touched with life by Venus, on one of the panels which decorate the music room at Sans Souci.

However, it was her destiny to inspire passion. One evening the son of the chancellor, Cocceji, fell at her feet and offered her his name, his heart, and his hand. Perhaps she loved him. In any case, she was very rich and tired of the theater; the idea of being a baroness was too much for her. At the expiration of her contract she braved the maledictions of the chancellor and the threats of the King; the marriage was celebrated in secret. In the height of fury Frederick sent the young baron to Spandau and then exiled him to Silesia as vice-president of the Chamber of Domains of Glogau.

The tale ended in German fashion. For some months Barberina played a dignified part as the vice-president's wife. But as she did not get on with her husband she obtained a separation and retired to her property at Barschau. She died in 1799, Countess of Campanini and Mother Superior of a convent for aristocratic young ladies. She bore as her arms two laurel crowns, a horse courant, three bells, a star, and two cranes each holding a stone in its lifted claw, with the motto, *Virtuti asilum*. In her life she endured only one rebuff: Frederick's successor refused her the title of Excellency.

II

WHEN Reinhold Koser is describing Sans Souci he laments the fact that the house had no mistress. The war and Barberina had succeeded in completing the detachment of Frederick from his wife. Thenceforward he was hardly aware of her existence. She was never invited to the palace of Potsdam or to Sans Souci. Frederick sometimes saw her at Berlin during the carnival season. On those days he took off his boots, put on silk stockings, and paid her a ceremonial visit which would last for a quarter of an hour. For the rest of the year he sent her detached little notes to assure her of his "complete friendship," to thank her for her good wishes, or to console her for the loss of some relative; "Madam, I was grieved to hear of the death of Madam your mother. I send you my condolences. She was aged and ailing; she now finds herself sheltered from all the misfortunes which are the lot of humanity, and we, however long we exist, will take the same path. . . ." Even so, he forgot to tell her of the death of her brother, who was killed at the battle of Soor. One day, when the Dowager Electress of Saxony compared him with Solomon, he replied, "Solomon had a seraglio of a thousand women, and by no means considered he had enough of them; I have only one and that is too much for me."

However, she was the Queen. She had maids of honor, a Grand Mistress of the Robes, and some chamberlains. She took part in ceremonies, was present in a carriage at the spring reviews at Tempelhof, held court, and received ambassadors. She was not in the least stupid, played the harp, collected books, and took an interest in the latest German literature. Frederick was gratified by the respect strangers showed her, but as he gave her only a modest pension she was always short of money. When she complained he sent her advice on how to economize, and paid her debts most unwillingly. At first she bore his neglect with touching resignation, saying prayers for her "dear prince" each morning and asking God every night to bring him back to her on the morrow. However, through sheer boredom she became a shrew and a dotard. In the summer at Schönhausen she spent her time playing blindman's buff with her ladies and in marrying off the peasants of the neighborhood. On one occasion she went on a visit in night attire: this prank amused her for a whole day. On the pretext that the sight of her was enough to sadden the gayest company, Frederick did not even invite her to the festivities he gave in honor of his mother in 1746. In private he called her "my grumpy old cat." Twenty-five years later their relations were no better but the King expressed himself in a more vulgar way. His sister Ulrica, Dowager Queen of Sweden, was passing through Berlin, and he introduced her to relations and friends, many of whom were new to her. He ended with the Queen: "And here is my old cow, whom you already know."

Frederick felt respect and affection for his mother: the rest of his family did not count at all. Except for pretty, naughty Amelia, who died as Protestant Abbess of Quedlinburg, all his sisters were already married by 1744. The Queen of Sweden and the Duchess of Brunswick had unlimited admiration for their brother. "You are my divinity," wrote the first. "You are my saint, whom alone I honor and revere," wrote the second. Her he saw quite often, as their capitals were near to each other. He called her Lottine or La Lotte and gave her little presents. On the other hand, he had only distant relations with Frederica and Sophia, Margravines of Ansbach and Schwedt. He never wrote to them himself and left the care of answering their letters to a secretary, according to a fixed scale—"compliments," "sincere compliments," "most sincere compliments."

During the second Silesian war he fell foul of his dearest Wilhelmina of Bayreuth because she had received Maria Theresa, who was passing through to go to Frankfort, and because a gazetteer in her state defamed Prussia in a broadsheet. In vain did Wilhelmina increase her advances to her brother, worry over his labors, rejoice at his victories, and send him her love and congratulations, he only answered her in a three-line note. "My dear sister, I am much obliged to you for interrupting your amusements to think of me. I trust that your health may be always of the best." He informed her of the peace of Dresden in a pointed way: "The interest you take in all that concerns the Queen of Hungary gives me the opportunity of announcing to you that we have just concluded a peace between ourselves. I flatter myself, my dear sister, that this will be all the more pleasing to you in that your predilection for that princess will not find itself hampered by any remnant of former friendship which you perhaps preserve for me. . . ." However, after three beautiful letters full of pathos they were reconciled with tears and took up their correspondence again on the old footing. Wilhelmina came to Sans Souci in 1747; she came again in 1750 and 1753; Frederick visited her home in 1754. She used to put on a lot of rouge and to deck herself out with diamonds. Potsdam society found her provincial. When fire destroyed the castle of Bayreuth Frederick was a party to the misfortunes which assailed her: he gave her some pocket money and some consolations after the style of Marcus Aurelius. Certainly, if he had possessed the lyre of Amphion, he would have lent it to the Margrave that he might rebuild the house "with the aid of its harmonious notes." As he had not got it, he merely sent him a flute, some music, a piece of linen for making shirts, and some secondhand theater togs to clothe his opera company. "If you knew the spirit in which I am doing this," he said, "you would not grudge me this pleasure of mine."

Last came his three brothers. Augustus William, his father's favorite, was eighteen years old in 1740, Henry was fourteen, and Ferdinand twelve. William was a good, obedient boy without the least harm in him, who ran after girls and did not possess a high level of intelligence. He behaved with bravery at the battles of Chotusitz, Hohenfriedberg, and Soor. Frederick was determined to leave no children himself, so he married his brother to the sister of the Queen and declared him heir presumptive with the title of Prince of Prussia. There was no friendship between them, however. Frederick, who had fits of sensibility after the fashion of the times, used sometimes to complain of not possessing his confidence. On such occasions he sent him letters full of affectionate reproaches: "This is not the first time that you have done me such an injustice. . . ." More often he preached at him with a severity which echoed the sound of another voice.

An affair between the Prince and a very nice young lady, Sophie Marie von Pannewitz, provoked a crisis. William was very much in love and wanted to divorce his wife. This enraged Frederick, so he married off the girl to a councilor in the legation and sent the couple away from Court. Thus ended the romance. However, many years later the King still made speeches to his brother against princes who gave themselves up to their passions and were only suited for the command of a harem.

William was easy and pliable. The strong character was Henry, who possessed, in addition to the tastes, vivacity, attractiveness, intelligence, and pride of Frederick, an ardent imagination, a faultless memory, and a prodigious capacity for work. The King put a respectable soldier called Colonel Stille as governor over him and Ferdinand. The two young men were to be treated strictly and trained to be Prussians. He once reproached Henry with too much fondness for music: "It is with grief that I hear that you are beginning to get slack. . . . If you want to get anywhere in the world, learn to distinguish the useful from the agreeable, the important from the frivolous."

But, truth to tell, Henry could never be a thing of more account in the world than the shadow of Frederick. He felt that he was born to shine and he came little by little to hate that avaricious, authoritarian brother of his who claimed that he

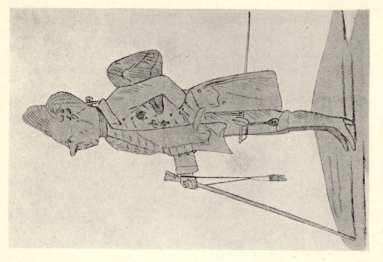

Caricature of Prince Henry

Caricature of Frederick

alone should have the whole stage. The King, looking upon him as a rival, took care to keep him in a state of strict dependence and make him conscious of all his bonds. "I have sought for your friendship," Frederick wrote in 1746, "I have been sparing of neither caresses nor approaches to gain your affection. . . . I have seen nothing but extreme coldness in your conduct; you have not lived with me as a brother but as a stranger. . . . I have modeled my conduct on yours. . . ." On another occasion he wrote, "We have nothing with which to reproach each other, we are equally cold toward each other and since you wish it to be so, I am contented also."

Henry, who had been made a colonel at sixteen, bore himself with honor during the Silesian wars, but his brother blamed him for having no keenness for the service and inflicted upon him the disgrace of having his regiment drilled by another colonel. "Sir, I have found it desirable to restore order in your regiment, because it was being lost. I am not accountable to you for my actions. If I have made changes, it is because they were desirable. You will also need to make some in your conduct. That is all I have to say at present."

Here the King's adolescence seems to be lived over again. So that their fates should be still more alike, Frederick obliged his brother to marry a princess of Hesse-Cassel whom he did not love. On that occasion there were huge festivities at Charlottenburg. The Queen Mother caught her foot in her dress and fell on the floor. Henry displayed the blackest gloom, but as a reward for the marriage the King lightened his slavery and made him a present of Rheinsberg. The Prince, wrote one of his biographers and admirers, abandoned himself "to the delights of a select society, which he knew how to gather round him by his affability, to retain by his attentions, and to animate by his wit." To tell the truth he also made some handsome young adventurers welcome there.

III

"FRIENDSHIP is essential to our happiness" is one of Frederick's sayings which depicts him best, but for him friendship was primarily a conversation. At Charlottenburg, at Potsdam he reunited the foreign legion of Rheinsberg, enlarged by some new conquests—Algarotti, D'Argens, Pöllnitz, and the two Keiths.

Algarotti was the same age as the King. He was the son of a rich merchant of Venice, was acquainted with France and England, sketched, and wrote verses; he had explained universal gravitation in dialogues, translated Petronius into French, and written a life of Caesar.

> Pupil of Horace and Euclid . . .
> A Newton for philosophy,
> Bernini as an architect,
> With Homer's voice for poetry.

He was to be found in the best company and in the worst. He was gay, amiable, frivolous, changeable, and a good talker on any and every subject. Frederick made him a count and gave him a pension. He called him the Swan of Padua, harmonious Swan, my sweet Swan. Algarotti repaid him in Italian engravings, in books of operas, in shafts of wit, in advice on artistic matters, and in letters stuffed with tender flattery.

D'Argens was a French marquis, son of a procurer general of the High Court of Aix and brother of a president. He had been a lawyer in Provence, a captain of cavalry in Germany, secretary to a legation in Constantinople, a writer in Holland, a lover in Italy, and the husband of an actress in Spain. Want forced him to be an intellectual. He wrote the *Jewish Letters,* which gained him the acquaintance of Voltaire but did not enrich him. He took refuge in the service of the Duchess of Württemberg, who was said to be a little mad. Frederick took him away from the Court at Stuttgart and appointed him chamberlain and director of the class of belles-lettres at the Academy, with a pension of 6,000 livres. D'Argens was a man of the world. He collected Dürer's engravings, ate too much, slept a lot, took no exercise, was afraid of draughts, and moaned about his illnesses, which were fear of dying, asthma, diarrhœa, piles, dysentery, several kinds of fever, and a scorbutic hemorrhage on his leg. He kept his urine in bottles, which he looked at several times a day to see if it became clouded. He wore five pairs of stockings in winter and grew pale if a saltcellar was upset in front of him. He did most of his writing in bed, propped up with a great number of pillows and with his writing desk on his knees. He knew the ancient languages perfectly and had published several works, some *Cabalistic Letters,* a *Common-sense Philosophy,* which was a discourse on the fallibility of human knowledge, and some *Secret Memoirs,* which were at bottom nothing but a review of the principal systems of metaphysics; he had translated Ocellus Lucanus, Timon of Locris, and the Emperor Julian's *Defense of Paganism,* a pretext for abundant commentaries. He resembled Bayle in having a certain ardor for research and erudition, but his style was soft and languishing. Voltaire defined him as "a very useful heathen, in spite of his chatter." He had as his mistress an actress of the French troop, Babette Cochois, whom he taught Greek and finished up by marrying. At the beginning of their affair Babette made him a present of a magnificent dressing gown which she had made out of a costume she wore in a queen's part. The marquis took the gown, tried it on, and found himself so becomingly attired that he took a fancy to wearing it throughout the evening. However, as he had to go to the King's, he sent word that he was ill and could not leave his room. Frederick did not like people to cut his suppers, and his intimates had to be punctual in the duties of wit. Being suspicious of the lie, he disguised himself as a priest, dressed his guests in black, and all the company went in a troop to visit D'Argens. A bell gave notice of the procession. D'Argens was warned by a valet and leaped into bed still dressed in the golden-flowered gown. The door opened; the spectators formed themselves into a semicircle, the priest mumbled a sermon, approached the bed, pulled aside the covering, emptied a bottle of oil on the marquis' dressing gown, and retired with the same ceremony as before. The master's jokes were not always agreeable.

If D'Argens loved peace, old Pöllnitz rushed about enough for ten. He was born rich and had been page and gentleman of the Bedchamber under Frederick I; then he had left Prussia to roam the world, magnificent, needy, hectic, beloved of the ladies. Flitting from capital to capital, he left in the gambling dens of Amsterdam, London, and Vienna the fortune of his fathers and the money he earned by writing startling society revelations. He was to be seen in Paris at the time of John Law's Mississippi scheme, converted to Catholicism and conspiring with Cellamare. After that he became a colonel in Spain and had himself

tonsured in Italy to obtain a canonry. He turned up again at
Berlin as a Lutheran and a contractor for hackney carriages. He
knew how to tell a tale, amused the King with his stories, and
always ended by getting out of him the money needed to pay his
debts. In 1744, as the sum was a large one, he again became a
Catholic and talked of entering a monastery. Frederick satisfied
his creditors so as to avoid losing him but imposed on the baron
a formal condition: "Every time you are at my table and find the
guests in a very good humor, you will take care to avoid assuming
the expression of a cuckold at the wrong moment, and you will
rather seek . . . to sustain and increase their joy." Pöllnitz had
invented an omelette; he bore the title of Premier Chamberlain
and he was a member of the Academy. At the age of sixty-five he
used to embroider satin purses and send them to the ladies in
the hope that they would return them to him full of money. But
in his latter days he was less sought after because he sometimes
forgot himself in his breeches.

The two Keiths were Scots and well born at that. They had
left the islands to avoid serving under the Hanoverian dynasty.
The younger, Jacob, had been a general in Russia: Frederick
made him a field marshal and governor of Berlin. The elder,
George, hereditary earl marischal of Scotland, was ambassador
at Versailles and governor of Neuchâtel. He was always called
"My Lord Marischal." He was a real character and had a heart of
gold. There were also some notorious atheists and some renegade
priests: La Mettrie, inventor of the mechanical man, a wretched
doctor and a jolly clown; Bastiani, a giant whom Frederick William had put in the grenadiers (Frederick made a canon of him);
the Abbé de Prades, whose thesis had been censured by the Sorbonne (he got taken on as a reader). "Really," observed the King,
"Potsdam is becoming a den of the excommunicated."

For some years there was also Darget, an intelligent, discreet,
hardworking man, who had the qualities of a fine clerk. He
played the part of private secretary, had charge of the library,
bought the books, went through the private and literary correspondence, corrected the copy of the royal works and saw them
through the press. . . .

> Your vexations never vary if you are the secretary
> Of an author who's a wit (and is well aware of it),

Who from morning until night loves to read and
rhyme and write. . . .

In each of his palaces Frederick had a library arranged in the
same manner: on the Rheinsberg basis with the addition of some
new French books. Once he ordered Darget to get the *Memoirs*
of Sir William Temple, the *Letters* of Cardinal d'Ossat, the
Essay on Commerce by Melon, and a new translation of Caesar's
Commentaries. "When I ask for a book," he added, "I mean that
I must be sent the finest, the most correct, and the most valuable
edition." Often he had printed for himself alone a few volumes
of authors he liked to reread, in specially chosen type and with
ornaments made to his orders. He took a store of reading with
him to the field. After the battle of Soor, when he lost all his
baggage, he asked Duhan to send him with all speed the works of
Boileau, Bossuet's *Discourse on Universal History,* the *Tusculan
Disputations,* the *Philippics,* and the *Orations against Catiline,*
Lucian (translated by D'Ablancourt), Chaulieu, Jean Baptiste
Rousseau, Feuquières, the *Campaigns of Turenne,* the *Persian
Letters,* the *Poem of Fontenoy,* and the *Henriade.* At his death,
however, the library of Sans Souci was more extensive than the
others: 2,288 volumes as against 1,038 at the castle of Potsdam.

IV

IMAGINE what the conversation must have been like between
such a variety of men—none of them was really a very original
thinker but all of them had lived in uncommon ways, possessed
a huge amount of culture, liked ideas and could tackle the most
daring ones with complete freedom. All the same the monastery
lacked the presence of the indispensable Brother Voltaire. More
than ever did Frederick desire to acquire his services permanently: the best method was to make life impossible for him in
France.

After the peace of Breslau Voltaire had sent the King a letter
of congratulation drawn up in imprudent and even in defama-
tory terms. "Sire, I received some verses, some very fine verses,
from my adored King at the time when we imagined that Your
Majesty was only thinking of freeing Marshal de Broglie from
anxiety. . . . I have learned that Your Majesty was then mak-

ing a very good treaty, very good for you no doubt, for you have trained your virtuous mind to be adept at statecraft. But whether this treaty is good for us poor Frenchmen is what people are doubting in Paris; half the world cries that you abandon our men to the discretion of the god of war; the other half is also crying out and knows not what it is all about; a few abbés of Saint-Pierre bless you in the midst of all this outcry. I am one of those enlightened persons; I believe you will force all the powers to make peace, and that the hero of the century will be the pacifier of Germany and of Europe. . . . Thus you are no longer our ally, Sire? But you are to be the ally of the human race. . . . Say 'I want everyone to be happy' and they will be; have a good opera, a good theater. Would that I could be a witness of your pleasures and your glory at Berlin." Several hundreds of copies of Voltaire's letter were broadcast over Paris one morning. All the ministers and all the ambassadors received a copy personally. That evening in the cafés people snatched it from each other to read it. The scandal and the fuss were universal, especially at Court, where everyone had a brother, a relation, or a friend in danger in the army of Bohemia, and cared little for the information that Berlin was to have a good opera. Naturally Voltaire repudiated it. But when he wrote to Frederick after the storm had blown over, he pretended to believe that it had been stolen by a clerk in the post office: the chances are that Frederick himself was responsible for the indiscretion.

In any case, when epigrams in which the philosopher had ridiculed the Bishop of Mirepoix were circulated in the same way, doubt was no longer possible. "Here is a letter of Voltaire's," the King commanded Rottenbourg on August 17, 1743, "which I beg you to send to the Bishop of Mirepoix by some underground means so that you and I will not be visible in this affair. My intention is to get Voltaire into such trouble in France that he will have no other course open to him but that of coming to my Court." This treachery was not even kept secret: "Talking of buffoons," wrote Frederick some weeks later, "Voltaire has unearthed, I know not how, the little betrayal we played on him and is strangely piqued by it; he will calm down, I hope. . . ." (October 14.) But as everything between them was turning into a comedy, Frederick went on writing to him: Come to Berlin "to withdraw your fragile skiff from the tempests and winds which have so often tossed it. You have endured too many affronts in France to be able to remain there with honor; you should leave a country where your reputation is torn to shreds daily."

For seven more years, while Madame du Châtelet lived, Voltaire turned a deaf ear. "I would rather live in a Swiss village," he said, "than enjoy the dangerous favor of a King who is capable of putting treachery into his friendship."

In 1750 he was a member of the Académie Française, Historiographer Royal, and a gentleman of the Chamber. The Court had no pleasures without him, Madame de Pompadour flattered him, Stanislas kindly invited him to his castles in Lorraine, Louis XV gave him a pension. But Voltaire was not the man to be content with honors which Boileau and Racine would have thought munificent. He wanted to receive letters from the King of France, to call him Trajan, to write him epistles in verse and sup privately with him and his mistress. That was not the custom at Versailles: he fell back on Potsdam. It can even be said that this time he made the first move. In one of the letters of guidance on poetry which he sent to Frederick he slipped in an offer of his services. "You have a prodigious genius and that genius is a cultivated one. But if, in the happy leisure you have obtained after so much glory, you continue to devote yourself to literature, if this passion of great minds continues with you, as I hope it will, if you wish to perfect yourself in all the finer points of our language and our poetry, *it will be necessary for you to have the goodness to work with me for two hours a day for six weeks or two months;* it will be necessary for me to make critical remarks on our finest authors in Your Majesty's company. You would enlighten me on all matters which are the concern of genius, and I would be not unhelpful to you on matters which depend on rules, matters which are a question of language and especially of different styles. A man's whole life is needed to acquire a profound knowledge of poetry and eloquence. I have plied this trade and this trade alone, and at the age of fifty-five I am still learning every day. These occupations are well worth a gambling party or a hunting expedition. The amusements of Frederick the Great should be those of Scipio."

The reply arrived by the next courier: "Sacrifice to me those two months which you promise me." Alas, the death of Madame du Châtelet upset the plans for the journey once again, but thereafter nothing held back the philosopher in his fatherland and no one prevented him from settling permanently in Berlin. Then came the question of terms. Voltaire asked for the Order of Merit: Frederick promised it him on arrival along with a chamberlain's key and a pension of 20,000 crowns. Voltaire asked Frederick to advance him the expenses of the journey: Frederick did better than that, he sent him a letter of exchange for 16,000 livres without a word about repayment.

> I wish to imitate the shower
> Her gallant poured abundantly
> Upon the breast of Danaë,
> For of your genius' lofty power
> The lover I have sworn to be.

And Voltaire replied while packing his trunks (June, 1750):

> Out from her humble, small retreat
> Your very aged Danaë
> Draws near the fine and starry seat
> Where age has got no right to be.
> Now Jupiter has done his part
> She yearns not for the golden dower;
> She loves with a devoted heart
> Her Jupiter and not his shower.
> But futile is the man who sneers
> At drops containing health untold,
> For we who live in iron years
> Cannot dispense with drops of gold.

At Cleve Voltaire found the King's coach waiting for him. Yet his joy was not unmixed. First, Louis XV had let him go like a person of secondary importance, accepting his resignation from his posts and himself playing a fine part by keeping up his pension. "One madman the more at the Court of Prussia," he said, "and one the less at mine." And then the news from Berlin related that Frederick was congratulating himself on having discovered a budding genius, the young Baculard d'Arnaud, whom it amused him to contrast with Voltaire as Apollo against decadence. The journey dragged because of bad roads, the coach broke down, and the traveler began to feel ill. At last on July 26 he addressed D'Argental with a cry of "My divine angels, I salute you from the Heaven of Berlin." At first everything was sunny. Frederick had kissed the poet's hand; Baculard had been dismissed into obscurity; Voltaire slept at Sans Souci in the room which had once been given to the Maréchal de Saxe; the Queens had given him a standing invitation to their table; he scrounged a pension for his niece, Madame Denis; he was free, he was flattered, he was beside himself with joy: "A hundred and fifty thousand victorious soldiers, no attorneys, opera, comedy, philosophy, poetry, a hero who is a philosopher and a poet, grandeur and grace, grenadiers and Muses, trumpets and violins, feasts like Plato's, good company, and liberty!"

A nocturnal carousal took place lit by 30,000 Chinese lanterns. "It is a carousal of the Great Louis' and a Lantern Festival of the Chinese rolled into one." When he passed through the amphitheater to get to his box, a murmur of admiration arose from the immense crowd of spectators, "Voltaire! Voltaire!" Balls, masquerades, receptions, and dinners followed each other almost without interruption. In the theater at Potsdam the King's brothers, the princesses, and the brothers of the monastery acted *Rome sauvée*, *Jules César*, *Zaïre*, *Mahomet*, *Mérope*, and *Brutus*. All the morning Voltaire had rehearsals. At eleven he went to see the King drilling his regiment of guards; then he walked with him till dinner at midday. After that came a two-hour interview with the royal pupil—literature, poetry, grammar, rhetoric—after which the master worked on his *Age of Louis XIV*, which was designed to crush the ill-advised Louis XV by mere comparison. At seven o'clock, a concert: the King played the flute. Lastly, supper: the meal was a good one and continued late. The King had two famous chefs in his kitchen, Joyard of Lyon and Noël of Perigueux. For himself he liked highly spiced dishes, venison pasties, botargo, truffles, game that was high, and ox tongues seasoned with pepper. He found Rhenish wines too sour for him and only drank champagne with a little water. At all times of the day and night baskets full of fruit were to be found on the consoles, which the King and his guests emptied in the middle of their chattering. "These suppers," Voltaire was to write later, "were very pleasant: I do not know if I am making a mistake, but it seems to me there was plenty of wit. The King possessed some and gave rise to it in others." And again, "Never did anyone in any spot on the globe talk with such liberty about all the superstitions of mankind, and never were they treated with more jesting and contempt. . . . A ghost listening to us would have thought he heard the seven sages of Greece at . . ." let us say, at a tavern.

They talked about everything. Frederick had his recognized butts—the Marshal de Broglie, whom he nicknamed the Quadruple Xenophon, because he had made his retreat into Bavaria with 40,000 men; the King of England; the Duke of Cumberland, whom he called a great blockhead; the King of Poland and his minister, the Count von Brühl, whose wardrobe at Dresden had drawn this exclamation from him, "What a number of wigs for a man without a head!" One day, when he had just finished tearing his neighbor to pieces, he asked the Abbé Bastiani, "When you become Pope, how will you receive me if I decide to go to Rome to prove my devotion at the feet of Your Holiness?"

"Sire," replied the Abbé, "I will say, 'Let the Black Eagle be admitted, let him cover me with his wings, but let him spare me his beak.' "

In December the King used to move to Berlin to spend the six weeks known as the carnival there. During this Prussian "Grand Season" he presented himself on fixed occasions at the Queens' dinners, which were very boring, at their evening parties where cards were played, at their ballroom where there was dancing to order. In the immense state rooms of the castle were held some great official receptions which were more boring still. The principal event was always the composition of an Italian opera, or rather of an opera sung in Italian. The music was by Graun, the book by Frederick after a fable or incident in ancient history, the words arranged or translated by Algarotti or by someone else. The King possessed the best voices in Europe. One year he himself gave lessons to the young tenor Porporino, for whom he wrote two cantatas and some fine melodies in the opera *Artaxerxes*. On these occasions many strangers came to Berlin: German princes, Englishmen, young lords who wanted to be presented, officers traveling to study their profession. Quantities of money were spent on clothes, wines, jewels, equipages, and crockery. The quarrels over etiquette were as lively and as ridiculous as at Versailles but they put the King in a spiteful mood. Having to settle a dispute about precedence between two ladies, he replied, "Let the stupidest go first."

Voltaire, however, already did not feel very secure. "I am a bit like Chie-en-pot la Perruque," he had written to D'Argental. "Perhaps you do not know the tale about him: he was a man who left Paris because the little boys ran after him; he went by stagecoach to Lyons and as soon as he got out was greeted by a mob of guttersnipes." The guttersnipes of Berlin were called Baculard, who did not leave without displaying his venom, and La Beaumelle, who had arrived by ship from Copenhagen and had just published a collection of tasteless maxims, which contained phrases of this sort: "There have been greater poets than Voltaire, there have never been any who were so well paid. The King of Prussia overwhelms men of talent with kindness for the same reasons which make a minor prince of Germany overwhelm a jester or a dwarf with kindness. . . ." Fortunately La Beaumelle behaved like an archlunatic and left before Voltaire could call in the arm of the law.

Thereupon the Hirsch affair broke out. By the latest treaty Saxony had undertaken to redeem at par for Prussian holders, but for them alone, certain bills which within her own frontiers had depreciated by 16 per cent. It was a trick of the stock jobbers to buy depreciated bills at Dresden, to smuggle them into Prussia, and to present them for refund. Voltaire requested a Jewish broker called Hirsch to buy him 80,000 thalers' worth of bills; to cover the transaction he sent him bills of exchange on Paris which he afterward recalled, undoubtedly through fear at the risk involved. The agreement was complicated by an obscure tale about diamonds which Hirsch had entrusted to the poet and was unwilling to take back on the plea that he could not identify them. Finally the agent still claimed a commission for the purchase of the bills and 500 crowns compensation. Voltaire replied that as he had canceled his order as soon as he had learned of its fraudulent nature, he had no obligation to anyone. Whereupon he lost patience and took Hirsch into court. The Jew's claims were overruled and Voltaire emerged victorious (February 18, 1751).

But the case he had won before the judges he lost at the bar of public opinion. The King forbade him to reappear at Potsdam till judgment was given: "I was very pleased to receive you here; I have a high opinion of your wit, your talents, your knowledge, and I naturally believed that a man of your age, tired of fencing with authors and exposing himself to the storm, came here to take refuge as in a tranquil harbor. . . . You have had the world's most dirty affair with the Jew. You have made a dreadful scandal throughout the town. . . . As for me, I have kept the peace in my house up till your arrival and I warn you that if you have a passion for intriguing and caballing you have come to the wrong place for it. I like people who are mild and peaceful, who do not infuse their conduct with the violent passions of a tragedy. In the event of your being able to resign yourself to the life of a philosopher, I shall be very pleased to see you; but if you have to abandon yourself to all the fury of your passions and feel aggrieved at everyone, you will give me no pleasure by coming here and you may just as well remain in Berlin."

Then, alluding to old brawls, he added, "I hope that you no longer have any quarrel either with the Old or with the New Testament; these sorts of dispute are dishonorable, and with the talents of the finest wit in France you will not hide the stain which this conduct will imprint on your reputation in the long run. A bookseller, a violin from the Opera House, and a Jewish jeweler—these really are people whose names should not be found in the company of yours in any sort of business. I write this letter with the heavy common sense of a German, who says what he thinks without making use of equivocal phrases and flabby extenuations which disfigure the truth; it is for you to profit by it."

Monsieur André Bellessort writes that nothing could be more pitiable than the replies Voltaire made to these outrageous remarks: his wit does not smile, it grimaces. "I have told H.R.H. the Margravine of Bayreuth that Brother Voltaire was in disgrace. Have pity on Brother Voltaire. . . . To whom would you show the products of your noble genius if not to your old admirer? He has no talent left but he has taste. . . . Reckon that

I am in despair. . . . If the Queen of Sheba had been in disgrace with Solomon she would not have suffered more than I. . . ."

When he had been pardoned, all occasions were appropriate for the adoration of his hero.

> Today, although they would have us believe
> This very day, Good Friday, was the day
> That a God suffered for the world's reprieve,
> To my true King of Glory I dare tune my lay,
> To my salvation's real source. . . .

Frederick accepted the repentance, the flatteries, and the baseness, and wrote to his brother William, "Voltaire is as meek as a lamb and as droll as a harlequin."

Although, in the midst of all this, the King had given his chamberlain a house which was called the marquisate, it was henceforth impossible for their relations to be as friendly as before. The affair had emboldened the envious: the clique which was overwhelmed by Voltaire's reputation proceeded to poison the atmosphere. They hawked anecdotes around. The poet was supposed to have said of the King, with a sneer, "That man is Caesar and a Grub Street hack." Another time when a raw poet was proffering him his works, a second pile of verses was handed to him: "There," said he, "the King has sent me his dirty linen to wash, yours must wait." Frederick, referring to his guest, was supposed to have calmed his impatient followers with these words: "Let be, I need him for another year at the outside; first squeeze the orange, then throw away the peel." Is this statement accurate? At all events he had written down harsher ones; to Algarotti, "Useful things can be learned from a rogue. I want to know his French, what do I care about his morals?"—to his sister Wilhelmina, "You ask me about this lawsuit between Voltaire and the Jew. It is the affair of a swindler who wants to cheat a sharper" —to Darget, "Voltaire has behaved like a cad and a consummate knave." But Voltaire had money to invest: he placed his capital with the Duke of Württemberg. Frederick knew this and was weak enough to be piqued by it. Whereupon the catastrophe arose.

Voltaire's principal opponent at Berlin was Maupertuis, the president of the Academy, a considerable scholar, mathematician, geometer, and physicist, a member of the French Academy and of the Paris Academy of Sciences. He had become famous through his expedition to Lapland, where he had gone to measure the length of a degree of the meridian in the neighborhood of the Arctic Circle. He was proud, boastful, pitiless to his scientific enemies, considered himself the high priest and protector of all the Frenchmen in Prussia, dared to make the wildest flights of the imagination, and had gained the confidence of Frederick, who always wrote to him on a particular note of respect, without familiarity or mockery, as to a distinguished official. "You are the Pope of our Academy," he told him one day. The King wanted hard-working academicians: Maupertuis knew how to keep them at it.

That year Maupertuis was convinced that he had discovered a new principle in physics. With all possible caution his friend König, the mathematician, denied the value of the discovery, making reference to one of Leibniz' letters, which was in his view at once the source and the refutation of the theory. Maupertuis called on König to produce the original letter; König admitted that he had only a copy of it; the great philosopher's papers were searched and nothing was found. Then Maupertuis formed the Academy into a tribunal and the letter was adjudged to be apocryphal. König replied by resigning and appealing to the public. Voltaire was conscious of Maupertuis' jealousy and could not bear him; he was revolted by his behavior and, unable to contain himself, published "A Letter from an Academician of Berlin to an Academician of Paris," which had four lines too many in it: "Several members of the Academy of Berlin have protested against this conduct and would have left the Academy which Maupertuis coerces and dishonors, if they were not afraid of displeasing the King who is its patron." A few days later a reply appeared, the author of which called Voltaire a wretched writer, a barefaced impostor, and an inept compiler of lampoons. "I pity these unfortunate writers," he went on, "who senselessly abandon themselves to their passions and are so blinded by their own wickedness that they betray at the same time their frivolity, their rascality, and their ignorance." Soon after a second edition of the reply was published with the crown, scepter, and eagle of Prussia at the head of the title page (November, 1752).

Voltaire was staggered: he had never realized that in finding fault with the Academy he was at the same time attacking Frederick, who had founded it with so much fuss. However, it was impossible for him to resist the pleasures of revenge. He flung himself upon the wild extravagances of Maupertuis' latest book and tore it to pieces for all eternity in a pitiless douche of buffoonery, *The Diatribe of Doctor Akakia*. No book was published in Berlin without authorization; Voltaire made use of a privilege which had been given him for the *Defense of Bolingbroke* to bring out the *Diatribe*. The King's annoyance can be guessed; Voltaire's denials exasperated him; he gave orders for all the copies of *Akakia* to be seized, had them burned by the common hangman, and sent the ashes to Maupertuis (December 24, 1752). On January 1 Voltaire asked for leave to go. "Sire, impelled by the tears and solicitations of my family, I see myself obliged to place at your feet my fortune and all the distinctions with which you have honored me. . . . I have made you my idol; an honest man does not change his religion, and sixteen years of boundless devotion cannot be destroyed by the misfortune of a moment." At the same time he returned him his chamberlain's key and the ribbon of the Order of Merit with this quatrain:

> These I received when days were bright,
> These I return now days are black,
> Ah, thus a lover hands his mistress' portrait back
> When passion is at topmost height.

Frederick returned the lot with a request that he should stay. A supper and a few forced jests sealed the reconciliation, but Voltaire thought of nothing but making his exit: "I see clearly that the orange has been squeezed," he wrote to his niece. "It is time to think of saving the peel." He asked leave to go and take the waters at Plombières, as an invalid. "There is no need whatever for you to find a pretext," said the King. "You can leave my service when you wish."

They supped together every evening for a week; finally on March 23, 1753, Voltaire drew the last quarter of his pension and left on the twenty-sixth for Leipzig, where he had *Akakia* republished with a postscript in his best style. From Saxony he traveled to Gotha, where the duchess received him like a prince;

then, calm and lively, he arrived at the free city of Frankfort along with Collini, his secretary.

Now while Voltaire was with him Frederick had had published under the title *Works of the Philosopher of Sans Souci, in the Keep of the Castle, Privileged by Apollo* several selections of prose and verse, a four-hundred-page history of Brandenburg, an *Art of War* in six cantos (which though Voltaire had corrected it word by word was packed with vulgar doggerel), odes, letters of prose and verse mixed, stanzas and *Epistles* wherein the banalities of a commonplace morality were developed more or less skillfully, but also in a limited edition a burlesque epic after the manner of *La Pucelle,* called *Le Palladion,* the subject of which was the abduction of Darget in 1745 by the panders of Maria Theresa, who thought they were getting hold of Valori, whose secretary he was. God and the saints were mixed up in this affair, Saint Hedwig, patroness of Prussia, came down to the Austrian camp to rescue Darget from the clutches of the enemy, Darget told his abductors how he had been brought up by the Jesuits and all the fine things they had taught him, sodomy included—in short, it was such a collection of blasphemies, smut, and obscenity as to make a king ridiculous forever.

Voltaire spent a night in Frankfort and was preparing to get into his coach (May 1) when he was arrested by the Prussian resident, a person called Freytag, a complete lackey, rogue, and imbecile, who demanded "dey vucks of poeshy of de King, mine master." Freytag had been prudent enough to bring the senator of the town with him. For eight hours he searched the trunks, coffers, money boxes, and portfolios. Voltaire was at the end of his tether and fainted, but the book had been left in a box at Leipzig. Freytag sent the travelers to the Black Lion Hotel: they would be able to continue their journey when the box arrived. Madame Denis rejoined her uncle; on June 17 the box and the "vucks of poeshy" arrived. However, Freytag was waiting for further instructions; Voltaire lost his head and tried to escape; he was recognized at the gate, arrested, treated as a thief, taken back to the town, insulted by the populace, robbed by the soldiers, and shut up in a hovel with Collini and Madame Denis. It was not until July 6 that the three prisoners were released. The whole episode had been contrived and carried out by Freders-

dorff, acting on the instructions of Frederick; Freytag had embellished it with the idiocy of a greenhorn, the magistrates of
Frankfort with their servile complicity. Frederick tried to cover
himself by an incredulous letter which he sent to his ambassador
in France but he deceived no one. Eight months later Voltaire
began to offer him his books once more.

V

POTSDAM was too small to house two kings, but Voltaire's flight
was the end of Sans Souci. Insensibly the setting disintegrated.
In the first place the King's tastes had changed. In 1754, when
pastorals by Lancret were suggested to him, he replied, "I have
no more taste for such things, or rather I have enough in that
style." His friends, especially D'Argens and Algarotti, had succeeded in making him believe that the frivolous art of the French
did not deserve his attention and that he ought only to interest
himself in the "great paintings" of Italy and Flanders.

"Watteau had considerable imagination," said D'Argens; "he
understood color well, his brush is sweeping, his touch light, his
fanciful notions contain much truth, his landscapes are well
treated; he has seldom painted anything but rustic pictures and
he has never done anything serious which merits the attention
of connoisseurs; his talent consisted in portraying balls, theater
scenes, and rural feasts; and the clothing of his figures is always
comic."

Frederick had acquired his first collection very cheaply, or according to his own way of putting it, "for a bit of bread." When
he started buying up Raphaels, Titians, and Correggios he was
robbed. "It is astonishing," he wrote naïvely to Wilhelmina,
"with what ease I have succeeded in making quite a large collection of pictures, well known and famous among connoisseurs.
. . . I have already collected nearly a hundred, among which
there are two Correggios, two Guidos, two Paul Veroneses, one
Tintoretto, one Solimena, twelve Rubens, eleven Van Dycks,
without counting other famous masters. I still need fifty pictures,
I expect some from Italy and Flanders. . . ." Oesterreich's catalogue shows under 1771 three pictures by Da Vinci, nine by
Titian, five by Raphael. . . . But some of these canvases had

never existed and the others have disappeared leaving no memory behind them, for they were fakes. Frederick's two buyers, Petit and Mettra, cheated him quite calmly: to quiet his doubts, it was enough to have the expert opinion of "enlightened" amateurs, academicians of some sort or other. At any rate among the alleged pictures by Correggio there was one genuine one which was very lovely, "Leda and the Swan," which Darget had bought at the Pasquier sale.

Pesne was growing old. Frederick looked for another painter. He wanted "the most famous," but Boucher and Natoire eluded him. He contented himself with "the most reasonable solution," Amedeus van Loo, the nephew of Charles, an understudy. He had also some sculptors who were not of the first rank, Francis Gaspard Adam, who apparently remained for twelve years without any scenes, and his nephew Sigisbert Michael, who made off, loudly demanding the price of works for which he had not been paid. In 1748 Thieriot, who kept Frederick in touch with life in Paris, also stopped working for him as a correspondent: he complained he had not received a third of the promised salary.

Besides the atmosphere of Sans Souci was too artificial, too manufactured. Usually the Court enjoyed amusements of a pretty shoddy variety. To amuse Prince Henry a bear dressed in woman's clothes was trundled about in a sedan chair. When Princess Amelia was elected Abbess of Quedlinburg, her brother William got up a fete for her at Oranienburg: he muffled up all the domestic staff in ridiculous tawdry robes, and led her past the servants, who sank down in bows and curtseys, presenting them to her—*la marquise de Pissenlit, la vicomtesse de Cul-Tendre.* . . . When Amelia reached her room after the masquerade, she found there a giant chamber pot as large as a barrel, inscribed "For the Mother Superior." Frederick himself often talked like a trooper. To Darget he ended up a letter with the salutation, "My hemorrhoids salute your pox." One day at a state dinner he made a terrific attack on Podewils, accusing him of going to houses of ill fame in the daytime, and cried, "I do not understand how old Grumbkow, who was a sensible fellow, could have given you his daughter!" Frederick's letters to his confidential chamberlain Fredersdorff are astonishingly full of low or common expressions. It is more surprising still that Fredersdorff, who was well versed in alchemy, should almost have succeeded in converting his master. The King began by mocking at charlatans; he feared ridicule and he cited the experience of the Duke of Brunswick, who believed in the philosophers' stone and was robbed of three millions; but in the end he became interested in the experiments of an old witch called Madame Nothnagel: "Write to me, then, on Monday, to say if she has really made gold. If it is true, I will put up the necessary money for beginning production on a large scale not later than next spring." Voltaire Apollo had left in March; in September Frederick Marcus Aurelius had become a disciple of Old Moore.

When telling one of his correspondents to engage some actresses for him, the King worded the command thus, "We want determined harlots, who act with spirit." That gives us the tone. Also at the theater and the Opera House desertions and revolts were frequent. One year the ballet master Pointier and the *première danseuse* Mademoiselle Rolland took to flight together: Frederick wrote an article against them in the gazette. In 1747 came a new desertion—Lani, the ballet master, disappeared, taking with him Noverre and part of the company. On another occasion a dancer called Lavoir let off a pistol at a sergeant who tried to recapture him.

The liberty with which Frederick flattered his friends was an illusion; they went to supper as to a military maneuver; they could not be absent without permission; their slightest gestures were spied upon and reported. The Platonic familiarity which ruled among those about the round table was no less deceptive. The master of the house possessed an extraordinary faculty for attraction, gaiety, and wit, and a great fund of ideas and information; he often paid charming compliments to people; but he was a scoffer and never knew when his banter had gone far enough. As the wretched people who became his butts dared not reply in the same tone, they had to endure the sarcasms and force a smile of agreement and of flattery. One evening he asked the guests how each of them would like to govern Prussia if they were king of it. When the turn of the Marquis d'Argens came, "Bless my soul," said he, "I would quickly sell my kingdom to go and eat away the price of it in Provence."

Algarotti left in 1742; he returned in 1747 but in 1753, after having begged the King for a suitable, permanent post in vain, he obtained leave to remain in Italy. Following a duel Chasot was clapped in jail. He made off in 1752 and succeeded a stable-boy in the favors of the Duchess of Mecklenburg-Strelitz, who was a frightful old body with the bosom of a wet nurse. She gave him a lot of money and a charming castle which he christened "What Will People Say?" In the same year Darget made a journey to Paris and did not return.

One after another all who had been the masters and companions of the Crown Prince disappeared: the aged Dessau, his son Leopold, Marshal the Duke of Holstein, Frederick von Borcke, Knobelsdorff, Rottenbourg, Stille. It seemed as though Death, by effacing the figures of the past one by one, wanted to place a desert, an impassable barrier of mourning, around Frederick. Suhm had not seen his friend again as King; he had died on the way back from St. Petersburg and had scarcely had time to send him a last farewell. "Sire, it is in vain for them to give me a little more hope. . . . A few more days, perhaps a few more hours, and I will be no more. . . . All that is left is for me to turn my heart from the earth, to turn it toward the eternal source of all life and all felicity. Ah, it is at this moment that I feel all the strength of the tender bonds which unite me to the most lovable, the most virtuous of morals. . . . The hour approaches, already I feel my strength deserting me, I must be gone. Farewell. One more tear, it bathes your feet. Oh, deign to look on it, great King, as a token of the tender, unalterable devotion with which your faithful Translucent was devoted to you unto death!"

In 1745 within three months of each other died the mild Jordan and Keyserlingk, who was the breath of life itself. Jordan had been suffering from chest trouble for a long time; he felt he was dying at the time when Frederick was busy with the second war of Silesia. He had the strength to await a visit of the King's, he saw him once again on his arrival, and died the next day. Frederick bought a number of his books: when he opened them and saw the inscription which Jordan put at the head of them all —*Jordani et amicorum*—he could not hold back his grief. "I confess to you that I had tears in my eyes and that it gave me real pain to think that this man whom I had loved so deeply is no more. I am afraid of Berlin for that reason. . . ."

Keyserlingk had got married in 1742 and the King had written a comedy in the manner of Molière for the wedding celebrations called *The Monkey à la Mode*. He fell ill in the winter of 1744, dragged on for a few months without taking care of himself, seemed to recover in the sunshine, and died suddenly during the first frosts of autumn. Frederick was prostrated. Jordan and Keyserlingk had been his friends, the one for eleven and the other for seventeen years; he had loved them before being King; they had come to him when he had almost nothing to give them; they kept him linked to the world by reminding him of sad and tender memories. For weeks he could find no consolation. He wept when he was alone. After the death of Keyserlingk he tried to put his grief into verse:

> Alas, I have lost all, have lost the friend I love,
> Thee gone, I am alone in this vast universe;
> Those days have passed from me like unto shadows vain,
> When our two souls, conjoined to form a single soul,
> Would intercommunicate their pleasure and their pain,
> And still the same delight would their two joys control.

He also said, "When I return to Berlin I will find myself almost a stranger in my own country, living all alone in that land, isolated among the living and only having acquaintance with the dead." While emptiness grew up about him, he surrounded himself with peaceful pessimism; amid solitude and hard work he built up a bitter and despairing philosophy which expected nothing of men and even less of God:

> This God may take delight in some vast enterprise,
> But he is deaf to all the idiot rabble's cries.

It is reminiscent of the despair of De Vigny. "I have lost almost all my friends and old acquaintances," he repeated to Maupertuis, "and I find consolation only in study and in work; one must learn to be self-sufficient. . . . That is difficult."

Ten years later he still wrote in the same terms: "My youth has been a school of adversity, and since then I have not escaped reverses and misfortunes in my much-envied position, which imposes on people with its puffed-up grandeur. One thing which has happened almost to me alone is that I have lost all the friends of my heart and my old acquaintances. These are wounds from which the heart long bleeds; philosophy can staunch but it cannot heal them."

Life completed the education arranged for him by his father. She snatched from the son his pleasures, his joys, his dreams, his tastes, his affections, and even the dear shadows of his youth. He might not, he could not, be other than Frederick the Great, King of Prussia.

IX

Fredericus Rex

I

FREDERICK used to get up at five in the morning in summer and at six in winter. Protected by the cupids who mounted guard along his beautiful silver balustrade, he slept on a camp bed hidden by a curtain. A footman used to wake him, light his fire, dress him, and shave him. He would put on his boots and his uniform; a page would bring him the ambassadors' dispatches, the letters which had arrived by the post and those which the secretaries of the cabinet had received from ministers. He read these letters until eight o'clock, having carefully examined the seals first to see if they were complete and intact. At eight o'clock a secretary used to come to get the answers, some already scribbled in the margin, others ready to be dictated. Toward nine or ten o'clock he would give an audience to his chief aide-de-camp and regulate all army matters in the same manner. Then he used to go and drill the Guards' regiment or inspect some other unit. In the afternoon he used to read, write, and meditate. At four o'clock his secretary would come back to get his signature, after which he devoted himself to his private correspondence, matters concerning the Academy, building operations, and artists.

In his study at Potsdam he held all the threads of policy and administration in his hands. Everything started from there and ended there. He wielded absolute power with anxious and almost morbid jealousy: "In a state like this one the prince must of necessity arrange his affairs by himself, because if he is wise he will only pursue the interests of the public, which are his own. . . ." It would not have been possible for Newton "to work out his system of attraction if he had labored in company with Leibniz and Descartes." In the same way a political system cannot "be made and upheld if it does not spring from a single brain. This must be that of the sovereign, the head of Jupiter must give birth to Minerva fully armed, that is to say that the prince should plan his system and execute it himself."

In fact his government was not only personal but also mechanical. The people he employed had to obey his wishes without appreciating them, if need be even without understanding them. "I will have my commands executed immediately and exactly, and when I demand and require something I must obtain it on the spot and promptly." In whatever form independent initiative showed itself—advice, influence, objections—he was always afraid of it and invariably rejected it. Never in his two-line orders did he give a reason, for fear that the reason should be discussed. He accepted no comment, however humble it might be: "I can do nothing about it; it must be carried out without argument." Or else when a minister was concerned, "My dear fellow, you understand nothing about it. Sir, mind your own business," and the question was closed. Lastly, never would he put up with anyone stimulating or soliciting him to action: everything, from the slightest of favors to the gravest of decisions, had to emanate from him. One day he asked the Directory of Intelligence about a candidate for a minor post. The Directory replied that the applicant was recommended by a general. "Since the general recommends him I will not take him." On another occasion, when General von Prittwitz begged to be given the Black Eagle, he drew upon himself the following retort, "My order is like efficient grace, it is given and not deserved."

Frederick mistrusted hasty reforms. He believed that the constitution of a country was the product of time, that the basic character of a people was a thing that was never obscured, that institutions adapted themselves to it in an imperceptible manner, and that as soon as they had been tested by long use they must be held to be the best available. Therefore he kept up his father's bureaucratic apparatus almost unchanged. At the center, the Ministry of Foreign Affairs, the Ministry of Justice, and the Central Office for Finance, War, and Domains; in the provinces, the seventeen Chambers of War and Domains with their secretaries and their clerks, district councilors (*Landräte*), commissioners of taxes (*Steuerräte*), and bailiffs.

The administration was collegiate, that is to say that it rested on the authority of a large number of persons, on Councils, the members of which were collectively responsible and could do nothing on their own. This collegiate organization as compared with French "one-man" administration provided greater facilities for information and inquiry, and guaranteed impartiality and tolerance more effectively. However, it called for the presence of an autocratic prince at the top to be the essential mainspring of it all—a man without whom decision and responsibility would be ground to powder between the infinity of forces and counterforces which immobilized each other. On the other hand, the monarch whose unhampered will was indispensable to the movement of business encountered no moral resistance from the colleges—met with none of those unwritten, all-powerful traditions which had been promoted in France to the status of fundamental laws. At Versailles it was possible for a minister, an intendant, or a senior assistant to gain a reputation and a position which the King would be compelled to take into account. In the Prussian collegiate system the commissioners kept a check upon and nullified one another in a dead level of obscurity. The more there were of them, the less individuality and distinction did each possess. Not only was the King the sole fount of will but also in the end he became the sole fount of knowledge, sole possessor of regular, detailed, and complete information on the resources of the State and the life of the kingdom.

Moreover, Frederick treated his assistants as mere quill-drivers, barely competent to carry out his orders effectively. He never brought them together and he only saw them very occasionally one by one, at the most a few times each year. There was indeed in June a sort of general inspection of ministers, in the course of which the King examined the budget and the state of each department, but in the normal course of events all business was done in writing. The Central Office, the presidents of Chambers and the councilors used to send in the reports: the King wrote his decisions in the margin. That was what was called an Order in Cabinet. He sometimes made fifty or sixty of them in a single morning, for the custom had grown up of sending on for his scrutiny everything a hairsbreadth outside the administrative routine. He did not trouble to set the public services in order according to strict logic, for he epitomized the State in his own

person. The Central Office, for example, was divided into four
sections and a legal section, which shared the correspondence
with the provinces between them according to a geographical
classification. Without worrying whether the division of business
by subjects did not run contrary to this territorial division, he set
up beside them four "real" departments, i.e., departments with
competence over the whole kingdom for one particular matter—
manufactures, military administration, mines, and forests.

The Prussian bureaucracy used a pedantic, verbose language,
bristling with latinisms and legal jargon. Frederick demanded
clear, brief reports, "short and precise abstracts" with "exacti-
tudes" and without "useless details" or "digressions." The Central Office was briskly told "not to make use henceforward in the
reports which are to be submitted to H.M. of words and expressions completely unknown to H.M., but to express themselves in a comprehensive way in words entirely well known,"
in such a way that, when H.M. decreed something, he might be
able "clearly to understand" what the matter was upon which
he was making a decision. Furthermore the ministers ought to
know that it is "unthinkable to send H.M. documents stuffed
with legal Latin, for although it is well enough known among
the legal profession and in the criminal courts" it is so much
"Arabic" to H.M. All these remarks were written by Frederick
in a fine, nervous hand, so elegant and neat that it might be
mistaken for the writing of a woman. When his letters were
in French he signed them *Fédéric* (without an *r*), as was also
the case with diplomatic dispatches. For administrative correspondence, on the other hand, he almost always used German—a caricature of German which has to be read aloud to be
properly understood, so unusual is the spelling. The same comments reappear with the greatest frequency. "He is mad!"
"What idiocy!" "Hot air!" "I am as poor as Job!" "No, thank
you!" "No money!" He was perpetually on the defensive, as if
his officials, and especially the smaller ones, thought of nothing
but robbing and cheating him. "I could hang 99 per cent of
them with a completely clear conscience," he wrote one day.
He deceived his ministers with false confidences, he aroused
their jealousy by hiding from one what he revealed to another,
and he disguised his most important decisions. In the spring of

1744 the excellent Podewils was quite ignorant of his master's negotiations with France; he did not know of the alliance until it had already been in existence for three weeks.

Frederick did not want to share his plans or his secrets. "I would tear off my shirt," said he, "if my shirt knew my secret." Still, as regards Podewils he imposed certain limits on himself: he only accused him of prevarication twice. However, he treated the others with tart contempt, with deliberate and insulting suspicion, which would have warmed the heart of old Frederick William and made an English envoy remark, "I would rather be a monkey in Borneo than a minister in Prussia."

Sometimes he made jokes. A president asked to be authorized to requisition twenty-four horses so as to move house, and he replied, "That's all very fine, but twenty-four can drag a cannon. The president is not important enough for such heavy transport. He may have eight horses and when he gets more corpulent he may have ten or twelve." An officer had been fined a hundred thalers for killing a deer in the royal forests and feared he would fall into disgrace: "This is a matter of no importance. At such a price most of my deer are at your disposal." However, more frequently he threatened or preached. "That is a first warning. Take care that nothing more serious comes your way."—"That will remain in my control, the rest is nothing but a ministerial maneuver to get jobs for their toadies."—"I get nowhere with Knobelsdorff. He does not carry things out as I wish, he is lazy as a gunner's horse."—"More lawyers' dodges."—"The draftsman is an ass and the ministers have not read the rescript, there is nothing in it. I have never read anything so stupid in all my life." This was his answer to an officer who pleaded his length of service: "It is not long services which matter but good ones; I have a stable full of old mules which all did service, but they do not claim for that reason to become grooms." To a president who asked for extended leave because of illness, "Gout when on leave, I know that one!" To a former member of the War Council who asked leave to go into France, "As he has robbed here, he can always go down there and rob them also." To a medical student who asked leave to go into the English army as a surgeon, "I would rather hang him!" To the president of the Chamber of Cleve, who had displeased him, "I must have been misinformed as to your character. Either you are an ass and you do not know the province, or you are a bladder full of wind who does no work. No one could make a more stupid report than that one you sent me." To the councilors of the Chamber of Königsberg, "You are archrogues who are not worth the bread you are given and you all deserve to be dismissed. Only wait till I visit Prussia!" Until his last gasp he wrote and dictated thousands of notes of this type.

Frederick kept a very careful eye on public opinion; during the first war for Silesia he pestered Jordan to keep him well posted: "I ask you for news of Berlin. . . . I want news. . . . Tell me what the public is saying, and in what circumstances it is said. Hide no part of the picture from me." In reply he sent him the general topics for conversations he must start and the remarks he must spread around. But as for this opinion which he humored, he despised it even more thoroughly than he watched it. In his opinion the majority of mankind were not by nature reasonable. They were "creatures of habit" who allowed themselves to be led "by rogues and cheats." The swinish multitude "wallows in an invincible ignorance." It loves the marvelous, the supernatural, and every sort of superstition. The greater part of its judgments rest upon "prejudices, fables, errors, and impostures." When the Berliners discussed the war they made observations which were "distorted." When the Parisians protested against the peace of Breslau "their jibes were like the screaming of parrots and their judgments as serious as the decisions of a baboon on questions of metaphysics."

Nevertheless he had himself many of the eccentricities of the society of his time, and for a start "sensibility"—a taste for righteous rhetoric and for studied emotion. In the *Mirror of Princes,* which he wrote in 1744 for the young Duke of Württemberg, he declared that humanity was "the cardinal virtue of every thinking being," and that his heart henceforth "blossoms at the sight of the fine spirits who love the good." He preached continually on his "generous" word of honor how "the weaknesses of a sensitive heart are preferable to the inhuman hardness of the Stoics." In the foreword of these memoirs he could not stop himself from slipping into a lachrymose tirade against "the horrible effusion of human blood which has taken place" and against the battles which transformed Europe "into a butcher's stall." But at a time when the "sensibility" of the age had often its counterpart in a facile and reckless skepticism, it was nothing but a literary diversion for Frederick; it would suddenly give way to the coldest and most calculating realism.

His own sphere was one of facts: facts desired and facts accomplished, interests, the land, and constant dealings with men, with war, and with public business. He thought in concrete terms. An idea came to his mind like a figurative representation of actual objects. His power of concentration was such that he could glance through twenty letters running and then answer each one of them in order and without reading them again. He had a positive and in some ways a visual imagination, a highly developed topographical instinct, and an astonishingly precise memory for places. To compensate for this he had a horror of the abstract: "Our reason," he said, "only works upon matters upon which our experience throws light. Put abstract matters before it and you set it straying in a labyrinth from which it will never discover the exit." Man was made for action and not for knowledge, for "the principles of things elude our most persistent research." Therefore he despised metaphysics, "a balloon blown out with wind," and since Bayle had diverted his mind from seeking after transcendent truths, this was the greatest advantage for which he had to thank him. As for mathematics, he admitted that he did not understand them; they appeared to him to be "a pure luxury" of the intellect. Although it was "sublime," geometry (the word he used to describe all the exact sciences) was not in the least made to be the business of men. "I leave it," he said, "to some empty dreamer of an Englishman; let him rule the sky just as it pleases him, I confine myself to the planet I inhabit." His writings naturally have their share of this horror of abstraction. When he took up his pen as a man of letters he wrote as an amateur—the language is often hackneyed and full of mawkishness and padding. When he wrote as King everything was different—the style is direct, supple, and full of life. He has at his command the appropriate, vigorous word, never a vague one; his turns of speech are lively, mocking, and enthusiastic, his phrases are rapid and compact. "Whipped cream" disgusted him, but he was not afraid to use trivial or even vulgar expressions, so long as they were expressive.

His usual conversation used to leave his companion breathless. It was an incessant sequence of questions to which he demanded frank, brief, and prompt replies. Thiébault was sent to him by D'Alembert as professor for the Cadet School, and he began by saying to him, "Good evening, sir, I am very pleased to see you and make your acquaintance." Then without a second's pause he asked him how his name was spelled, in what part of France he was born, if his parents were still alive, what his father's position was, what he had been doing up till then, where he had lived, if he was married, what his wife's family was, what his principal studies had been, if he had had anything published, in what state of health he had left the Abbé d'Olivet and D'Alembert, which way he had come, why he had made a detour to Dresden, how he had managed to make himself understood in the inns, who had been his traveling companions, if Saxony looked prosperous, if people there were working, if he knew what the curriculum of the school was like, who were the best living writers, why he had not put Voltaire in the first rank, if ellipsis was allowed in French, if Racine could have written grammatically "I loved you fickle, faithful what would I not have done?" Then he thanked him in a word and dismissed him.

After the grand reviews at Berlin, Potsdam, and Spandau, Frederick devoted two months to touring the provinces. Every year he revisited Silesia, Brandenburg, and Pomerania—the compact territories of the monarchy—nearly always Prussia, more rarely the small estates on the Rhine, which he did not care for. He made the regiments perform maneuvers, visited the Courts, the Chambers, the tax collectors; inspected the crown domains, the magazines, the arsenals, the manufactures, the markets, the canals, the towns; questioned everybody and dictated orders and plans everywhere. He took with him a very detailed documentary survey, which he completed and annotated as he went along. The memoranda which the cabinet gave him when he set out have been preserved—they are little books bound in leather containing provincial accounts, population statistics, catalogues of trades and manufactures, livestock census, etc. He sent before him a general questionnaire, sometimes running to a hundred items, for which the Chambers had to collect a complete set of answers.

One day he visited a piece of reclaimed land near Fehrbellin in his carriage. The district bailiff walked beside the door of the coach ready to satisfy his curiosity.

"Sire, here are two new ditches which we owe to Your Majesty's kindness; they keep our clearing dry."

"Ah, ah, very pleased to hear it. Who are you?"

"The bailiff of Fehrbellin."

"What is your name?"

"Fromme."

"Ah, ah, you are the son of District Councilor Fromme?"

"Sire, by your leave, my father was the councilor bailiff of the bailiwick of Loeme."

"Councilor bailiff, that's not true. Your father was district councilor. I knew him very well. Tell me, has the drainage of the clearing I have had made been of use to you?"

"Oh yes, Sire."

"Have you more livestock than your predecessor?"

"Yes, Sire, I have forty cows in this steading and seventy more in all."

"That is very good. You haven't got murrain in your canton?"

"No, Sire."

"Has there been any?"

"Yes, Sire."

"Make your cattle eat a lot of rock salt and they won't get it."

"That is what I do, but common salt is almost as good."

"Don't you believe it. Rock salt must not be ground but put within reach of the cattle so that they can lick it."

"I will do so without fail."

"Are there any other improvements to be made here?"

"Oh yes, Sire! Here is the lake of Kremmen, if it was drained Your Majesty would have 1,800 acres of meadowland, where colonists could be set up. It could be used to make a waterway to lead out of the district, which would benefit Fehrbellin and Ruppin greatly. Many goods could be taken from Mecklenburg to Berlin by water."

The King was anxious about the expense of it and the profit

anticipated. Then he questioned the bailiff about the neighboring landowners, and went on, "What is the bailiff of Old Ruppin called?"

"Honig."

"Since when has he been there?"

"Since Trinity Sunday."

"Since Trinity Sunday? Where was he before that?"

"He was a canon."

"A canon? A canon? Who the devil made a bailiff out of this canon?"

"Sire, he is a young man of means, whose ambition it was to be one of Your Majesty's bailiffs."

"But why didn't the old one stay?"

"He is dead."

"His widow could have kept the bailiwick."

"She has become poor."

"Female economy, I suppose?"

"Pardon me, Sire, she planned things very well, but accidents ruined her. It might happen to the best of stewards. Myself, I suffered from the death of cattle two years ago and got no compensation at all. I do not know how I shall ever get back on my feet again."

"My child, I am suffering from deafness in my left ear today; I can hear nothing from that side."

The bailiff drew back.

"Come on, bailiff, come near me. Keep close to the coach but take care no accident befalls you. Only speak a bit louder. Tell me, what is this village on the right called?"

"Langen."

"To whom does it belong?"

"One third to Your Majesty, one third to Herr von Hagen, and the Chapter of Berlin has vassals in it."

"You're wrong, it's the Chapter of Magdeburg."

"Sire, I ask your pardon, but it is the Chapter of Berlin."

"That's not true. The Chapter of Berlin has no vassals."

"Sire, I should be a very bad bailiff if I did not know who had jurisdiction in the sections of my bailiwick."

"Ah, in that case, you're right."

The inquiry continued. The quality of the ground, of the

crops, of the woods, names of lords, the state of their fortunes, mortgages, markets for produce, experiments on new crops— everything was included. Finally, after having collected the bail- iffs and the inspectors of buildings together, the King ordered more land to be cleared.

"This must be arranged. I do not want it done gratis. You have only to write to my financial department about the land I want cleared. I will put up the money. . . ."

Undoubtedly the anecdotist who reported this episode made a bit of a caricature of it, but at bottom it does show the Frederick of the *Political Correspondence* and of the *Acta Borussica*, with his mania for information, his care for detail, his unflagging at- tention, his fear of being duped, his curbed desire to be always in the right. This tyrannous, circumstantial, suspicious realism is indeed the explanation of a certain weakness of character which made the King misjudge his neighbors quite frequently. Truth to tell, he had good enough pretensions in the difficult art of summing people up; in his *Political Testament* of 1752 he even inserted a little psychological treatise on the virtues of the perfect ambassador, having regard for the Court to which each was accredited. At Vienna a caviler expert in the art of wrangling was needed; at Versailles a wise and prudent man, who would not let himself be taken in by the witticisms in which French ministers used to indulge; at London a pleasant debauchee, who could hold wine better than the English and could keep up an appearance of being frank without giving anything away; in Holland, where state secrets ran around the streets, nothing but common sense and simple manners were needed. . . . But in the back of his mind was the proud, narrow notion that he was capable of dealing with anything and everything, and so he did not always take the trouble to distinguish the mediocre from the good. One of his secretaries mentioned a number of times that he judged people "not as they are, but as he has summed them up in his own mind for character and abilities." And it was all the more serious, added the Marquis d'Argens, that "when our philosopher has a fixed idea about someone, good or bad, he does not easily abandon it. What he decides is decided beyond all appeal." For example, this presumption of his made him make the gross mistake of offering 500,000 crowns to Madame de Pompadour to get her on his side, and it cramped his choice of officials often enough.

From those who worked immediately under him he demanded persistent labor, unimpeachable discretion, and a total forgetfulness of self. Old Eichel, who had been left to him by Frederick William and was secretary to the cabinet until his death in 1768, was a celibate. He lived in absolute retirement, spoke to hardly anyone, and had not half an hour's leisure in a whole year. An ambassador wrote that a stranger could have lived seven years at the Prussian Court without seeing him or even suspecting his existence. He had no successor: the men who later shared the responsibilities which had been his—Laspeyres, Müller, Galster, Mencken—were not his equals. Galster was dismissed and confined in a fortress—a unique occurrence in the history of the cabinet. Without doubt his crime was a small one, since he was released at the end of a year and pensioned, but when he was being sent off to Spandau he said that he was just changing one prison for another.

Unquestionably Frederick made the Prussian bureaucracy more homogeneous, more methodical, more hard working and even more prompt; he improved its output, he made it into a more effective instrument of unification, he inspired it with a feeling of duty and a sense of public service which enabled it to survive the collapse of the Frederican system after Jena, and even the fall of the Hohenzollerns. On the other hand, throughout the hierarchy from top to bottom he thwarted, if he did not stifle, the spirit of initiative, personal inquiry, and all taste for responsibility. Councilor Ursinus, one of the most prominent members of the Central Office, stood out against the King's commercial policy: he was thrown into jail on the charge of having been in the pay of some traders. His trial only exposed minor negligence on his part; he was cashiered none the less and kept several months at Spandau. Though he arranged for several dismissals of this sort (four presidents after the wars of Silesia), Frederick did not like changes of personnel for all that: "My horse stumbles," said he, "and I know it, but I would rather keep him than take another one, the faults of which I do not know." The trouble was that for every vacancy he had difficulty in finding a single man of talent amid the flat monochrome picture presented by his staff. So as to fill certain positions he had a documented list sent him of landed proprietors, retired staff officers, and provincial councilors. At times he used to call together a dozen or so candidates and question them himself. As he had a far better memory for faces than for names, it once happened that he had a search made between Liegnitz and Schweidnitz for a district councilor whose name he had forgotten—a tall dark man, whom he had noticed at the time and had thought the right sort to be called to Berlin. He ended by having gifted young people taught by the Central Office and by the Chambers rather after the manner he had himself been taught at Cüstrin, but above all he kept on for years people whom he had himself to correct and guide almost daily. President von Siegroth in the Kurmark held his position from 1766 to 1782, although Frederick incessantly reproached him with his "negligence," his "unpractical way of thinking," and his "idiotic proposals."

However, the good type of servant was not completely lacking. It is the privilege of great men, even if jealous of their authority, to draw to themselves intelligent and devoted people: Podewils, Finckenstein, and Hertzberg for foreign affairs; Goerne and Blumenthal for the domains; Katt for the administration and the army; Boden for the finances; Cocceji and Carmer for the law; Heinitz for economy; Zedlitz for the churches. Moreover, unlike his father, Frederick made a habit of choosing his ministers from among the presidents of provincial Chambers. A certain number of these acquired a high reputation, among others Domhardt in East Prussia, Aschersleben in Pomerania, and Platen and Lenz, who remained more than twenty years at their posts, the first at Magdeburg and the second in East Prussia.

II

FREDERICK had a sanguine temperament. Ever since his youth he had complained of "very violent," "unbearable" beating of the heart, of feelings of suffocation, and of hemorrhoids. At thirty-four he endured his first attack of gout; nearly every winter both his legs and his left hand were attacked. At thirty-five he had an attack of some form of hemiplegia, mild enough it is true but it left his neck and legs swollen. And on top of this came fever, colics, cramps of the stomach, and "bloody fluxes," which must have been intestinal hemorrhages. "My soul makes my body work," he used often to say. He must indeed have had a prodigious power of endurance to overcome these ills and trials while leading the life of a "fettered galley slave." From 1758 on he believed he was condemned to an early death, but during a reign of forty-six years he made his bodily "machine" work "at any price," by treating it "like a sorry old nag and digging in the spurs with vigor."

He displayed other symptoms of the sanguine type—mental ones. Firstly, habitual gaiety and a slightly whimsical good humor of which misfortune never deprived him completely, for sometimes at tragic moments he still spoke of his reverses with a smile and with brilliant flashes of wit at the "raps" he was giving the enemy. Further, he had fickleness of character, impatience, sensitivity to passing impressions—youthful faults which diminished with the passing of years. He possessed brilliant physical courage, which made him, according to his officers, habitually expose himself too much upon the battlefield. He had enthusiasm, the fundamental optimism of a man of action which showed him the profit behind each trial rather than the hazard of it: one of his close friends said that with him a display of confidence was always the prelude to some reverse, and one of fear to some success. Finally, he had extraordinary vivacity, exuberance of speech, transports of anger, and fits of violence. For a man of such a temperament to want and to act were necessities, were instinctive and irresistible natural functions. Decision and action were synonymous to giving way to a nature of irrepressible strength, giving way joyfully as to a delicious and tyrannical passion. "In short," said he one day, "only the founders of empires can properly be described as men."

The man's political imagination was always in labor, for his mind restlessly fathered plans and projects. He had one for every eventuality: some prepared and precise, others roughed out on bits of paper, summarily "sketched" so as to be "digested" afterward by ministers. In the *Political Testament* of 1752 there is one for the conquest of Saxony, a second for the acquisition of Polish Prussia, others again anticipating a civil war in Russia, the succession of a minor in England, and a vacancy on the throne of France by the extinction of the elder line of the Bourbons. Never did he give himself over to the lazy calm of routine, never was he tied down to a system or a formula. He was not even bound by his signature, except under conditions of evident and durable advantage to himself. He was on the watch for the smallest changes so as to adjust his plans to them, but in the course of his reveries he had turned over so many ideas, gone into so many possible combinations, that he could hardly ever be caught napping. He merely remarked, as in 1756, "The old systems are no more, to wish to reëstablish them would be like chasing a shadow."

In the details of his work he used an inexhaustible variety of methods. Anything was good enough for him so long as it succeeded: designing provocation, calculated delay, false news, deceitful cordiality, veiled menace, stubborn incomprehension, corruption, espionage, familiar waggery—every mortal thing, noisy movements of bluff included. "Penetrating minds count upon uniform behavior, that is why it is necessary to change one's game as often as possible and to disguise it; to transform oneself into Proteus, sometimes appearing lively, sometimes slow, sometimes warlike, sometimes peaceful. That is the way to make the enemy lose his bearings." This was a mistake, for he overdid it. He provided refinements of perfidy for his adversaries and allies which were quite foreign to them, he sensed treacheries which did not exist, he changed his behavior because of vague impressions, he got in a fever about nothing. He was showered with blessings by Fortune from the very start, so he thought he could take every sort of liberty with the older Courts. Thus he would become uselessly haughty, patronizing, and sarcastic, he chaffed and wounded everybody and kicked up "the devil of a row" for a bagatelle. As an ally of France he wanted to get a promise of vigorous action in Germany from Louis XV and he gave Valori a memorandum which bore this significant title—"Project Which the French Should Follow If They Are Reasonable." The ministers were so afraid of his ways that they agreed with the secretary of the cabinet to stop en route such and such a provocative reply to George II and such and such an insulting letter to Louis XV.

However, he knew his faults too well not to keep an eye on

his own conduct. One of the most constant features of his life was precisely the ceaseless restoration of an equilibrium between imagination and calculation. First, he was completely frank with himself: in his *Testament* of 1752 he even went so far as to write of Maria Theresa, "I have not a clear conscience in regard to this princess." Besides, like a gambler who is winning, he had a sense of risk, a "secret instinct" which told him the moment to take a risk and the moment to leave the game. "You must know when it's right to stop; forcing luck is the way to lose it, and always wanting more of it is the way never to be lucky." Finally he meditated powerfully and minutely. His system was always to consider things in writing by drawing up comparative tables: *Reasons which I might have for remaining in alliance with France, reasons which I might have for making peace with the Queen of Hungary,* or else, *Items which give rise to just apprehensions the King should have at the pernicious designs of the Queen of Hungary and of the King of England; items which should reassure the King upon the designs of the Queen of Hungary and of the King of England.* These are not vague reasons but carefully qualified possibilities which lead up to an induced conclusion by a process of elimination.

He distrusted easy victories. "A lightning stroke, such as the conquest of Silesia, is like a book, the original of which succeeds while the imitations fall flat." He was equally suspicious of the gigantic edifices raised by visionaries. "A village on the frontier is worth more than a principality sixty leagues away." The height of wit was to see the opportunity approaching and seize it as it passed, for "policy consists rather in drawing profit from favorable events than in preparing them." The light of his mind played upon two types of plan: a long-term plan, which he called his metaphysic, concerned with acts of aggrandizement, which might or might not mature sooner or later, and in the second place, limited but terribly precise applications of this grasping metaphysic applied as chance directed.

When he did not see his way clearly he drew back. He evaded all conversation with ambassadors or else he refused to receive them without being informed of the subjects on which they intended to touch. One day, when England had put an embarrassing question to him, he wrote to Podewils, "I do not want to bother with that. Reply like an Austrian in polite but completely vague terms, which are neither negative nor affirmative but simply incomprehensible." Three times did the minister present a draft of the letter and three times did the King tear it up because it was too clear, until at last he grew tired of the struggle and himself drafted a twenty-line note in German, which contained a single sentence, so cut up into clauses that it was hopeless to expect to find a main verb and a subject in it. On the other hand when he took a decision nothing could stop him. In his faults, as in his failures, what always saved him was suddenness of action, daring, and promptitude which baffled the enemy. Most important was the fact that he had an obedient army which was always on the alert. "I am not rash enough to give you advice," in view of the uncertainty of events, he wrote to instruct his successor, "I am content to repeat what I have told you in greater detail—control your finances wisely so as to have money when you need it; only make alliances with those who have precisely the same interests as your own; never make treaties to guard against far-off events, wait till the situation arises before you make up your mind and act accordingly; beware of placing confidence in the number and good faith of your allies; count only on yourself, then you will never be deceived." The preservation and extension of the power of Prussia—that was the essential task.

III

THE tradition had crystallized at least a century earlier: the Hohenzollerns were peasants who administered their kingdom like a farm. The State had no debts. Moreover the land had too little currency to subscribe to heavy loans—one million thalers, perhaps two in cases of extreme danger. At no time had the prince the opportunity to relax or go in for extravagances. "If he wished to be respected, he must keep his finances in order; never has a poor government exacted consideration for itself. Saxony could have played a part in the war which began in 1740, but as she was loaded with debt she loaned herself to the highest bidder and suffered misfortune on all sides. . . . If France continues to run amok as she is doing today, in spite of her great power she may pass into eclipse and become an object of contempt to her rivals." The budget, then, was to be rigorously balanced, the smallest detail of the expenses checked, and in addition there would be a secret fund, containing sufficient savings for waging a good and profitable war at five million thalers per campaign, if the need arose.

The fiscal system set up by the Great Elector and by Frederick William had a robust simplicity about it; there was no simpler one in all Europe. First came the revenues of the royal domains which covered a quarter of the country and were leased out to bailiffs. They included forests, fields, pasture lands, real estate, and also the salt pits, the posts, and the tolls. Second came direct taxation, the "Contribution," paid only on land (34 per cent of their revenue from peasants, 28 per cent from the nobles of Prussia; other nobles paid nothing). Last came indirect taxation, excise levied at the gates of towns on the most varied objects and types of produce (nobles were exempt for their personal needs). The sums received were sent to two central treasuries—the treasury of the Domains on the one hand, and on the other the treasury of War, into which went the Excise and the Contribution. This was entirely devoted to the army estimates; while the first treasury paid the King's expenses, the appanages, the pensions, and the costs of colonization which could not be met by the provinces. It also served to make up the deficit of the treasury of War and to build up the Treasury Reserve. According to the terms of the Settlement of 1748 the Chambers sent the King detailed statements monthly, and finally all the statements were submitted to the Court of Accounts six weeks after the close of the financial year.

A brief table will save lengthy explanations.

| | Millions of thalers | | | NUMBER OF SOLDIERS | MILLIONS OF POPULATION |
| | Credit | | Debit | | |
	DOMAINS	TAXES	ARMY		
1713	1.6	2.4	2.5	38,000	1.6
Accession 1740	3.3	3.6	5–6	72,000	2.2
+ Silesia 1752	4.5	7.7	9.4	135,000	3.9
Death 1786	6–7	10–11	12–13	195,000	5.7

From comparing these columns it would appear that Prussia had only been created, only lived, and only worked to keep up an army which was at one and the same time the goal and the instrument of its greatness. "Policy, the army, and the finances are branches so closely connected that they could not separated." The King was his own Commander in Chief, and the nobility, from whom the officers' corps was recruited, was the highest class in the nation, the only one which was to be honored. "Every man of birth who is not a soldier is nothing but a scoundrel." At the time of Frederick William there was still mistrust and rancor between the King and the nobility. The struggles of the provincial estates against royal absolutism were not yet forgotten. Frederick William especially dreaded the proud, jealous, turbulent lordlings of Prussia. Under Frederick the reconciliation was completed. The nobles were at one with the monarchy: they were its "foundation and support." Not only were all the higher ranks in the army reserved for them (for if common people had to be roped in to command troops "that would be the beginning of decadence") but also almost all the high civilian posts in the ministries, the Central Office, the Embassies, and the Chambers of Domains.

In his castle the noble was lord, for the feudal system subsisted in all its rigor: the peasants were serfs or mere tenants for life, subjected to tithes and forced labor, and suitors to the lord's court. The lord took charge of the payment of land tax and the levying of recruits for his overlord the King. In the army and out of it the King and his nobles were united by a sort of military comradeship—the King lent them money when they were in debt, he helped them to set up their sons, to marry off their daughters, and to safeguard their domains and their privileges; he prohibited the purchase of their lands by townsmen in such a way that the landed resources of the nobles as a class should never diminish. When he prepared to transform his own peasants into hereditary tenants by slow and cautious stages, in imitation of France, he was careful not to force the same reform upon the aristocracy. After the inquest of 1748 he did no more than attempt to humanize the forced labor system, which was "unbearable, grievous, absolutely Egyptian," and to suppress the abuse of corporal punishments. Still, in Pomerania the proprietors, with the support of Cocceji and Podewils, succeeded in obtaining the repudiation of the president, Von Aschersleben, whom they accused of favoring the peasants. To judge by the numerous cases of flight and abandonment of lands mentioned in the administrative correspondence, the lot of the serfs remained wretched. In spite of the King lords continued to exact four, five, or even six days of forced labor a week.

Thus under Frederick the monarchy became more narrowly aristocratic than in the past, but this aristocracy, with its special feeling of duty toward the dynasty and of scorn for all who were not in uniform, was not born with a natural taste for arms—Frederick constantly complained that many young gentlemen still preferred "a low, feeble life"—no, that was not the product of a love of the fatherland, for the fatherland was only just beginning to develop out of the royal domain; it was the product of a pride of caste, of military training, of forced obedience to the crown, and of rivalry under the eyes of the King.

As for the townsmen, their function was to be townsmen, that is to say, they were to make a lot of money so as to pay a lot of taxes. Each man had to stay in his own class. Education consisted in distributing better practical knowledge to the people without giving individuals the means of raising themselves to a higher social position. Apart from duly authorized exceptions, industry and commerce were confined to the towns in such a way that activities were kept quite distinct, and no product escaped paying tolls. In the country only small trades fulfilling primary needs were allowed—that of the baker, the miller, the shoemaker. . . . Every year after Trinity Sunday the Chambers submitted a trade balance extracted from the excise books to the King, from which he saw what merchandise had entered and what had gone out of each province and what manufactures the country still needed. On these statistics he regulated his economic policy, which consisted of large sales abroad to attract specie and the smallest possible foreign purchases so as to keep it in the country. "There are three sorts of trade. The first is to export goods and receive money in exchange. Two, foreign products can be obtained and sent elsewhere: transit. Three, products are exchanged for other necessary products. All three are good, but the first is best. For the second our outlet from Poland must always be kept in view, and the third must be used when nothing better is available. Our trade depends on wheat, wood, and all sorts of woolen goods: that must be protected in every possible way. The greater part of the money which goes abroad is for wine, brandy, sugar, and silks. Wine can be more highly taxed to raise the sale of beer. Sugar refineries can be set up. Silk manufacture has already been dealt with, but the Central Office is recommended to protect these factories and see to it that foreign products shall be forbidden as soon as we can stand on our own feet." It was a Prussian version of the mercantile system with all its consequences—authoritarian State intervention, regimentation, control of prices and movements of goods, prohibitions, customs, creation of protected industries. "For example, we take Prussian butter to Berlin instead of Holstein butter; that is why they ought to buy velvet from Berlin or Potsdam in Prussia instead of foreign velvet, Silesian instead of Dutch linen, and muslin from here instead of from France, and thus it should be in every province so that one gives a helping hand to the other for mutual profit."

But what if customers preferred some article manufactured outside the kingdom? The customer would buy what the King thought good to provide: "The paper of Silesia and Prussia must be used even if it is less good than the foreign kind." It was for the Chambers to improve the quality of it and to compel the mills to produce the right weights and sizes. But what if the Central Office feared reprisals and protested that it was clumsy to protect beer by prohibiting wine? That was because the Office was full of drunkards suffering from thirst. And it was not only wine that was prohibited, but also Swedish grain and livestock from Mecklenburg. "When I return to Berlin, there will be fine ructions if all foreign produce, butter, stuffs, and merchandise are not heavily taxed." In the shade of this protection not only did the silk industry improve but in 1743 the first manufacture of cutlery began at Eberswalde and in 1744 cotton weaving began at Berlin. Close to mineral deposits in the district of Halberstadt and also in Silesia small foundries developed which did work for the arsenals. Finally, thanks to the State and army granaries, the Central Office succeeded as by a miracle in stabilizing the price of grain.

However, the countries affected replied to these prohibitions with other prohibitions. There was a fierce customs' war with Saxony and Austria: Silesia suffered from it, for the Prussian market was not big enough to take all her linen. Frederick's two great enemies were Hamburg and Leipzig, Hamburg as a warehouse for English goods and Leipzig as an international fair. Since Prussia had no roads but mere tracks in the soil which were only kept up near towns, the bulk of her trade went by water. Therefore Frederick strove by means of tolls and customs to divert trade from down the Elbe to go down the Oder, which was Prussian almost the whole of its length and the main highway of the kingdom. The port of Stettin was improved and the river was embanked and joined to neighboring rivers by canals.

Undoubtedly Frederick was more interested in things than in people, more absorbed in manufacture than in the workmen, more concerned with the land than with the peasant, whom he protected mainly because he considered him as a potential soldier. But here again, though he continued his father's work, he brought to it a more enlightened idea of progress, a more methodical effort not only to extend the area under tillage but also to improve the methods of cultivation and the breeds of livestock. Otherwise it was the same obstinate struggle to clear and colonize the hinterland. Two offices for recruiting colonists had been established at Frankfort and Hamburg. To them came Bohemians fleeing from the famine of 1747, Hussites, Hessians, Saxons, and Mecklenburgers who complained of being crushed by taxes. In all from 1740 to 1756 50,000 persons were established as hereditary tenants, with their labor service and dues exactly stipulated and strictly limited. These subjects were not always of a very high grade, for it was no longer common, as in the seventeenth century, for groups of first-class citizens to emigrate in a body to preserve their faith; it was more often isolated families who were attracted by the promise of material advantages. There were disappointments and desertions. "I am disgusted," Frederick wrote in one of his minor works, "at the trouble people take to make pineapples, pisangs,[1] and other exotic plants grow in this harsh climate, and the small care that is taken for the human species. Say what you like, one man is more pre-

1. Early name for the fruit now known as bananas.

**Harvest Thanksgiving to the
Goddess of Plenty**

cious than all the pineapples in the world; he is the plant which should be cultivated, the one which is worthy of all our care and labor, for he it is that stands forth as the ornament and glory of the fatherland." In this connection, however, Frederick was not thinking of racial purity but of the moral upbringing of his lords of the manor. During his reign he took many measures for preventing Jews from seizing upon too big a share of trade, but he also thought of setting up a Tartar horde of Mohammedans in East Prussia.

It was a matter of great concern to him to adapt the administration of each province to the local needs, and even to the local customs. "The genius of the people" and "the position of the country" were expressions which often came from his pen. The Central Office and the Chambers had received general instructions from Frederick William which applied to all the domains under their control. These instructions were revised in 1748 by Frederick to put them in keeping with new conditions, but the most delicate problem he had to solve was that of the annexation of Silesia.

He set up two Chambers there, one at Glogau and the other at Breslau, under the same president, who received, as a further complication, the title, rank, and powers of a minister, so as to be responsible to the King alone over the head of the Central Office. For this post Frederick chose the son of his old teacher at Cüstrin, Von Münchow, whom he even refused permission to marry, because, he wrote, "It seems to me impossible for you to be able to divide your time between the businesses of which you are in charge and the cares which a family demands." Münchow was the man for the mission; young, courteous, pleasant, and a great organizer. He threw overboard the solemn manners of the past administration, surrounded himself with Silesians, and gave the province the illusion it was its old self again. Without delay he introduced the Prussian fiscal system, which was more equitable, more productive, and more easy to work than the Austrian system. He arranged a cadastral survey, and the Contribution on landed property was limited to the sum total of taxes paid by the land in 1739, the last year of Hapsburg rule. Its imposition was arranged in such a way as slightly to benefit the laborers, who formed a majority of all the occupiers. As the greater part of these were only tenants for life, it often happened that the lord took advantage of the death of one of them to take the tenement away from his children and join it to the domain proper. Then the former occupiers were compelled to become domestic servants, or manual laborers, or to move off into Poland with their livestock. A law of 1749, extended later throughout the kingdom, forbade proprietors to reduce the superficial area of peasant tenures.

But the rule of Prussia brought with it a troublesome and unpopular novelty, obligatory military service. Furthermore in the days of Charles VI there had been only 3,000 or 4,000 men garrisoned in the fortresses, but Frederick settled 40,000 in them, and their presence entailed other burdens, lodgings, requisitions, transports. . . . To counter the discontent he set out to win his new subjects with personal attentions. For the last one hundred and thirty years no sovereign of the House of Austria had visited Breslau. He went every year in August. His ease of access, his intelligence, his gaiety, his simple attractive manners gave him popularity and a sort of legend grew up around him. He showed himself frequently, kept open house, distributed places at Court, received everybody, accepted all petitions, even the most ridiculous. The countryfolk came in a body to speak to him; a Jew asked him for authorization to wear a beard against the counsel of his coreligionists; a member of the War Council who had not been able to find a wife applied to him to discover the woman of his dreams. Frederick read, listened, replied. Once, however, he was out of patience with all that he had heard and advised a peasant to apply direct to the Chamber of Domains. Then without listening further the good man cried to his wife, who was an admirer of the King's, "Come, you see they are all of a piece." And he made off very upset.

The Provincial Estates had fallen into disuse and no longer represented anything or anybody, yet the more or less equal division between the two religions—eight Catholics as against every nine Protestants among the population—might have constituted a danger, which was the more serious because almost all the Catholic nobles were educated by the Jesuits of Schweidnitz and because the clergy, especially the regular clergy, remained faithful to the House of Austria. Although the peace treaties had guaranteed to religion and to the clergy their liberties, privileges, goods, and lands, Cocceji, the Minister of Justice, a strict and pedantic Lutheran, would willingly have regulated everything by means of the civil authority, without worrying about "the Bishop of Rome." It was to Frederick's credit that after some useless friction he reëstablished good relations with the Holy See. He helped the Catholics of Berlin, who were few in number, to build a new church dedicated to St. Hedwig near the Opera House facing his forum; the architect intended it to be magnificent and like Agrippa's Pantheon. In fact it is an abortive Pantheon, with too large a cupola and a basement which seems to sink into the ground beneath the weight of the building above it. However, the Pope recognized the gesture for what it was worth. Above all, the Prince Bishop of Breslau, Philip Louis von Zinzendorf, was absolutely the right person to allow himself to be seduced, or rather fooled, by Frederick.

Imagine a little old man crippled with gout, always pushed about in a wheel chair, a lover of the opera, the world, and worldly honors, vain, talkative, witty, but without common sense and moreover very easy to convince because his character was not of the strongest. He was the son of an Austrian chancellor, had been arrested during the course of the first war and then exiled to Vienna. He came back in 1742 and Frederick set to work to make him accept as his coadjutor a twenty-six-year-old canon, scion of one of the richest and noblest families of Silesia, the Count von Schaffgotsch—a handsome, bedizened young man, with curled hair and a wide circle of acquaintances; a gay dog with unedifying morals but popular at Sans Souci because of his conversational powers. Zinzendorf refused: the ribbon of the Black Eagle for himself and the rank of commander of the Order of Malta for his chamberlain, Falkenhayn, overcame his intransigence, and a very strange chapter of diplomatic history developed as Zinzendorf, Schaffgotsch, and Frederick plotted and maneuvered to overcome the distaste of Benedict XIV, who had seen the prospective coadjutor at Rome and felt nothing but aversion for him.

Zinzendorf redrafted Frederick's letters to the Papal Curia, and the Holy Father was ironically surprised to find a heretic so well up in the usages of the pontifical chancellery. Frederick on

his side tried to make Schaffgotsch presentable. He handed him
over to Münchow, who had him tonsured and cut off his ringlets.
Then he set about intimidating the Chapter. "The Holy Ghost
and I have resolved that the prelate Schaffgotsch shall be erected
coadjutor of Breslau, and those of the canons who are opposed
to it will be considered as souls devoted to the Court of Vienna
and to the Devil." He also talked about grenadiers and prison.
When the canons remained firm, he decided to proceed himself
with the nomination by laying down that he should henceforth
exercise the same right over all the benefices in the province. At
the death of Zinzendorf in 1747 nothing had yet been settled
with Rome. At the end of the year the Pope resigned himself to
the preconization of Schaffgotsch as Bishop of Breslau but without making the slightest allusion to the royal nomination. The
question of appeals to the Nuncio's court was also settled, and to
rebut the arguments of the Austrian Jesuits Frederick called in
the French Jesuits—the men who had brought up Monsieur de
Voltaire.

IV

THE Hohenzollerns were a Calvinist dynasty ruling over a people containing a majority of Lutherans, and religious toleration
was a tradition of theirs. However, Frederick William took his
part of father and spiritual head very seriously. As for Frederick,
he was an unbeliever; a simple, natural unbeliever, whose personal lack of faith hardly concerned other people, for it did not
involve the least element of tyranny nor any great zeal to effect
conversions. In that he was as much an exception among princes
as he was among the "enlightened."

Throughout his reign he only went nine times to divine service but he never dissuaded anyone from going to church or
chapel. Certainly the revealed religions were absurdities and
impostures in his eyes, but, he added repeatedly, they were absurdities agreeable to the man who took spiritual delight in error
and did not like to be shaken out of his rut. To attack established religions so as to found a natural religion would be an im-
practicable and foolish enterprise. All a prince could do was to
watch over the tranquillity of his subjects' souls and stop the
mouths of madmen who wanted to preach a war of religions.

Furthermore, the King of Prussia had the advantage of ruling over subjects who were mostly Protestants and in general quieter and more submissive than other peoples. In the instructions given to Major von Borcke for the education of one of his nephews Frederick summed up his doctrine quite unambiguously in a few lines. "When he is a few years older," he wrote of the young prince, "he may be given a short account of the opinions of the philosophers and of the different religions, without inspiring him with hatred for any of them, and making him understand that they all worship God but in different ways. He must not have too high an opinion of the priest who instructs him and he must not believe things until he has examined them. The Catholic religion is widespread in Silesia, in the Duchies of Cleve and elsewhere. If this child were to become a fanatical Calvinist all would be lost. It is very necessary to forbid even the priest from sanctimoniously attacking the papists; however, the governor must skillfully make his pupil understand, by referring to persecutions and to the ambitions of popes, that nothing is more dangerous than when the Catholics have the upper hand in a state, and that a Protestant prince is much more the master of his own house than a Catholic prince."

At his supper parties Frederick took pleasure in parading his impiety, but in front of Fouqué whom he loved deeply he abstained from all sorts of raillery which might have hurt the old man, as he never failed to say a prayer when he sat down at table. Even among his closest friends he seldom joked with those who were frank and sincere Christians. Though he indulged in a certain amount of gaiety on this subject, he was easily brought to a standstill. Thiébault relates that one of his generals was a devout Catholic and never charged the enemy without making the sign of the cross with his saber. As the King laughed at this habit, he silenced him by saying, "Sire, do not concern yourself with that. These are things which are not part of my service to you, which cannot harm it, and are no business of yours. Provided I do my duty and serve you zealously, what do my devotional practices matter to you and what would you gain by poking fun at one of your most faithful servants?"

However, at the same time Frederick overwhelmed people with pitiless sarcasm when they appeared to be going against their consciences from mere obsequiousness. He liked to see just how far their weakness would carry them, he fought them to a finish and afterward had the satisfaction of despising them. Like many another unbeliever he enjoyed theological subtleties and Biblical exegesis. Pen in hand he read the Church historians, parodied the sacred orators, and freely prided himself on having odd scraps of erudition and a refined knowledge of dogma.

"I am in some ways," he wrote in the *Testament* of 1752, "the Pope of the Lutherans and the Protestants." In virtue of the *summum jus circa sacra* he did in fact watch over the order and discipline of the churches, nominated the pastors, controlled the administration of ecclesiastical property, and granted marriage dispensations. This required a great deal of correspondence with the church consistories which he joyfully sprinkled with all sorts of impertinences. Often the faithful flock objected to the doctrines of their pastors. Some Pomeranians talked of dismissing theirs because he did not firmly believe in the resurrection of the body. "Let the vicar remain. If on the Day of Judgment he does not want to be resuscitated, he has only to remain lying down." The people of Valangin asked for the recall of another who doubted the eternity of the pains of Hell. "If my subjects at Valangin want to be eternally damned, I have no reason to complain of it." As for the townsmen of Charlottenburg, they had to bear with the Reverend Eberhard though he maintained that Socrates could be admitted to Heaven. "Let Socrates be saved and Eberhard be vicar." On the other hand, the pastors complained of their salaries. Some asked to be paid in wheat. "Your kingdom is not of this world," replied the King. "The soldier is given bread but the priest lives on celestial manna which cometh from on high. Peter and Paul were not paid in wheat and throughout the New Testament there is no trace of an apostolic granary." An ass's head drawn in the margin put a full stop to the discussion.

Undoubtedly these ecclesiastical jests of Frederick's were not all very successful, but an extraordinary number of them were current and the pages of the anas are full of them. It was said that a good priest paid homage to him with a mediocre book entitled *The Sins against the Holy Ghost,* and that he replied with this message: "I have received your sins against the Holy Ghost and I trust that God takes yours under his august and holy care." Another time in Silesia some Catholic priests had arrested a soldier who was breaking open church alms boxes. In his defense the soldier maintained that the coins found in his bag had been brought to him by the Virgin as a reward for his devotion to her. The King saved his man by a piece of low comedy. He summoned a council of canons and asked them if, according to the tenets of their religion, this miracle was possible or no. The canons did not dare deny it positively but all the same they objected that such miracles were rare. "I therefore spare the accused," announced the King, "since according to the theologians of his belief the miracle would not be impossible. But I forbid him under pain of the most rigorous punishment to accept any gift of the Virgin or of any other saint in the future." This anecdote is authentic. Many others could be cited, but it is not hard to guess with what mocking satisfaction these stories were received in Paris by all who were concerned in the Encyclopaedia. This was the way in which Frederick was the colleague of the philosophers; it was by his religious "enlightenment" that he occupied a place in the life of his time which was not only that of a king and a warrior but also that of a political innovator—one might almost say the head of a school or the leader of a crusade.

The expression "enlightened despotism" which is often applied to his reign was invented by the German historians of the nineteenth century: it serves to designate a current of ideas which inspired the sovereigns, ministers, and reforming writers of the eighteenth century, not only Frederick but also Catherine, Joseph II, Gustavus III, Leopold of Tuscany, Pombal, Struensee, Turgot, the Physiocrats, and the great provincial administrators of France. But for so many different citizens of diverse countries to be grouped under one flag or one definition, the flag must be very drab or the definition very vague. Henri Pirenne has said that enlightened despotism is the rationalization of the State. One is tempted to object that at all times and in all places there have been thoughtful despots, methodical and open-minded men who have had the wisdom to surround themselves with intelligent counselors, men who have encouraged human progress, assisted agriculture, commerce, and industry, protected artists and scholars, dug canals, planned roads, and drained marshes. But the contemporaries of Voltaire and Diderot held those sovereigns to be enlightened who possessed the spirit of the age. Now from Bayle to the Encyclopaedia the spirit of the age was above all else antireligious. The "light of reason" was opposed to obscurantism, that is to say, to the Church, to the monastic orders, to the dogmatic authority of the Pope and the Councils, to the Holy Books, to faith, to miracles, and to revelation. This is the sense in which Pirenne's epigram must be understood. From Frederick William to Frederick II there was no antagonism, no break in the practice of government, but Frederick William ruled beneath the eye of God in fear of the Last Judgment, while Frederick abstracted the idea of monarchy from its religious background. He deprived it of its character as a divine institution: this was the intellectual revolution, this was the revolution of principle which enraptured the philosophers who devoted both life and talents to a struggle against "the Beast."

Since his *Considerations on the Present State of Political Forces in Europe* (1738) Frederick had not changed his system, but he never ceased to enrich it with new arguments. His political writings were numerous. *The Mirror of Princes* (1744), the *Dissertation on the Reasons for Enacting or Abrogating Laws* (1750), the *Instruction to Major von Borcke* (1751), the *Political Testaments* of 1752 and 1768, the *Discourse on Satires* (1759), the *Discourse on Libels* (1759), the *Examination of the Essay on Prejudices* (1770), the *Critical Examination of the System of Nature* (1770), the *Account of the Prussian Government* (1775), the *Essay on the Duties of Sovereigns* (1777)—all these developed with the same clarity a theory of government very similar to that advocated in France by Quesnay and his school of economists, which can be summed up more or less as follows.

Peoples found it to be necessary for their peace and preservation to have judges to regulate their differences and protectors to keep them safe from their enemies; they chose from among themselves those whom they thought to be the wisest, the most disinterested, the most humane, and the most valiant to govern them and to unite "their different interests into one simple common interest." Such was the origin of monarchy, and monarchy should be held to be the best system or else the least defective, because "the sovereign is joined by indissoluble bonds to the main body of the State: he feels the repercussions of all the ills which afflict his subjects, and society suffers equally from the misfortunes which affect its sovereign. If the prince loses some provinces he is no longer as able to assist his subjects as in the past; if misfortune forces him to contract debts, it is the duty of the poor citizens to pay them. On the other hand, if the population is too small, if it is sunk in misery, the sovereign is deprived of all his resources. He and his people are one and cannot be happy except when united in concord."

Undoubtedly hereditary succession was not without its disadvantages: "It is impossible for talents and merit to be transmitted in a family from father to son without interruption during a long term of years." It might therefore happen that the throne would be occupied by an unworthy prince, but self-interest would at least make him choose worthy ministers. "Princes born to the throne have less arrogance and vanity than recent upstarts who are puffed out with their grandeur and, in disdain for men lately their equals, take pleasure in displaying their superiority at every opportunity. But notice especially that a prince who is sure that his children will succeed him feels that he is working for his family and will exert himself with much more zeal to promote the real good of the State which he looks upon as his patrimony, as opposed to sovereigns in elective monarchies, who only think of themselves, of matters which will continue during their own lifetime and of nothing else. They try to enrich their families and allow everything to deteriorate in a state which, as far as they are concerned, is a precarious possession destined some day to pass out of their hands. If anyone wishes to confirm this statement, he has only to inform himself of what occurs in the bishoprics of Germany, in Poland, in Rome itself, where the evil consequences of election are all too striking." In conclusion, monarchy owes its origin to the benefits the people expect of it and is upheld by those which it gives to them.

History teaches that in course of time most republics fall back into the hands of despots: it is probable that it is a misfortune which awaits them all, for the ambition of party leaders, the

bribery of foreign powers, the divisions and the corruption of
the citizens continually bring them to the brink of disaster by
exposing them "to internal wars, a thousand times more dangerous than foreign wars." On the other hand, the prince up-
holds the laws, enforces justice, prevents the corruption of
morals, and defends the State against its enemies. He is attached to the interests of the public "as a permanent watch-
man," but as he keeps his power only by the continued indulgence of his subjects and not by a decree of Providence, he has
"no rights over the citizens' ways of thought" and he cannot
conscientiously force a religion upon them.

Thus in the full meaning of the words Frederick was the only
"enlightened despot" of the eighteenth century, for he was the
only one to cut himself off completely from the Churches; this
he did not do for reasons of public order, to reduce the fiscal
privileges of churchmen, or to confiscate the property of con-
vents; but in his role as a well-known unbeliever he wished to
give monarchical power a sanction other than divine approval,
to endow it with a positive right of its own to exist. So influen-
tial was his example that because of it the philosophers were
prepared to forgive the King everything. And they had a great
deal to forgive! Not only the arrest of Voltaire at Frankfort, not
only his outbursts and his sarcasms, not only his wars and his
conquests, but even the Prussian administrative system in detail, as it was the very opposite of all that they extolled on paper. They preached civil equality: Frederick would not allow
the common people so much as a sense of honor. They advocated free trade, free movement of grain, the free play of supply
and demand: Frederick applied the most niggling and the most
oppressive regulations. They believed in mankind's inherent
goodness, they taught that in social matters evident truths could
be unearthed and a natural order could be discovered, which
the State need do no more than protect against superstition and
error: Frederick had a pessimistic opinion of his fellow men; he
thought it impossible to cure them of their delusions; he considered it essential to supervise their activities continuously and
forcibly to hold the balance between various interests, orders,
and countries, because it would not establish itself automat-
ically and because it was always unstable. He only resembled his

friends in a kind of urge for the simplification and unification of the old institutions of the past. Still, he was prudent in practice and resigned himself to trial and error, to reversals of policy which gave pure theoreticians an impression of timidity and self-contradiction.

Unquestionably the support of the philosophers was equivalent to an increase of strength and prestige to Frederick. They were prejudiced in favor of all his undertakings and bestowed their praise and their applause upon them. They diverted public opinion in favor of the heretic hero—Voltaire's expression—or, as an American historian puts it in the language of today, they conducted his propaganda for him. For half a century the Republic of Letters was the ally and auxiliary of Prussia, just as though the victories of Prussia were the victories of unbelief, the revenge of writers harried by the forces of tradition. But what of the invasion of Silesia? Maybe its moral effects were bad, but after all it was so much pure gain over obscurantism, so much taken from the Jesuits of Vienna, from "the tools of Rome," and from that bigot Maria Theresa.

Voltaire's letters give a distorted picture of the part played by these Imlacs as grenadiers of Brandenburg: the patriarch was too whimsical, too personal; he had too many grudges and too many memories. It is better to read D'Alembert's, for he was an honest ranker and a moderate enthusiast. His pen depicts Frederick as the head of a kind of International, a kind of Free Masonry at war with the Church. "Your Majesty will find in me the docility which a philosopher owes to him whom he regards as his leader and his model" (December 12, 1766). "The philosophers and men of letters of all nations, and in particular of the French nation, have long regarded you as their leader and their model" (July 6, 1770). "You were, Sire, the leader and the model of those who think and those who write; you are at present . . . their rewarding and avenging deity" (August 12, 1770). "Your Majesty imagines that Voltaire and I are merry at his expense, while considering him of use to the advance of philosophy. Not only of use, Sire, but also very necessary; necessary because of your works which serve at once to enlighten and to instruct us; necessary because of the example you give to sovereigns never to put their light under a bushel, when it only cries out to be displayed; necessary lastly because of the protection you grant to those who try to make their works useful to mankind. That, Sire, is what we all think and what we all say in chorus, in all places and on all occasions" (November 26, 1770).

D'Alembert was pensioned by Frederick, and the King of Prussia found the Catos of the Encyclopaedia were by no means sparing of fawning flattery toward him. To thank him for a portrait D'Alembert wrote phrases such as these: "I will bear it perpetually upon my person and at night I will hang it at the head of my bed, in the place where believers put their crucifix and their stoup. . . ." But, when allowance has been made for flattery, the insistence with which the philosopher repeated the word "leader" is not without significance.

By means of his correspondence and through his literary friendships Frederick had made his presence and authority felt on every hand. This European "publicity" was all the more useful to him because his policy was most resolutely and egotistically a Prussian policy. His personal philosophy willed it to be so. In fact, as against the sovereigns of the past, who believed themselves to be responsible to God and remained at least outwardly subservient to the rules of Christian morality, the "enlightened" prince had no rule except that of reasons of state, no justice except the interests of the State. His conscience did not tell him to obey a law coming from on high but to hand on to his successor a kingdom greater in strength, population, arms, riches, and extent. Success was his criterion, success as a legislator, as a builder, as an economist, as an educator but also success as a soldier and as a conqueror. Order, prosperity, and public education were elements of his glory, but so also were those more brilliant and more transient triumphs which fell to him when battles were gained and provinces subdued. If the State was an end in itself the prince could not help being a man of ambition and a warrior.

The service rendered Frederick by the philosophers was precisely that of deceiving contemporaries and posterity as to the characteristics of his reign. They toned them down, obliterated them in a mist of words and of incense. It is probable that they were themselves deceived, for if they had not acted in good faith they would not have succeeded so completely: their own fanaticism made them blind. Frederick was a great Prussian, perhaps the greatest of them all, but they succeeded in making people believe that he was the political incarnation of free thought.

V

ONE of the truisms of the age was that the will of the prince ought to make itself felt through general laws, without arbitrary or personal intervention at the expense of individuals: thanks to his friends Frederick had also the reputation of being a legislator. His kingdom had been groaning under barbarous or archaic customs and he was supposed to have succeeded in giving it a complete code, a monument of science and of humanity. It was a question of the radical simplification of a horribly confused problem which went back almost to the origins of the Prussian State. As the domain of the Hohenzollerns had been gradually built up of territories patiently cemented together, each province had kept its own traditions and institutions. Justice and the laws were thus in a dreadful tangle: a tangle of customs, procedures, and jurisdictions, in a system festering with courts of all sorts—feudal, municipal, administrative, privileged, royal, and corporate—which met now here, now there, had overlapping competences, cost the plaintiffs dear, and judged badly and slowly without the suitors ever being able clearly to know their rights. For the last century the Electors of Brandenburg had been striving to put some order into this chaos. The suppression of useless tribunals, hostility to independent jurisdictions, the better recruiting of magistrates, the simplification of procedure, the unification of law, the reduction of the costs of justice—from one reign to the next the program did not vary, but its results were still second rate. At the death of Frederick William among the most notable reforms were the suppression of all appeals to imperial justice, the institution of a Supreme Court of Appeal at Berlin, and the end of trials for witchcraft.

In this matter nothing could be less revolutionary than Frederick's ideas. The *Dissertation on the Reasons for Enacting or Abrogating Laws* which he had read to the Academy in January, 1750, was quite full of the maxims of a prudent empiricism. Laws must conform to the spirit of each nation; the best were not always those which seemed to agree most closely with natural equity; it was even necessary to keep some which were not good because men did not like to be disturbed in their habits. The essential thing was for them to be simple, few in number, "since too much medicine is harmful," for the procedure not to be too lengthy or to pass through too many courts, so as to give no advantage to rich people who could wear down the poor with appeals. All this was reasonable and commonplace enough.

As early as 1737 Frederick William had set up a High Commission of Judicial Reform under the control of his minister, Samuel Cocceji, who had borne the title of Chief Justice for the last ten years with at least a nominal preëminence over his colleagues in the same department. Frederick continued the investigation which had been begun. Cocceji was the son of a professor, had once been a professor himself, and was quick tempered, curt, authoritarian, and systematic. He met with opposition from other ministers, especially from Arnim, a sour, distrustful lawyer as deeply attached to traditional forms as was his rival to brutal changes. The antagonism between the two schools did not die down during the new reign. Finally on January 12, 1746, by an Order of Cabinet, Frederick made legal reform his personal business, and in 1748 Cocceji was given the title of chancellor.

The greater part of the chancellor's duties consisted of a grand circuit of redress and expedition of justice to all the tribunals of the kingdom. He traveled in the company of a staff of jurists, took the chair in the courts himself, issued decrees, and did not move on until all his work was done. The mere news of his approach inspired the magistrates with an unusual burst of speed. In 1747 he sat for six months at Stettin and Koeslin in Pomerania; in 1748 at Berlin; in the summer and autumn of 1749 at Cleve, the main stronghold of pettifoggers; from May to August, 1750, in Silesia; in the spring of 1751 in Prussia. He himself judged 927 cases at Koeslin, 1,364 at Berlin, and 2,101 at Stettin, one of which was a fiscal dispute that had been dragging on for two hundred years and had a dossier running to seventy volumes. Later on this type of inspection was regularized and took place once every three years.

On his rounds Cocceji visited not only the royal courts but also seigniorial and municipal proceedings. Relying on this experience, he issued a series of detailed ordinances which aimed at the simplification and better functioning of the judicial machine—the recruitment of seigniorial and municipal judges from among graduates in law; the division of competence between the courts and the Chambers of Domains; the suppression of appeals to the Faculties; the suppression of three out of five Courts of Appeal (one of which was the French court reserved for refugees); the regulation of the legal profession; the institution of examinations for the selection of magistrates; the simplification of procedure in Pomerania and Brandenburg; the reduction of certain punishments (torture was already abolished). However, the great work was to have been the construction of a single code for the whole country. Frederick, who had no knowledge of the making of laws, gave his chancellor complete freedom of action in this matter. From 1744 to 1752 Cocceji published a copious treatise, the *New System of Natural and Roman Jurisprudence,* but his principles were not sufficiently definite, for he attacked Roman and yet despised customary law. He claimed that he had rediscovered Germanic law, under the exclusive inspiration of natural law, and he even overrode the prejudices of his master, who paid the greatest respect to local traditions. In reality the *Corpus Juris Fridericianum* remained a project and no more than that. It is true that two volumes were printed in German, but when Cocceji died in 1755 after two years of illness the third was forgotten and the manuscript mislaid. Of the official scheme only the articles relating to marriage and to the guardianship of minors received the force of law and then only in certain provinces. In 1779 Frederick appointed Carmer chancellor and in 1780 commissioned him to codify Prussian law. But it was not until 1794 that the famous Prussian Code was promulgated. Thus not much actual reform was completed under Frederick. Contemporaries were fooled by the praises of the philosophers and had rosy illusions about his judicial work. It would also appear that

Frederick himself overestimated the work done by Cocceji and his two immediate successors, Jarigues and Fürst, who had merely carried on the day-to-day administration of affairs; after the Seven Years' War the King began to complain of the delays of judgment and the cupidity of magistrates once again. Furthermore, in 1779, the notorious business of Arnold the miller showed to what extent he wished to remain master of his judges and of their judgments.

This fellow Arnold had a mill on a little river in the Circle of Züllichau. Upstream of him the river passed through the lands of a municipal councilor, Von Gersdorf, who had had a carp pond dug in the middle of his park; into this he had made the river flow, but in such a way that afterward it flowed out into its normal bed once more. Arnold had certainly been inconvenienced during the actual filling of the pond, but he then claimed that he could no longer grind corn for more than a few days each year and on this pretext he refused to pay rent to his landlord, the Count von Schmettau. Schmettau took him into court; Arnold lost the case but persisted in refusing to pay. At the end of the respite allowed by law the court ordered a distraint upon him. Arnold appealed to the High Court of the Neumark and lost the appeal. Accusing the judges of violence and injustice, he complained to the King, who ordered an administrative inquiry to be held: its results were doubtful, but two of the commissioners admitted that there was a possibility of prejudice against the accused. Frederick was convinced that the judges had wished to do the noble councilor a good turn and that they had nonsuited Arnold through loyalty to their class; therefore he sent the case before the Berlin Court of Appeal. After minute investigation the court confirmed the two previous judgments.

On the afternoon of December 11 the King, who was suffering from gout, summoned Fürst, the chancellor, and the three councilors concerned to the castle at Berlin; he was in a furious temper and rained reproaches and insults on their heads. Fürst, who protested, was chased from the room and learned a minute later that his successor had already been appointed. The councilors, stammering and dismayed, left the castle only to be taken to prison. Step by step through Orders in Cabinet the decree of the Court of Appeal was revised, the miller restored to the possession of his mill, Councilor von Gersdorf recalled, his pond filled in, the president of Cüstrin recalled, and the three Berlin magistrates condemned to a year's detention in a fortress. Frederick was praised by D'Alembert for having taken the part of the weak, but in actual fact he was so unsure of himself that he freed the prisoners before their sentences expired. After his death, when the matter was reconsidered, it was found that Arnold was an expert pettifogger, famous for his litigious temper and for his bad faith. Besides, on the same river between the carp pond and the mill there was a sawmill worked by water power: the owner of the sawmill had given evidence that the pond had never caused him any inconvenience, and this decisive testimony invalidated Arnold's claims. The courts had therefore given a right judgment but without making the point of fact upon which their decision rested stand out intelligibly.

Modestly must it be confessed that a legend is always more powerful than the truth. The names of the imprisoned councilors should have gone down in history as those of courageous, honest magistrates: however, what confirmed the popularity of the "judges of Berlin" in the eyes of the world was the childish tale of another miller, the one at Sans Souci, who never spoke the words put in his mouth. According to the contemporary taste for rusticity his famous windmill was the necessary adjunct of a park "in the English manner," like the Chinese pagoda and the Greek temple; so far was the King from the least desire to demolish it that in the end he exempted the miller from taxes so that he might be willing to play his decorative part with a good grace.

Carlyle defined Frederick in a single word: he said he was a Reality. He surpassed the conventional picture of the philosopher king at all points and he appears to us as a reality—a reality too strong, too active, too independent to have himself succeeded in setting up the sovereignty of law, which would have confined his own action in a well-adjusted net of legal rulings. No, for half a century the Prussian State consisted of Frederick himself with his qualities, his defects, his capacity for work, and his ubiquitous will.

The legendary Frederick would have been a very insipid person. The true man was sometimes terrifying: to know him properly it was not enough to have seen him at table or traveling around his kingdom, he had to be observed at the head of his armies. Force is in fact the basis of all states and "it is under the protection of the soldier's art that all the other arts flourish." Prussia was an army and the Hohenzollerns were its hereditary leaders. If ever the troops were neglected, "it would be all up with this country." It was true that the barren soil of northern Germany only brought forth "iron and soldiers," but if "the first duty of a prince was to maintain himself and the second to improve his position," it provided the dynasty none the less with everything it needed to establish and develop its power.

The Hohenzollerns were crowned emperors after a victory and have disappeared before our eyes in the whirlwind of defeat: their ambitions came very near to being shattered a hundred and sixty years earlier. Frederick's endurance, his military genius, the valor and discipline of his troops, and also a run of luck saved the King and the kingdom on that occasion. The terrible crisis lasted for seven years, seven mortal years of agony, suffering, and danger, and it was because he surmounted all this that Frederick seemed so great to the men of his time.

X

Riding the Whirlwind

I

THE peace of Aix-la-Chapelle had left all Europe either discontented or anxious. There had been leagues and battles after the old pattern of the reign of Louis XIV. On one side stood France and half the Germanic states, on the other Austria and the maritime powers—the same combatants and often even the same fields of battle. "If Villars and Marlborough had come back to earth they would have recognized and could have resumed all their old positions." What results had emerged from this repetition of a play so often acted before? A confused struggle and a treaty which satisfied nobody. France gained no advantages from her victories; England was forced to restore all she had taken in Canada; Austria had regained the imperial crown but had lost one of her finest provinces; even the King of Prussia, the ravisher of Silesia, saw no security in his conquest. Each thought himself ill-used and laid the blame not on his own faults, not on bad luck, but on the treachery, hesitation, and weakness of his allies. There was a muted chorus of recriminations, and everybody had a vague feeling that the system of coalitions inherited from the seventeenth century no longer answered to the actual conditions of the balance of power in Europe.

Maria Theresa was the first to understand this fact. In her eyes the real enemy of the House of Austria, the implacable enemy, was no longer the Bourbon monarch but Prussia. Against Frederick Austria could find no satisfaction in an English alliance, for England was busy extending her colonial and maritime power and had become indifferent to the fate of the Continent and especially to the internal affairs of the Empire. Had she not hurried on the peace of 1748 just when Russia was about to give powerful assistance to the Empress? But if the Hapsburgs needed an ally on the Continent the only possible one was France. Besides, from 1750 onward Kaunitz, the ambassador at Versailles, had been suggesting to Louis XV that old quarrels should be forgotten and that his country had friendly inclinations. The King received these offers with extreme politeness, smiled upon the diplomat and displayed much confidence and feeling toward Maria Theresa personally; however, France did not change her allies. On the other side, although the hatred the merchants of London felt for popery inclined them toward Frederick, King George was still too much of a German, too closely attached to his Electorate of Hanover and to the enmities of his youth to join with a good grace in a reversal of policy. He strove to keep Austria as an ally by removing her every pretext for discontent. In short, for five more years Europe persisted in a routine of which she was weary because she shrank from breaking free of it through fear of the unknown.

Peace worried Frederick more than war. He was at loggerheads with Russia, Saxony, Austria, and Hanover, and none of his frontiers seemed to him to be safe. Besides, it was essential for him not to let the Court of Versailles become either estranged or indifferent. He pestered it with his complaints, his grievances, and his fears both real and imaginary. Every other minute he required, he even demanded, the active aggressive intervention of France. They must send an ambassador after King George into Hanover, for it was in Hanover that "the most pernicious schemes were brought forward," they must see that their ministers spoke with vigor in St. Petersburg and with firmness in London, they must arouse the Turks, they must increase their subsidies to the minor German princes, they must give less dry and laconic answers; all this advice was mingled with respects, flattery, remonstrances, and shafts of sarcasm. The French hardly found Frederick a reliable or accommodating companion, they complained of his bad temper, they did not share all his suspicions, they did not always put much conviction into the steps to which he primed them, but on the whole they did take them, and on their side the alliance was never betrayed except by the sub-acid words which escaped them in moments of fatigue.

Decisive action came from London, for London had decided

to break up the chain of French posts which stretched from Canada to Louisiana, from the St. Lawrence to the Mississippi, and so encircled the English colonies in America as to prevent every chance of expansion in depth toward the interior. Though officially peace had been restored, skirmishes and ambuscades continued to occur along the ill-defined boundary between the two empires, and as the French nearly always got the better of these in spite of their numerical inferiority, the British ministers were urged on by their colonists and merchants to the point of desiring open warfare, so that they might make some use of the superiority of their fleets by preventing French troops from leaving the Continent.

Though Frederick was in the first instance deeply concerned with the affairs of Europe—unrest in Sweden, plans for the succession in Poland, the possible election of the Archduke Joseph as King of the Romans—it did not take him long to see through the tactics of the English. He was in dispute with them over some vessels of his which had been seized during the last war; in a fit of impatience he had indemnified himself for them by confiscation of the interest due on the capital sums laid out by London bankers in mortgages on Silesia. However, his perspicacity went far beyond this business of his own. From the winter of 1753 onward the tone of his political correspondence changed, as though he had a presentiment of great troubles ahead. His questions were more searching, he demanded more precise information and more detailed bulletins. In February, 1755, he wrote to his chargé d'affaires, "I think that the odds will be ten to one that a war will ensue, and that armaments will lead to more armaments and thence to diplomatic ruptures in a manner at once unplanned and unappreciated." Frederick then was mistaken on only one point: English policy was much more conscious and much more deliberate than he imagined. In fact on April 16, 1755, Admiral Boscawen, commander of the American squadron, received secret instructions. They ordered him to place a cruiser in the mouth of the St. Lawrence, to capture the merchant vessels seen in the vicinity, and finally to attack and sink without preliminary declaration the French warships and transport vessels which were assembling at Brest and were due to start for Canada a fortnight later.

On April 28, as war was a certainty, King George embarked for Hanover, but the English ministers had been imprudent to hurry into aggression in this way, for their continental coalition was not yet ready. It was true that Spain promised to remain neutral, but her interests as a great colonial power were too sharply opposed to England's plans of conquest for her neutrality to be reliable. Austria would not commit herself, as she did not wish to send to Belgium the troops she needed to cover Bohemia. The Low Countries, upon whom fell the defense of the Barrier fortresses, were incapable of putting a man into them or even of bearing the cost of keeping them in repair. The vast size of the subsidies demanded by Russia was sure to arouse the opposition of the Commons. In short, apart from the 8,000 men of the Landgrave of Hesse-Cassel who were always up for sale, England had not yet acquired any military support when in mid-July came the news that Admiral Boscawen had indeed attacked the French squadron but had missed his mark, for the greater part of the convoy had escaped in the mist, thanks to the sacrifice of two ships. Such was the dismay in London that the Duke of Newcastle had to rearrange his cabinet in a hurry. As for George II, he refused to leave Herrenhausen until the "continental system" had been built up.

But if the Commons was determined to keep its credits for naval warfare, how was the support of other German princes to be bought? By force of circumstance English policy was drawn toward the King of Prussia; he had either to be intimidated or won over. On July 23, that is to say about ten days after the arrival of the packet from America, Newcastle decided to enter into negotiations with him through the mediation of the Duke of Brunswick, who was much in need of money and was ambitious to marry his eldest daughter, Frederick's niece, to George II's grandson, who was now Prince of Wales and heir to the throne owing to his father's death. "If the King of Prussia," wrote Newcastle, "could be restrained either by fear or by a pretended regard for the peace of the Empire, or by attentions to his sister and his family, this disposition must certainly be encouraged." The advantages of Prussian neutrality would be considerable: "In this way the expenses of the Prussian troops would be spared if they were in our pay and the German possessions of the King would obtain a most solid and substantial security."

Up till then Frederick's main anxiety had been that France would become absorbed in her colonial operations and would leave him alone face to face with his enemies. And so he preached incessantly at Versailles the need of a great diversion in Europe. Let France collect a decent body of troops and at the first act of hostility march it into the Low Countries and Hanover! In a talk with the French minister he even added, in reference to his uncle, George of England, "That's the surest way of making that old ——— sing!"

However, at the same time he was careful to hold back his own full coöperation. When Louis XV's Council took, or pretended to take, his kindly suggestion that they should seize the initiative as being the announcement of a common plan, he was evasive. By every courier he continued to upbraid the lifelessness, indolence, credulity, false moves, and lethargy of the "ministers of cotton," but he spoke no more of Hanover and he ordered his ambassador, Knyphausen, to remind Rouillé, the Secretary of State, that their alliance did not concern the colonies and that in any case he himself could not get on the move without a year's notice.

In the month of June he went on a tour of inspection to Wesel and he took advantage of the journey to have a little spree in Holland disguised as a musician. The Berlin road in Westphalia passed very near to Hanover—a slight detour would have brought him to his uncle's house. Both times he passed by there was a vague suggestion that the two kings might meet, but the plan got no further than that. When an opportunity arose to open conversations in a more discreet manner, Frederick hesitated to believe in such a piece of good luck. Nothing was more painful for him than to be bound by a formal treaty when he felt that destinies were being linked together elsewhere without his participation. Was he going to find himself, thanks to England, in one of those ambiguous situations from which he had always profited—desired by both sides, "haggling" first with one and then with the other and making up his mind quite egotistically? Nevertheless, he feared it was a trap and only displayed his hand with the greatest caution. He took good care not to make the least promise, he hid behind generalizations, he demanded information, he offered his mediation and, when pressed, pleaded the fatigues and discomforts of maneuvers for not having answered promptly. "At bottom," he wrote to the Duke of Brunswick, "I see that the King of England is sweating with fear for his Electorate, and I begin to suspect that he is not satisfied with the Court of Vienna, otherwise he would never have approached me."

Reticence and flirtation of this type went on throughout August. George II was about to return to England without anything having been decided, when Frederick took one step further forward: "I have been thinking," he wrote once again to his brother-in-law, "that my treaty of alliance with France will end in the spring of the coming year, which will leave me free to act in accordance with my interests and my convenience. Though I will not undertaken [sic] any engagements before the period of this treaty shall have expired, nevertheless I will not disavow Your Highness if he wishes in the meanwhile to give the English ministers to understand . . . but always as if it came from him and without involving me in it as yet, that *provided that reasonable propositions are made to me on the part of the King of England it might be possible to reach the goal which was proposed in relation to the neutrality of the States of Hanover, upon which it was nevertheless not to be expected that I should broach the subject first.*" (September 1.) However, he also took care to warn Rouillé that "rather unusual and important overtures" had been made to him, details of which he intended to put before the Duc de Nivernais, the ambassador nominated to negotiate the renewal of the alliance.

It is clear that at that moment Frederick had not taken any decision except that of playing his usual game of offering himself to the last and the highest bidder. However, the English ministers knew far more of all this than he imagined, for all the correspondence of Mitchell, his chargé d'affaires at London, was intercepted, read, and deciphered by government agents. From it Newcastle arrived at the conviction that the King of Prussia had not the least desire to be involved in a colonial war which seemed to him to be completely futile, as its aims were no concern of his. Also, as first minister he was absorbed in preparations for the next session of Parliament and did not reply in a hurry; when he did reply it was in riddles. This exasperated Frederick: "Is it not singular that these people ask me to join their faction while in actual fact I have two big quarrels with them which have not been settled? It seems that the whole world is obliged to sacrifice the particular interests of each part and to undertake the defense of this damned country. At a moment when they are giving no explanations themselves, they demand declarations of me. They want me to throw over France and repay myself with the glory of having preserved their land of Hanover, which is no concern of mine either way. These people either want to make a vulgar dupe of me, or else they are mad and blown out with a ridiculous self-esteem." This diatribe was made on November 24. On December 2 Frederick, having learned that the secret of his negotiations was beginning to leak out, issued a denial of "the malicious insinuations of his enemies" at Versailles and an affirmation "that he had made no arrangement with the Court of London." Five days later he ordered Mitchell to sign the agreement.

What then had happened in the interval to force Frederick to make up his mind in such a hurry? Something which was very commonplace at first sight. He had received a detailed account of the Anglo-Russian treaty which had been signed on September 30 after endless bargaining and had just been ratified at the end of the two months allowed for the exchange of signatures. By this treaty each of the two states reciprocally guaranteed all the possessions of the other, including the German possessions of the King of England, which were specifically mentioned by name. For this purpose a body of 55,000 men was to be kept by Russia on the frontiers of Livonia along with fifty transports ready to put out to sea. To ensure the execution of the pact England undertook to advance Russia £100,000 payable in advance and £500,000 on the day the Russian troops began to move. The text of these articles had been given Mitchell by Fox, the Secretary of State, who was leader of the House of Commons. He added that in the mind of King George and the Empress Elisabeth the convention had no other aim than to preserve their German lands from possible attacks by French armies—nothing to disturb the King of Prussia, nothing directed against him. "Your master," he concluded, "is in a most brilliant position; he holds the sword in one hand and the olive branch in the other: let him say the word and all the differences we have with him would be settled."

No doubt the English ministers were sincere in affirming that they had only been thinking of France, but as for the Tsarina, she had only been thinking of Prussia. After having allowed her chancellor, Bestucheff, constantly to raise his price on the proposed subsidies without coming to an agreement, she had only consented to get down to business when pressed by the new English envoy, Sir Charles Williams, who came from Saxony bubbling over with enthusiasm for Austria and described Frederick as the "common enemy," the enemy who must be overthrown. Williams knew nothing of the Brunswick negotiations and therefore he played his part with perfect candor. However, when the alliance was at last concluded the English cabinet used it not as a weapon for crushing its enemy but as a threat and as a means of gaining a new ally by pressure. "It must be admitted," wrote the Duc de Broglie, "that seldom in the annals of diplomacy has there been a more skillful or a more successful sleight of hand."

It did not require much attention on Frederick's part to see that, if he did not ward off the blow, he and he alone would be struck down. The extent of the empire of the Tsars frightened him; the Russian Army could do him a great deal of harm, but if he beat it he would not be able to pursue it. If—and to judge by the constant friendship of the two sovereigns it was highly probable—if similar agreements existed between St. Petersburg and Vienna, he was in danger of being crushed by an enormous coalition without even a hope that France would detain a part of the Austrian forces, as Maria Theresa would rather abandon Belgium than withdraw a single battalion from Bohemia. England had scored a palpable hit, and from that moment there was no question of shilly-shallying or hairsplitting. In a few days a convention was prepared and finally settled at Berlin on the first day of 1756.

It consisted of four articles, one of which was secret. The first and the third contained vague declarations of alliance and friendship. By the second the two Kings of Prussia and England undertook, "whatsoever foreign power upon whatsoever pretext desires to march its forces into Germany, to unite their forces to prevent the entry or passage of the troops aforesaid." The text bore the word "Germany" and not "Holy Roman Empire" so as to exclude the Austrian Netherlands from the guarantee, and this exclusion was repeated in the secret article. The convention was agreed to by the English ministry on January 16, 1756, under the name of the Treaty of Whitehall. To put it briefly, England removed Prussia from the threat of Russian attack; Prussia in return undertook to defend the German possessions of England against her own ally, France.

The Duke of Brunswick was the only one not to be rewarded for his zeal in the political field, for his matrimonial dreams were not satisfied. Poor Princess Amelia did not marry the Prince of Wales, who had no desire to take her. However, she did not remain single, and as the wife of the Duke of Saxe-Weimar she had the glory of protecting Goethe and Schiller and of being their friend.

II

From the beginning of September onward the government of Versailles had been importuned with the most lively entreaties by the Court of Vienna. Schooled by Kaunitz, the chancellor, the ambassador, Stahremberg, forcefully exhibited to Louis XV that Frederick's ambitions were a direct danger to his kingdom. "France," said the Austrian, "is at this very moment nursing a snake in her bosom. It is incompatible with the true interests of France to allow the strength of the said king to increase and to provide the maritime powers with the opportunity of putting him in due time in the place of your august House and of making use of him to overcome the supremacy of France." In addition to this the Empress warned Louis XV that negotiations were under way between Prussia and England and before many months were passed he would be abandoned for the third or fourth time.

The deepest interest was shown in the remarks of Stahremberg, but he received no other reply than a reminder of the treaty which still bound France and Prussia. The note read as follows: "Faithful to his agreements and to the laws of honor the King could not, without reasons of the utmost gravity and proofs of the greatest clarity, not only break with his allies but also entertain doubts of their good faith and consider them capable of infidelity and treachery." As a consequence France was only ready to treat with Austria on the basis of the *status quo,* that is to say, with Frederick guaranteed in the peaceful possession of Silesia. All the same Bernis, whose job it was to follow up the conversations with Stahremberg, could not hide from him the deep concern his master felt at the alleged defection of the Prussian King. Kaunitz was quite certain that Frederick would commit what Louis XV had branded in advance as infidelity and treachery, so he resigned himself to a waiting game and to postponing the discussion until such time as a positive and official act should hallow the reconciliation of England and Prussia. Nevertheless, as the gazettes of Amsterdam and Leyden contained the clearest allusions to it, Rouillé dispatched the Duc de Nivernais to Berlin, although up to that time he had not hurried him, so confident had he been of the strength of the alliance.

Frederick awaited the interview without pleasure. He had signed in a hurry so as to confront the duke with an accomplished fact, and faithful to his system of lampooning people toward whom he felt guilty, he had filled his dispatches to Knyphausen with bitter complaints against France. However, he foresaw that coming after the Convention of Klein-Schnellendorf, the peace of Breslau, and the peace of Dresden, the Treaty of Whitehall would arouse a storm of anger in Paris—an anger which would be all the more sharp since Louis XV, after having tried every sort of mildness and conciliation in vain, had at last issued an ultimatum claiming the restitution of the ships held in English ports and the liberation of the sailors who were victims of Boscawen's piracies. The French demands had reached London on January 3, on the tenth the English ministry had decided to reply with a refusal, and it was on the sixteenth that it ratified the agreement with Prussia which had been drawn up on the first of the month.

Certainly France had not decided to attack Hanover but she had no hope of winning the war at sea, and the sending of reinforcements across the Atlantic might be considered too risky;

therefore it was certain she would be forced to seek for successes in Europe—to occupy territory and thus seize counters which could be exchanged at the next peace for all she might have lost in India and America. Hanover was England's vulnerable point. By covering the Electorate Frederick cheated France of one of her chances of victory: "I am the ally of France," he himself wrote to the Duke of Brunswick. "In truth, our treaty is simply and purely defensive, but under what pretext and with what colors could I disguise so peculiar a move on my part as to lay down the limits up to which it should hold good?"

The Duc de Nivernais was the great-nephew of Mazarin, sweet-natured, showy, and a perfect gentleman. He arrived at Berlin on the twelfth and had his first audience on January 14. It would all have been painful enough after the opening compliments had not Frederick taken refuge in generalizations, putting off the embarrassing details till later. "You know," said he, "that England had made proposals for an alliance to me: I had you informed of this, but since that piece of information those people have pressed me very hard. I will acquaint you of all this on another occasion."

The interviews which followed were far more ticklish to handle. After much ambiguous talk Frederick had to inform the duke of what had been done, and with an ingenuous air he finally exposed before his eyes a copy of the text he had initialed, which was about to be brought back from London. For a moment Nivernais was struck dumb.

Frederick pleaded his case with great dexterity and brought forward all sorts of reasons. Russia was a formidable power with an inexhaustible supply of men which could ravage his lands in a single campaign. Between Russia, Austria, England, and Saxony he was "encircled," "besieged." He had been frightened. . . . He had had to give in. But what harm was he doing to France? None. On the contrary, he was protecting her from the Russians! Besides, never would the French armies have been able to push their way into the Empire for *there the English were thought of as gods, and there was a scramble to hold out one's hat to get the guineas.* Let the French take Belgium—it was well worth Canada. And then this convention of his was only the result of the preoccupations of the moment. If his interests were to change he would easily find a pretext for going back on his word, they could count on him for that. Whereupon he unfolded a map of the British Isles and improvised a plan of invasion for the ministry of Versailles, underlining those points for landing which he thought to be the least well defended.

Nivernais replied that it was a matter of indifference to know whether France intended to attack Hanover tomorrow or next year, for the mere uncertainty of it compelled England to keep back a part of her forces and her money to safeguard this much-prized possession. Prussia was allowing her to devote everything henceforth either to the defense of her own coasts or to the development of the struggle at sea, where she already enjoyed a formidable superiority. Moreover, if Germany was kept completely intact England could collect bands of mercenaries there which France would have to fight on some other battlefield. Finally, even admitting that the security of Prussia demanded peace in Germany, Frederick could have made this the subject of direct negotiations with France instead of arranging it with her enemy behind her back. In addition to all these grievances Nivernais did not mention the personal affront which the other had thrust upon him by allowing a man of his rank to arrive on such a mission when a word in advance would have been enough to stop him from coming. He was too much of a nobleman to let his distaste come to the surface but he wrote to his friend the Comte de Broglie a little later, "Your patriotism would have been as bewildered as mine if you had arrived here on January 12, while the convention was being signed in London on the sixteenth. . . . As to the form, that is to say, the manner and the circumstances of it, I think the best thing to do is to be silent, and that is just what I am doing. There are some actions which should be allowed to speak for themselves."

Nevertheless the exchange of views was continued until the end of March. Nivernais was much flattered by the King and had a lively appreciation of the charm of his behavior and conversation. After a stay at Sans Souci he even came to imagine that he could get a new defensive treaty signed and he produced a draft of one. France would have guaranteed Frederick in the possession of Silesia, in exchange for which he would have promised to send a small force of 10,000 men in the event of her territory being attacked. Nivernais added naïvely enough that it hardly mattered whether Frederick subscribed in good or in bad faith, the essential thing being to get from him some sort of document to annul the moral effect of the neutrality agreement. In reality it was most improbable that this arrangement would have seemed very glorious or very safe to the French. However, Versailles refused it point-blank by bringing Nivernais' mission to a conclusion. Then Austria once more put herself forward to fill the place of the fickle ally, making a great show of bringing Russia and Saxony with her, but allowing it to be understood that if she were to be rebuffed once again she would be obliged to fall back upon the other camp. "In the event of France persisting in her spiteful prejudice," wrote Kaunitz, "there will always be a further choice open to us, that is, to rally to the side of the big battalions and fall in with the views of England."

The Franco-Austrian treaty was signed at Rouillé's house at Jouy-en-Josas. It bore the name of the Treaty of Versailles and comprehended several conventions by which Austria renounced her English and France her Prussian alliance. The two states gave each other a mutual guarantee of their European possessions, and promised that if one of them were to be attacked the other would send help to the tune of 24,000 men or else an equivalent subsidy. Taken at its face value the pact was purely defensive, but in reality the conversations already under way went further in every respect than the text upon which agreement had been reached. Maria Theresa's goal was not, in fact, to maintain the *status quo* on the Continent but to recapture Silesia and to weaken the power of Prussia to the point of making her inoffensive. Also, in the light of the events which followed it, the Treaty of Versailles seems to have been the bait used to collect the great anti-Prussian coalition which Maria Theresa was trying to bind together from St. Petersburg to Versailles.

The Tsarina was furious over the way she had been tricked by the English, and her anger was so genuine that she refused the 100,000 crowns they offered as the first installment—a thing never seen before in Russia. As soon as she learned of the conclusion of the Treaty of Versailles she offered her good friend and sister Maria Theresa a force of 80,000 men, backed with a promise not to lay down her arms so long as Frederick retained Silesia and the County of Glatz. The adhesion of Russia decided that of Poland and Saxony. France was eagerly listened to at Stockholm, and her ambassador had more influence in the Senate than Queen Ulrica, who had compromised her position by a fruitless and unskillful attempt to make herself absolute. Furthermore, the time was ripe for Sweden to reconquer the port of Stettin and the Pomeranian duchies which Frederick William had taken from her. To balance this, in exchange for Silesia Austria was ready to cede Luxemburg, Ostend, and Nieuport to France, while Belgium was to go to Louis XV's son-in-law, the Infante of Parma. Thus there would have been created on the frontier itself a completely French, semivassal State comparable to Lorraine under the compliant sovereignty of Stanislas. However, even in July Louis firmly maintained that he would not be obliged to engage in an *offensive* war against the King of Prussia.

It is impossible to know and fruitless to conjecture in what way and at what moment the negotiations would have been concluded if Frederick, by one of those sudden and unforeseen decisions which were always the hallmark of his policy, had not invaded the Empress' dominions and thus cast himself for the part of aggressor. In fact, in the middle of June he had been informed by the English envoy of Russia's change of front and by his spies of the movement of troops which was taking place in Livonia. He also had in his pay a secretary of the Austrian minister at Berlin and an employee of the Saxon Chancellery who both of them gave him news of mysterious correspondences and military preparations, with the exaggeration usual to reports of this type. On the twenty-second, the very day of the arrival of a courier from Dresden, he wrote to his sister Wilhelmina, "War seems to me inevitable, I have done what I could to avoid it and have not succeeded; I wash my hands of what is about to happen"; the next day he sent Marshal Lehwaldt, commander in East Prussia, highly detailed instructions anticipating a Russian invasion. Not only did he outline a plan of operations for him but he foresaw the defeat of the army of the Muscovites and gave him full powers to treat with them. If the victory was complete, if it coincided with a success gained by the King over the Austrians, the marshal was to demand the cession of Polish Prussia, with indemnities for Poland at the expense of Russia.

The British ministers took a very poor view of the martial ardor of the King of Prussia. As they had not been able to unite the Continent against France, they feared that open warfare waged by Frederick would involve them in the very expenses and risks which they had hoped to escape by means of the convention of neutrality. One day, when their minister Mitchell pointed out to the King the exaggerated nature of the news from Vienna and tried to persuade him that the Queen-Empress was maneuvering so as to force him into an act of aggression, the King lost his temper and looked him straight in the face: "What do you see, sir, in my face? Do you think that my nose is made to be pulled? By God, I will not stand for it!"

When Mitchell protested that his character was well known and that "among all his royal qualities it had never been said that patience and submission must be included," he started to laugh and cried out, pointing at a portrait of Maria Theresa, "It can no longer be avoided. This lady wants war. Well, she will get it soon enough!"

Nearly all those around him were against the adventure—his brothers, his ministers, all his generals except Winterfeldt. A long conference was needed to convince Schwerin and Rochow. In an audience held on July 21 old Podewils twice insisted on the dangers of an act of aggression. The first stages of the war might be brilliant and easy but in the long run Prussia, virtually without support, would remain exposed to the attacks of three powers. Was it not better to gain time, to make sure of the support of the Protestant princes in the north, to try once more to get an understanding between France and England, and to leave the English to deal with the Court of St. Petersburg, the twistings and turnings of which were innumerable? When Podewils had finished Frederick was quite unshaken and dismissed him with the famous words, "Farewell, Sir Timorous Policy!"

Nevertheless, perhaps on Mitchell's advice, he asked Vienna three times to explain the concentration of troops in Bohemia and the alleged treaty with Russia to dismember Prussia. Was he still thinking of intimidating Austria? Did he want to put appearances on his side? Historians are still discussing this, especially as the third demand was made a few days after the beginning of hostilities. However that may be, Maria Theresa replied to the second questionnaire by saying that no offensive alliance between Russia and herself existed, that the King of Prussia was misinformed, and that his accusations were self-evidently false. The reply arrived in Berlin on August 25. On the twenty-eighth at four in the morning Frederick left the capital. On the twenty-ninth he entered Saxony, the frontier of which lay at that time a few miles south of Berlin.

The Elector King Augustus III and his minister, Count von Brühl, were not expecting any such event. They had been out hunting the day before and were peacefully sleeping. When they learned that the frontier had been crossed by all the roads, they tried to have a parley with Frederick, who refused to answer them. Instead of making for Bohemia at full speed to join the Austrian forces under Marshal Browne, Augustus III and his army withdrew into a bend of the river Elbe, at the camp at Pirna, and awaited events. They had scant provisions, were encircled by the Prussians, and failed to force the blockade. Browne was first held up at Lobowitz and then made a fruitless advance to within four miles of the camp to support an attempt to force a way out on the right bank of the river. On October 15 the Saxon Army surrendered as prisoners of war. Augustus III was allowed to withdraw into Poland, while his soldiers were at once incorporated into the Prussian Army. At the first opportunity they almost all deserted.

The Elector King was out of the fight, but the lateness of the season prevented Frederick from carrying the war into Bohemia. Furthermore, Maria Theresa took advantage of the indignation aroused in Europe by the invasion of Saxony, a neutral state, to get from Russia the convention of February 2, 1757, and from France the second Treaty of Versailles (May 1, 1757). The Tsarina undertook to send 80,000 men into the field against Prussia, Louis XV 105,000 and 24,000 auxiliaries. Furthermore on January 25 the German Diet passed upon Frederick the ban of the Empire and decreed the mobilization of the army of the Circles against him. A division of his dominions was to be made according to the plan mentioned above (see pp. 315–316). No one in his senses could have believed at that time that Prussia could long resist such a redoubtable gathering of forces.

Such was the upsetting of alliances which for nearly two centuries has caused rivers of ink to flow and has aroused controversies which have not yet subsided. A childish but persistent legend lays the blame or the merit for it on Madame de Pompadour. It is enough to trace events in their chronological order to be convinced that England was responsible for everything, because she was the only power resolved to make war in all eventualities and whatever came of it. Austria, by her passivity and her unwillingness to garrison the Low Countries, facilitated the Hanover negotiations, but however much she desired to recover Silesia she could not act apart from France, whose assistance she only got with difficulty and after two events: firstly, after the neutrality agreement between England and Prussia and because of that agreement; secondly, after the invasion of Saxony by Prussia and because of that invasion. France submitted to events more than she controlled them. Because Louis XV feared war "as a calamity" and clung to peace "with immoderate devotion" (both these phrases are Knyphausen's), Boscawen's attack took him by surprise. Because he had honored his own signature and refused to treat with Austria at a moment when he could have got a high price for the betrayal he might have made of the King of Prussia, he found himself isolated on the Continent and forced to accept Maria Theresa's terms instead of imposing his own on her.

As for Frederick, he has many a time been accused of lies and perfidy. The precipitation, imprudence, and ill-success of his moves are still more striking. After having tried to tack between France and England he decided on friendship with England in a sudden moment of fright. His movements were so maladroit that after antagonizing France so as to avoid war with Russia he was compelled to make war on Russia and France simultaneously. In none of his plans had he ever admitted the possibility of a Franco-Austrian alliance: none the less this alliance was concluded, and for this he was himself to blame. From fear of encirclement he invaded Saxony, and it was the invasion of Saxony which cemented the coalition by which he was to be encircled.

When he occupied Dresden he had the government offices broken into and the archives burgled to find proof that Saxony,

Russia, and Austria had plotted to divide his lands among them: the documents thus obtained simply made it clear that he was hated by his neighbors but that it was only in the event of his attacking them that the three powers had agreed to coöperate. He had played Maria Theresa's game, he had provided her with arguments for convincing Louis XV, he had borne the odium of being the aggressor, but from this aggression he did not even obtain a military advantage sufficient to outweigh the moral loss.

So astonishing was this series of mistakes that German historians have sought for a hidden meaning in Frederick's conduct. In their eyes the conquest of Saxony was his main aim and he simply took advantage of the uncertain state of Europe to make a war of conquest look like a war of defense. This hypothesis was formulated more than half a century ago—it has aroused controversies which still continue. Frederick's most recent biographer has tried to justify his hero by taking it upon himself to explain that the invasion of Saxony in 1756 was quite as legitimate and free from ulterior motives as the invasion of Belgium in 1914.

To be honest, the discussion is a pointless one. That Frederick had views on Saxony cannot be denied, as he has taken care to tell us of them himself. In his *Political Testament* of 1752 he ranked it among the acquisitions to be made "by right of convenience." "Of all the provinces of Europe," he wrote, "there are none more suited to our State than Saxony, Polish Prussia, and Swedish Pomerania because all three of them round it off. Saxony, however, would be of most use; it would set the frontier back farthest and cover Berlin. . . . No doubt you think that it is not enough to indicate the countries that would suit us but that means for acquiring them must be suggested. Here they are: we must dissimulate and hide our plans, take advantage of circumstances, wait patiently for favorable ones and act with vigor when they arrive. What would facilitate this conquest would be if Saxony was in alliance with the Queen of Hungary and if that princess or her descendants should break with Prussia. That would be a pretext for entering Saxony, for disarming the troops and strengthening our position in the country." In fact, everything happened in 1756 as Frederick had imagined it in 1752. Furthermore, it is certain that coalitions were a nightmare to him. In June, 1756, he sincerely believed that he was in danger and on the point of being overwhelmed by a league which Maria Theresa was struggling to bring into being but which was as yet nonexistent. This mixture of fear and rapacity was much the most extraordinary explosive force which history had ever seen.

III

FREDERICK had been applying his mind to the art of war without cessation. He had been considering the example of great generals and drawing lessons from his own mistakes. His most important writings date from these ten years. Among them the *Regulations* are concerned with the purely technical sides of the Service, the part called the little service in Germany and in England recruit drill, company drill, and battalion training. . . . On the other hand, the *General Principles of War Applied to the Tactics and Discipline of Prussian Troops, The Opinion of M. de Folard, Knight, Drawn from His Commentaries on Polybius,* and *The Reflections and General Rules for Warfare* are devoted to that side of the science of battles which possesses "most grandeur and sublimity." Without doubt it would be idle to look for a systematic account of the matter here. Frederick treated the various topics which came into his mind with equal attention but in a rather loose order. He even cut short a train of thought sometimes as if he was afraid he had said too much, or as if he thought it was no use explaining his ideas to readers who were not capable of understanding them. Nevertheless in the first and last of these works he set out in admirably clear and concise terms the highly novel principles of modern warfare.

The essential idea was that the aim of warfare was not the occupation or defense of a piece of territory but the destruction of the forces of the enemy. "A completely defensive plan of action is worthless; it reduces you to taking up strong positions; the enemy turns your flank, and as you dare not fight, you retire. The enemy again outflanks you, and it turns out, when all is said and done, that you lose more ground by your retreat than after the loss of a battle, and that your army melts away more rapidly by desertion than after the bloodiest of actions. A modified defensive plan is worthless, for you have everything to lose and nothing to hope from it." Of all possible methods for the efficient conduct of a great war the best was that which consisted of resolutely taking the offensive on enemy soil and of forcing the other side to subordinate its movements to your own. "Our wars must be short and lively. It does not suit us in the least to spin things out. A long-drawn-out war would imperceptibly destroy our admirable discipline; it would depopulate the land and drain our resources." However, such operations were difficult. Revictualing on foreign soil posed some thorny problems. You had to expect to traverse a land without roads, emptied of inhabitants and livestock, with harvests destroyed or buried. Even though an army carried in its wagons and ammunition carts a month's bread, field ovens and hand mills, yet it remained dependent upon its magazines, unless it could gain control of the whole course of a river—the only reliable and convenient thoroughfare—such as the Oder in Silesia or the Elbe in Bohemia.

Therefore if it happened that you were compelled to fall back upon the defensive, you had to give it all the appearance of an offensive war, to make it mobile, cunning, and active, in short turn it into "a trick to flatter the vanity of the enemy and thus tempt them to make mistakes of which the general will be able to take advantage."

How should you get to work so as to lead your army into battle with the best chances of success? The main principle was that you must not attempt to prevail on all sides at once but only at one well-chosen point, the result of which decided that of all the others. "If you separate your forces you will be beaten in detail; if you wish to give battle, collect the greatest number of troops you can; they cannot be more usefully employed. . . . Petty minds wish to preserve everything, men of understanding keep their eyes on the main object alone. . . . He who preserves everything preserves nothing." From this maxim Frederick briefly deduced another which was to become Napoleon's especial maxim, that of *simultaneous movements made by forces mutually supporting each other*. "In battles the only good dispositions of troops are those which give each other mutual support, in which no body of men is exposed on its own but is continually supported by others. In the same way it is necessary to support the war on a large scale."

The dispositions taken by Frederick during the winter of 1756 were at once in agreement with and opposed to these ideas. He had at his disposal 200,000 men including the Hanoverian troops and the Hessians in the pay of George II. After taking counsel with Schwerin and Winterfeldt he decided to leave a mere covering force to face the Russians and the French, so as to unite the main body of his forces and fall upon the Austrians before they had emerged from their winter quarters; after that he would double back against the most menacing of his opponents. It is hard to imagine anything more coherent and better planned; but when his troops went out at the beginning of April he divided them into four separate bodies which were joined together in pairs: the first two coming from Saxony under the command of the King, the others from Lusatia and Silesia under Schwerin. Frederick's army advanced on Prague along the left bank of the Elbe and Schwerin's on the right bank along the valley of the Iser. They were separated at their point of departure by sixty leagues of difficult country. Their junction had to take place almost under the walls of the town and in the presence of the enemy. This time the amazing thing was the boldness of the plan, completely opposed to the principle of forces giving each other mutual support. The fact is that war does not depend upon conventional rules to which leaders are bound down as if they were chess players. The man who gets the worst of it by applying the principles is in the wrong; the man who is victorious by neglecting them is in the right. In the general arrangement of operations Frederick remained faithful to his own ideas; in matters of detail, face to face with generals who, being weak tacticians, felt a kind of superstitious fear for him, he could allow himself to take many risks.

To begin with, the Austrians did not know how to make the best use of their central position; they wanted to cover every point simultaneously and divided their army into four isolated masses which the Prussians drove before them. Yet they did this slowly and lost several days themselves in forming up their columns again. On the other hand, as the Prussian offensive struck the two extremities of the country, the Austrians found their forces concentrated by their own retreat, so that when Prince Charles arrived at Prague he had at his disposal a compact body of 61,000 men, whereas Schwerin and Frederick were still separated by the Moldau and the Elbe. Yet the Prince remained motionless: Frederick crossed the Moldau unmolested three miles from his camp, and Schwerin passed over the Elbe ten miles off, as little harassed as his master.

The battle began on May 6. The Austrians were drawn up to the east of the town on a line of arid, rocky heights, very steep in places but sloping away toward the right with the lower portions merging into some marshy meadows, scattered with ponds and divided up by dykes which were used for transport purposes. At this period the infantry generally used to draw up in three ranks, in a thin line, and in very extended order so as to make the most of the firing line. Behind this first line a second one was placed which repaired the gaps made in the front line. The cavalry used to be stationed on the two wings. At daybreak Frederick issued the order to attack the enemy's right, which could be reached across some reasonably small foothills. However, Prince Charles sensed the danger and drew back that wing, so as to arrange it in the shape of a hook behind a very broken piece of ground, in such a way that his front formed a right angle pointing toward the enemy. This defensive battle order, which tacticians call the gibbet formation, is a remedy worse than the disease according to Jomini. In fact, the extreme end of his line had to be as well covered as if it had been a straight one, and on the other hand the troops around the salient could not withdraw without pressing against each other, while at the same time they could not advance without leaving a great gap in their center. Nevertheless Prince Charles had gained something by his new position, for the Prussians were forced to make a wider extensive movement in order to attack him.

Their first assault under Schwerin was repulsed for want of preparation, and Schwerin was killed while waving a flag to encourage a battalion which was hesitating. The second, led by General Zieten with sixty-five squadrons, broke the Austrian cavalry. Marshal Browne had a leg smashed to bits and had to be carried off the field. Prince Charles, rushing to stop the fugitives, succumbed to an apoplectic fit and could not return to his place until the end of the day. The Austrian Army lost its unified command, and the battle split up into a medley of minor engage-

ments which were confused and hard to describe. Nevertheless
Zieten's success was not enough to gain the victory, because his
horsemen dispersed to pillage the Austrian camp, cut up the baggage train, and get drunk. A decision was reached through a surprise attack by the Prussian right, which Frederick had kept in
reserve till then, for it flung itself into the struggle just as confusion was beginning to appear on the other side. The regiments
of Prince Henry, Prince Ferdinand of Brunswick, and Winterfeldt performed prodigies of valor. They advanced under fire as
if they were at a review and only fired themselves at point-blank
range. The Austrians had lost about 16,000 men as against 13,-
000; half the army withdrew into Prague, the rest escaped to the
south to join forces with Marshal Daun, who was coming up with
reinforcements.

The fugitives were not harried. Frederick hardly ever pursued
a routed opponent. Most often he had no reserves fresh enough to
do so. Secondly, as his army was composed of individuals of all
sorts and of all nationalities, he was afraid that a swift and
scattered movement would dislocate the order of his units and
would give volunteers a chance to desert against their better
judgment. That is why, although he let it be understood on a
number of occasions that the aim of a battle was the annihilation
of the enemy, he could only count in practice on their more or
less complete demoralization and disorganization. Therefore he
merely had Daun's retreat followed by an observation corps
under Marshal von Bevern, and he began the blockade of Prague
since he had neither enough artillery nor enough men to be able
to take it by assault. As for Prince Charles, he had provisions to
last till June 20. Daun used this breathing space to reorganize his
men and on the twelfth he took the offensive with 54,000 men
against Bevern, who had less than half that number. Bevern withdrew in a hurry to Kolin, while Frederick marched to his assistance with far too small a reinforcement—four battalions and six
squadrons. The movements of the two bodies were so very unplanned that they nearly failed to meet. When they did meet it
was by chance on the evening of the fourteenth, and the battle
was fought on the eighteenth.

Frederick wished to repeat his Prague maneuver in detail, that is to say attack with his left wing while refusing with his right, but this time he was faced by a general of much greater merit. Daun, guessing his intentions, changed front during the night and, when he was positive that Frederick was persisting in this plan, made his reserve and his second line slip over to the threatened point with such effect that not only did the Prussians meet with unexpected resistance but they were even taken by surprise themselves in the course of their flanking march. The Austrian cavalry completed the rout. Of his 18,000 foot soldiers Frederick lost 12,000. Daun's losses amounted to a mere third of this number (battle of Kolin, June 18, 1757). After his defeat the King had to raise the siege of Prague, and he arranged to retreat in two bodies, one commanded by himself and the other by his brother William. Daun was wise enough to keep his army united. He followed up William, whom he forced into a series of aimless, disastrous marches, in the course of which the Prince lost his baggage train and his artillery. The two brothers joined forces again in Saxony at Bautzen. William, along with his generals, went to meet Frederick, who watched him approach and then without a word turned his back on him. Some hours later he sent him the following message by General Goltz: "Tell my brother and all his generals that I ought to cut off their heads."

In the depths of despair William at once asked for permission to leave the army. "You have reduced my affairs to a desperate pass," replied the King. "It is not my enemies who destroy me, but the false steps which you have taken. . . . Your ears are only used to the language of flatterers; Daun has not flattered you, you see the result. As for me, nothing remains for me in this sad situation but to take the most desperate chances. I shall fight, and we will all be massacred if we cannot win. . . . The misfortune which I foresee has been caused partly by you. You and your children will bear the pain of it more than I. . . ." And he also said that his brother was good for nothing but commanding a harem of Maids of Honor.

The Prince was furious and could scarcely hold in the anger aroused in him by this treatment but he gave way to old Eichel's advice, restrained himself, and went into complete retirement. Disappointment and illness ensured that he did not long survive his disgrace, and he died in 1758.

IV

AT the end of September, 1757, the King's position seemed desperate. The Austrians had driven him out of Bohemia and were threatening Silesia. The Russians had invaded East Prussia by way of Memel and defeated Marshal Lehwaldt at Gross-Jaegersdorf. The French under D'Estrées and Richelieu had occupied Wesel and the Prussian possessions on the Rhine, crossed the river Weser, occupied Emden, Hanover, and Brunswick, then cornered the army of the Duke of Cumberland at the mouth of the Elbe and forced it to capitulate. The Swedes had joined the coalition, entered Pomerania, and seized his territory up to the Oder. Finally the army of the Empire, strengthened by a French auxiliary force, was assembling between Erfurt and Weimar to liberate Saxony. None the less, Prussia was saved within three months. Never was there a more brilliant campaign in the whole of Frederick's life. His genius was inspired by misfortune and gave the impression of being more irresistible than force of arms or force of intellect. By his choice of opponents, combination of maneuvers, calculation of marches, disposition of armies, and complete command of the map he produced his masterpiece.

His affairs were in so critical a state that a victory was indispensable. That was what decided him to turn first against the army of the Circles, which was provided by the whole Germanic body. It consisted of an omnium-gatherum of hoboes, beggars, and escaped jailbirds recruited by a staff office of princes. One of the best contingents, the one belonging to the Prince of Hesse-Darmstadt, had neither baggage train nor victualing nor any means of subsistence apart from the good offices of fifty Jews whose commercial ingenuity had to make up for the lack of provisions. Their ammunition consisted of a few cannon balls for each cannon and thirty rounds per musket. The French auxiliary force was in better trim, but the majority of the soldiers had not yet been under fire, they were badly led, and from contact with the Imperialists they had picked up habits of indiscipline and pillage. The Commander in Chief was the Prince of Saxe-Hilburghausen, a nonentity; the commander of the French force the Prince de Soubise, a mediocrity. At the approach of Frederick the first thing they did was to draw back, taking up good defensive positions in the Harz Mountains—the wisest thing to do, for they had only to keep the King busy for a few weeks to give the Austrians time to complete the conquest of Silesia, after which winter would have held up all further operations.

"What plagues me," wrote Frederick to his sister Amelia, "is that I can do nothing. When I advance the enemy runs away; while I retire, he follows me but always out of my reach. If I leave here and go and look for the haughty Richelieu in the neighborhood of Halberstadt, he will do the same thing, and my enemies here, who are as motionless as stone statues at present, would straightway come to life and rebuff me near Magdeburg. If I turn toward Lusatia, then they seize my stores at Leipzig and Torgau and go for Berlin. To conclude, my dear sister, I am in despair."

Luckily for him, the allied generals plucked up courage. They had 30,000 Germans and 24,000 Frenchmen at their command. Frederick had only 21,000 men. When the two armies met at the village of Rossbach on the west of the river Saale the King once again considered it unwise to attack an enemy drawn up on easily defensible heights, and he himself drew back behind a stream with marshy banks. The two princes were taken in by this apparent timidity and now imagined that they could force him to retreat without a fight by a simple turning movement. However, the maneuver was carried out with bewildering incompetence and disheartening slowness. The columns set out quite uncovered, without scouts or flank guards, and described a huge semicircle around Rossbach. When their intentions had become quite clear, Frederick made his army carry out a movement parallel to theirs but screened by some hills, in such a way that at half-past four the "combined" army was suddenly attacked in front and on the flank, without having had time to deploy so as to take up its fighting formation. While hoping to turn the enemy it had itself been outflanked. The Imperialists broke under the first volley. The Walloons and the French bore themselves bravely, but so great was the confusion that the whole army was swept away in the collapse. At nightfall the plain was covered with a crowd of fugitives who were sabered by Seydlitz' horsemen. However, the Allies lost no more than 8,000 men, only five or six hundred of whom were killed. On the Prussian side there were only 165 dead and 376 wounded, one of whom was Prince Henry (November 5, 1757). "The battle of Rossbach," Frederick wrote in his memoirs, "merely allowed the King freedom to go and look for new dangers in Silesia. The only importance of this victory was the impression it had on the French and on the wreckage of the Duke of Cumberland's army." In a letter he also called it "a genteel engagement."

Daun and Prince Charles had invaded Silesia, taken Schweidnitz, beaten Bevern, and relieved Breslau. Frederick flew to the help of the province with 14,000 men whom he combined with the remainder of the army that had been beaten. On December 4 with 33,000 men he came upon the Austro-German forces which numbered 70,000. They were encamped ten miles to the west of Breslau on a chain of wooded hummocks between the villages of Leuthen and Lissa. This battle provided the military writers to the end of the century with a nice cup of tea. It was to become the type of Frederick's battles, which he was to attempt in all circumstances, and it was to give the key to his genius. It can be described in the maxim already quoted—attack with one wing while refusing the conflict at the other extremity. This was the oblique approach. Prague, Kolin, and Leuthen had in fact been battles of this type, but though Prague had been a victory Kolin had been a defeat, and even at Leuthen success was due not to the oblique approach but to surprise. The weather was misty; the Austrian Army had not used patrols to reconnoiter the whole front but only a large body of cavalry, which watched the main road and was dispersed by the Prussians. This occurrence made Prince Charles believe that he would be attacked on the right; he put his best regiments on that wing. Frederick attacked on the extreme left in echelon after some clever wheeling movements, which were to become subsequently the *ne plus ultra* of military pedantry. The battle was decided in the long run by the cavalry of the retarded wing. There is no fixed system for winning battles: Frederick's merit was to have adhered to simple principles and to have varied his application of them according to circumstances. Each of the two armies lost 6,000 men dead or wounded, but as the Austrians were fighting with their backs to a river, their retreat was difficult and they also left behind them

24,000 prisoners. Frederick occupied Silesia once more except for Schweidnitz.

V

SELDOM has a victory been more brilliant and a victor more eager to come to terms. The campaign finished with a miracle, but in the spring the miracle had to be repeated. Frederick compared himself to a man attacked by flies—"When one flies off my cheek, another comes and sits on my nose, and scarcely has it been brushed off than another flies up and sits on my forehead, on my eyes, and everywhere else."

While he was maneuvering against Soubise the Austrians under General Hadick had made a successful detour to Berlin, occupied the town for several days and levied contributions. There was a fine panic. While the enemy were coming in at one side, the Queen and the Princesses were rushing wildly from one townhouse to the next. Carts were loaded only to be unloaded again, jewels and cash boxes were piled up at the palace to be taken back a minute later and carried away somewhere else. At last they leaped into carriages. At six o'clock the Court alighted at the castle of Spandau, which had not been lived in for the last forty years. Neither fire nor furniture was to be had. Benches were found and straw was spread out. The chambermaids remained sitting on the baggage and no one had a wink of sleep that night. In a room full of people the Queen took counsel with the ministers round a single candle. The Grand Mistress of the Robes, Madame de Camas, sat a little farther off and was much moved. What was to be done? Stay? Go? Ask the King for orders? Wait for help to come? Make for Magdeburg at once? "My children," said Madame de Camas from time to time, "speak a bit louder; I want to deliver myself of some wind which is troubling me." At last arrived the news that Berlin was soon to be relieved. However, a month after Leuthen Richelieu occupied Halberstadt for the second time in midwinter and made the citizens pay an indemnity.

If Prussia with her forces almost intact was still so vulnerable in spite of two victories, what was going to happen in the years to come? Frederick felt that he was walking on a tightrope and the least false step would destroy him. In fact all the campaigns up to and including 1762 were like the campaign of 1757. There were the same marches from one enemy to the next, from the Oder to the Elbe, from the Elbe to the Weser, from the Russians to the Austrians and from the Austrians to the French. However, each time Frederick grew weaker and weaker. While Prince Ferdinand of Brunswick was flinging back the French on the Rhine in 1758, he could take the offensive again in Moravia, but he was stopped by the resistance of the town of Olmütz, lost a convoy of 3,000 wagons loaded with grain and ammunition, raised the siege, and till the end of August allowed Daun to maneuver him into a series of marches and countermarches which exhausted him to no purpose. His fight against the Russians at Zorndorf (August 25) was nothing but a shambles, and the autumn campaign in Saxony ended in a defeat. He was surprised and beaten at Hochkirch (October 14). During the action Marshal Keith, Prince Francis of Brunswick, and Prince Maurice of Anhalt were fatally wounded, but thanks to the steadiness of his troops he managed to make good his retreat.

In 1759 Prince Ferdinand moved backward and forward between the Weser and the Rhine; there was a war of skirmishes on all sides and a single big battle at Kunersdorf near Frankfort on the Oder. Frederick was crushed by the Russians under Soltikoff. He had two horses killed under him and his clothes were pierced by two bullets; as evening came on he tried to drive his men back into the fight by seizing a flag and crying, "Let all brave soldiers follow me!" However, he was surrounded by a wave of fugitives and swept away amid the disorder of the regiments which were disbanding (August 12). To cover Silesia Prince Henry had to abandon Saxony to the army of the Circles, which recaptured Leipzig and Dresden. In November during terrible weather Frederick was still trying to maneuver against Daun. His soldiers, being ill-clad, ill-fed, and almost without fire, put up with terrible suffering. A large number died of the cold. To cut the Austrian marshal's communications and force him to retreat Frederick sent off an isolated body of 15,000 men under General Finck. Daun surprised and surrounded them at Maxen; Finck surrendered complete with arms and baggage train (November 21).

That was the most dreadful year of all. "I am a galley slave in chains!" cried the King, but he did not endure "his martyrdom" with that proud impassivity, that unshakable self-control which has often been attributed to him. Undoubtedly he tried to deceive himself: "Stoicism suits the position in which I find myself," he said. "Stoics are good fellows who bear up under misfortune. . . . Marcus Aurelius is my baton, I make use of him."

However, his whole temperament rose in revolt against this inhuman calm. When he was waiting for news the least noise—the opening of a door, the passing of a horse—put him into a wild state of agitation. Blood rose to his cheeks, he trembled as he opened his dispatches, he could not sleep, he was "in an agony of high fever." The evening of the disaster of Kolin he declared, sobbing, that he was incapable of drawing up a plan of retreat. After Kunersdorf he gave up the command of his army to General Finck and remained for two days in a state of complete stupefaction. He was overcome by discouragement through physical and moral exhaustion during the long, lonely days spent in winter quarters: "God! How weary I am," he cried, "I am fit for nothing but a common sewer! . . . Was it worth the pain of being born? . . . My fires are low. . . . It is almost nonsense for me to go on living. . . . Oh, how much happier are the dead than the living!" He was haunted by a vision of final catastrophe, "of a death blow"; he was often ill, spat blood, had attacks of giddiness three or four times a day, and gout in both feet and in the left arm; he was nothing but a "skeleton on two sticks," "an old man going gray, without gaiety, without fire, without imagination," an "encumbrance to the army." Even politics had no further interest for him. One day he was brought letters from Constantinople, and as he handed them back to Finckenstein he said, "I have not troubled to read them, I am so discouraged that I leave public business to chance."

He had nightmares. He was lying in a room, when the door opened and his father came in with six soldiers who flung themselves on him and bound him. He was being sent to Magdeburg. "But why?"—"Because you do not love your father well enough!" Or again he drew near to kiss the hand of the Queen, and Frederick William drove him back with his stick. The terrors of his childhood returned to rob him of sleep. "I am so worn out by the reverses and disasters which come upon me," he wrote to

D'Argens after the capitulation of Maxen, "that I have wished a thousand times for death and I grow more and more tired of inhabiting a worn-out body condemned to suffering. . . . Astonishment, despair, indignation, and vexation combine to rend my heart." This was not the first time he had thought of suicide. Since the beginning of the war he had carried eighteen pills of opium, "quite a big enough dose to send the soul to those gloomy banks whence it never returns," in a little gold box which hung on a ribbon under his shirt. The idea of voluntary death haunted him and he often talked of it. Indeed, he talked too much about it, for each time fortune was against him he could not resist the temptation of putting his iron resolution into writing. "How can a prince survive his State, the glory of his nation, and his own reputation? . . . No, no, my dear sister, your thoughts are too noble for you to give me such cowardly advice. Shall liberty, most precious of prerogatives, be less dear to the sovereigns of the eighteenth century than it was to the patricians of Rome? And where is it said that Brutus and Cato pushed generosity further than princes and kings? . . . Assuredly life is not worth the determination with which some people cling to it, etc. . . . etc. . . ."

The extraordinary thing was this—that Frederick was at no time more of a man of letters than in the thick of a war, though undoubtedly he had other counterirritants at his disposal. At the least rift in the clouds he recovered his gaiety and hope. "The great storm will pass once again. . . . We are going to give them a fine pommeling. . . . You will see me extricate myself from all this much better than I could have thought possible. . . ."

One evening at the siege of Olmütz he called for his reader, De Catt, a Swiss he had met in Holland. He told him that in his youth he was a good dancer and that he could still do an *entrechat*. And lo and behold, he did five or six, took De Catt's hand and gave him a lesson in how to do the minuet!

At other times he lost his temper; he revenged himself on objects: he had Augustus III's countryhouse despoiled, a suburb of Dresden burned, and the castle of the Count von Brühl sacked. On such days his enemies were incendiaries, barbarians, assassins, brigands, and sharks; his army a hotchpotch of ruffians; his lieutenants rookies absolutely fitted to pile one "asininity" upon another. After the fall of Schweidnitz he was so pleased with Balbi, his colonel of engineers, that he dedicated an Epistle to him, which began like this:

Accept, my dearest Balbikin,
These lines of my enchanted Muse.

But dearest Balbikin, having failed to take Olmütz at the appointed time, changed overnight into nothing but an incompetent, a —— bad engineer and an oily brute. "He is not worth a fill of tobacco. . . . He has put me in such a hole. . . . He has opened the trench *à la Pantagruel*. . . . Instead of a civic crown I will send him an ass's cap, should it cost me the ears of my best mule." Next day for an hour by the clock he deluged the poor fellow with his whole vocabulary of abuse.

But his great remedy was poetry, ideas, conversation, and music, as in his happier days. In 1757 at Christmas he summoned D'Argens to Breslau. The marquis came with a trunk full of pills, quite smothered in furs, wearing footwarmers under his feet, and fortified against draughts. They spent three months supping, writing, and talking together. During the other years the King had no company but De Catt. Almost every day, even during a campaign, when he was not on the march he had him in toward five o'clock and kept him for an hour or two or sometimes more. He played on the flute to him, spoke to him of his childhood, of his houses, of his books, of his friends, and especially of Voltaire. He would recite to him some tragedy, whole scenes of which he knew by heart—*Andromaque, Phèdre, Britannicus, Mithridate, Athalie*. Between each act he took a pinch of snuff, and every now and then he would stop at a certain line to emphasize its beauties: "How skillful is Racine! How promptly and in how few words does he announce the subject of the piece! What bewitching devices! How well he knows how to improve upon common expressions! What a true and living picture!" Sometimes at the pathetic passages tears interrupted the recitation. "I cannot go on. This fellow Racine rends my heart."

He did not like new writers. "Their verses and their dialogues get nowhere near to those of Racine." However, he made bold to read Monsieur de la Touche's *Iphigénie,* but he was pulled up short by these lines:

    . . . That with astonishment he learns a king can teach
    How far the noble laws of amity may reach.

"Monsieur de la Touche," said he, "Monsieur de la Touche, put not your trust in those blackguards." And that was the last that was heard of *Iphigénie.*

The point was that in his own eyes he was still one of Racine's heroes. He saw himself living and acting in the person of a stage prince. After the defeat of Hochkirch he greeted De Catt with a passage from *Mithridate:*

    A year is gone—once more you see me, Arbates,
    Who in the balance held *Vienna's* impending fate,[1]
    That 'twixt her power and mine the globe was in debate.
    A vanquished man am I. *Daunus* has seized his chance. . . .

In each of his internal crises Frederick instinctively felt that the trouble which floored him was much too great to yield to frontal attack. Far from pretending to rationalize his gloom, he only tried to "benumb it" at first. Then it was that he flung himself body and soul into reading and worked away at it, for "nothing is as calming as hard concentration." He read straight off, for example, the sixteen volumes of Jacques Auguste de Thou's *Universal History* and was "very pleased" with it, or the thirty-six volumes of Fleury's *Ecclesiastical History.* He wrote at length to his sister at Bayreuth and to D'Argens "more to calm himself than to amuse them." But of all the devices he had for benumbing himself the one he found most effective was poetry. When he was rhyming he used to forget everything, and forgetfulness "cleared his head" for him. "Often," he explained to Princess Amelia, "I would like to get drunk to drown my disappointment but as I cannot drink, nothing relaxes me like writing verses, and as long as the distraction lasts I am not conscious of my misfortunes."

Hence "this deluge of verse which inundates each of his campaigns." He sent pieces to his relations, to his friends, to his generals, even to Voltaire. Between times he compiled a rhyming dictionary and wrote pamphlets against Kaunitz, against Daun, against the Pope, against Madame de Pompadour. He encour-

---

1. There were, of course, twelve syllables in Racine's alexandrines: he wrote *de Rome* and *Pompée*—"great Rome's" and "Pompey."

aged De Catt to follow his example: "I will correct you rigorously and I will make you go back to the beginning until the work is well done. That was how Voltaire behaved with me, and I will be your Voltaire. But, tell me, do you not find something of the cadence of Racine in my verses?"

As De Catt had left a flirtation unfinished at Breslau, he provided him with poetical declarations.

> A certain god, at Cythera adored,
> Had placed me, Phyllis, underneath your sway.
> I sighed, I hoped some pleasure to afford. . . .

The Queen Mother died in 1757, ten days after Kolin; Wilhelmina died the following year on the same day as the battle of Hochkirch. They were beyond all doubt the two people whom Frederick loved best in all the world. At the Margravine's death his desperation reached its zenith. Each time he said her name tears started to his eyes. For several weeks he complained that he could not write any more, but then he recovered his calm by learning some funeral orations by heart and reciting them to De Catt. Some weeks later he made use of this knowledge to write a parody, the *Funeral Oration of Matthew Reinhault, Master Shoemaker,* and as he had also read Massillon's *Little Lenten Sermons,* he composed a sermon on the Last Judgment which he painstakingly copied out on mourning note paper with black edges. As an edition of his poems had just come out in France, he had a second and then a third edition printed at Berlin wherein he suppressed or corrected certain satirical passages and added some stanzas paraphrased from Ecclesiastes to flatter his Protestant readers.

When he had lulled his trouble with these rough and ready sedatives, he recovered his strength by a more profound meditation. Of all the philosophical doctrines which he had patronized there was one to which he remained faithful for the whole of his life—it was what is nowadays called determinism. It sustained him at Cüstrin by making him believe in his star. It sustained him in his defeats by convincing him that nothing could save him from the demands of his position. In this world "that destiny treats as it will," "where politicians and fighters are only marionettes" moved by "an invisible hand," all that came to pass had to come to pass. "To require that fortune should be constant is like wanting a dog to have scales on its back. . . . Fortune has to be fickle, a butterfly has to have wings, our destiny has to be mixed, sometimes agreeable, sometimes unpleasant." Above all, kings must play their part as kings. "My body is worn out, my mind is dull, my energies are departing from me, but honor speaks, it makes me think and act." Life, which was too short for idle speculations, was also too short for long-drawn-out sorrows. "To murmur or complain is to go against universal laws . . . whosoever cannot stand up to bad luck is unworthy of good fortune."

> Blown as I am toward the rocks,
> I ought to face the tempest's shocks
> And think, live, die as fits a king.

On the day he overcame his depression he was at it again, enlivened with sudden energy, drawing up his troops once more, arranging a thousand intrigues to get peace or to stir up diversions. He spoke only of "victory or death," of getting himself and his rabble "bashed about." "All lukewarmness is out of season! . . . We must willy-nilly throw ourselves into great ventures and stake double or quits. . . . For desperate ills desperate remedies are needed."

VI

TRUTH to tell Frederick was too exhausted to pitch his demands very high. Using Voltaire as a go-between, he began to correspond with the new French minister, Choiseul; there was a tacit agreement that Voltaire should inform each of his distinguished friends of the contents of the letters he got from the other. It was an exchange of treacherous compliments, of sour consolations, of malicious remarks and epigrams, among which serious matters were intermingled. To reach Choiseul Frederick also made use of a bailiff of the Order of Malta. Finally at The Hague, where were to be found the ambassadors of all the belligerent powers, negotiations continued for several months. However, England rejected any sort of compromise and wanted to crush France. The fight was on. Frederick gained two victories over Daun, one at Liegnitz in Silesia (August 15, 1760), and the other at Torgau in Saxony (November 3), but at the beginning of the campaign Fouqué had got himself and 12,000 men captured on the border of Bohemia; Daun covered Dresden, and in October the Austro-Russian forces made another move against Berlin. They occupied the town for four days, raised a contribution of 1,700,000 thalers, freed all prisoners, destroyed the gun foundry and the powder mill, emptied the arsenal, sacked Charlottenburg, and religiously preserved the castles at Potsdam.

Throughout the year 1761 the King maneuvered to hold up the enemy and yet to avoid the battle which might have been the end of him. He succeeded in reaching the winter almost without a fight but he lost two important fortresses—Schweidnitz in Silesia and Kolberg on the Baltic. He ought long since to have been overwhelmed by weight of numbers. He was preserved by the "divine idiocy" of his enemies, who could never coördinate their operations. If they had acted at the same time, he told D'Argens, "you would only have had to write my epitaph." There was no real understanding between the Russians and the Austrians, and the elaboration of a common plan was made even more difficult by distance. As for the French, for seven years they had only had mediocre generals, and their warfare had been perpetually hamstrung by internal troubles. Frederick was kept well informed by D'Argens and knew that the writers and philosophers had worked so well for him that they had made his cause a popular one: he was the hero of liberty. And then the courts of justice were in open revolt against the crown. While the armies went without common necessities from lack of money, the magistrates ordained a tax strike. Within seven years eight men occupied the post of controller general in quick succession, and each of them was worn out by the contumacy of the judges: "Withhold your subsidies from the King of France," wrote Frederick to Voltaire, "and he will see himself forced to make peace" (March 26, 1760).

But what was he himself to make of his own State? The Westphalian duchies, East Prussia, almost all Pomerania, and part of Silesia were held by the enemy. Since he had drawn his alliance with England tighter (April 11, 1758), he lived partly on help from London and for the rest he squeezed Saxony dry. When he had invaded it, it was the richest province of all Germany; if he were to leave it, it would be emptied, drained, almost reduced to famine. Yet he felt he was at the mercy of a "fatal moment." His army had melted away; every winter recruiting became more and more difficult. No doubt he could find men in Mecklenburg, Thuringia, and even in Saxony—but what sort of men? "A collection of scamps, thieves, bootblacks, chimney sweeps" who did not want to fight. At Kunersdorf they had deserted: things were going quite well if he could retain 3,000 men out of 40,000 to make their retreat in good order. What more had he? Deserters, prisoners who were forcibly brought in. In 1759 at Berlin they formed a plot to set the town on fire: it had been stopped by arresting three hundred of them. One hundred and twenty of his generals had been killed. Fourteen were prisoners in Austria.

His closest associates complained. If he had not broken the French alliance and attacked Saxony, the State would not have been brought to the brink of destruction. His pride was blamed, so were his obstinacy, his rashness, his thoughtlessness, and his whims. He had had violent quarrels with his brother Henry. Perhaps someone had told him the dreadful expressions the Prince had applied to him, accusing him of loving human blood just as tigers love raw meat? Till on his deathbed William had cursed him without ceasing, him and Winterfeldt. He had counted on the Turks; he had intrigued at Constantinople so as to fling them at Austria; nothing happened. In vain had France been torn apart, "a great kingdom can always produce the cost of a campaign." What was to be done? Collect all the armed forces in a single body and seek a battle? Was that not the choice of despair? "After all, are not destruction in detail and destruction in a body the same thing?" His normal remedies no longer worked. "I do not feel well," he said one day to De Catt, "but how am I to feel well with the gloomy idea that I will be overpowered sooner or later?" And he wrote to the marquis, "To conclude, my dear fellow, the whole concern is going to the dogs."

A hairsbreadth from destruction, Frederick and Prussia were saved by the disloyalty of Russia. The Tsarina was tired of life and died on January 7, 1762. Her nephew and successor was an idiot of German extraction. He played with dolls, got drunk with his menservants, and spent a good part of his time making his army of wax soldiers maneuver. One day his wife, Catherine of Anhalt-Zerbst, caught him in the act of hanging a large rat. When she asked him what was the meaning of this execution, he replied that according to the military code the rat was liable to capital punishment for having demolished the wall of a cardboard fort and knocked down a sentinel. His great pleasure was to make love to hunch-backed and one-eyed women, to comb dogs, and to teach Prussian drill to his guard of soldiers from Holstein. In secret he dressed as a Prussian general and he had the plan of campaign which Vienna was sending to St. Petersburg passed on to Berlin by a treacherous secretary. On the very day of his accession he ordered the army to suspend operations and had the jackets of the infantry shortened so that they should be no longer than those of the Prussian infantry.

Frederick hastened to send Peter III an ambassador, Baron von Goltz, who was given the rank of colonel, aide-de-camp, and chamberlain for the occasion. To get peace Goltz was authorized to give up Prussia until a general peace conference and even to hand it over finally in return for an indemnity. Goltz found an emperor who swore by no one but his old friend Frederick. He gave up all the land he held—Pomerania, Königsberg, and Prussia (May 5, 1762). Better still he signed an offensive treaty of alliance with Frederick to recover Silesia for him (June 19). "If the King gives me the order to do so," said he, "I and my whole Empire will make war on hell itself." Frederick could not believe in such a piece of good luck. He sent Peter distracted letters of gratitude: "Our ruin is terrible; I could have despaired of my position, but I find a faithful friend. . . . If I were a pagan I would erect a temple and altars to Your Imperial Majesty as to a divinity. . . . As for me, my body, my soul, my heart are yours. . . ." In all his letters he repeated the same words—the Tsar is a divinity.

Soon his imagination fired him with the thought of approaching revenge. He saw Hungary invaded by 100,000 Tartars, and the Turks making straight for Budapest: "A most sweet calm springs up again in my heart and hopeful feelings, to which I have not been accustomed for six years, sooth my agitation. . . . I will say a mass before the Queen of Hungary and I will have the *De Profundis* sung at her. . . ." However, his dreams only flared up for a very short time. Catherine, with the support of the army, expelled her weak-minded husband and proclaimed herself

Empress with the title of Catherine II. "The peace which I have made with Russia will stand but the alliance has come to nothing. The troops are going back to Russia and here I am on my own again. . . . I am fortune's spinning top, she makes a fool of me. . . . At heart I am disappointed, my position is most embarrassing, but what's to do?" Nevertheless, the defection of Russia involved that of Sweden also (treaty of May 22, 1762) and disorganized the coalition.

The people of England were desirous of tasting the fruits of victory. They were victorious on the sea and in the colonies and cared little for Frederick and Silesia. Except in the days of Pitt relations between the two capitals had never been very confidential. In the backs of their minds His Britannic Majesty's ministers considered the King of Prussia as a salaried prince, one of those contractors for troops for which Germany had long been notorious. Their disdain was always peeping through. When the envoy Mitchell came to announce the loss of Port Mahon to the King, "This news," he added, "is sad but not discouraging. We are hurrying up new armaments and everything leads us to hope that with God's help we will balance this reverse with some immediate successes."

"God?" cried Frederick in surprise, "I did not know that He was one of your allies."

"He is however, Sire, the only one who costs nothing."

Frederick replied to this allusion to the subsidies he obtained in the same spirit: "So you see what he gives you for your money!"

There was no friendship in such repartee.

Spain entered the war on the French side and a Franco-Spanish army invaded Portugal. On the other hand, the English began the conquest of the Antilles, the sugar islands. The war continued to spread and the further it extended the harder it was to bring it to an end. Without taking the least notice of the interests and desires of Prussia, the new King, George III, and his minister, Bute, entered into direct negotiations with France. Throughout the year 1762 Frederick, feeling he was being pushed on one side, stormed against Bute as he had stormed against Fleury in the past. Meddlesome minister, inept politician, filthy gossip, a man without decency, without system, without manners, unworthy betrayal, wretched villain—the whole litany of recriminations and insults. He kept two ambassadors at London. He ordered them to overthrow Bute by hook or by crook. "You will let slip no opportunity of arousing and embroiling the nation against him. . . . You will encourage the pamphleteers. . . ." All this work was in vain. The Anglo-French preliminaries were signed at Fontainebleau in November and the final treaty at Paris on February 10, 1763. War could no longer be carried on in Germany: the mediation of Catherine II had to be accepted. Discussions began in the last days of 1762 at Hubertsburg, a little castle near Leipzig. The peace treaty was finally signed on January 31, 1763: everything was restored to the State in which it had been in 1756. Prussia kept Silesia and Austria had fought to no purpose for seven years.

Frederick assumed an air of deep calm. "Had the State obtained some further province, that would have been of advantage without a doubt; however, as that did not depend on me but on fortune, this idea in no way disturbs my tranquillity. If I succeed in repairing the ravages of war I shall have been of some use, and it is to this that my ambition confines itself."

Nevertheless his pride had been galled by the behavior and the "perfidies" of England. "In seven or eight years," he reckoned, "the French will avenge us." And then he had passed "through a school of patience, which was hard, long, cruel, nay, even barbarous." What deaths there had been around him! His mother, his favorite sister, his best generals, Schwerin, the companion of his earliest conquest, the audacious Winterfeldt, Keith, his noblest and most faithful friend, and so many others . . . What devastation too, what bleeding wounds! He walked among ruins and among tombs. At times he was struck by waves of disgust— "Follies of politics, follies of ambition, follies of interest, these should not sway the heart . . ." But a moment later he became a king again and "alive to glory." Yet he was tired of living. Someone told him that January 31 would be the happiest day of his life, to which he replied quite simply, "The happiest day of a man's life is that upon which he leaves it."

XI

Frederick the Higgler and Frederick the Conqueror

I

I AM so accustomed to reverses and mishaps, I grow so indifferent toward events that the things which would heretofore have made the most profound impressions upon me at the present float gently upon the surface of my mind. . . . My heart is imperceptibly becoming detached from the shows of this transient world which I am soon to leave behind. . . . My sensitive faculties have dried up."

Frederick returned to Berlin aged, shriveled, gray-haired and "half crippled with gout." He had not seen his capital for six years and he feared he would recognize nothing but its walls. On March 30, the day fixed for his entry, he made a pilgrimage to the battlefield of Kunersdorf, and on the way he delayed to hear the complaints of the Provincial Councilors, who described the poverty of the peasants to him. He did not turn up till half-past eight in the evening. The whole town had been afoot since the morning. The citizen companies had taken up their arms and lined the road well before midday. Fifty thousand spectators were leaning out of windows and hanging round the streets with torches. At the Frankfort gate Frederick received the compliments of the magistrates but he did not get into the state coach which they had ready for him. He stayed in the old berlin which had seen him through his campaigns. The coachman whipped up the horses, turned unexpectedly down a side road, and reached the *Schloss* along a dark, empty street. The Court was waiting in full ceremonial dress. The King gave a long embrace to his brothers Henry and Ferdinand and to Prince Ferdinand of Brunswick. He greeted the ambassadors and thanked the Dutch envoy for having opened his embassy to the wretched inhabitants, who had been left without a refuge by the Russian invasion.

Then he moved on toward the room where the ladies were sitting; the Queen came forward to welcome him—"Madame is much fatter," he said to her and turned toward the Princesses. He embraced old Camas, was full of loving attentions for his little niece Wilhelmina, and stayed at supper until nearly midnight. The next day he gave audience to the Corporations, the merchants, the butchers, and the archers, and he paraded the town in the gala coach provided by the gallant townsfolk. In the days which followed there were a ball and illuminations. The houses of bankers and Jews were the best decorated. The King gave some presents—5,000 thalers to the Queen, 4,000 to his sister Amelia, and jewels to his sisters-in-law. Then he revised the list of pensions. Podewils had died of apoplexy: the Count von Hertzberg was appointed minister.

On April 1 the Provincial Councilors of the Kurmark arrived. Landrat von Nussler began to speak on their behalf. He had already harangued the King when on tour and he was beginning a new oration. "Let him be silent," Fredrick cut in. "Has he a pencil? Good. . . . Let him take my orders. . . . These gentlemen must calculate the quantity of grain which is absolutely necessary for bread and for the sowing in their districts; how many horses, bulls, and cows they need. Think this over and return tomorrow."

Eichel showed them the requests for help running to whole volumes which the King had already received. They all examined them and arranged them in order of urgency. In May the King gave himself a few days' rest at Sans Souci so as to enjoy the spring and then undertook a tour of the provinces beginning with Pomerania, which he found less devastated than he had feared it would be. Prince Ferdinand of Brunswick came with him into Westphalia and showed him the battlefields. At Cleve the King spent some hours visiting one of his former friends, Von Spaen, the lieutenant to whom he had confided his plans of flight; he had passed into the service of the Low Countries and had become a general. Frederick saw once again the bloody shadows of his youth, but imperious needs called him back— "Has he a pencil? Good. . . . How many horses, bulls, and cows does he need?"

From time to time he groused that it was not worth his trouble to have made war for so long just to set up as a higgler in peacetime but he plied the higgler's trade with the same tenacious zeal as the general's. D'Alembert came to rejoin him at Wesel and went with him to Berlin. They traveled through Brunswick: there the ducal Court was so formal that the philosopher allowed the chamberlains to announce him as a marquis. He stayed three months at Sans Souci, dining and supping with the King, D'Argens, and My Lord the Marischal. It was like a subdued resurrection of the good old days. "You do my soul good," said the King. He was calm, relaxed, almost happy. He talked about everything simply and without bitterness. One day he praised the good qualities of Louis XV; another time as they walked in the park he offered D'Alembert a rose: "I would like to give you much more than this," he added. However, D'Alembert was not willing to take on the post of president of the Academy, vacant since the death of Maupertuis. He loved the calm of a cloistered life, the coldness of the north frightened him, and he was afraid of getting bored. "The King," he wrote to Mademoiselle de Lespinasse, "is almost the only person in the kingdom with whom it is possible to converse, at least with that kind of conversation met with hardly anywhere but in France, which becomes a necessity when once it has been experienced." Apart from him "society is very insipid and quite worthless." When he entertained ministers, councilors, and generals, "all these gentlemen say not a word and are content to laugh at some stories that we tell." The last supper was a sad one. The King assured D'Alembert of his good will, offered him the money he needed for a journey into Italy, and gave him a long embrace, desiring to see him again. D'Alembert never returned.

Frederick's work remained his best friend. The restoration of Prussia was a harassing and detailed task. The demobilization of the army and the disbanding of the commissariat equipment set free 30,000 men and 35,000 horses. The provisions of wheat, flour, and oats collected for the next campaign put off the major problem of reorganization until the next harvest. For years the King's heaviest work was making censuses, recruiting new colonists, lecturing in favor of artificial grassland, giving out assistance, allowing relief from taxes and relief from rents, signing contractors' accounts, buying cows, and calculating the fertility of sheep.

In the first year Pomerania had a right to 8,766 head of livestock at 25 thalers apiece; each peasant whose house had been burned down (there were 1,246 in all) received 50 thalers and wood to rebuild it. In the Neumark Cüstrin had been almost entirely destroyed by bombardment and had lost 68,866 sheep—no more and no less. The Kurmark (Berlin) had lost 25,000 horses, 17,000 bullocks, 20,900 cows, 121,000 sheep, and 35,000 pigs. In Silesia the open country accounted for 3,223 houses, 2,225 barns, 3,495 stables burned or fallen into ruins; the towns for 2,917 houses, 399 barns, and 1,380 stables. The province had also lost its archbishop, Schaffgotsch, who had gone over to the side of Austria, but Frederick did not class this desertion among the disasters. During his travels in 1766 he wrote to Voltaire: "I am in a province where the physical is preferred to the metaphysical; fields are cultivated, 8,000 houses have been rebuilt, and thousands of children are begotten every year to replace those done to death by political and martial fury." He wrote up his facts a little to make them look better than they were; yet at that date, according to his papers, only 644 houses, 95 barns, and 829 stables were still to be rebuilt. On the other hand, the textile industry never recovered from its loss of custom.

If Frederick could stand the expenses of reconstruction, calculated at the lowest possible price to be sure, it was because his finances were not in too bad a way. England and Saxony had financed Prussia. After Kunersdorf he had himself advised "prosperous folk" to fly to Hamburg with their capital: it served as a reserve. Elsewhere the province of Königsberg had been gently handled by the Russians and it could pay its taxes in full from the start. He had still to repay various loans and to withdraw from circulation the debased coinage which had been minted since 1758. Though having the usual nominal value, these coins were only one third composed of silver—and equivalent, one might say, to banknotes made of metal. Frederick arranged to pay off the debt by installments, and the debased coins were recalled but only at their real value, that is to say at a third of their face value. This meant considerable losses for individuals.

Amid all this poverty the King allowed himself to indulge in one expense which was merely for show and he himself described it as a bit of swagger. At the end of the park of Sans Souci he made Bühring and Manger, two talentless architects, put up a second palace which was called the New Palace, or the New Sans Souci. It was a huge building in pink, white, and green embellished with three ill-proportioned cupolas like bell glasses, the most monumental of which rested upon a kind of convex cover that served as a connection with the walls below. The domestic offices made up two other palaces with monumental staircases, cupolas, columns, and obelisks. The whole effect was heavy, theatrical, unbalanced, and without grace—frankly ugly.

For interior decoration the King had remained faithful to the style he liked when he was twenty, but by 1763 the originality of the rococo style had been exhausted. In spite of strokes of luck, in spite of some successful little rooms, the artists were obviously breathless at the excessively great surfaces they had to cover. They used the same designs too often—quivering stalactites and gilded latticework on the ceilings, around mirrors, above doors, in window recesses. This was a long way from the fantastic and charming inspiration of Sans Souci and the *Stadtschloss*. The work went on until 1769. In the final years Carl von Gontard and Legeay put up the colonnade of the domestic offices. Gontard also built two little temples in the park, the Temple of Friendship and the Antique Temple, which thenceforth housed part of the Polignac Collection.

The building of the New Palace helped to support the artists of Berlin, but Prussia did not escape the economic crisis which swept over Europe at the end of 1763. It began with the failure of the brothers De Neufville, one of the greatest financial houses of Amsterdam. Then bankruptcies spread from place to place, from bank to bank, from customer to tradesman. At Hamburg ninety-five businesses suspended payments. It was soon the turn of Gotzkowski, the man who was reputed to be the richest person in Berlin, to be struck down. During the war he had collected a huge fortune by providing military equipment and carrying through very complicated exchange operations. However, he was too deeply involved financially and connected with too many concerns to be able to resist the storm. Frederick tried to save him by lending him some money, but three months later Gotzkowski was insolvent once more.

The King was deeply amazed by this crisis, the mechanism of which he could not understand. "Since I came into the world," he said, "I have seen nothing like it," and at first he believed it was a traders' conspiracy. However, it hurt him most of all to feel that Prussia was dependent on foreign banks. As early as 1752 he had thought of setting up an issue, discount, and credit bank in Berlin, but the business was too novel and too difficult for the routine officials of the Central Office. This time he was advised by a projector who came from the homeland of money-changers, a very obscure Italian called Calzabigi, who lived in London after having been a subordinate or a director at the Genoa Lottery. Ministerial opposition was still very lively; the collapse of Law's bank and the failure of the banks of Copenhagen and Stockholm were recalled. However, the King stuck to his guns—difficulties only stiffened his resolution. With lively appreciation of how to sway public opinion he would have liked the bank to have been independent of the State but he found no buyers for his shares and he had to subscribe the whole of the capital himself. The foundation decree (June 17, 1765) expressly mentioned that the concern would not be under any branch of the administration but under the King alone. The capital, which was originally 400,000 thalers, was raised by decrees to 8,800,000 thalers (1785).

The early stages were very difficult, as no one had confidence in the institution. The public was sure that Frederick wished to draw the currency of the realm into his coffers and then pay out in paper. The bank drove away capital instead of keeping it in the country, and the trade in silver, which up till then had centered on Breslau and Berlin, moved to Leipzig, Frankfort, and Prague. The bank's statutes were modified, and under Minister von Hagen's control it gradually acquired connections, thanks to its businesslike conduct of operations. In 1768 its bills were accepted at Hamburg in preference to commercial drafts, and it was doing so well that the King was able to decide that thenceforth it should be the only authority qualified to hold the liquid assets belonging to minors in wardship. The profits, which were only 22,000 thalers for the financial year 1767–68, rose to 216,000 for 1785–86.

The Berlin bank had a branch at Breslau, but from 1770 onward another bank did business in that town, a mortgage bank which was a sort of coöperative concern of the nobility. The landed proprietors had in fact suffered badly from the invasion and the war; the majority of them were deeply in debt and the help given by the King was not enough to restore their fortunes. The bank acted in the name of the nobles collectively, each landowner being liable for the debts of all the rest. As initial capital it received an advance of 200,000 thalers from the State, and little by little it took over all the debts of its members, but made do with a very moderate rate of interest. Six years later a similar institution was set up in Pomerania. The nobles had at first rejected the idea, claiming that the system of collective responsibility involved a risk of a few ruining all the rest, as would infallibly have happened during the Thirty Years' War. "Evidently," the King replied, "if the sky falls on the earth all the birds will be caught. And if the Last Judgment comes upon us we shall all be bankrupt. However, if it happens that a whole province is devastated the sovereign ought to apply a cure to it, for he and his estates are one."

The least contradiction annoyed him. In his *Political Testament* of 1768 he wrote of his subjects, "This nation is heavy and lazy. These are two defects against which the government has to struggle without ceasing. They are masses which move under pressure and stop if you cease to press them on for a single moment. No one knows of anything but the habits of his fathers; little reading is done; hardly anyone is eager to learn what is done elsewhere, so that all novelties terrify them, and *as for me, who have never done them anything but good, they think that I am going to put a knife at their throats as soon as it is a question of making some useful reform or some necessary change.*" Also he became more and more annoyed with the formal methods and delaying tactics of the bureaucracy, the habits and hierarchy of which he used intentionally to override by sending junior officials on extraordinary missions invested with full powers in such and such a province. The reconstruction of Pomerania and the Neumark was the work of one of these confidential agents, Schönberg von Brenckenhoff, who was neither a minister nor a president but a mere finance councilor. After him Councilor Schütz fulfilled the same office of overseer and temporary controller.

At the annual review in the month of June the King no longer received his ministers in a batch but two by two. Sometimes he made them stay to supper and they drew up an account of what had been decided in the course of the meal during dessert. He was not afraid of being overreached by them, for as of old he scarcely saw them except on this occasion. But as he took decisions piecemeal, he had inevitably to allow himself to be guided by the documents and figures which they submitted to him. It was through these that he was taken in. For example, in 1770 Schulenburg, president of the Chamber of Domains of Magdeburg, was invited by the Central Office to falsify his grain statistics a little so as not to give the King the idea of forbidding the exportation of corn. Later Hoym, the minister for Silesia, added 20,000 inhabitants to the census of his province—the King loved fertility. The same Hoym was guilty of a still more serious piece of deceit. One of the things which concerned the King deeply is known to have been the changing of peasant serfs into hereditary tenants; Hoym's predecessor, the energetic Schlabrendorff, had tried to force the nobles of Silesia to submit to the royal will but had only met with resistance. Scarcely had Hoym been installed at Breslau when clashes died down and complaints stopped: the recalcitrants had given in. However, in 1785 an extraordinary commission discovered that, although His Majesty's orders had been scrupulously carried out on paper, not one of the peasant serfs had felt the least real improvement in his condition.

Another episode is most revealing. During his first journey into Pomerania after the peace of Hubertsburg Frederick had dictated a peremptory cabinet order to the president of the Provincial Chamber: "All serfdom in the villages of the domains, in those of the nobility, and in those which are the property of the towns must be suppressed this very hour, completely and without questioning. If opponents are encountered, they must be led by kindness, or if need be by force, to conform to the irrevocable will of the King." The nobles replied with feigned innocence that serfdom had indeed once existed in Pomerania but that it had been long ago transformed into a simple bond of hereditary dependence, which had nothing in common with serfdom, properly so-called. The Provincial Chamber even added that, whatever the state of the case, the ordinances of 1610 and 1670 had guaranteed the lords the continuance of a rigorous form of serfdom. Before this resistance the King beat a retreat, and the ordinance of 1764 sanctioned an almost unameliorated version of the existing situation. Peasants could be neither sold nor given away; they could freely dispose of their household effects and of anything they bought; they owed the lord of the tenement they occupied an annual quitrent and certain labor services; they lent him their children so that he could make servants of them; they could not leave the property without permission of the lord but they could not be expelled from it without a valid reason. Such were the bounds set by the nature of things to the reforming zeal of Frederick.

Truth to tell, his intentions were not in doubt, but he not only came in collision with what were called the acquired rights of real estate, rights acquired often enough by violent or fraudulent acts, he also came up against the very framework of the social edifice. There were no small rural proprietors; everything depended on the almost uncontrolled exploitation of the serfs of the countryside. A long chain of dependence ran from the top to the bottom. Without a complete breakdown the last link of the chain, the serfdom of the peasants, could not be broken. The aristocracy lived on this serfdom and would not allow it to be touched. This was perhaps the true reason for the collapse of Prussia at the beginning of the nineteenth century. The Napoleonic conquest encountered a rural population which was amorphous, almost indifferent, and incapable of a spontaneous outburst of patriotism and self-sacrifice. It needed the landslide of 1806 to bring about a remodeling of the social structure. The men who revived Prussia after Jena endeavored to free the peasants, or at the very least to reduce their hardships: it was only then that they became one of the living forces of the nation.

judged in a great variety of ways. Professor Schmoller portrays the department as one of the pillars of the idea of monarchy, *Traegerin des monarchischen Staatsgedankens;* Walter Schultz, the specialist, writes that it was a "completely useless" institution. One thing stands out clearly: it was a costly institution and it involved a disproportionate increase of rigor and inspection to produce a very small increase of revenue.

The Prussian State already possessed a monopoly of salt, which was administered on the same principle as the Gabelle, that is to say that each family was compelled to purchase each year at the public storehouses a minimum quantity of salt which represented its estimated consumption. In this way smuggling was made not impossible but futile. The Administration of the Posts was reorganized in 1766 on the model of the Excise Department; a monopoly of tobacco was set up in 1765 and an Excise Office for coffee in 1781.

Coffee was a special cause of complaint to Frederick. He knew the taste his subjects had for *café au lait,* he computed the total cost of it, and gloomily reckoned up the number of millions which went out of Prussia each year to pay for the dirty fluid. "The wretches," he used often to say, "are they of better breeding or of more delicate complexion than I am? Well, I was brought up on bread soaked in beer and no one would say that I am doing too badly. Their fathers knew of nothing but beer: it is the right drink for the climate. They are in danger of destroying their temperament and leaving nothing behind them but a race of degenerates. Besides they are ruining the country." After the monopoly had been established the Prussians continued to drink what they liked, but the King at least reaped some benefit from this "unnatural taste."

The creation of the Excise Department dismembered the competence of the Central Office; the unity of control and administration established with such difficulty by Frederick William was destroyed and replaced by the expedients of close, suspicious avarice. In fact, the profits of the department were turned over thenceforward to a special treasury, which was not subject to the inspection of the audit office: it was the privy purse. To the same treasury came the excess of receipts accruing from the old and new provinces, without anybody except the King being able to check the use made of these funds. The construction of the New Palace, the losses of the war, the cost of colonization, in general all extraordinary expenses were paid from this mysterious source. From these changes it can be guessed that Frederick was tired of the comments of the Central Office. He had a feeling that his most categorical orders were going to get lost there, were going to become immeshed in its routine. The older he got the more jealous he was of his authority and the more did he wish to be served "at full speed" and to the letter. If need be to save time he would do everybody's job, he would be banker, exciseman, inspector, director, controller, minister, and audit office. This exceptional man, who was being hardened and rigidified by age, came to incarnate the monarchy more thoroughly every day that passed.

<h1 style="text-align:center">III</h1>

SILESIA was the richest province in the kingdom and paid most in taxes: a historian has ventured to say that Frederick's first conquest was the column which supported the whole reign. To keep his acquisition he had had to fight for seven years, he had held out, he had conquered, yet the peace left him almost completely isolated in Europe—on bad terms with England, without diplomatic relations with France, always the enemy of Austria and Saxony. The Russian alliance was truly a compulsory alliance for him in this isolation. Yet how are we to define friendship? Long ago this was done in Latin in a concise and classical manner: *Eadem velle, eadem nolle*—to have the same likes and dislikes. On what subjects and against whom could Russia and Prussia agree to say yes or to say no? Firstly, Prussia, like Russia, was a newcomer on the great stage of the world. The ambitions of Russia in the East were not in the least antagonistic to the aims of Frederick, who must rather have viewed with satisfaction the embarrassment they were about to cause to Austria. Finally, in Poland it was equally in the interest of each of the two states to nullify the influence of Austria, to support a king who would be under their control, and on the pretext of defending the Polish constitution to maintain the anarchy which crippled that unhappy republic.

The death of Augustus III, which occurred unexpectedly on

October 5, 1763, led Frederick and Catherine to reaffirm their friendship by a treaty which was signed on April 11, 1764. It was to last eight years; it laid down a reciprocal guarantee of territories, neither peace nor a truce was to be made without mutual consent, and in case of war assistance to the tune of 10,000 men, for which a subsidy of 480,000 thalers might be substituted, was promised either on the Rhine or in the Crimea. As for Poland they promised to arrange for the election of Stanislas Augustus Poniatowski, "long known to the Empress and personally pleasing to her," as Frederick said in a gallant euphemism. The fact was that Poniatowski, who had been during the lifetime of Peter III if not the first at least the dearest of Catherine's lovers, appeared wonderfully suitable to fulfill the subordinate part for which he was cast. However, it was not enough to give Poland a king incapable of helping her, the Poles themselves had also to be prevented from making an end of their quarrels, should patriotism open their eyes one day, and a pretext had to be kept open for disturbing their affairs.

In the republic the real power did not belong to the elected king but to the two chambers of the nobility, the Senate and the Chamber of Nuncios which made up the Diet and met every other year. Since the seventeenth century a custom had grown up that all decisions had to be taken by a unanimous vote. A single opposing voice was enough to annul and hold up everything—this was called the *liberum veto*. Then the Diet was said to be divided and an appeal was made to the whole body of the nobility. A "confederation" comprising several tens of thousands of armed horsemen used to collect at the gates of Warsaw and its decisions were taken by a simple majority. Prussia and Russia were therefore agreed that they could not allow the *liberum veto* to be abolished, nor the elective monarchy to be transformed into a hereditary monarchy. As for a pretext for intervention, there was one to hand. There were religious minorities in Catholic Poland, Orthodox Greeks and Lutherans, who were classed together as Dissidents. Since 1736 they had been excluded from almost all public posts. The Greeks had turned to Russia and the Lutherans to Prussia. Catherine and Frederick agreed to make a combined effort to restore the Dissidents to their rights and prerogatives.

The treaty gave the Tsarina all the securities she needed. She lost no time in taking advantage of it: Russian troops massed on the Polish frontier and on September 7, 1764, Poniatowski was elected king. Instead of 100,000 gentlemen only 5,000 had taken part in the voting. Catherine thought she had won a great victory, but events took a course which could not have been foreseen. The new sovereign went over to the side of the reformers, converted by his cousins, the Csartoryskis. In a few months great progress was made, a military academy was opened, the central administration rapidly organized, and the budget balanced. At the Diet of 1766 Stanislas Augustus even got the deputies and senators to agree that unanimity should no longer be required for voting taxes: a majority was to be sufficient. At once Repnine, the Russian ambassador, protested and asked for a return to the *liberum veto* and the recognition of all the rights of the Dissidents. The Diet refused, the Lutherans and Orthodox Christians revolted, Russian troops crossed the frontier, Repnine had the recalcitrant bishops kidnaped, and on November 19, 1767, the Diet voted all that he desired. Finally, on February 24, 1768, a treaty between Russia and Poland confirmed the latter's subjection. Russia bound herself to preserve, defend, and assure the integrity of the republic, which in return placed its constitution under the guarantee of its powerful neighbor. In short, Poland had sworn to live and die in anarchy.

Frederick had made a supplementary agreement with the Tsarina to oppose Austrian intervention should the need have arisen, but his special function was to give the tuning note to his philosophic friends. As might be guessed, Russian intervention was a victory for liberty of conscience over "christed superstition." Poor Poniatowski could not get the better of his mitered fanatics; the Empress had been obliging enough to send "arguments reinforced with cannons and bayonets" marching to his assistance. Nothing could be more legitimate, nothing more happy for the propagation of enlightenment. "It is a very pleasant thing," replied Voltaire, "which has an air of contradiction, to uphold indulgence and tolerance with arms in one's hand, but then intolerance is so odious that it deserves to be given a box on the ears. If superstition has made war for so long, why should not we make war on superstition?" This point of view was assiduously spread and did not help Louis XV's efforts to help the old and faithful friend of France.

However, in spite of an outward show of zeal, Frederick was not eager to see the Tsarina succeed too soon or too completely. He had come to an understanding with her to encourage Polish anarchy, not to turn Poland into a Muscovite protectorate. Besides, he had always been afraid of Russia because "her commodious frontiers," her "rough and barbarous" climate, her very immensity protected her from the attentions of Prussia, while Prussia lay open to hers. When the laws of necessity made him enter an alliance with her, he still had the same feelings of fear and antipathy. He believed the Empire of the Tsars to be "fatal to its neighbors and dangerous to all Europe." He called the Russians the savages of the north, the ursomaniacs, the Scythians, the barbarians on the frozen sea. Though he adored Catherine as a divinity in the letters he sent her, he jeered at her without pity in his private correspondence.

His system was never to swim against the current, and to interfere everywhere, all the time, and at any price. He trusted in the good goddess of politicians, Opportunity, in Her Sacred Majesty Chance, for in general it was those who indulged in the greatest activity who made the biggest mistakes. It was for others to take advantage of this. The forecast was a good one: in quick succession two important events came to hinder Russia's action, on the one hand, the rising of Polish patriots united in the Confederation of Bar; and on the other, the intervention of Turkey, which was secretly stirred up by Choiseul and Vergennes and used a frontier incident as a pretext for attacking the Tsarina. "With a new field of action lying open before one, one must be without skill or engulfed in stupid torpor not to draw the least profit from so advantageous an opportunity." Austria feared that the balance of power would be destroyed in the East; Russia, taken unawares by the Sultan, attached an importance to the Prussian alliance which was magnified by her own embarrassments. In short, once again Frederick was going to find himself courted by both sides and in the position of arbiter.

Arbitration, to be sure, was not at all simple. If there was much to gain, there were also great risks to be run. In fact, if Austria and Russia came to an understanding Prussia would find herself caught between two empires which would dictate terms to her. If on the contrary Austria was persuaded by France to support the Confederates and the Turks, Frederick as an ally of Russia would be forced into a new war, with France on his hands. Luckily it was autumn, operations would not start until spring, and it was probable that Europe would let the Russians and the Turks fight a campaign without interference. Lastly, there was room for everyone in Poland. The plan of partition was not Frederick's any more than it was anyone else's—it had been in the air for a long time—but it appealed to the King's mind as the ideal solution. What was the use of making war so far from home at such expense, when with so little trouble, by just stooping to pick it up, one could find the desired advantage under one's hand?

Frederick's plans touched those of Maria Theresa and her son, the Emperor Joseph II, at a tangent. In November, 1768, Nugent, the Austrian ambassador, proposed to Frederick that the two Courts should combine to keep Germany neutral. "We could do nothing more reasonable," cried Frederick. "We are Germans, what does it matter to us that the English and the French are fighting for the isles of America, that Paoli is keeping the Frenchmen's hands full in Corsica, that the Turks and the Russians catch each other by the forelock? . . . The Queen Empress and I—we have long sustained ruinous wars: what has that left between us?" Nugent could have replied that it had left Silesia but he thought it better to be silent. Frederick let it be understood that the Russians would do better to increase their dominions in Asia than in Europe, and it was agreed that he should meet Emperor Joseph next summer.

The interview took place on August 25, 1769, at Neisse in Silesia. On the Austrian side Joseph's visit to this fortress was a most striking confirmation of past treaties. The Emperor traveled under the name of Count von Falkenstein, accompanied by only a few aides-de-camp. Frederick received him attended by his brother Henry, his nephew, and a crowd of officers. The two sovereigns embraced. It was a fast day; the King had his guest served with meals without meat. Dinner and supper lasted three hours. Frederick talked all the time; the Emperor answered him back; the princes and the Prussian generals did not dare to open their lips; if their Austrian neighbors asked them a question they answered swiftly and in low voices, not wishing to interrupt the King's conversation nor to lose a word of it. At supper some of the generals were sated with eloquence and fell asleep. Next day reviews were held and troops marched past. Meals, maneuvers, and conversations followed each other until the morning of August 28.

For Joseph the conversations were the great interest of the visit. Frederick put himself out to dazzle and charm him. He overwhelmed him with politeness, extolled the tactics of Marshal Daun, praised the marches of Lascy and Laudon, and passed a verdict on the French Army which flattered the Austrian Army: "Their officers," he said, "have a military jargon which is deceptive: they are parrots who have learned to whistle a march and know no more than that." He spoke highly of Kaunitz, "the first head in Europe," and returned to the art of war. "When he speaks of it," Joseph reported to Maria Theresa, "it is enchanting, and all is vigorous, sound, and very instructive. No verbiage, but he proves the axioms he advances by facts with which history and an excellent memory provide him." Frederick made a show of being frank. "When I was young," he said, "I was ambitious; at this hour I am so no longer." Or again: "You think I am full of bad faith, I know I have deserved this in some ways; circumstances demanded it but they have changed." Next there was much talk of German patriotism and of the "patriotic system." During the last days there was an exchange of letters. First Joseph sent a rough draft, then Frederick sent a letter, and Joseph an answer.

These began and ended with balanced compliments. "It is impossible for my heart to be the enemy of a great man," said Frederick. "I have been able," replied Joseph, "to make the personal acquaintance of one who gives the lie to the proverb . . . that great objects grow less when looked upon too closely." Frederick was unwilling to express the impression made on him by the Emperor—"I respect his modesty." Joseph in the same way was silent, for "the unvarnished truth would seem a flattery." The King of Prussia recorded "perfect reconciliation between the two Houses." Joseph declared "that being sincerely reconciled" nothing prevented them from establishing mutual confidence and friendship. Finally, in identical terms they promised that "if ever the flames of war are rekindled between England and the House of Bourbon, they will maintain the peace so happily restored between them, and even in the event of another war breaking out, the cause of which it is at present impossible to foresee, they will observe the most exact neutrality for their present possessions." It was the beginning of an understanding and the way was open for a common policy. In any case, it was enough to upset the Tsarina.

Never had Frederick been more alert or more master of himself than in this crisis. Never was gambler more bold or more circumspect at one and the same time, more fertile of feints and expedients, and above all more adroit at discovering his opponent's plans and at unmasking them. On the pretext of amusing the Russian ministers with the mad projects of a certain Count de Lynar, an arm-chair diplomat "who governed Europe from the depths of his village," he had already sounded the government of St. Petersburg. A bantering reply had convinced him that at the right moment Russia would not shrink from compensating herself at the expense of Poland. He went to work in the same way to make the Count de Nugent talk, and from a few phrases which escaped that diplomat he learned that the Court of Vienna would not find his claims in the least excessive on the day when he should be in a position to assert them. The main point was to use the Empresses as bugbears to frighten each other. In fact, after having floundered about on the banks of the Dnieper for some weeks, the Russians had beaten the Turks, destroyed their fleet, and occupied the Rumanian plains. The Turks were in a bad way and asked for Frederick and Maria Theresa to mediate. Austria would have to adopt a pretty high tone to hold the victors back, after which Russia, robbed of victory in the East, would turn on Poland again of her own accord, and to preserve the balance of power each would help itself according to its appetite.

In September Frederick repaid the Emperor's visit of the year before. The interview took place at Neustadt in Moravia. Frederick had offered his guest Italian low comedy, Joseph replied with the ballet of Noverre. One day at dinner, as Marshal Laudon was late, Frederick took advantage of this to change his place at table: "He's a man," said he, "whom I would rather have at my side than facing me." Then as someone was talking of the last war he followed this up by saying, "I beg your pardon for having harassed you so often. I am sorry for it in all humanity, but what a good war of apprenticeship! I made enough mistakes for all you young people to learn how to do far better than I! My God, how I love your grenadiers! How well they marched past me yesterday on parade! If the god Mars wished to raise a bodyguard, I would advise him to take them without looking further!" One evening he sang the praises of Louis XIV: "That man was the patriarch of kings."

The Prince de Ligne replied, "A king of France, Sire, is always the patriarch of men of wit."

At that Frederick cut in with, "That's the worst lot of all, to govern them is not worth a curse. Far better be the patriarch of the Greeks like my sister of Russia, that is worth and will be worth far more to her."

This time, however, the Emperor was accompanied by Kaunitz. The chancellor kept serious matters for himself, leaving his master nothing but reviews, marches past, music, and the courtesies of the dinner table. Frederick loved desultory conversations favorable to shock tactics wherein every subject was lightly skimmed, for this suited his incisive manner. Kaunitz had a good rule of thumb. He always had some memorandum under eight headings in his pocket which he used to inflict on the ears of the King, who bubbled with impatience and tried to stop him by flinging his arms around him. Finally agreement was reached to propose a joint mediation to Catherine II, and Prince Henry set out for St. Petersburg charged with this ticklish mission.

Henry was short, ill-proportioned, very ugly, and very agreeable. He had big blue eyes, which were animated but hard and squinting, so that they gave him a forbidding air. Once he had opened his mouth this impression faded away, such goodness, charm, and intelligence did he put into his remarks. Just as Frederick was lively and hurried, all witticisms and epigrams, so had he a serious, argumentative mind with a special taste for vast speculations and broad systems. Catherine made friends with him immediately but all the same she would not consent to divulge her intentions until the end of December. She agreed to a triple alliance in principle, it is true, but she was unwilling to give up any of her conquests. At the very least she agreed to a concealed protectorate over Moldavia and Wallachia.

"A snook was cocked at me," growled Frederick, "when I received the peace terms presented by the Russians. Never can I take it upon me to propose them to the Turks or the Austrians, for indeed they are not acceptable. The one regarding Wallachia can in no way fit in with the Austrian system. Firstly, they will never leave their alliance with France, and in the second place they will never endure the Russians in their neighborhood. You can look on this document as a declaration of war. . . . States proceed according to their own interests and one can have some courtesy for one's ally, but everything has its limits!"

Austria was possibly not as determined on war as Frederick said. Nevertheless she had mobilized, and as the plague had broken out in Poland she had lined all her frontiers with a cordon of troops which was at once an observation corps and a sanitary protection. However, these frontiers were very uncertain in several places. Wherever there was doubt as to ownership the Austrians took care to plant their imperial eagles on the far side of the points in dispute. Thus it was that they incorporated in their lines the little district of Zips, which had belonged to Hungary and would perhaps still belong to it had it not formed an enclave on Polish territory in the south of Galicia. These threatening tactics succeeded. On January 8, 1771, during a social evening the Empress flippantly told Prince Henry that the Austrians had taken two starosties [1] and that they had hoisted the imperial standard over them. She added, "But why didn't everybody take some too?" The Prince replied that at all events the Prussians had not occupied any starosties. "But," insisted the Empress, who was always flippant, "why not occupy some?" And after her Count Czernichew also said, "Why not take the Bishopric of Ermeland? After all each power must have something."

This opening did not surprise Frederick. It occurred at the right time and he had made every effort to provoke it. Yet he knew the strength of ideas. Although he was ready to scandalize his contemporaries by bold strokes, he held it to be imprudent to goad them with pinpricks. Venial sins are those for which his-

1. See page 366 for a definition of a starosty.

tory has the least compassion: the man who gains fame by taking a province is dubbed a rogue if he takes a district. In his eyes the Bishopric of Ermeland was not worth "sixpence." "It is such a wretched scrap," he said, "that it would not repay the protests it would arouse. . . . When trifles are snatched with eagerness, that produces a reputation for avarice and insatiability which I do not want to have laid at my door more than it is already in Europe." If there was to be a partition the operation must be substantial and effective. If a din was to be raised let it be for something considerable! "Polish Prussia would be worth the trouble." It would unite Royal Prussia and Brandenburg, "which would be a matter of importance," and it would give the royal House all the trade of the Vistula. At once he ordered Fincken-stein to get his judicial claims and titles in order. By truly exceptional good luck he found that the ancient rights provided by the archives of Prussia exactly coincided with those which rested on convenience and decorum.

The Tsarina allowed herself to be persuaded easily enough, but it needed more than six months to win over Maria Theresa, whom Kaunitz and Joseph had dragged into a formal alliance with the Turks (July 6) and led to hope that everything could be arranged in the Balkans without letting Frederick interfere or aggrandize himself. But this plan was too complicated and above all it laid Austria open to a new war. Now she did not wish "to come to blows," and everyone ended by being immeshed in his own intrigues. As the Russian chancellor wrote, the more each was "sunk in the rut of treacheries" the greater grew the temptation to finish once and for all by falling in a body on the weak and the innocent. "And that," wrote Frederick, "will unite the three religions, Greek, Catholic, and Roman, for we shall all communicate upon the same eucharistic body, which is Poland, and if this is not for the good of our souls, its great object will surely be the good of our States."

The first convention was signed at St. Petersburg between Russia and Prussia on January 15, 1772, the second at Vienna on February 19, the third at St. Petersburg on July 25. Maria Theresa had not given in without many a protest and many a jeremiad. She consoled herself by taking the largest portion, Lemberg and Galicia, with two million and a half inhabitants.

Russia had the lands between the rivers Dvina and Dnieper, with Polock, Mohilev, and Vitebsk; Prussia what was until recently called the corridor, except for Thorn and Danzig, with 400,000 inhabitants. The treaties were ratified by the Diet in April, 1773. The three Courts had pooled some money to buy the voices of dissident members. The operation was done very cheaply, for consciences were not a dear commodity. A prince sold himself for 60 thalers; the two Chambers together cost no more than 100,000, high dignitaries included.

The partition aroused no indignation, for Europe had been prepared for it, and who could take up the cause of such pious Catholics as the Poles in the century of the Encyclopaedia? Frederick made much ado to keep his friends in the true faith. To D'Alembert and Voltaire he depicted Poland as "the last people of all Europe," without honor or virtue, given over to the grossest debauchery. As for the patriots of Bar, they were "dastards," brigands, "minds brutalized by the most imbecile superstition," quite "capable of the sort of crimes in which cowards indulge." He even took upon himself to ridicule them in verse and he wrote a poem against them in six cantos, *The War of the Confederates*, which D'Alembert read aloud at receptions.

In all his letters he made efforts to run down "the little scrap of anarchy" which had been given him to reform. "To excite less jealousy, I say to all who will hear me that I have seen nothing throughout my journey but sand, fir trees, mist, and Jews." But he was well content with his share. In the first place he had conquered it without shedding blood, with a pen and a little ink, and then in spite of disorder and poverty these regions were full of natural resources which judicious exploitation would raise in value. Once again he took up his job as higgler. Survey of lands, introduction of the Prussian fiscal system, reform of the courts, opening of schools, foundation of villages, attempts to germanize the country by setting up colonies of German artisans or cultivators, limitation of forced labor services, transformation of serfs into hereditary tenants, digging of a canal from the Oder to the Vistula, formation of a trading company at Elbing to compete with Danzig: these were the same tasks inspired by the same general principles, yet they were carried out somewhat more systematically and inflexibly than before.

As in Silesia, Frederick kept the direct administration of the new Prussia to himself over the head of the Central Office, but this time he was not harassed by any treaty. Thus one of his first moves was to transfer to the State the management of the goods of the Church and to pay for his kind offices he pocketed half the revenues. "Our bishops keep 24,000 livres yearly income, our abbots 7,000. The apostles had not so much. . . . They are disembarrassed from worldly cares that they may devote themselves without distraction to the attainment of the heavenly Jerusalem, which is their true fatherland. . . ." In the distant past crown lands had been granted to lords in life tenancies which later became hereditary. These alienated lands were called starosties. They were recovered from the nobility for a meager indemnity and joined once more to the royal domain. Some resistance was made to this, and Frederick took advantage of these signs of ill will to quash the indemnity as often as possible. Frederick William had congratulated himself on increasing the rent of a farm by twenty thalers: had he ever dreamed of such a "bit more"? And then these expropriations had the advantage of drawing the teeth of the only two effective social and moral forces remaining in the country.

Frederick's itineraries henceforth bear the names of new stages —Bromberg, Kulm, Graudenz. In the summer peasants and woodmen saw his old berlin go past, raising the dust of the sandy roads or trundling noiselessly over the rich black soil of the valleys. Sometimes they saw the King's silhouette as he leaned through the window to follow with his glance a flock of geese which made off with a great commotion. And then the carriage used to stop at the beginning of some village near a farm in the shade of the birches. The bailiff, the surveyor, and the provincial councilor would come up hat in hand, and the King's voice would be heard to say, "Has he a pencil? Good. . . . Let him take my orders. How many horses does he need? How many bulls, how many cows?"

XII

Old Fritz

I

ON June 14, 1773, Monsieur de Guibert arrived at Potsdam. He was a colonel twenty-nine years old and he claimed to have considerable talent. He had in his pocket a tragedy on the Constable de Bourbon, and he had just published an *Essai de tactique* prefixed by an essay on the state of European politics and military science. He hoped to be present at the Prussian Army maneuvers, and as he was Mademoiselle de Lespinasse's lover D'Alembert had given him letters of recommendation to Monsieur de Catt, the King's secretary. It was fashionable to go and look at old Fritz in his glory: a journey in the great world was not complete without a visit to Sans Souci.

Monsieur de Guibert was astonished by the appearance of the town, which contained only 6,000 inhabitants as against a garrison of 12,000. He admired the streets, which were straight, broad, well laid out, and continually being embellished by the King, who had new Italianate façades built each year with a great abundance of columns and statues. However, as retired soldiers could ply any trade they liked—as cabmen, hired servants, or match sellers—he saw military trousers hanging down from Corinthian pilasters and beer-house signs fixed to walls rich in demigods. No one could appear at Sans Souci without being summoned there: Monsieur de Guibert sent his letters of introduction to De Catt, and as Frederick was on a tour of inspection, he took advantage of this to present himself to the King's friends, who received him with much politeness.

Since 1763 the circle had broken up. D'Argens had left to end his days in Provence. Right through the war the King had written serious letters to him full of affection and confidence. When he went back to being treated on his old footing after the peace, the good marquis could not endure coming down to the rank of

common courtier or submitting anew to the sarcasms and banterings which he had put up with for twenty years. Besides, he was
homesick. In the autumn of 1764 he had gone to Aix to take
possession of an inheritance. The lawsuit, the rest, and the lovely
sunshine had kept him there for more than a year. He returned
discontented with himself and discontented with the King, who
had tried to frighten him and amuse himself by having a tale
spread all along his route in inns and at posts of a bogus order
of the Bishop of Aix denouncing the traveler as an unbeliever,
a perverse, impious, bigoted blasphemer and enemy of the human race. "Take up your arms like those brave Levites who in
saintly homicide massacred their brothers in the desert. Purify
the castles of Argens and of Eugilles; root out from the number
of the living this spirit which rebels against the Church! . . ."
After having quaked with fear and changed his name out of
prudence, D'Argens discovered the imposture. A mistake in the
title put him on the track of it, as there was no Bishop of Aix
but only an Archbishop. When he presented himself at Potsdam
expecting protestations of friendship, the King pretended not to
recognize him on the pretext that he was wearing a white shirt
and clean trousers and had pulled up his stockings. For several
months they lived together coldly enough. A *Praise of Idleness*
printed anonymously with an epistle of dedication containing a
wretched portrait of the marquis completed the misunderstanding. Nicknamed a madman and a renegade, D'Argens for all that
got leave to go (1768). From Dijon he sent his former master a
letter of farewell full of respect for the King of Prussia and
severity against the philosopher of Sans Souci. "How great would
have been the astonishment of posterity if Plutarch, who was so
to speak Marcus Aurelius' companion in philosophy, had been
obliged, that he might shelter himself from the harsh pleasantries
and humiliating contempt of that Emperor, to sell the one and
only resource left to him, his plate and his wife's jewels, so as
to go and live quietly at the foot of the Alps, esteeming himself
happy to hear no more discourses, some of which were revolting
to humanity, such as the proposal that Plutarch should marry his
dog to a talented girl whom he had brought up like his own
daughter, and again such as sending for ostlers to rub him down
and cure his rheumatism? Does the philosopher of Sans Souci

think that Plutarch could be accused of having done wrong to leave Marcus Aurelius, because he had given him three gilded rooms in his palace, whence this philosopher never emerged except in terror, and to which he scarcely ever returned without his heart being rent with grief?"

D'Argens had been replaced in Frederick's friendship by Colonel Quintus Icilius. In reality his name was Charles Théophile Guichard, he was born at Magdeburg of French refugees and had taught belles-lettres at the University of Leyden. He was a naturalist, a historian, a philologist, a numismatist, an amateur of old pottery, old manuscripts, and of everything that was Greek and Roman. One day when Frederick was talking to him he asked him who had been the best aide-de-camp of all the officers around Caesar. Guichard replied that Quintus Icilius was his man, and, "Very well," his master replied, "you shall be my Quintus Icilius; I give you that name, confident that you can deserve it." While he was a professor Quintus dreamed of nothing but strategy and battles. He came to enlist at the beginning of the Seven Years' War, but during his first conversation with the King he had the misfortune to maintain that the equipment a legionary had carried was heavier than that of a grenadier. Frederick called him to his house a few days later and, smiling broadly, put him in the middle of the room, made him hold himself like a soldier who is being drilled, raised his chin, put a hat on him, as per regulations forced down to the ears, girded a saber on him, loaded him with a rifle, a cartridge box, and a haversack, and then after having cluttered him up in this way, cried, "It must be agreed that you look well, you really look to me like a Prussian soldier, you'll see that you will prefer it to your Romans."

Without another glance at him he took De Catt into a corner and began to hold moral and philosophical discourse with him which went on and on. At the end of three quarters of an hour he set the classical soldier free: "Well, sir, do you not find our soldiers' equipment to be tolerable? At present we are going to make some great marches. I hope that you will agree that they will be as strenuous as those the Romans made. You will see operations of which they had not and could not have the least idea. Farewell, sir, be just a bit of a Prussian and you will have cause to be pleased with me."

Guichard did not like Frenchmen; he blackguarded them as much as he could and thwarted them whenever he had the chance. He put up with the King's banterings but when he was driven into a corner he would sometimes lose his temper. One day at Sans Souci Frederick, who always tormented him at supper, asked him how much he had stolen when clearing the Count von Brühl's castle in Saxony of furniture. "It's an old affair," insisted the King, "and dimmed by time. Moreover, you have drunk your cup of shame to the dregs; all the world knows that you are out for loot: it is a reputation for which you have already paid the price. Make a little effort: how much was that answer to a burglar's prayer worth to you?"

"Your Majesty should know well enough," replied Quintus, red with anger, "I did nothing save by your orders. I have given you an account of everything and you shared it with me."

Straightway he rose from the table and went out. For a year the King addressed not a word to him. When Guibert came to Potsdam a reconciliation had taken place, but Quintus, who was by then being accused of having dabbled in the shares of the Bank of Berlin, spoke of Frederick without respect. He said that his reputation was excessive, that the Seven Years' War had not been won by his military genius but by the bravery and discipline of his troops, and that there was more routine than intelligence in the Prussian Army.

From the old days there still remained the Abbé Bastiani, who lived at Breslau and came very seldom to Sans Souci. Our colonel dined with him and questioned him hungrily. Like D'Argens and Quintus he was bitter and disillusioned. "The King," he said, "has never known friendship and he is incapable of feeling it. He takes delight in the idea of what he was when he came to the throne and what he is today. His subjects are in his eyes nothing but common livestock designed to fertilize or embellish the land which he governs. Love of power and vanity are his most lively passions. Music, the arts, literature, philosophy, friendship—all this is to him so much recreation, padding, tomfoolery."

Thus forewarned, Guibert was at last presented to the King. In the twinkling of an eye all he had heard was forgotten. "A kind of magical vapor," he wrote, "seemed to me to surround his person." Guibert was not the only person to get this impression. "In spite of his lack of height," Ségur reported, "the mind saw him as greater than all other men." He was "radiant with majesty" said someone else in confirmation. It is hard to imagine it today. The portraits painted of him in his old age are worthless. The best is still Chodowiecki's *gouache* which has so often been engraved—it dates from 1777. Chodowiecki had seen a lot of the King at the spring maneuvers and he painted him in profile on horseback reviewing his troops. He is an almost emaciated old man, the skin of his neck is wrinkled and hanging, his back is rounded, his lips thin and set. He usually wore a blue coat, threadbare as his body, always tightly buttoned, trousers of shabby velvet, an old silver sash, a small brass-hilted sword with only the wooden center of the tassel left on the sword knot, a huge three-pointed hat, and boots which had once been black but were yellow with age pulled up above the knee and fixed with a ragged cord to the middle of his thighs. He took Spanish snuff to excess and his clothes were always stained with it. "I cannot do without it," he said to De Catt, "it is a fixed habit. Admit, my dear fellow, that it is disgusting. Admit that I look a bit of a pig."

He also said, "I am almost as slovenly as our good marquis." And he added, "When my mother was alive I was more tidy or, to be exact, less untidy. My tender mother made me a dozen shirts with fine cuffs every year, which she sent to me wherever I was. Since the irreparable loss I have sustained in her death no one has taken care of me at all." He slept on a very dirty little bed with his head sunk deep in a pillow tied up in a handkerchief. As he perspired heavily, in the morning the sheets were dried before the fire. His wardrobe was kept by a hussar who fixed buttons onto his clothes with white thread and put patches on his shirts.

What fascinated strangers in that withered face of his was his glance, which no artist could catch because it was strangely expressive, lively, and profound, with the fire of youth and life still alive in it. When Frederick wished to please he could give his countenance a singular expression of softness and benevolence, all his features became animated, and in his face could be seen the impulses which stirred his heart. He expressed himself clearly without raising his voice, in a confident tone, with intonations "as agreeable as the movements of his lips, which were inexpressibly graceful" (Ligne). He did a lot of talking and his hearers regretted that he did not talk more. From the first they were captivated and at their ease.

Passing Frenchmen and frequenters of Versailles were always welcome. They brought back to him the air he had once breathed, and with them he found again that brilliant, easy, rapid conversation which he had missed ever since the days when it had been his greatest recreation. Once when he had just quoted Vergil the Prince de Ligne took the opportunity of saying, "He was a great poet, Sire, but what a bad gardener!"

"To whom are you telling that?" answered the King. "Have I not tried to plant, sow, work, and dig with the *Georgics* in one hand? 'But, Sire,' my gardener used to tell me, 'you are mad and so is your book. That's not the way to work.' But, in God's name, what a climate this is. Will you believe it, it refuses me everything? Look at my wretched orange trees, my olives, my lemon trees—they all die of cold."

"That is the reason, Sire," replied the Prince, "that nothing but laurels thrive in your garden." Then, as the King made a gracious little grimace at him, he quickly added, to gloss over the tameness of the compliment, "And then there are too many grenadiers in this country; they eat everything!"

The King began to laugh, because, we are told, nothing but nonsense made him laugh. In 1769 Frederick received Grimm, whom he found to have "a philosophical brain and a memory garnished with fine learning." They exchanged letters; Grimm, who was frequently invited to St. Petersburg by the Tsarina, stayed several times at Berlin, and the King subscribed to the literary correspondence which his guest sent to the German princes. However, men of wit were rare, and more and more Frederick lived among ghosts. Once or twice a year he used to go to Magdeburg "as an old friend" to ask the aged Fouqué for soup and a plate of spinach. "I am coming alone: this demands no festivity or expense. Common fare will do." Fouqué was the last companion of his youth left in Prussia. In his company he could call up Rheinsberg and the dawn of his reign. He clung to his affection, he sent him souvenirs, fruit from Sans Souci, truffles which came from France, and coffee from Turkey. Once he gave him a big glass which had belonged to Frederick William, and another time a bottle of Hungarian wine which had been laid down sixty years before. "Good day and good year to you, my dear friend, I send you a present as one old man to another: a handy chair which you can raise and lower according to your fancy, some real balm of Mecca to restore your strength, and some trinkets from my porcelain factory to amuse you." But Fouqué was nothing but a ruin. He was deaf, paralyzed in the legs, and as he could not pronounce certain sounds, he used a machine to make in writing the syllables he could not say. He died in 1774, closely followed by Guichard and by Pöllnitz, who cheated till his last gasp and was much regretted by his creditors. Dead also were Seydlitz the cavalry commander, Valori, Bielfeld, Mitchell, and Quantz the flute master. At the peace settlement My Lord the Marischal was reconciled with the Hanoverian dynasty and went to live in Scotland, but since the fall of the Stuarts everything had changed: he recognized neither the people nor the things there. He returned to Potsdam, and the King gave him a house near the castle. Daily they walked together down the avenues of the park, Frederick round-shouldered and leaning on a long stick with diamonds set in the handle, Keith upright and hearty. At eighty-six he read Father Suarez' work *De Matrimonio* for his own amusement and complained that the author awoke in him ideas which sometimes worried him. When he was on his travels the King used to send him news of the garden: "My honeysuckle is out, my elders are going to bud, and the wild geese have already come back." However, the old Scot was struck by paralysis and condemned never to leave his room again. The King used to go and see him, and spent some long moments in his company, stirring the embers of a fire which had lost its power of heating them. The Lord Marischal died in 1778 at the age of ninety-two.

For eighteen months Frederick had about him an extraordinary personage whom he had met in Moravia, Count Hoditz, a distant relation of his from having married the Dowager Landgrave of Bayreuth in the prime of his youth. Count Hoditz was a very handsome man with a long face and a madness of the most charming variety. He had contrived his lands and castle at Roswald as a perpetual theater where his serfs were the actors, the dancers, the musicians, the painters, the decorators, and the turn-cocks. In the park there were Roman ruins, a pagoda, Druid caves with altars, mysterious grottos cut in the living rock, Christian hermitages, the mausoleum of Arminius, a Lilliputian hamlet, the vale of Tempe, artificial mines, a subterranean labyrinth where the passion of Christ could be seen, canals, a fleet of boats, and six thousand fountains. Helped out by a stupendous collection of costumes, a troop of ninety persons under a Frenchman called Count Duhamel as stage manager animated any part of his fairy realm as the whim of the owner directed. He gave pastoral comedies, illuminations, Indian ballets, Chinese dinners, Druid sacrifices, processions, and water festivals where naiads and sea gods appeared. Frederick was filled with curiosity at this astounding man. On a number of occasions he invited him to spend some weeks at Potsdam, and when the magician found that rockets and music had ruined him completely, he took him in and pensioned him off. Hoditz was crushed by the infirmities of age and died of the stone in 1778.

In the same year Voltaire died also. The King and the patriarch hated one another, but they always considered each other as the greatest men of their age, and each could not get on without the other. In private Voltaire called Frederick *"Luc"* which was the name of a very nasty monkey but might also be considered as an anagram. He called him a perfidious friend, a wretched poet, an ungrateful heart, a bad relation, a faithless ally, born for the misfortune of the human race. He could not forgive Soubise for letting himself be beaten at the battle of Rossbach, for this defeat had deprived him of the godlike vengeance of consoling Luc amid irreparable misfortunes. On his side, Frederick referred to Voltaire as a vicious man, a miser, a dirty rogue, a coward, and a liar. Yet they exchanged several letters a month. In moments of bitterness they reiterated their old reproaches. "You have done me harm enough," said Voltaire; "you have set me at odds with the King of France forever; you have made me lose my posts and pensions; you ill-treated me at Frankfort, me and an innocent woman, a respectable woman who was dragged in the mud and thrown into prison. . . ." You behaved "as a disturber," replied Frederick. . . . "You have wronged me in every sort of way. . . . I forgave you everything and I am even willing to forget everything. But had you not been dealing with someone madly in love with your noble genius, you would not have got out of it so well with anyone else. Take it all as said, as I will hear no more of that niece of yours who bores me. . . ." However, Voltaire would not keep his mouth shut and reproached the King for having a heart full of gall, corrupted by "a perverted delight . . . of wishing to humiliate everybody else." Then they had a reconciliation: "I could have loved you faults and all," wrote Frederick. "You are necessary to my happiness," agreed Voltaire. "I could not live without you nor with you. . . . You are the most attractive person I know. . . ." And they returned to metaphysics, literature, confidences, and jests against religion. "I console myself that I lived in the age of Voltaire: that is enough for me," wrote the King before signing his letter. "From afar I kiss the victorious hands which have written such inspired and profitable things," replied Voltaire.

Astronomers and mathematicians kept the brilliance of the Academy of Berlin alight in the world of learning, but Frederick was not interested in the sciences. The schools of the humanities and philosophy were falling asleep. They had no more boisterous disputes with foreign institutions; they had no La Mettrie and no D'Argens to arouse the clamors of Christian philosophers; intestine strife had also come to an end. The vacant posts went to Swiss professors, grammarians, honest clergymen, and industrious, uninspired writers, whose names no longer mean anything to anybody—Prévost, Formey, Thiébault, Toussaint, Wéguelin, Mérian, Bitaubé. Besides these came a French Benedictine monk called Dom Pernety as director of the public library, and Carlo Denina, an Italian priest, who began as a lively abbé but soon became as boring as the rest of them. Several taught at a military school which the King had founded in 1766 for the education of indigent young nobles. Casanova was employed there for some weeks in the position of a supervisor. From time to time Frederick had one of his academicians to see him. He would deliver a monologue before him and give him some memoir to copy out or correct. He did not even take the trouble to chaff them, for they had long ago dulled the fine edge of his wit.

At times he had the feeling that he had outlived his own existence. "Prudence demands that you leave the world," he said, "before the world leaves you. The human race is all too easily bored by the same set of features. . . . It is as well to anticipate your public and not to give them time to get bored." He signed his letters "The Hermit of Sans Souci," as if his tastes and friendships had made him into a man of the past. Truth to tell, he continued to be a disciple of Bayle, a "libertine" of the seventeenth century, as he had been in his youth. With that great period he associated Voltaire, but after Voltaire there was nothing but decadence and corruption. "A few centuries ahead the great writers of the times of Louis XIV will be translated, just as those of the times of Pericles and Augustus are translated today." And again, "Our poor century suffers from a dreadful sterility both of great men and of great works. Of the century of Louis XIV, which was an honor to the human mind, only the dregs are left us. Soon nothing will be left at all." He foresaw an age when everything would be subordinated to physical and analytical research.

He was disgusted with the generation of 1760, with its ideas, with its style, with its license, with its daring, and above all with its imperious way of reasoning and of laying down the law in the abstract. He saw nothing there but "runts of Parnassus, false wits, paradoxical and sophistical philosophers." He offered Rousseau an asylum in the principality of Neuchâtel because he considered him an invalid down on his luck but he could not get through his *Emile:* "It is a rigmarole of things we've known for ages. . . . Nothing original, little concrete reasoning, lots of impudence. This boldness which springs from effrontery annoys the reader, so that the book becomes unbearable and he throws it away in disgust." On another occasion he classed Jean Jacques as a demoniac because of his *Discourse* on the arts. Diderot revolted him "by his self-satisfied tone and his arrogance"; Raynal by his intrepid maintenance at any price of what he had decided to be true: "He risks banishment for daring to maintain that the trade of a power is some millions more profitable than it is given out to be." Voltaire recommended him a Monsieur Delisle, author of a *Philosophy of Nature,* to fill the post of librarian. He skipped through the work and found nothing in it but "a shapeless rhapsody of fantastic ideas" which might be pardoned "in a man who wrote when drunk" but not in a writer who gave himself out as a thinker. He advised Delisle to become a cab driver, for if the worst came to the worst "it is better to be the first coachman in Europe than the last of the authors." As for D'Holbach, he irritated him so much that he took the trouble to refute his *Essay on Prejudices* and his *System of Nature,* those middens of humbug, impertinence, and idiocy. "What have I learned by reading them? What truth has the author taught me? That old churchmen are monsters fit to be stoned, that the King of France is a barbarous tyrant, his ministers are archrogues, his couriers cowardly, servile rascals, the great men of the kingdom ignorant fools full of arrogance, the judges sordid prevaricators, the financiers Jack Sheppards and Dick Turpins . . . and that no one in the kingdom is wise, laudable, or worthy of respect except for the author and his friends, who have assumed the title of philosopher." He ended by shrugging his shoulders: "If our author had been syndic in the little village of Pau in Béarn for six months, he would have a far greater appreciation for these men, whom he will never learn to know through his wild speculations." In a letter he compared D'Holbach to a mad dog which attacks everybody and rushes at the passers-by, satisfied with anyone so long as he can bite.

It annoyed him to be taken for the patron of all the pamphleteers with pretensions and with systems who were banished from their fatherland because of their morals or their quarrels with the Church. "You could not believe," he wrote to D'Alembert, "what caravans of literary insects arrive here—it is difficult to get rid of them." He blushed at the absurd, shabby intrigues in which his friends tried to involve him. He had of his own free will taken in young D'Etalonde, who had been condemned to death for contumacy at the same time as the Chevalier de la Barre, and given him a place in his army, but when D'Alembert asked him to suppress the *Lower Rhenish Courier,* which had committed the atrocious crime of casting doubt on the nobility of Loyseau de Mauléon, counsel for the Calas family,[1] and on the talents of D'Alembert himself, he replied ironically that the philosophers had demanded liberty for themselves and should

1. Jean Calas and his family were Calvinists. They were the victims of fanatical persecution by the Catholics of Toulouse, which led to the death of Jean and the exile or confinement of his children. The family was rehabilitated by the efforts of Voltaire.

have the decency to allow it to their opponents also. He advised Loyseau to take some sedative powders and a regular course of emulsions. However, he added, "If this distressed family needs consolation, here in Germany we will find learned men who will make the deceased lawyer be descended in a direct line from the ancient kings of Leon and Castile, and I dare promise that the *Lower Rhenish Courier* will print this fine discovery. That is all that I can accomplish for the reconciliation of these two illustrious parties: I shall take pride in it and insert in my memoirs that having contributed to the pacification of the disorders of Poland and Turkey I was also sufficiently favored by fortune to succeed in restoring peace between the Mauléons and the *Lower Rhenish Courier*. Come, my dear Anaxagoras, after this I hope that your philosophy will be content with mine."

Alas, D'Alembert was indefatigable. He would have liked Frederick to place a bust of Voltaire in the Catholic church at Berlin so as to profane it just a little: Frederick replied that the patriarch would get bored in such a position and would enjoy himself much more at the Academy in the midst of his admirers. Then for another whole season the philosopher harried the King with the utmost seriousness to make him insert a clause in the treaty of mediation between the Porte and Russia compelling the Sultan to restore the temple at Jerusalem; a glorious piece of tomfoolery which would give the lie to the predictions of the Holy Scriptures and cause the Sorbonne the greatest embarrassment. Frederick reached the end of his patience and asked him if the Sultan should also rebuild the tower of Babel—but on that day he discovered that Anaxagoras was a fool. They had another scuffle over the Jesuits. When the company was expelled from France and suppressed by Rome Frederick made haste to open his realms to the Jesuit fathers, who were excellent educationalists and had only to wear different clothes to obey the Pope's orders. When D'Alembert wrote to him in an acid tone reminding him that in the past he had himself described the Jesuits as vermin and as caterpillars, Frederick read him another lesson: "I treat men with kindness and act with humanity to all my species without differentiation. . . . Believe me, we ought to practice our philosophy and talk less metaphysics. Good deeds are of more use to the public than the most subtle systems. . . ."

Frederick had immense popularity in Germany: his fight to
the death against the House of Austria and the Bourbons had
made him into the idol of Protestantism. Seven years of victories,
disasters, trials, and hardships had given the war a legendary
character for heroism which inflamed men's imaginations. Young
people burned with enthusiasm for him. The pride of Germany
awoke at the spectacle of his life. A poet published the *War
Songs of a Prussian Grenadier;* and Lessing had *Minna von Barn-
helm* performed, a play which portrayed an officer of the Seven
Years' War and glorified the King. However, Frederick had not
the least curiosity about this literature. In 1780 he had a memoir
which was an insulting condemnation of everything written in
Germany read at the Academy. The German tongue was a half-
barbarous jargon; it was diffuse, difficult to control, not sonorous
enough, and burdened with too many heavy and disagreeable
syllables. "It is physically impossible for an author of the highest
merit to control this rough language." Besides, German literature was still at the stage of its first stammering utterance: a few
scrappy little stories, a comedy, a history book, a few oddments of
poetry, one or two sermons. The rest was nothing but cumbrous
verbiage. As at the age of twenty, Frederick was untouched by
everything which was the rage or was beginning to be the rage
with his fellow countrymen—pietistic phraseology, misty senti-
mentality, individual lyricism, the bursting forth of the first person singular, and the torrents of *Sturm und Drang.* "To reckon
up the lack of taste prevalent in Germany you have only to go
to public performances. You will see the abominable plays of
Shakespeare acted there, translated into our language, and all the
audience swooning with delight at the sound of these idiotic
farces, which are worthy of the savages of Canada. . . ." Where
were the rules of drama? Where was all probability? "There are
porters and gravediggers who walk on and make remarks quite
in character; then in come princes and queens. How can this extraordinary hotchpotch of lowliness and grandeur, of buffoonery
and tragedy touch and please the heart?" Still, Shakespeare lived
in a barbarous age and could be forgiven, but a certain Goethe
had just appeared, the author of *Werther* and of *Götz von Ber-
lichingen* (1774), who dared to repeat "these disgusting plati-
tudes!" A century after Racine! It was a cause for despair. But

perhaps he could still find a few Germans who would put themselves to school under Malherbe, Boileau, Bossuet, Montesquieu,
and the great authors of the past. While awaiting those distant
days it was easiest to speak French: "This tongue has become the
skeleton key which lets you into every house and every town.
Travel from Lisbon to St. Petersburg and from Stockholm to
Naples talking French and you will be understood everywhere.
By the use of this idiom alone you will reduce the number of languages you must know; these used to overload the memory with
words, in the place of which you can fill it with facts—a thing
much to be preferred."

Wrapped in solitude, the King shut himself up in Sans Souci
with his dogs. He had no suppers and went to bed early. For a
few hours each morning he used to walk from room to room playing on the flute, but since Quantz's death he had had no one to
accompany him. He played old tunes which he knew by heart,
tunes which had lulled his sorrows or accompanied his victories.
He often said that the taste for noble songs was lost and that the
music of Gluck and Haydn was a shindy which flayed the ears.
He had shut up the guest rooms. The four or five rooms which he
inhabited were very dilapidated, the gilt tarnished, the silk of the
arm chairs worn out in big patches, and the curtains soiled and
torn by the dogs, but he did not want any repairs made. Scraps
of paper, maps, and books were scattered on all the tables, with
heaps of "Fredericks," rolls of gold coins which gave him the
physical delight of riches. His great luxury was snuffboxes to the
number, it is said, of one hundred and thirty, in jasper, agate,
chrysolite, and especially in gold, veritable pieces of jewelry
covered with precious stones, which were worth millions. He
always had four or five of them in his pocket or within reach.
When he moved to his capital at the beginning of winter a chest
of snuffboxes was loaded onto a camel, which was a present from
the Tsar Peter, and the animal ambled slowly across the sands of
Brandenburg to carry the treasure to Berlin.

Round about one o'clock Frederick used to dine with his
aides-de-camp and he certainly enjoyed himself at table. Daily
he was brought the kitchen program and modified the menus
himself, adding very indigestible and highly flavored dishes, eel

pasties, goose livers, and soups so heavily spiced that they gave him terrible stomach trouble. He made up potions for himself, to which he attributed curative powers. One year he would drink nothing but cold coffee mixed with champagne. When someone gave him a smart answer, he recovered his gaiety with the greatest ease. He repeated little stories which had made him laugh in the past, he spoke of his youth and of his campaigns, he soliloquized on God, on Voltaire, on the arts, and on the sovereigns of Europe. One day he amused himself by reallotting heraldic emblems to the Great Powers. He gave Austria a thundering Jupiter to adorn its shield, France the star of Venus, England the pirate captain Mercury, god of merchants and thieves, and for ourselves, he said, an ape, for we ape the Great Powers without being one.

Three times a week he still used to exercise his regiment. On the other days he went for a walk which often took him to the experimental garden, where he tried out agricultural novelties imported from England, beetroots, kohlrabis, clover, lucerne, and rhubarb. Sometimes he went off on horseback to Berlin followed by a page and an officer. Guttersnipes touched his boots and veterans said good day to him, calling him "Father" or "Father Fritz." He used to inspect the porcelain factory which he had founded in imitation of Meissen with a scepter as its trade-mark. He would pass several hours with Princess Amelia, who was disfigured, almost blind, her eyes half out of their sockets, her head shaking, her limbs paralyzed, only speaking with a raucous whistling sound like someone who is being stifled. The carnival took place at Berlin each year as usual on his return. At the conclusion of the reviews at Potsdam he used to give a great banquet at the New Palace in the grotto on the ground floor, to which all the officers were invited.

His calling kept him going. "It is very true," he said, "that glory comes to nothing much when we examine what it is. To be judged by the ignorant and valued by imbeciles, to hear one's name pronounced by a populace which approves, rejects, loves, or hates without reason, this is nothing to be proud of. Yet what would become of virtuous and praiseworthy deeds if we did not cherish glory? All those who have deserved well of their country have been encouraged in their work by an earnest of future fame." He had made no changes in the routine of his strenuous life but the older he grew the more he was horrified by vagueness, by "whipped cream." In 1780 he was introduced to the Marquis Lucchesini, a young Italian nobleman of good family who was touring Europe for his own amusement. He kept him at his side in the position of a chamberlain. Every evening for two years Lucchesini wrote down in his diary a précis of the subjects the King had discussed at table or in private conversation. Population, taxes, money, banks, trade, crops—the precise, even arid nature of his usual monologues is very striking. He quoted a large number of figures and discussed them. Much more rarely than in the past did he indulge in chatter which ran from one epigram to another and had no subject. He only recovered his biting vein to satirize the princes of Europe or to make mock of the geometrical mind.

Each year when spring came round, a little thinner, a little more bent, supporting himself with an invalid's stick in the form of a crutch, he began his tour of the provinces again. The dilapidated old carriage rolled once more along the roads of Silesia and Prussia. The bailiffs, hat in hand, lined up at the entrance of the village, and with fingers deformed by gout old Fritz wrote in his notebooks: "On the property of Count Wallis they sell their flax in Bohemia. Why is it not spun in the County of Glatz?—The town of Striegau complains it has no manufactures nor any possibility of enriching itself. I do not see how to help it, unless a factory could be set up there for the preparation of vitriol or something of the same sort.—At the towns of Schweidnitz and Neisse there is still a lack of roofing tiles. N.B. This must be considered.—The bailiff of the Count de Wallis has told me he could found a colony of thirty families. Verify if this would work.—There could be more sheep in the land of Glatz if they were made to pasture in the forests which grow on the mountainsides. The question is whether their wool would be good or not. At the least this would be a help to the poor peasant, who could feed himself on ewe's milk.—I am giving 1,000 thalers to each of the two nobles, Arnold and the other whose name I forget, who suffered from the flooding of the Oder between Crossen and Glogau.—The new road for china clay; Pfaer has the plans of it. . . ." And Frederick felt he had lived a full life.

Frederick on Tour with His
Old Berlin

Frederick Hears of His
Nephew's Death

II

HE was cut off from the world at Potsdam, and even in Europe his only ally was Catherine, for whom he had no love. The agreement with Austria was only provisional; diplomatic relations with France had been resumed but without much warmth. In 1772 he would have liked to use the death of King Adolphus Frederick and the constitutional anarchy of the country to apply to Sweden the maneuver which had succeeded so well against Poland. However, the new king, Gustavus III, son of Ulrica of Prussia, was supported by Louis XV and nipped the plans for intervention in the bud by violent military action, which restored order and confirmed the traditional privileges of the monarchy. Frederick grumbled, tried to intimidate his sister, and gave in. In 1776 he courteously bowed out the ambassadors of the American colonies which were in rebellion against England. To his friends he said that he was keeping his seat in the theater but did not want to get onto the stage. At every turn he used to quote at them some lines of Chaulieu's:

> Melancholy and Care, begone!
> Your tardy poison shall not deaden my last hours.
> Most of my road is past, is gone;
> The rest I mean to sow with flowers.

However, it needed very little to transform the hermit into a warrior. On December 30, 1777, Maximilian Joseph, Elector of Bavaria, died without issue. The lawful heir was the nearest cousin of the dead man, Charles Theodore, Palatine of Sulzbach, whose title was confirmed by a number of solemn acts— a family compact, a will, and a pact of part ownership. However, as at the death of Charles VI, the inheritance had already been contested, firstly, by the Dowager Electress of Saxony, Maximilian's sister, who in fact preserved certain rights over his personal property; and second, by Joseph II, who appealed to complicated and doubtful arrangements dating from the days of the Emperors Sigismund and Matthias. To begin with, to the terror of the prudent Maria Theresa, Joseph succeeded in the extraordinary exploit of getting the validity of his claim admitted by the man who had the strongest reasons for contesting it, the heir

Charles Theodore himself. Backed by this recognition, he ordered the Austrian Army to take possession of the territory which had been ceded to him, the parts called Lower Bavaria—the regencies of Landshut and Straubing between the rivers Inn, Isar, and Danube.

Out came Frederick, thirty years younger, ready to have it out with "Dame Theresa" and "Joseph Caesar." At the first news of it he annulled the credits reserved for building purposes and ordered his superior officers to hold themselves in readiness. He rushed letters to Baron von Goltz, his ambassador in Paris, wherein may be seen the feverish haste of a young king making his bow to the world: "You will strive to put all your Moscas to work. . . . You will employ your best efforts. . . . As this is the first and the most important business in which you can display your sagacity and your penetration in all their maturity, the success of your endeavors will let me see if you have enough energy to satisfy me in everything I desire to know." And Goltz had to run round the drawing rooms, to hear "the warbling" of certain well-informed ladies. How Frederick urged him on! "Go on, now is the moment to bestir yourself; perhaps this will lead to a closer connection; you must handle these people through their love of glory and the shame they will feel at sacrificing the Münster guarantee to the cupidity of Austria. Display all your eloquence. Even France might have something to gain. I would sign anything."

However, Louis XVI was busy preparing his revenge for the Seven Years' War against England and had no desire to complicate the war at sea by a quarrel on the Continent. His alliance with Austria was only defensive: nothing obliged France to help the Emperor in his plans of conquest. As for assisting Prussia so that she could be sure of stopping her rival, he had still less idea of doing that. Therefore Frederick was forced to set the ball rolling himself, but good policy counseled him to dissimulate his own personal interests and pose as the champion of Germanic liberties, as the protector of small states, yet remaining free to seize on a piece of land when the moment came. On his advice the Duke of Zweibrücken, the Palatine's heir, refused to ratify the cession of the regencies as far as he was concerned; Saxony protested in due course; finally Prussia asked the Diet to intervene at the Court of Their Imperial Majesties so that the succession might be regulated by judicial means and that in the meantime Lower Bavaria might be evacuated.

Frederick was in a laughing mood. He had light meals served him, went to bed at a fixed hour, and ate very sensible food; his conversation treated of the pleasures of his last campaigns which he expected to enjoy during his next one. On April 5, 1778, he called together his generals and his officers. He told them that he was old and infirm, that he would make use of a post chaise during the marches, but on the day of battle he would be among them on horseback as in the past. The next day he set out for Silesia. The negotiations still dragged on for a few weeks. In exchange for Lower Bavaria Joseph offered to recognize in advance the King's possession of the two margravates of Ansbach and Bayreuth which were already joined in a single principality and were due to return to him by a family arrangement, as their joint sovereign had no heir. Frederick would not agree to connect the two matters. A personal appeal by Maria Theresa had no greater success. The Prussians entered Bohemia on July 5, with Frederick at the head of the advance guard.

His plan consisted of a rapid march on Vienna by way of Olmütz and Moravia, culminating in a "good battle" which would place the capital in his hands. The operation was to be carried out by his own main army of 80,000 men, while Prince Henry with 60,000 Prussians and Saxons was entering Bohemia up one of the two banks of the Elbe. However, contrary to his expectations, the Austrians pinned themselves to their positions in the Prague area. Prince Henry did indeed succeed in storming the Mountain of Giants by surprise, but the King did not dare to push on with his offensive against Vienna and he remained stuck on the frontiers of Silesia.

Joseph II had none of the qualities of a leader, neither a cool head, nor true perseverance, nor a steadfast heart, but he was assisted by Laudon and Lascy, veterans of the Seven Years' War, who were past masters in the arts of the defensive. They covered the heights round the Elbe and the Isar with "formidable" entrenchments and transformed the center of the province into a gigantic fortified camp, taking care not to allow Frederick's maneuvers to draw them into a pitched battle. The autumn was very rainy. From September onward the roads became impassable. Along mountain paths cannon were dragged by hand; convoys failed to arrive; horses died by hundreds; every day field kitchens, hay wagons, and munition carts got stuck in some quagmire and had to be abandoned. The King tried a turning movement; while on the march he saw the battlefield of Soor once again, but after several stages he was beaten by fatigue and by the mud and had to stop. He had his revenge by "devouring" the areas occupied by his troops. In October they took up their winter quarters in a very demoralized condition.

Frederick watched the rain falling and found life insipid; his brother Ferdinand had been unwilling to take part in the campaign; Henry, who disapproved of the war, was a prey to deep melancholy and kept complaining of insomnia, vertigo, eye trouble, and nervous depression. The King was surrounded by automatons, by worn-out generals, and logically minded young officers, who criticized his dispositions and laughed up their sleeves when one of the convoys he had arranged and directed himself came to grief. The army behaved like a spiritless, grating machine. "We have fallen very low," groaned Henry, and laid the blame on his brother's despotism, which had replaced honor by servitude. He also said that he was more distrustful of the King's errors of judgment than of the enterprises of the enemy. The soldiers were drilled to the blows of a stick, beaten by noncommissioned officers, and liable to horrible punishment such as flogging: thus they were only retained by fear and hunger. In this mountainous region, cut up by forests and drenched in mists and bursts of rain, the regiments were badly fed and slackly commanded and melted away through sickness and desertion. On September 8, on Frederick's orders, the ministers, Finckenstein and Hertzberg, told the French envoy, the Marquis de Pons, that if Louis XVI could move the Austrians "to less invidious propositions" Prussia would "willingly" agree to his mediation. Frederick's offer was accepted at Vienna as it was supported by a threatening move by Russia. The King spent the winter at Breslau, "living like a rat in a hole" and covering reams of paper with his scribblings.

A congress met in March at Teschen, a large village in Austrian Silesia. It would have been difficult to have chosen a more odious and inconvenient place. "The most ordinary amenities of life are completely absent," wrote the Baron de Breteuil, the French delegate, to Vergennes. . . . "We are unsuitably lodged here. . . . The mountains drain into this town; it is difficult to get here in a carriage and quite as difficult to walk here with dry feet. . . . Deep snow surrounds us and the cold is intense. We lack provisions or at least they are scarce and bad." The powers were pretty nearly agreed to accept the plan of the French mediators, yet for two months they argued over the indemnities to be granted to the Electress of Saxony, over the revenues of the Duke of Zweibrücken, and over the admission of his signature as a "contracting" or as an "acceding party." At last everything was settled. Frederick was enchanted by the behavior of France and received the Marquis de Pons with all sorts of "courtesies," cracked a thousand and one jokes with him, and ended up with, "You have never seen My Lord the Prince von Kaunitz. Well, then, I am going to give you a glimpse of him"; and he aped the imperial chancellor by mimicking his pomposity and solemn manner. Peace was signed on May 13, Maria Theresa's birthday. Austria annexed a small portion of Bavaria called the quarter of the Inn, that is, the piece of land between the rivers Danube, Inn, and Salzach, including the town of Braunau. On the other hand, the Emperor bound himself to raise no obstacle to Brandenburg recovering the Margravates of Ansbach and Bayreuth on the extinction of the ruling branch of the family. The conclusion of the treaty was known at Berlin on the twenty-second and proclaimed to the sound of the trumpet. The authorities wished to give Frederick a state entry: he replied by refusing it, as he did not consider himself as a soldier returning home but as a defendant who had just won a suit.

At the end of the negotiations Frederick wrote to one of his agents, "All thanks for the present situation are due to France." In a review of the respective actions of the two mediating powers, he contrasted "French sagacity" with "Russian ineptitude," declared that the success obtained by Vergennes' diplomacy did infinite honor to Louis XVI, and began to dream of a new friendship with France, his favorite ally. In fact he was fully conscious that the Russian alliance could not last because Austria and Russia were bound to come together one day, willy-nilly, to

divide the carcass of the Ottoman Empire. The death of Maria
Theresa in 1780 precipitated this event: Joseph II and Catherine
immediately opened discussions upon it. Nevertheless, out of
courtesy to Russia and to give France an open proof of his good
will, Frederick joined the League of Armed Neutrality formed
by the Tsarina during the American war to compel His Britannic
Majesty's fleets to respect the trade of neutrals. As, however,
Russo-Austrian friendship grew more close, he made offers at
London and at Paris, which both powers listened to sympatheti-
cally but both politely shelved. In 1784 Henry made a journey
to Paris. His reputation, his amiability, his intelligence, his flattery of the French nation and the memory of the generous way
in which he had treated captured officers insured him an enthusiastic reception. He said on his departure, "I have spent half
my life wishing to see France, I am going to spend the other half
missing it." However, he did not bring back the desired treaty.
Nothing was left for Frederick but to search for allies inside the
Empire itself and to play the part of defender of the little states
against "Austrian despotism," as at Teschen.

Thus in defiance of the Emperor and his incalculable ally,
Russia, Frederick appealed to the independence of the princes,
to the particularism of the country, to all the disruptive forces
which retarded the unification of Germany and perpetuated its
impotence. He formed a League of Princes, the *Fürstenbund*,
the members of which engaged themselves mutually to uphold
the integrity of their possessions and their rights against the
Caesar of Vienna. To the League adhered the Elector of Hanover,
the Dukes of Saxe-Weimar, Saxe-Gotha, Zweibrücken, and
Mecklenburg, the Princes of Anhalt, the Margrave of Baden, the
Duke of Hesse, and the Bishop of Osnabrück (1785). But this was
nothing but a last resource and Frederick looked to the future
with anxiety. The great Bourbon-Hapsburg-Russian coalition
which had almost crushed him in the past had in fact nearly
come into existence again. A formal alliance with England,
which had been defeated in North America by France, was not
of itself enough to restore the balance. At least the League of
Princes gave Frederick the advantage of a revival of popularity
among the Germans: from the point of view of his legend it
would have been a pity for him to have died without having

been the idol of Germanic anarchy for just a few months. Truth to tell, the precarious position his State was in made the League of Princes a necessary expedient for him, but politically he was not nor had ever wished to be other than King of Prussia.

III

EACH summer Frederick took the waters at Landeck or Eger, and for some years they did him much good, but during the winter of 1775–76 he had eighteen attacks of gout in the feet, the knees, the hands, and the elbows, which left him weak and distorted. He could scarcely get up a few steps and he put on rouge to hide the pallor of his cheeks. In the years that followed his gout was a little less severe, but he suffered from erysipelas, bleeding hemorrhoids, colics, abscesses in the ear and on the knee, and a high fever which would not leave him. In spite of discomforts and suffering he used to get up at five o'clock in the morning and played his normal part as king. During the War of the Succession of Bavaria he once stayed on horseback ten hours at a stretch and started off again the following day. "It is not necessary for me to live," he said, "but for me to be active." In his letters he spoke of his "old carcass," his "cadaverous limbs," his "half-hoary head," his "blood which grows cold." He complained of loss of memory and loss of sight, of the difficulty of working, of having regrets "just like other men," but, he added, "this litany of infirmities does not stop me from being gay and I will keep a smiling countenance until they put me under ground."

He awaited death without the least change in his life. He looked at his pictures; he reread tattered notebooks wherein he had collected his notes on reading for the last fifty years; he returned to the books he had loved; for hours he labored on poems which he had corrected twenty times already, but he had no more illusions about his "limited" talent. He still had the delight of hearing *Mithridate, Œdipe,* and *Zaïre* played at the theater of the New Palace by Aufresne and Lekain. He imagined he heard Voltaire declaim and he wept. "A man loves to find his heart again," he said. In 1784 he was visited by an apparition from the past, Chasot, who was a septuagenarian, a married man with sons in the army as officers, and was finishing his days as governor of Lübeck, cultivating melons and inventing kitchen recipes. Could this good old soldier, this jovial fellow who talked of eatables, be Chasot the lively little Frenchman who once copied out the letters to Voltaire and played on the flute? How he had laughed in the good old days! He returned in 1785. Once again the King could say out loud the name of Rheinsberg, which was still his talisman of happiness and friendship.

Alas, these memories were too far off. "When everything in the world has been seen, when it has all been tasted, then one can make ready to leave it without regret. There is indeed little enough to lose. Youth, it is true, can be attached to life, because everything smiles on it, because its inexperience paints everything in rosy colors and it believes it will be carried on fortune's wings to the summit of its desires." But truth exposes quickly enough "the emptiness of mortal vanities. Then come reflections."

His own were in order. For two years from one courier to the next he had passed the systems of metaphysics in review with D'Alembert. He expected neither rewards nor punishments of God, for the divinity was only the order of things, the intelligence which presides over the universe, the principle of life and motion. It could neither change the laws of the world nor judge creatures which the necessities of their globe condemned to imperfection. Poor men! Despicable men! Blind, mad, and vicious gang. They did not even deserve to be instructed; it was a waste of energy to preach a truth at them of which they were not worthy. They were amused by illusions and led by lies. Yet they thought themselves free, though liberty was the privilege of the strong, of those who had the power to act or refrain from action.

As for him, he had possessed that power, he had held peace and war in his hands, he had ordered men to life and to death, he had filled the century with his name, he had enlarged Prussia and had made her name feared. The treasury was full, the people drilled to obedience, the succession assured. Yet he had only loved one of all his nephews, grandnephews, and relations, Henry, the second son of his brother William—dead at the age of nineteen and mourned for without end just as if he had been the King's own son. The other boy, the heir, was good for nothing. He had considered giving him Prince Henry as counselor and tutor, but what weight have the wishes of a monarch when he is dead? Undoubtedly for a long time past nothing got done in the kingdom except through the will and exertions of the sovereign; he had taken hold of everything, grasped upon everything. Would his successor be able to bend himself to this inhuman way of life? So much the worse for him if he could not! Let each do his own work! "If my nephew slumbers in idleness," if he lives "in negligence," if "prodigal as he is, he squanders the funds of the State and does not brace up all the faculties of his soul, I foresee that Mr. Joseph will easily get the better of him and that in thirty years from now there will be no more talk of Prussia nor of the House of Brandenburg." Might fortune spare the realm that affliction!

In August, 1785, Frederick set out for Silesia according to his usual routine. He appeared before the troops a haggard skeleton, like a specter of the wars of the past. On the twenty-fourth he made a regiment maneuver in driving rain which fell on him for several hours without his troubling to cover himself with a mantle. Next day he had an attack of fever but he refused to pay any attention to it. At Breslau he had a discussion with Professor Garve. The mass of mankind, he told him, were so much riffraff.

"But," objected Garve, "when Your Majesty arrived in the town yesterday and all the people ran to see their great king, they were not riffraff!"

"My dear fellow," replied the King, "put an old monkey on a horse, make him gallop down the streets, and the people will run up in just the same way."

Once at Potsdam, he had to stay in bed; on September 18, when he had got back to all his usual occupations, he had a stroke. His first words when he came round again were "Do not speak of it," delivered in an imperious tone. However, he could not be present at the autumn maneuvers. He spent the winter at the castle of Potsdam, less feverish and coughing badly. In the new year he received a visit from Henry but he forgot the Queen at Berlin. On April 17, 1786, he had himself taken to Sans Souci by a roundabout road and gave audience to a Frenchman called Mirabeau whom he did not like. His legs were swollen and festered. He summoned Dr. Selle, the most celebrated medical man in Berlin, to a consultation but he was a difficult patient to treat because he imagined he knew something of medicine, questioned all the remedies, and applied them in his own way.

His cough gave him no rest. On his best nights he only slept two or three hours. After midday he used to have himself hoisted onto his white horse, Condé, but after a few steps he would collapse in the saddle and he had to be seated on a bench. He dragged himself from one arm chair to the next without getting any rest and he breathed with difficulty. For a tip his guards showed him to strangers while he took the air on the terrace. The Marquis de Toulongeon hid in a thicket and saw him come forward supported by two hussars. He had on a dressing gown of crimson velvet, an old plumed hat, one leg booted and the other wrapped in damp linen. He sat "downcast, crushed by illness, his face blanched and altered by suffering," with attacks of coughing which, wrote the onlooker, "echoed even in my own chest." He remained for a few minutes in the sun and then, having probably heard a noise, had himself taken back into the castle.

He began work at four o'clock in the morning, dictated letters until seven, received General von Rohdich, governor of Potsdam, and his aides-de-camp, gave orders for the army, called for Lucchesini, Count Pinto, and Hertzberg and talked to them or had them talk to him. In the evening Voltaire's *Summary of the Age of Louis XV* was read to him. In June he summoned a doctor from Hanover, Dr. Zimmermann, whose conversation had pleased him when he had seen him some years earlier.

Zimmermann arrived on the twenty-third and was brought before the King the next morning at nine o'clock. Frederick was attended only by his hussars and a few servants. He was dressed in a very dirty jacket of blue satin and he was in boots, with the swollen leg resting on a footstool. He wore two rings with two very large brilliants on his left hand and on his right one with a green Silesian chrysoprase.

"You find me very ill," he said to the doctor.

"The eye of Your Majesty is as bright as when I had the honor of seeing it fifteen years ago. I do not observe the least diminution in the fire and vigor with which Your Majesty's eyes are animated."

"Oh, I have aged a lot and I am very ill."

"Germany and Europe do not perceive the least signs of age or of illness in Your Majesty."

"My occupations go on as usual."

"Your Majesty rises at four o'clock in the morning and thereby prolongs and doubles his life."

"I don't get up at all, as I don't go to bed any more. I spend all my nights on the arm chair where you see me now."

"Your Majesty has written to me that during the last six months his respiration has become very painful."

"I am asthmatic but I am not dropsical. Yet see how swollen my legs are."

Zimmermann examined the invalid. He had a waxen complexion, discolored and dried-up hands, legs swollen up to the thighs and full of water, a hard stomach, was very feverish, and spat blood several times a day.

"I cannot be cured?"

"Your Majesty can at least be relieved."

Zimmermann advised sedatives, which worked wonders. On his next day's visit the King scarcely allowed him to get in a word about medical matters; he spoke to him about Locke, Newton, and Hume, and questioned him on Gibbon, the author of a history of the Roman Empire which he had not read. On July 4 he felt well enough to take a ride on horseback in the park, but in proportion as his condition grew better his appetite increased. One day at dinner he had a soup seasoned with nutmeg and ginger, beef *à la russe,* that is to say, stewed in brandy, a polenta with plenty of garlic, and a huge plate of eel pasty, so spiced that it seemed as if it had been prepared in hell. "I simply taste the dishes," said he, "I only eat to fortify myself."

However, he was seized with spasms and vomitings. Some days later he had indigestion from eating meringues and then again from fresh herrings. When Zimmermann besought him to show some moderation, he began to talk to him about the League of Princes: "Germany is a kind of republic. It was in danger of losing this republican form: it has given me the most sincere pleasure to see it reëstablished." On July 10 Zimmermann took his leave. Frederick begged his pardon for having kept him from his patients, thanked him for his pains, and then raised his hat, saying, "Farewell, my dear Mr. Zimmermann, do not forget the good old man you have seen here."

For the next few days he had himself taken about in a little carriage. On August 4 his left leg began to run with pus very abundantly so that the King felt better and was able to sleep again. He slept in an easy chair without any pain, lying on his right side. He dictated the plan for the maneuvers in Silesia and he arranged the program of land reclamation for 1787 with Councilor Schultz. He was worried about the flooding of the Oder. A number of times he asked if the three hundred sheep which he had bought in Spain had arrived. On August 15 he worked as usual, but his signature was almost illegible. On the sixteenth he fell into a kind of stupor. In a moment of lucidity he called General Rohdich and tried to give him the password but could not speak. That evening he walked a few paces held up by his hussars and then he dozed off. His extremities began to grow cold. His greyhound bitch was trembling beside him: he had its covering rearranged, asked the time, and began to rattle in his throat. Two menservants took turns at holding him in an upright position to help him to breathe. After a spasm of coughing he murmured, "The mountain is passed, we shall do better. . . ." In a room near by were Hertzberg, Selle, and two aides-de-camp. At twenty past two Frederick died quietly and without convulsions in the arms of his hussars. Hertzberg closed his eyes. The new King arrived almost at once and the garrison of Berlin took the oath that very day.

"Everything is dismal," wrote Mirabeau, "nothing is sad; everyone is busy, no one is afflicted. Not a face which does not express relaxation and hope, not a regret, not a sigh, not a word of praise. So many battles won, such glory, and a reign of nearly half a century so full of mighty deeds lead only then to this? Everyone wished for it to end. Everyone rejoices at it."

IV

FREDERICK had asked to be buried under the terrace at Sans Souci among his dogs. His body was carried to the chapel of the garrison where his father's was already lying.

It is a large rectangular hall in gray and white, with two galleries of gilded woodwork one above the other. Crystal candle lusters and stacks of flags upheld by eagles are its only ornament. The entrance to the crypt is in the middle of one of the longer sides, behind the altar, under a twisted pulpit which rests on a triangle surrounded with rays of the sun. The crypt is small and icy cold. On Frederick's tomb is a crown of laurel leaves in gold. It was placed there on March 21, 1933, by Field Marshal Paul von Beneckendorff und Hindenburg, after Hitler, as chancellor, had stepped before the King's coffin to proclaim the birth of the Third Reich.

BIBLIOGRAPHICAL NOTE

THE literature of Frederick is almost as extensive as that of Napoleon. As many of the works used in the course of this book are in German or French or else little known to the English public, a summary bibliography of the whole subject is given here.

For a complete survey reference should be made to Dahlmann-Waitz, *Quellenkunde der deutschen Geschichte* (9th ed., 2 vols., 8°) edited by Hermann Haering, 1931–32. To bring this up to date consult the *Jahresberichte für deutsche Geschichte* (Leipzig).

Bruno Gebhardt's *Handbuch der deutschen Geschichte* includes a summary catalogue of events, bibliographies, and critical notes (7th ed., 2 vols., 8°) edited by R. Holtzmann, 1930–31.

In French under the general title of "L'Allemagne de 1648 à 1806" Albert Waddington has written two critical articles in the *Revue de synthèse historique* (Paris, Vol. 18, 1909), which consider all the sources for the history of Frederick's reign; in spite of their date it is worth while referring to them in order to begin one's acquaintance with German historical literature and the manuscript sources. Lastly the *Bulletin de la société des professeurs d'histoire et de géographie* has published four bibliographical articles on Prussia in the eighteenth century by Pagès and Lhéritier; Nos. 65 (November, 1930), 85 (November, 1935), 89 (November, 1936), and 90 (January, 1937).

FREDERICK'S WORKS

Frederick's own writings are still the most important source. A bibliography of his literary works, including translations and apocryphal works, appears in the *Miszellaneen zur Geschichte Koenig Friedrichs des Grossen,* published at the instigation and with the assistance of the keepers of the Royal Archives of Prussia (Berlin, 1878, 8°).

The basic collection is the *Œuvres de Frédéric le Grand,* imprimerie royale (R. Decker), 30 volumes and an atlas, which came out from 1846 to 1857 under the direction of J. D. E. Preuss. There was a de luxe edition in quarto distributed by the King of Prussia, but the normal edition is in octavo (see Sainte-Beuve, *Causeries du Lundi,* Vols. 3 and 7).

However, the edition of Preuss does not fully live up to the original design of its editor. Not only has Preuss omitted all political and military correspondence but he has made numerous cuts and has not been sufficiently critical in his treatment of the text. That is why the *Œuvres* must be supplemented by a large number of other publications. Of these the most important is the *Politische Korrespondenz* which began being published in 1879 (Berlin, 8°) under the direction of J. G. Droysen, and has reached its 44th volume under G. B. Volz. As a supplement to the correspondence in 1920 the same editor gave us the political testaments, only parts of which were available under the monarchy (*Die politischen Testamente F.d.G.*, Berlin, 8°).

Another very important source is the correspondence between the Margravine Wilhelmina of Bayreuth and her brother. There are 347 items in the edition of Preuss and 528 in that of G. B. Volz and F. von Oppeln-Bronikowski (*Friedrich der Grosse und Wilhelmina von Bayreuth,* 2 vols., Leipzig, 1924, 8°). The editors have translated the correspondence from its original French into German. The late Professor Volz was good enough to send me the original text of the letters I have quoted, and I am deeply indebted to him for this.

To these may be added Frederick's correspondence with his friends the Borckes (*Briefe F.d.G. . . . an die Gebrüder Friedrich Wilhelm und Friedrich Ludwig von Borcke,* an octavo pamphlet, Potsdam, 1881); with Grumbkow and Maupertuis (*Briefwechsel F.d.G. mit Grumbkow und Maupertuis, 1731–59,* edited by R. Koser in "Publikationen aus den koeniglichen preussischen Staatsarchiven," Vol. 72, Leipzig, 1898, 8°); with King Stanislas of Poland (*Correspondance inédite de Stanislas Leszczynski . . . avec les rois de Prusse Frédéric-Guillaume Ier et Frédéric II,* edited by Pierre Boyé, 1906, 8°); with Voltaire (*Briefwechsel F.d.G. mit Voltaire,* edited by R. Koser and H. Droysen in "Publications of the Prussian Archives," Vols. 81, 82, 86, in 1908, 1909, 1911, with a supplement on the Voltaire-Maupertuis dispute, Vol. 90, 1917); with the Princes of Anhalt-Dessau (edited by O. Krauske in *Forschungen zur brandenburgischen und preussischen Geschichte,* Vol. 7, Leipzig, 1894); with his valet Fredersdorff (*Die Briefe F.d.G. an seinen vormaligen Kammerdiener F.,* edited by J. Richter, Berlin, 1926, 8°); with his doctors (*F.d.G. Korrespondenz mit Aerzten,* edited by G. L. Mamlock, Stuttgart, 1907, 8°).

The journal kept by Crown Prince Frederick during the campaign of 1734 has been published by R. Koser in *Forschungen z.b.u.p.G.* (Vol. 4, 1891), and the 1746 version of the *Histoire de mon temps* by Max Posner in the "Publications of the Prussian Archives" (Vol. 4, 1879).

As it is not always easy to get hold of Preuss's edition of the Works, it is worth mentioning that under the title of *Mémoires de Frédéric II, roi de Prusse* (2 vols., Paris, 1866, 8°) Boutaric and Campardon have issued all together the *History of My Times,* the *History of the Seven Years' War,* and the *Memoirs* from the peace of Hubertsburg to the end of 1778.

ITINERARY. Nothing is more useful for the biography of Frederick than a knowledge of his movements and his public acts. Reference should be made to H. Droysen, "Tageskalender F.d.G." (Part I, 1732–40, *Forschungen z.b.u.p.G.,* Vol. 25, 1913; Part II, 1740–63, *ibid.,* Vol. 29, 1916).

MEMOIRS

Frederick's remarkable character dominated his age and hypnotized his contemporaries. All who came in contact with him felt the urge to depict him, to describe his life and study his methods.

First came the memoirs of his brothers, sisters, sister-in-law, niece, and nephew, which raise delicate personal problems and have not all been published in full: the *Mémoires* of Wilhelmina, Margravine of Bayreuth, which go up to 1742 (first ed., 1810, Brunswick, in 2 vols., translation, London, 1812, both frequently reissued since that time); those of Ulrica, Queen of Sweden (written in French and edited in Swedish by R. M. Klinkowström, as an appendix to the collection of speeches and historical writings of Field Marshal Axel de Fersen (7 books in 4 vols., Stockholm, 1867–72, 8°). A large number of letters from the Queen to her relations in Prussia have been edited by Fritz Arnheim, *Luise Ulrike, die schwedische Schwester F.d.G.* (2 vols., Gotha, 1909–10, 8°). Numerous quotations of the original French version occur in O. G. von Heidenstam's *Une Sœur du grand Frédéric*, Paris, 1897, 8°); the French diary of Prince Henry's wife, Wilhelmina (edited by E. Berner and G. B. Volz, in Vol. 9, of E. Berner's series "Quellen und Untersuchungen zur Geschichte des Hauses Hohenzollern," under the general title of *Aus der Zeit des siebenjährigen Krieges* (1908, 8°), along with letters from Prince Augustus William to his sister-in-law and letters from Queen Elisabeth to her brother, the Duke of Brunswick); the brief memoirs of Princess Wilhelmina of Orange (*Erinnerungen der Prinzessin W.v.O. an den Hof F.d.G., 1751–67* by G. B. Volz, *ibid.*, Vol. 7, 1903); the notebooks of Duke Ferdinand of Brunswick (*Tagebücher des Herzogs Ferdinand von Braunschweig, 1756–66*, short extracts from which have been published by H. Bornowski in *Forschungen z.b.u.p.G.*, Vol. 12, 1899).

Reference may also be made to an article by Albert Naudé, "Aus ungedruckten Memoiren der Brüder F.d.G." (*Forschungen z.b.u.p.G.*, Vol. 1, 1888), to one by Otto Hermann, "F.d.G. im Spiegel seines Bruders Heinrich" (*Historische Vierteljahrsschrift*, Vol. 26, 1931–32), and finally to one by R. Tabournel, "Considérations sur la guerre de sept ans," an unpublished work by Prince Henry of Prussia (*Revue historique*, Paris, 1902).

From among the King's servants and dignitaries of the Court, the Queen's second chamberlain, Count E. A. H. von Lehndorff, kept a diary in French, which has been translated into German and edited by Karl Eduard Schmidt-Loetzen under the title of *Dreissig Jahre am Hofe F.d.G., 1750–75* (Gotha, 1907, 8°), but the text is abridged and expurgated. The portions omitted are the subject of two supplementary volumes which go up to 1784 (*Nachträge*, 1910 and 1921). Henri de Catt, the reader, kept a diary and made notes of his conversations with the King during the Seven Years' War (*Mes Entretiens avec Frédéric le Grand*, edited by Reinhold Koser, "Publications of the Prussian Archives," Vol. 22, 1884, translated by F. S. Flint as *Frederick the Great: the Memoirs of His Reader Henri de Catt*, London, 1916, 8°). Another reader, Dantal, has done the same thing for the years 1784–86 (*Les Délassements littéraires ou heures de lecteur de Frédéric*, Elbing, 1791, 8°). One degree lower comes the sincere Schoening, hussar and valet (*Friedrich der zweite, ueber seine Person und sein Privatleben*, Berlin, 1808).

Among literary friends and Academicians of Berlin first comes Voltaire, who was ready to flatter and bite by turns, not only in his *Vie privée du roi de Prusse* (1759) (or even in his *Mémoires pour servir à la vie de M. de Voltaire,* in Vol. 1 of the Moland edition of his complete works—which were previously translated, London, 1784, 8°) but throughout his correspondence, varying from day to day; then comes Bielfeld (*Lettres familières et autres,* 2 vols., La Haye, 1763, 12°; and translated, 4 vols., London, 1768–70, 12°); Pöllnitz (*Mémoires pour servir à l'histoire des quatre derniers souverains de la maison de Brandebourg,* 2 vols., Berlin, 1791, 12°); Formey (*Souvenirs d'un citoyen,* 2 vols., 1789, 12°); Dieudonné Thiébault (*Mes Souvenirs de vingt ans de séjour à Berlin,* 1st ed. Paris, 5 vols., 1804; and London, as *Original Anecdotes of Frederick the Second,* 2 vols., 1805, 8°; it was reissued a large number of times with additions which are more or less suspect); the Abbé Denina (*Essai sur la vie et le règne de Frédéric II,* Berlin, 1788, 8°, and also his *La Prusse littéraire sous Frédéric II,* 3 vols., 1790–91, 8°—a very useful catalogue); the Marquis Lucchesini, who Mirabeau said was not a friend of Frederick's but a man who listened to him (*Das Tagebuch des Marchese Lucchesini,* 1780–82; in Italian, edited by F. von Oppeln-Bronikowski and G. B. Volz in "Romanische Bücherei," 1926, 12°).

Dr. Zimmermann, who attended the King during his last illness, has left some memoirs, *Über F.d.G. und meine Unterredungen mit ihm kurz vor seinem Tode* (Carlsruhe, 1788, 8°), with an English translation (*Dr. Z.'s Conversations with the Late King of Prussia,* London, 1791, 8°).

Among officials, E. F. von Hertzberg, *Mémoire historique sur la dernière année de la vie privée de Frédéric II, roi de Prusse* (Berlin, 1787, 8°); the memoirs of President C. C. W. von Dohm, *Denkwürdigkeiten meiner Zeit* (5 vols., Lemgo, 1814–19, 8°), where personal reminiscences are worked into a general account.

Among ambassadors accredited to Berlin, *Mémoires des négociations du marquis de Valori,* edited by his descendant, Count H. de Valori (2 vols., Paris, 1820, 8°), and *Memoirs and Papers of Sir Andrew Mitchell,* edited by Andrew Bisset (2 vols., London, 1850, 8°).

Among visitors who pressed to see old Fritz in his glory after the Seven Years' War there is D'Alembert ("Frédéric le Grand d'après des lettres inédites de d'Alembert à Mlle. de Lespinasse," *Revue historique,* Vol. 26, 1884, and G. Maugras, *Trois Mois à la cour de Frédéric: Lettres inédites de d'Alembert,* Paris, 1886, 8°); Guibert (*Journal d'un voyage en Allemagne fait en 1773,* 2 vols., Paris, 1803, 8°, and his *Eloge du roi de Prusse,* London, 1787, 8°); the Prince de Ligne (*Mémoire sur le roi de Prusse,* an octavo pamphlet, Berlin, 1789, and his *Mélanges,* Vols. 6, 7, Dresden, 1795–1805, 12°); the Comte L. P. de Ségur (*Mémoires,* 3 vols., Paris, 1824–26, 8°; translation, London, 1825–27; *Memoirs and Recollections of Count Ségur*); the Marquis de Bouillé du Chariol (*Mémoires sur la révolution française,* new ed. Paris, 1821, 8°; translation, London, 1797, 8°); the Marquis de Toulongeon (*Une Mission militaire en Prusse en 1786,* edited by Finot and Galmiche-Bouvier, Paris, 1881, 12°); the Duc de Lévis (unpublished letters reproduced in the *Revue de France,* July 15, 1929). Goethe visited Sans

Souci in the King's absence (see his letters to Merk of August 5, 1778, and of November 14, 1781).

There are innumerable anecdotes about Frederick—for the best of these refer to Koser's biography, Vol. 4 (see below). This volume classifies the accounts of contemporaries and the King's earliest historians. The most reliable anecdotes are recounted either by the geographer, A. F. Büsching (*Charakter F.d. zweiten,* 2d ed., Halle, 1788, 8°, a translation of which was issued the same year in French at Berne, 2 vols. in 1, 8°, and *Zuverlässige Beiträge zu der Regierungsgeschichte Koenigs F. II,* Hamburg, 1790, 8°); or by the librarian and author, Christopher Frederick Nicolaï (*Anekdoten von Koenig F. II,* 6 pamphlets, Berlin und Stettin, 1788–92, 8°); or by J. C. T. de Laveaux in the fourth and last volume of his *Vie de Frédéric II, roi de Prusse* (a compilation published anonymously, 7 vols., Strassburg, 1788, 8°); or by S. F. Bourdais (*Portrait de Frédéric le Grand,* Lausanne and Paris, 1788, 12°).

G. B. Volz has collected these descriptions, portraits, and judgments relating to the King and translated them into German under the title of *F.d.G. im Spiegel seiner Zeit* (3 vols., 1926–27, 8°).

BIOGRAPHIES

The moment the King died his life and reign became a subject to be recorded. The best known of these writings is Mirabeau's *De la Monarchie prussienne sous Frédéric le Grand,* which came out in 1788. It is the work of a physiocrat who admired the King but criticized his economic policy harshly. Since then interpretations of Frederick have varied greatly. The vicissitudes of his fame follow the same curve as the vicissitudes of the Hohenzollern dynasty, of Prussia, and of Germany. A graph of this is given by Veit Valentin, "Some Interpretations of Frederick the Great" (*History,* September, 1934).

To pass over the bold portrait painted by Macaulay in his *Critical and Historical Essays* (new ed. London, 1852) and Carlyle's six volumes, it is interesting to run through Franz Kugler's popular work, *Geschichte Friedrichs des Grossen* (1840, 8°; translation, London, 1844), less for its text than for Menzel's famous woodcut illustrations, which crystallized the legendary Frederick in the same way as Charlot and Raffet popularized the epic of Napoleon. Kugler's book with its illustrations was reissued on the occasion of the 150th anniversary of Frederick's death (Leipzig, 1936, 8°).

The biography of J. D. E. Preuss will always be very valuable because of the large number of original documents it contains (*Friedrich der Grosse, eine Lebensgeschichte,* 10 vols., Berlin, 1832–34, 8°).

The most important work is Reinhold Koser's *Geschichte Friedrichs des Grossen* (4 vols., latest ed. Berlin, 1921, 8°). In actual fact Koser's work is more than a biography, and much more the history of Prussia under Frederick than that of Frederick himself.

On the other hand, L. Paul-Dubois, *Frédéric le Grand d'après sa cor-*

respondance politique (Paris, 1903, 8°, originally two articles in the *Revue de deux mondes,* July 15 and August 1, 1902) had produced a psychological study based on wide research.

Arnold Berney, *Friedrich der Grosse, Entwicklungsgeschichte eines Staatsmannes* (1934, 8°), takes Frederick up to the Seven Years' War.

For the 150th anniversary of the King's death Gerhard Ritter published the course of lectures he gave at Freiburg University (*Friedrich der Grosse: Ein historisches Profil,* Leipzig, 1936, small 8°) and Walter Elze, professor at the University of Berlin, published a *Friedrich der Grosse* with the subtitle of *Geistige Welt, Schicksal, Taten* (Berlin, 1936, 8°), which deals particularly with military history and contains extremely clear plans of battles.

Under the title *Fridericus* W. Hegemann published fictitious conversations on Frederick and his place in German history (Berlin, 1924, 781 pp., 12°). A shorter version was translated as *Frederick the Great* (London, 1929, 8°), and as an exile in France he has brought out the substance of this discussion as *Le Grand Frédéric* (Paris, 1934, 12°).

Among all popular works only W. Wiegand's *Friedrich der Grosse,* "Monographien zur Weltgeschichte," No. 15, need be mentioned (Leipzig, last ed. 1922, 8°); it is very fully and finely illustrated.

PERSONAL LIFE

YOUTH. SOURCES. The documents of his trial were printed for the first time in 1936 by Carl Hinrichs, *Der Kronprinzenprozess, Friedrich und Katte* (Hamburg, 8°). Queen Sophia Dorothea's letters quoted in the present volume were edited by H. Droysen, "Aus den Briefen der Koenigin Sophie-Dorothea" (*Hohenzollern-Jahrbuch,* Vol. 17, 1913). Frederick William's correspondence with old Dessau is edited by O. Krauske as a supplement to the collection of the *Acta Borussica* (1905, 8°). Baron Seckendorff's "Journal secret" has appeared as an appendix to the memoirs of the Margravine of Bayreuth (Tübingen ed., 1811). There are also the reminiscences of the two clergymen, *Sieben Tage am Hofe F.W.I. Tagebuch des Professors J. A. Freylinghausen,* edited by B. Krieger (Berlin, 1900, 8°), and those of Francke in G. Kramer's *Beitraege zur Geschichte A. H. Franckes* (Halle, 1861, 8°). The references taken from the Saxon correspondence are to be found in Carl von Weber, *Aus vier Jahrhunderten, Mitteilungen aus dem Haupt-Staats Archiv zu Dresden* (new series, Leipzig, 1857–61, 4 vols., 8°). F. C. Foerster's old work, the only biography of the soldier king that exists, contains a large number of documents in the appendix to prove his case (*F. W. Koenig von Preussen,* 3 vols., Potsdam, 1834–35, 8°).

WORKS. The best beyond all comparison are Ernest Lavisse's two works, *La Jeunesse du Grand Frédéric* (Paris, and translation, London, both 1891, 8°) and *Le Grand Frédéric avant l'avènement* (Paris, 1893, 8°), which render all mention of earlier works quite unnecessary. To these need only be added the lengthy article by Krauske on the Court of Frederick William I (*Hohenzollern-Jahrbuch,* Vol. 5, 1901); one by Koser, "Aus den letzten

Tagen Koenig F.W.I." (*ibid.*, No. 8, 1904); one by G. B. Volz, "Die Krisis in der Jugend F.d.G." (*Historische Zeitschrift*, Vol. 118, 1917); one by H. Droysen, "Graf Seckendorff und Kronprinz Friedrich" (*Forschungen z.b.u.p.G.*, Vol. 28, 1915); one by F. Meinecke, "Des Kronpr. Friedr. Considérations sur l'état présent du corps politique de l'Europe" (*Historische Zeitschrift*, Vol. 117, 1917). Last comes F. Arnheim's book, *Der Hof F.d.G.* ("Der Hof des Kronprinzen," Vol. 1, Berlin, 1912, 8°).

PHILOSOPHICAL IDEAS AND LITERARY TASTES. In addition to Frederick's works already mentioned above there are his marginal notes to the *Considérations* of Montesquieu. Frederick's copy fell into Napoleon's hands at Potsdam in 1806 and was lent to Mollien, who copied out the notes in it. The edition by Louis Vian (Paris, 1879, 12°) is based on his copy.

The catalogue of Frederick's first library is given by Bratuscheck, *Die Erziehung F.d.G.* (Berlin, 1885, 8°), the catalogue of his later collections is to be found in the first two of three articles by Krieger in the *Hohenzollern-Jahrbuch* (Vol. 15, 1911, and Vol. 16, 1912). The third, appearing in 1913, deals with his readers and his literary correspondence.

G. Pariset's thesis, *L'Etat et les églises en Prusse sous Frédéric-Guillaume Ier* (Paris, 1897, 8°) is indispensable for a real understanding of the religious and philosophic atmosphere in which Frederick grew up. L. Lévy-Bruhl's little volume, *L'Allemagne depuis Leibniz* (Paris, 1890, 8°) is as valuable as ever. The most important study in German is W. Dilthey, "F.d.G. und die deutsche Aufklaerung" (*Studien zur Geschichte des deutschen Geistes*, 3 vols., Berlin, 1907, 8°), which should be supplemented by E. Zeller's old book, *F.d.G. als Philosoph* (Berlin, 1886, 8°), H. Droysen's article on his relations with Wolff, "Friedrich-Wilhelm, F.d.G. und der Philosoph Ch. Wolff" (*Forschungen z.b.u.p.G.*, Vol. 23, 1910), W. von Sommerfeld's article, "Die philosophische Entwicklung des Kronprinzen F." (*ibid.*, Vol. 31, 1919), Arnold Berney's article "Ueber das geschichtliche Denken F.d.G." (*Historische Zeitschrift*, Vol. 150, 1934), and finally W. Langer's important thesis, *F.d.G. und die geistige Welt Frankreichs* ("Publications of the Seminar für romanische Sprachen und Kultur," Hamburg, Vol. 22, 1932).

Frederick's relations with Voltaire naturally occupy an important place in all biographies of Voltaire, especially in the one written by André Bellessort (Paris, 1925). There is an old book by Le Brisoys Desnoiresterres, *Voltaire et Frédéric* (1870), and the whole story has been retold by Emile Henriot in *Voltaire et Frédéric II* (Paris, 1927, 8°). Add to these F. Baldensperger, "Les Prémices d'une douteuse amitié, Voltaire et Frédéric de 1740 à 1742" (*Revue de littérature comparée*, Paris, 1930, 8°), and R. Koser, "Voltaire als Kritiker der Œuvres du Philosophe de Sans-Souci" (*Hohenzollern-Jahrbuch*, Vol. 10, 1906).

ICONOGRAPHY AND THE ARTS. Two articles in the *Hohenzollern-Jahrbuch* (Vol. 1, 1897) give the main points on Frederick's appearance and his portraits: one is by R. Koser, "Die äussere Erscheinung F.d.G.," the other by P. Seidel, "Die Bildnisse F.d.G." Most of the relics of Frederick, clothes, shirts, flutes, snuff boxes, etc., are preserved at the Hohenzollern Museum, at the castle of Monbijou.

The castles and suites occupied by Frederick have undergone numerous transformations. Many of the rooms have been destroyed or redecorated; even the room in which he died at Sans Souci has not been spared. As for Rheinsberg, it was lived in by Prince Henry. The most valuable contemporary descriptions are as follows: C. W. Hennert, *Beschreibung des Lustschlosses und Gartens des Prinzen Heinrichs zu Reinsberg* (Berlin, 1778, 8°); C. F. Nicolaï, *Beschreibung der koeniglichen Residenzstaedte Berlin und Potsdam* (three eds., 1769, 1779, 1786, the second in 2 vols., the last in 3, all 8°), which was abridged as the little *Guide de Berlin, de Potsdam, et des environs* (Berlin, 1793, 8°); M. Oesterreich, *Description de tout l'intérieur des deux palais de Sans Souci* (Potsdam, 1773, 4°), and *Beschreibung der koeniglichen Bildergallerie und des Kabinetts im Sans-Souci* (2d ed., 1770, 8°). The German museums sell English guides with good photographs, one of *Potsdam, Palaces, and Gardens* by B. Meier, and one of *The Palace of Sans Souci* by P. G. Hübner.

A part of Frederick's collection of pictures was to be seen at the Paris Exhibition of 1900 (*Die Kunstsammlung F.d.G. auf der pariser Weltausstellung*, 1900, 12°), and at the Exhibition of French Art in 1937.

Paul Seidel, the keeper of the royal museums, has devoted his life to the study of art in Frederick's times. His writings are authoritative. Many of them have appeared superbly illustrated in the *Hohenzollern-Jahrbuch*, of which he was the editor. It is simpler to refer to his basic work, *F.d.G. und die bildende Kunst* (latest ed. Berlin and Leipzig, 1922, 8°).

Pesne is the subject of a study and a catalogue by Pierre du Colombier in L. Dimier's *Les Peintres français du dix-huitième siècle* (Vol. 2, 1930, 4°), which may be completed by the catalogue of the exhibition organized at the royal palace at Berlin in 1933 for the painter's 250th anniversary (Antoine Pesne, *Ausstellung . . .*, with a note by Director Gall).

Frederick as a musician is dealt with by Georg Thouret, *F.d.G. als Musikfreund und Musiker* (Leipzig, 1898, 8°).

FREDERICK'S CIRCLE. The old but very copious work of Preuss, *F.d.G. mit seinen Verwandten und Freunden* (Berlin, 1838, 8°), is the only one to cover the whole of the King's life. All those who came in contact with him have been the object of detailed studies, among which may be cited the series by G. B. Volz, "F.d.G. und seine Leute" (*Hohenzollern-Jahrbuch*, 1907–8 and 1910–11), dealing with Winterfeldt, the Schwerins, Jordan, Madame de Wreech, etc., and Elsie Johnston, *Le Marquis d'Argens* (University doctoral thesis, Paris, 1928, 8°).

For Barberina see J. J. Olivier and Willy Norbert, *Barberina Campanini* (1721–99), (Berlin, 1909, 8°; in French, Paris, 1910, 8°), and G. B. Volz, "Die Barberina Legende" (*Aus der Welt F.d.G.*, Dresden, 1922).

For all the persons around the King reference can be made to the well-known *Allgemeine deutsche Biographie*, published by the Munich Academy of Sciences between 1875 and 1912; its articles are very reliable and it runs to 56 octavo volumes.

FREDERICK AS KING

The position occupied by Frederick makes it necessary to cite a good half of the political histories which deal with Europe in the eighteenth century. Therefore only summary indications, heads of chapters, and works which have been found particularly useful will be given.

Not to mention the classical histories of Prussia and Germany (Ranke, Droysen, Lamprecht) or general histories of a more or less recent date (*The Cambridge Modern History,* Lavisse et Rambaud, Oncken, *Propylaeen-Weltgeschichte,* etc.), the French public has at its disposal Halphen and Sagnac's "Peuples et civilisations," Vol. 2 by P. Muret, *La Prépondérance anglaise* (Paris, 1937, 8°). This covers the period 1715–63 and incorporates the most recent research.

Albert Waddington's *Histoire de Prusse* (two octavo volumes have appeared, 1911 and 1922) stops at Frederick's accession to the throne. A. Himly's work, *Histoire de la formation territoriale des états de l'Europe centrale* (2 vols., Paris, 1876, 8°), gives a good short account.

GOVERNMENT AND ADMINISTRATION. SOURCES. The essential documents are to be found in two great octavo collections, the *Acta Borussica, Denkmaeler der preussischen Staatsverwaltung, im 18. Jahrhundert,* and the *Publikationen aus den koeniglichen preussischen Staatsarchiven.*

The *Acta Borussica* includes a general section, "Die Behoerdenorganisation und die allgemeine Staatsverwaltung," in 15 volumes from 1701 to 1772, successively edited by G. Schmoller, O. Krauske, O. Hintze, and various collaborators (1892–1902). In Vol. 6 there is a monumental description of the State under Frederick by Otto Hintze (1901). Beginning in the same volume the acts of the reign are also printed here.

Another section is devoted to different branches of the administration: the silk industry by G. Schmoller and O. Hintze (3 vols., 1892, 8°); the trade in grain stocks for war purposes in two volumes with an introduction, statistics, and documents for the period 1740–1806 by W. Naudé, G. Schmoller, and A. Skalweit (1906 and 1910); the monetary system in four volumes with a sketch by F. von Schroetter (1904–13).

In the "Publications of the Prussian Archives" referred to above, see M. Lehmann, *Preussen und die katholische Kirche seit 1640* (Vols. 10, 13, 18, and 24 of the series deal with Frederick's reign); R. Stadelmann, *Preussens Koenige in ihrer Taetigkeit für die Landeskultur* (Vol. 2 of the series deals with Frederick's reign); M. Baer, *Westpreussen unter F.d.G.* (Vols. 83 and 84 of the series). The volumes contain both original documents quoted entire, abstracts, and studies, often of great length, e.g., 240 pp. by R. Stadelmann and a complete volume by M. Baer.

La Haye de Launay himself wrote a defense of the French system of the

Excise Department in answer to Mirabeau, *Justification du système d'économie politique et financière de Frédéric II* (n.d., 8°).

WORKS. On the question of enlightened despotism reference should be made to two articles which appeared under the same title—"Die Epochen der absoluten Monarchie in der neueren Geschichte"—in the *Historische Zeitschrift*, the first by R. Koser in 1889 (Vol. 61), the second by Fritz Hartung in 1931 (Vol. 145). Furthermore the latest state of historical studies can be discovered by referring to the inquiry of the International Committee of Historical Sciences which came out from 1930 to 1937 in Nos. 9, 20, 34, and 35 of its Bulletin. The German report by Fritz Hartung is to be found in No. 34 (March, 1937), and the general report by Michel Lhéritier in No. 35 (June, 1937).

Pariset's thesis (see above) contains a very clear account of the political and administrative organization of the Prussian State at Frederick's accession to the throne. L. Dorn, "The Prussian Bureaucracy in the Eighteenth Century" (*Political Science Quarterly*, Vols. 46 and 47, 1931 and 1932) is a study less of the institutions than of the working of various pieces of administrative machinery. It should be supplemented by Lehmann, "Der Ursprung des preussischen Kabinetts" (*Historische Zeitschrift*, Vol. 63, 1889), by M. Hass, "F.d.G. und seine Kammerpraesidenten" (*Festschrift zu G. Schmollers 70. Geburtstag*, Leipzig, 1908, 8°), and, on the way in which Frederick was taken in, by E. Pfeiffer, *Die Revuereisen F.d.G. und der Zustand Schlesiens* ("Historische Studien," edited by E. Ebering, Vol. 44, 1904).

There is an excellent short account by a legal writer which gives a general view of Frederick's economic policy—Anton Zottmann, "Die Wirtschaftspolitik F.d.G." (*Gesellschaftswissenschaftliche Abhandlungen*, Vol. 8, Leipzig and Vienna, 1937, 182 pp., 8°). For more detailed studies refer to the works which follow.

On Silesia, C. Grünhagen, *Schlesien unter F.d.G.* (2 vols., Breslau, 1889–92, 8°), and the huge, overpowering work of Hermann Fechner, *Wirtschaftsgeschichte der preussischen Provinz Schlesien in der Zeit ihrer provinziellen Selbststaendigkeit, 1741–1806* (Breslau, 1907, 8°). The author maintains against Schmoller and his school that Frederick's mercantilist policy did Silesia more harm than good.

On the Excise Department, Walther Schultze, *Geschichte der preussischen Regieverwaltung* (Vol. 1, the only one to have been issued, stops at 1770), which is Vol. 7 of the "Staats- und sozialwissenschaftliche Forschungen" (edited by G. Schmoller, Leipzig, 1888, 8°), G. Schmoller, "Die Einführung der franzoesischen Regie durch F.d.G." (*Koenigliche Akademie der Wissenschaften, Berlin, Sitzungsberichte*, 1888, Part IV, and *Deutsche Rundschau*, April, 1888), E. P. Reimann, *Das Tabaksmonopol F.d.G.* (Berlin, 1913, 8°).

On the finances, G. Schmoller, "Die Epochen der preuss. Finanzpolitik" (*Jahrbuch für Gesetzgebung, Verwaltung, etc.*, Leipzig, 1877), and the two articles by R. Koser on the finances during and after the Seven Years' War (*Forschungen z.b.u.p.G.*, Vols. 13 and 16, 1900 and 1903).

On judicial reform, O. Hintze, "Preussens Entwicklung zum Rechtsstaat" (*Forschungen z.b.u.p.G.*, Vol. 32, 1920), M. Springer, *Die Coccejische Justizreform* (Munich, 1914), R. Koser, "Die Abschaffung der Tortur durch F.d.G." (*Forschungen z.b.u.p.G.*, Vol. 6, 1892). On the trials of Miller Arnold, see K. Dickel, *Beträge zum preussischen Rechte, F.d.G. und die Prozesse des Müllers Arnold* (Marburg, 1891), with the articles by Holtze and by Graner in *Forschungen z.b.u.p.G.* (Vol. 17, 1904, and Vol. 38, 1926).

On the peasants, Henri Sée, *Esquisse d'une histoire du régime agraire en Europe aux dix-huitième et dix-neuvième siècles* (Paris, 1921, 8°), G. Cavaignac, "L'Etat social en Prusse jusqu'à l'avènement de F.-Guillaume III: Les populations rurales et le servage" (*Revue historique,* Vol. 42, 1890), O. Hintze, "Zur Agrarpolitik F.d.G." (*Forschungen z.b.u.p.G.*, Vol. 10, 1898), A. Skalweit, "Agrarpolitik F.d.G." (*ibid.,* Vol. 21, 1908).

For population statistics I have made use of R. Koser's figures in his "Zur Bevoelkerungsstatistik des preussischen Staats" (*Forschungen z.b.u.p.G.*, Vol. 7, 1894).

At the beginning of his *Geschichte des preussischen Staatswesens vom Tode F.d.G. bis zu den Freiheitskriegen* (2 vols., Leipzig, 1880–82, 8°) Martin Philippson has painted a somber enough picture of the state of Prussia at Frederick's death. The work started a controversy following which the author left Germany.

FOREIGN POLICY. SOURCES. In addition to the sources already mentioned (*Politische Korrespondenz,* Valori, Mitchell) there are the collections of propaganda, manifestoes, and declarations given out by the Prussian cabinet, *Preussische Staatsschriften aus der Regierungszeit Koenig F. II* (3 vols., Berlin, 1877–92, 8°), edited by J. G. Droysen and M. W. Duncker, the sequel to which is the *Recueil des déductions, manifestes, déclarations, traités, et autres actes et écrits publics, qui ont été rédigés et publiés par le ministre d'état, comte de Hertzberg depuis l'année 1756 jusqu'à l'année 1790* (3 vols., Berlin, 1789–95, 8°).

For France, it is always useful to refer to the relevant volumes of the twenty-six comprising the "Recueil des instructions données aux ambassadeurs de 1648 à 1789" (*Prussia,* by A. Waddington, 1901), and for England to those of the seven-volume *British Diplomatic Instructions* published from 1922 on.

WORKS. For the whole period the German public has at its disposal, in Below and Meinecke's *Handbuch der mittelalterlichen und neueren Geschichte,* a full summary by M. Immich, "Geschichte des europaeischen Staatensystems von 1660 bis 1789" Munich and Berlin, 1905, 8°), while the French public has Emile Bourgeois' classic, the *Manuel historique de politique étrangère* (Vol. 1, latest ed., 1926, 12°). It is half a century since

J. G. Droysen in his *Geschichte der Preussischen Politik* laid down the famous theory of Prussia's mission in Germany from its political standpoint. In spite of his preconceived ideas, his rank prejudices, and his obscure and ill-digested style, the work is one of those which no one can afford to neglect (5 vols., Berlin, 1855–86, 8°).

However, there is no doubt (see a critical article by P. Muret in the January-February number of the *Revue d'histoire moderne* for 1932) that the history of the eighteenth century has too often been considered as a mere expression of the rivalry between Frederick and Maria Theresa, whose vicissitudes throw other problems into the shade. The works of Sir Richard Lodge help to correct the prospective—*Great Britain and Prussia in the Eighteenth Century* (Oxford, 1923, 8°), *Studies in Eighteenth-Century Diplomacy, 1740–48* (London, 1930, 8°), and "Continental Policy of Great Britain, 1740–60" (*History*, Vol. 16, 1931–32).

None the less it goes without saying that throughout Frederick's reign it is necessary to contrast Prussia's history with Austria's. The main authority is still Alfred von Arneth, *Geschichte Maria Theresias* (10 vols., Vienna, 1863–79, 8°).

THE TWO WARS OF SILESIA. SOURCES. Add *Das Tagebuch Kaiser Karl VII aus der Zeit des oesterreichischen Erbfolgekriegs,* edited by K. T. Heigel (Munich, 1883, 8°), and the *Correspondance de Louis XV et du maréchal de Noailles,* edited by C. Rousset (2 vols., Paris, 1865, 8°).

WORKS. Herbert Tuttle, *History of Prussia, 1740–56* (2 vols., Boston and New York, 1888, 8°; also issued the same year at London); C. Grünhagen, *Geschichte des ersten schlesischen Krieges* (2 vols., Gotha, 1881, 8°); Duc J. V. A. de Broglie, *Frédéric II et Marie-Thérèse* (2 vols., Paris, 1883, 8°), *Frédéric II et Louis XV* (2 vols., 1885, 8°), and *Marie-Thérèse impératrice* (2 vols., 1888, 8°); M. T. Sautai, *Les Préliminaires de la guerre de la succession d'Autriche* (Paris, 1907, 8°), and *Les Débuts de la guerre de la succession d'Autriche* (1909); G. B. Volz, "Das Rheinsberger Protokoll" (*Forschungen z.b.u.p.G.*, Vol. 29, 1916), and "Die Politik F.d.G. vor und nach seiner Thronbesteigung" (*Historische Zeitschrift*, Vol. 151, 1935); R. Koser, "Der Zerfall der Koalition von 1741 gegen Maria-Theresia" (*Forschungen z.b.u.p.G.*, Vol. 27, 1914).

For military operations there is the great publication of the Prussian General Staff, *Die Kriege F.d.G.* (6 vols. for the two wars of Silesia, 1890–96, 8°). A very detailed work by Major Z. (Count Weil), *La Guerre de la succession d'Autriche,* mainly based on the publications of the Austrian General Staff, stops at 1745 (6 vols., 1897–1914, 8°). For French military operations, see also General Pajol, *Les Guerres sous Louis XV* (7 vols., 1881–91, 8°) from Vol. 2 on (Vols. 4 and 5 deal with the Seven Years' War). For Frederick's earliest military exploits as king, see A. Chuquet, *Episodes et portraits* (3d series, Paris, 1911, 8°), R. Koser, "Zur Schlacht bei Mollwitz" (*Forschungen z.b.u.p.G.*, Vol. 3, 1890), and O. Hermann, "Von Mollwitz bis Chotusitz" (*ibid.*, Vol. 7, 1894).

The Seven Years' War. sources. The origins of the Seven Years' War have given rise to a controversy extending over several years between the German historians Lehmann and Delbrück on one side and Naudé and Koser on the other: the former maintain that Frederick wanted the war and took military measures before Austria did; their opponents deny the facts of mobilization and retort that the situation was of a nature to discourage the most intrepid of gamblers. The items of this controversy are enumerated in No. 11,966 of Dahlmann-Waitz, *Quellenkunde*. . . . The discussion has had the happy result of making G. B. Volz and G. Küntzel publish the relevant official documents, *Preussische und oesterreichische Akten zur Vorgeschichte des Siebenjaehrigen Krieges* ("Publications of the Prussian Archives," Vol. 74, 1899).

For French diplomacy the *Correspondance secrète inédite de Louis XV*, edited by E. Boutaric (2 vols., Paris, 1866, 8°), the *Mémoires et lettres* of Cardinal Pierre de Bernis, edited by F. Masson (2 vols., Paris, 1878, 8°), the dispatches of the French Embassy at Berlin from 1746 to 1756, edited by R. Koser and appearing in *Forschungen z.b.u.p.G.* (Vols. 6 and 7, 1893 and 1894), and for the mission of Kaunitz, the *Correspondance secrète entre le comte A. W. Kaunitz-Rietberg . . . et le baron Ignaz de Koch* (secretary to Maria Theresa), edited by H. Schlitter (Paris, 1899, 8°).

works. The story of the reversal of alliances has been told in a manner hostile to Frederick by Duc J. V. A. de Broglie, *L'Alliance autrichienne* (Paris, 1895, 8°), and by R. P. Waddington, *Louis XV et le renversement des alliances* (Paris, 1896, 8°). For the Duc de Nivernais, see L. Perey, *Un Petit-Neveu de Mazarin . . . duc de Nivernais* (Paris, 1890, 8°), G. Küntzel, "Entsendung des Herzogs von Nivernais an den preussischen Hof. 1755" (*Forschungen z.b.u.p.G.*, Vol. 12, 1899), and the same author has written an article on Franco-Prussian relations on the eve of the Seven Years' War in a series called "Zur Geschichte F.d.G." (*ibid.*, Vol. 15, 1902). For the negotiations carried on through Voltaire, see Pierre Calmettes, *Choiseul et Voltaire, d'après les lettres inédites du duc de Choiseul à Voltaire* (Paris, 1912, 8°).

For the Prussian offensive and the final negotiations with Austria, see G. B. Volz, *Kriegführung und Politik F.d.G. in dem ersten Jahre des Siebenjaehrigen Krieges* (Berlin, 1896, 8°).

For the history of the war the main authority is R. P. Waddington, *La Guerre de sept ans* (5 vols., Paris, 1899–1914, 8°, stopping at 1762). See also A. Schaefer, *Geschichte des siebenjaehrigen Kriegs* (2 vols., Berlin, 1867–74, 8°), and A. N. Rambaud, *Russes et Prussiens* (Paris, 1895, 8°). The German General Staff has devoted 13 volumes of "Die Kriege F.d.G." to a detailed account of the operations up to 1761 (*Der Siebenjaehrige Krieg*, 13 vols., 1901–14, 8°).

For the reëstablishment of diplomatic relations with France, see R. Hammond, "Le Rétablissement des relations diplomatiques entre la France et la Prusse" (*Revue historique*, Vol. 25, 1884), and his "Mission du comte de Guines" (*ibid.*, Vol. 37, 1888). Also G. B. Volz, "Die Wiederherstellung der preussisch-franzoesichen Beziehungen" (*Forschungen z.b.u.p.G.,* Vol. 17, 1904).

LAST YEARS. For the partition of Poland, see A. Sorel, *La Question d'Orient au XVIIIe siècle* (2d ed., Paris, 1889, 8°; translation, London, 1898, 8°), A. Beer, *Die erste Teilung Polens* (3 vols., Vienna, 1873, 8°), also three articles by G. B. Volz (*Forschungen z.b.u.p.G.,* Vol. 18, 1905; Vol. 23, 1910; Vol. 35, 1923), and J. P. Garnier, *La Tragédie de Dantzig* (Paris, 1935, 8°).

For the succession of Bavaria, see P. Oursel, *La Diplomatie de la France sous Louis XV* (Paris, 1921, 8°). All other German works are prior to Koser's biography except for G. B. Volz, "F.d.G. und der bayrische Erbfolgekrieg" (*Forschungen z.b.u.p.G.,* Vol. 44, 1932), and Werner Hühne, *F.d.G., die europaeischen Maechte und das Reich am Vorabend des bayrischen Erbfolgkrieges* (Göttingen dissertation, Uelzen, 1935, 8°).

Add to Koser, for relations with the Turks, G. B. Volz, "F.d.G. und die Osmanen" (*Hohenzollern-Jahrbuch,* Vol. 19, 1915), and for relations with France before the League of Princes, F. Braun, *Preussische-franzoesische Bündnisplaene in den Jahren 1778–84* (Emsdetten, 1936).

ART OF WAR. The most important of the innumerable studies on Frederick's strategy and principles of warfare cannot be neglected—"Précis des guerres de Frédéric par Napoléon" (*Frédéric: Œuvres historiques,* Vol. 3 (1740–63), edited by C. F. A. Rousset, part of the "Bibliothèque de l'armée française," Paris, 1872, 8°); Jomini, *Traité des grandes opérations militaires* (3 vols., 4th ed. with atlas, Paris, 1851, 8°; translated as *Treatise on Grand Military Operations,* 2 vols., New York, 1865); Clausewitz, *Friedrich der Grosse* ("Œuvres," Vol. 10, 1837–63). F. T. von Bernhardi, in *F.d.G. als Feldherr* (2 vols., Berlin, 1881, 8°), ranked Frederick far above Napoleon, an assertion which gave rise to a series of restatements and discussions by Lieutenant Colonel Taysen, Delbrück, General Bonnal, Lieutenant Colonel Rousset, and Schlieffen (*Friedrich der Grosse,* 1912). The clearest account of Frederick's military technique is to be found in A.G. (Lieutenant Colonel A. A. Grouard), *Stratégie napoléonienne: Maximes de guerre de Napoléon 1er* (Paris, 1898, 8°). On Frederick's reflections between 1745 and 1756 the Prussian General Staff has published as Part XXVII of *Kriegsgeschichtliche Einzelschriften* (1899, 4°) a learned study called "F.d.G. Anschauungen vom Kriege in ihrer Entwicklung von 1745 bis 1756."

For the development of the Prussian Army before Frederick's time nothing more clear has been written than G. Schmoller, "Die Entstehung des preussischen Heeres 1640–1740" (*Deutsche Rundschau,* 1877).

Index